HMH

into Literature™

Front Cover Photo Credits: (outer ring): ©Mike Liu/Shutterstock, (inner ring): ©Nigel Killeen/Moment Open/Getty Images, (c) ©Carrie Garcia/Houghton Mifflin Harcourt, (c overlay): ©Eyewire/Getty Images, (bc overlay): ©elenamiv/Shutterstock

Back Cover Photo Credits: (Units 1-6): ©Print Collector/Hulton Archive/Getty Images; ©Christophel Fine Art/Getty Images; ©A. Dagli Orti/De Agostini Editorial/Getty Images; ©Tonktiti/Shutterstock; ©jgorzynik/iStockphoto/Getty Images; ©Friedemann Vogel/Getty Images

Printed in the U.S.A.

ISBN 978-1-328-51107-2

4 5 6 7 8 9 10 0877 27 26 25 24 23 22 21 20 19

4500762147 B C D E F G

GRADE 12

Volume 2

Program Consultants:

Kylene Beers

Martha Hougen

Elena Izquierdo

Carol Jago

Erik Palmer

Robert E. Probst

PROGRAM CONSULTANTS

Kylene Beers

Nationally known lecturer and author on reading and literacy; coauthor with Robert Probst of *Disrupting Thinking, Notice & Note: Strategies for Close Reading,* and *Reading Nonfiction;* former president of the National Council of Teachers of English. Dr. Beers is the author of *When Kids Can't Read: What Teachers Can Do* and coeditor of *Adolescent Literacy: Turning Promise into Practice,* as well as articles in the *Journal of Adolescent and Adult Literacy.* Former editor of *Voices from the Middle,* she is the 2001 recipient of NCTE's Richard W. Halle Award, given for outstanding contributions to middle school literacy. She recently served as Senior Reading Researcher at the Comer School Development Program at Yale University as well as Senior Reading Advisor to Secondary Schools for the Reading and Writing Project at Teachers College.

Martha Hougen

National consultant, presenter, researcher, and author. Areas of expertise include differentiating instruction for students with learning difficulties, including those with learning disabilities and dyslexia; and teacher and leader preparation improvement. Dr. Hougen has taught at the middle school through graduate levels. In addition to peer-reviewed articles, curricular documents, and presentations, Dr. Hougen has published two college textbooks: *The Fundamentals of Literacy Assessment and Instruction Pre-K–6* (2012) and *The Fundamentals of Literacy Assessment and Instruction 6–12* (2014). Dr. Hougen has supported Educator Preparation Program reforms while working at the Meadows Center for Preventing Educational Risk at The University of Texas at Austin and at the CEEDAR Center, University of Florida.

Elena Izquierdo

Nationally recognized teacher educator and advocate for English language learners. Dr. Izquierdo is a linguist by training, with a Ph.D. in Applied Linguistics and Bilingual Education from Georgetown University. She has served on various state and national boards working to close the achievement gaps for bilingual students and English language learners. Dr. Izquierdo is a member of the Hispanic Leadership Council, which supports Hispanic students and educators at both the state and federal levels. She served as Vice President on the Executive Board of the National Association of Bilingual Education and as Publications and Professional Development Chair.

Carol Jago

Teacher of English with 32 years of experience at Santa Monica High School in California; author and nationally known lecturer; former president of the National Council of Teachers of English. Ms. Jago currently serves as Associate Director of the California Reading and Literature Project at UCLA. With expertise in standards assessment and secondary education, Ms. Jago is the author of numerous books on education, including *With Rigor for All* and *Papers, Papers, Papers,* and is active with the California Association of Teachers of English, editing its scholarly journal *California English* since 1996. Ms. Jago also served on the planning committee for the 2009 NAEP Reading Framework and the 2011 NAEP Writing Framework.

Erik Palmer

Veteran teacher and education consultant based in Denver, Colorado. Author of *Well Spoken: Teaching Speaking to All Students* and *Digitally Speaking: How to Improve Student Presentations.* His areas of focus include improving oral communication, promoting technology in classroom presentations, and updating instruction through the use of digital tools. He holds a bachelor's degree from Oberlin College and a master's degree in curriculum and instruction from the University of Colorado.

Robert E. Probst

Nationally respected authority on the teaching of literature; Professor Emeritus of English Education at Georgia State University. Dr. Probst's publications include numerous articles in *English Journal* and *Voices from the Middle,* as well as professional texts including (as coeditor) *Adolescent Literacy: Turning Promise into Practice* and (as coauthor with Kylene Beers) *Disrupting Thinking, Notice & Note: Strategies for Close Reading,* and *Reading Nonfiction.* He regularly speaks at national and international conventions including those of the International Literacy Association, the National Council of Teachers of English, the Association of Supervisors and Curriculum Developers, and the National Association of Secondary School Principals. He has served NCTE in various leadership roles, including the Conference on English Leadership Board of Directors, the Commission on Reading, and column editor of the NCTE journal *Voices from the Middle.* He is also the 2004 recipient of the CEL Exemplary Leader Award.

UNIT 1

ORIGIN OF A NATION

PAGE 1

ESSENTIAL QUESTIONS

- What makes someone a hero?
- What is true chivalry?
- Can we control our fate?
- What happens when a society unravels?

Key Learning Objectives

- Analyze characteristics of an epic poem
- Analyze Old English poetry
- Analyze narrator
- Analyze conflict
- Make predictions
- Analyze characterization
- Make inferences
- Analyze tone

Visit the Interactive Student Edition for:

- Unit and Selection Videos
- Media Selections
- Selection Audio Recordings
- Enhanced Digital Instruction

UNIT 2

A CELEBRATION OF HUMAN ACHIEVEMENT

PAGE 138

ESSENTIAL QUESTIONS

- What can drive someone to seek revenge?
- How does time affect our feelings?
- What's the difference between love and passion?
- How do you defy expectations?

ANALYZE & APPLY

COLLABORATE & COMPARE

UNIT 2

Key Learning Objectives

- Analyze dramatic plot
- Analyze conflict
- Analyze soliloquy
- Analyze arguments
- Analyze key ideas
- Analyze sonnets
- Analyze metaphysical conceits
- Interpret figurative language
- Analyze speaker
- Analyze rhetorical devices
- Analyze text features

Online Ed

Visit the Interactive Student Edition for:

- Unit and Selection Videos
- Media Selections
- Selection Audio Recordings
- Enhanced Digital Instruction

UNIT 3

TRADITION AND REASON

PAGE 360

? ESSENTIAL QUESTIONS

- How can satire change people's behavior?
- What is your most memorable experience?
- What keeps women from achieving equality with men?
- Why are plagues so horrifying?

ANALYZE & APPLY

COLLABORATE & COMPARE

COMPARE ACROSS GENRES

Key Learning Objectives

- Analyze satire
- Analyze mock epic
- Understand author's purpose
- Analyze tone
- Connect to history
- Evaluate arguments
- Analyze counterarguments
- Analyze graphic features
- Analyze historical setting
- Analyze narrator

Visit the Interactive Student Edition for:

- Unit and Selection Videos
- Media Selections
- Selection Audio Recordings
- Enhanced Digital Instruction

UNIT 4

EMOTION AND EXPERIMENTATION

PAGE 490

? ESSENTIAL QUESTIONS

- What can nature offer us?
- How do you define beauty?
- How can science go wrong?
- What shapes your outlook on life?

ANALYZE & APPLY

COLLABORATE & COMPARE

COMPARE THEMES

Key Learning Objectives

- Analyze Romantic poetry
- Analyze imagery
- Analyze stanza structure
- Analyze rhyme scheme
- Analyze science fiction
- Analyze motivation
- Evaluate essay
- Analyze form
- Analyze diction
- Analyze symbols

Visit the Interactive Student Edition for:

- Unit and Selection Videos
- Media Selections
- Selection Audio Recordings
- Enhanced Digital Instruction

UNIT 5

AN ERA OF RAPID CHANGE

PAGE 586

ESSENTIAL QUESTIONS

- What is a true benefactor?
- How do you view the world?
- What brings out cruelty in people?
- Which invention has had the greatest impact on your life?

Key Learning Objectives

- Analyze setting
- Analyze first-person point of view
- Evaluate documentaries
- Analyze allegory
- Analyze mood
- Analyze characterization
- Analyze compare-and-contrast essay
- Analyze sound devices
- Analyze imagery
- Draw conclusions about speakers

Visit the Interactive Student Edition for:

- Unit and Selection Videos
- Media Selections
- Selection Audio Recordings
- Enhanced Digital Instruction

UNIT 6

NEW IDEAS, NEW VOICES

PAGE 690

? ESSENTIAL QUESTIONS

- What makes people feel insecure?
- Why is it hard to resist social pressure?
- What is the power of symbols?
- When should the government interfere in our decisions?

ANALYZE & APPLY

COLLABORATE & COMPARE

COMPARE THEMES

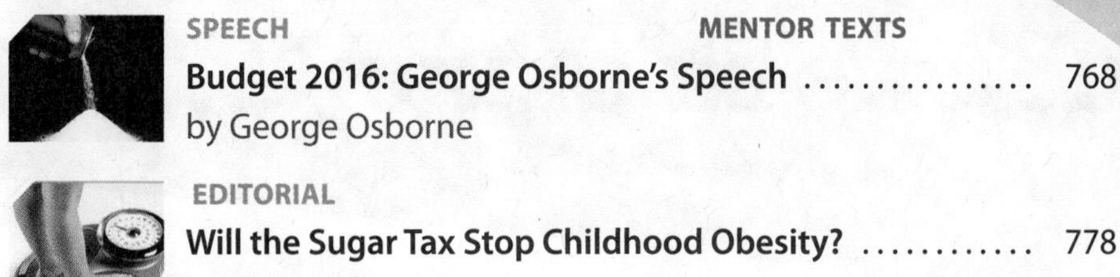

Key Learning Objectives

- Analyze third-person point of view
- Analyze stream of consciousness
- Analyze reflective essay
- Analyze irony
- Analyze setting
- Understand symbolism
- Analyze rhythmic patterns
- Evaluate persuasive techniques
- Analyze inductive reasoning

Visit the Interactive Student Edition for:

- Unit and Selection Videos
- Media Selections
- Selection Audio Recordings
- Enhanced Digital Instruction

SELECTIONS BY GENRE

FICTION

NOVEL

SHORT STORY

NONFICTION

ARGUMENT

MEMOIR/DIARY

POETRY

SELECTIONS BY GENRE

DRAMA

MEDIA STUDY

HMH

Into Literature Dashboard

Easy to use and personalized for your learning.

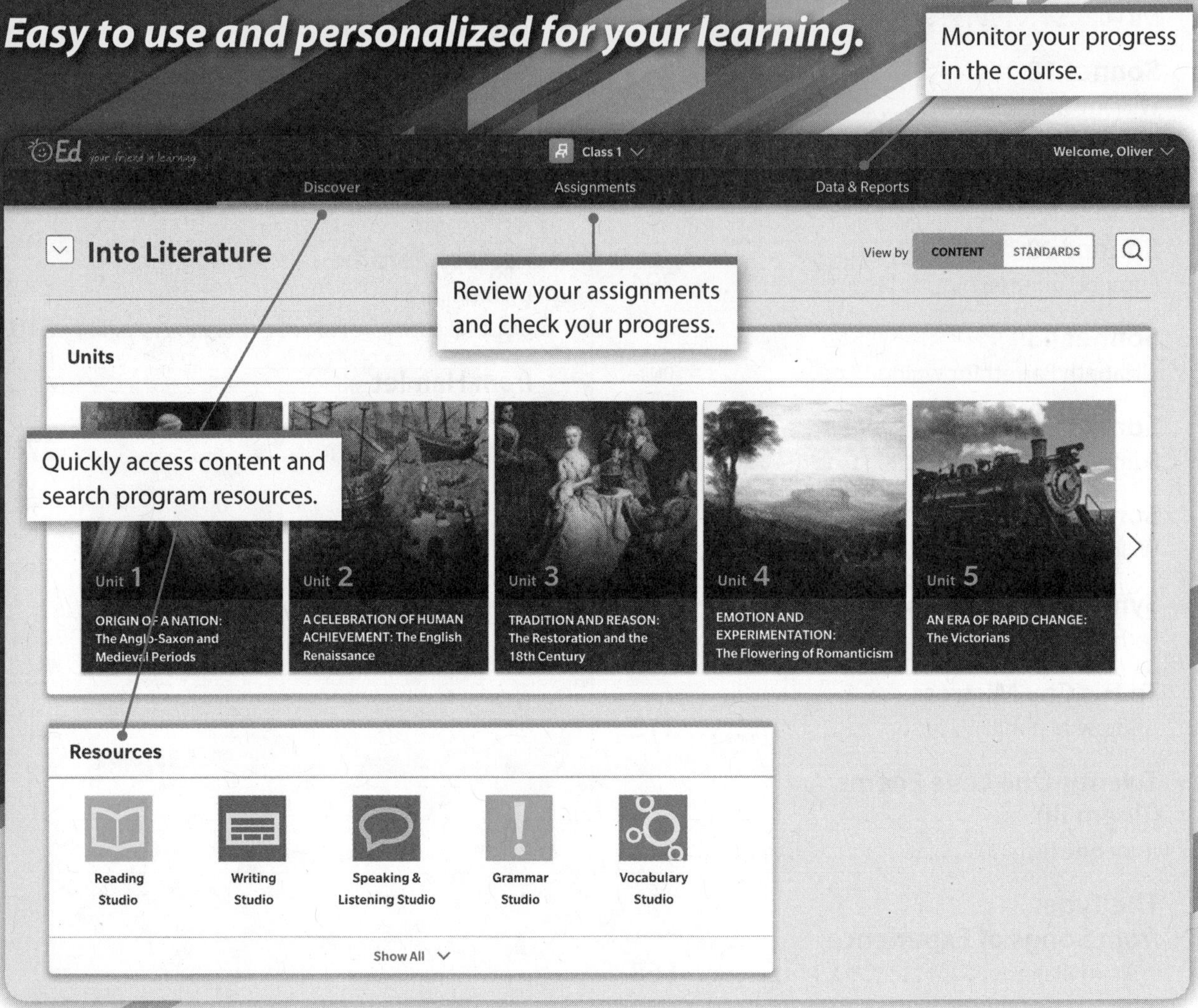

Monitor your progress in the course.

Ed your friend in learning

Class 1

Welcome, Oliver

Discover

Assignments

Data & Reports

Into Literature

View by CONTENT STANDARDS

Review your assignments and check your progress.

Units

Quickly access content and search program resources.

Unit 1 ORIGIN OF A NATION: The Anglo-Saxon and Medieval Periods

Unit 2 A CELEBRATION OF HUMAN ACHIEVEMENT: The English Renaissance

Unit 3 TRADITION AND REASON: The Restoration and the 18th Century

Unit 4 EMOTION AND EXPERIMENTATION: The Flowering of Romanticism

Unit 5 AN ERA OF RAPID CHANGE: The Victorians

Resources

Reading Studio

Writing Studio

Speaking & Listening Studio

Grammar Studio

Vocabulary Studio

Show All

Explore Online to Experience the Power of HMH *Into Literature*

All in One Place

Readings and assignments are supported by a variety of resources to bring literature to life and give you the tools you need to succeed.

Supporting 21st-Century Skills

Whether you're working alone or collaborating with others, it takes effort to analyze the complex texts and competing ideas that bombard us in this fast-paced world. What will help you succeed? Staying engaged and organized. The digital tools in this program will help you take charge of your learning.

Ignite Your Investigation

You learn best when you're engaged. The **Stream to Start** videos at the beginning of every unit are designed to spark your interest before you read. Get curious and start reading!

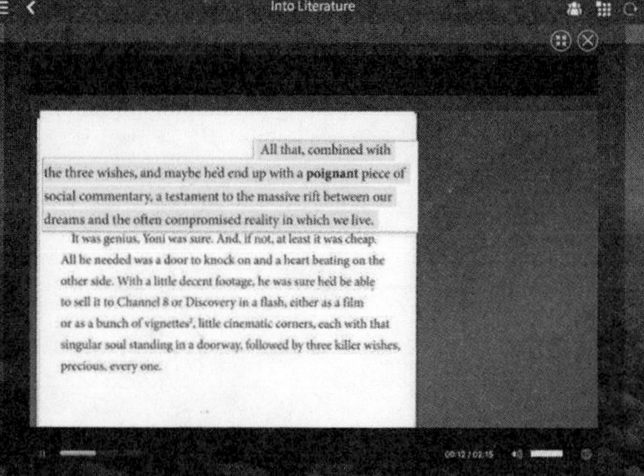

Learn How to Close Read

Close reading effectively is all about examining the details. See how it's done by watching the **Close Read Screencasts** in your eBook. Hear modeled conversations on targeted passages.

Personalized Annotations

My Notes encourages you to take notes as you read and allows you to mark the text in your own customized way. You can easily access annotations to review later as you prepare for exams.

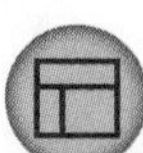

Interactive Graphic Organizers

Graphic organizers help you process, summarize, and keep track of your learning and prepare for end-of-unit writing tasks. **Word Networks** help you learn academic vocabulary, and **Response Logs** help you explore and deepen your understanding of the **Essential Questions** in each unit.

No Wi-Fi? No problem!

With HMH *Into Literature,* you always have access: download when you're online and access what you need when you're offline. Work offline and then upload when you're back online.

Communicate "Raise a Hand" to ask or answer questions without having to be in the same room as your teacher.

Collaborate Collaborate with your teacher via chat and work with a classmate to improve your writing.

HMH

Into Literature STUDIOS

All the help you need to be successful in your literature class is one click away with the Studios. These digital-only lessons are here to tap into the skills that you already use and help you sharpen those skills for the future.

Easy-to-find resources, organized in five separate STUDIOS. On demand and on ED!

Look for links in each lesson to take you to the appropriate Studio.

READING STUDIO

Go beyond the book with the Reading Studio. With over 100 full-length downloadable titles to choose from, find the right story to continue your journey.

WRITING STUDIO

Being able to write clearly and effectively is a skill that will help you throughout life. The Writing Studio will help you become an expert communicator—in print or online.

SPEAKING & LISTENING STUDIO

Communication is more than just writing. The Speaking & Listening Studio will help you become an effective speaker and a focused listener.

GRAMMAR STUDIO

Go beyond traditional worksheets with the Grammar Studio. These engaging, interactive lessons will sharpen your grammar skills.

VOCABULARY STUDIO

Learn the skills you need to expand your vocabulary. The interactive lessons in the Vocabulary Studio will grow your vocabulary to improve your reading.

Dr. Kylene Beers and Dr. Robert E. Probst

In reading, as in almost everything else, paying attention is most important.

You wouldn't stand in the batter's box, facing a hard-throwing pitcher, with your mind wandering to what you may have for dinner that evening. The prospect of a fastball coming toward you at 80 miles an hour tends to focus the mind.

And you wouldn't attempt to sing a difficult song in front of a large crowd with your thoughts on what dress you're going to wear to the dance this coming weekend. The need to hit the high note, without cracking, in front of 500 people evokes concentration.

Paying attention is essential.

It's the same with reading. Of course, if you don't concentrate while reading, you won't suffer the pain of being knocked down by the fastball or the embarrassment of failing to hit the notes in front of the crowd, but you'll miss what the text offers. If you don't pay attention, there is barely any purpose in picking up the text at all.

But there is a purpose in reading. And that purpose, that point, is to enable us to change. The change may be slight, or it might be dramatic. We might, at one extreme, simply get a little more information that we need:

- Where is tonight's game?
- What time is band practice?
- What pages do we need to read for homework?

Reading for that sort of information doesn't dramatically change who we are, but it does change us slightly. Or, at least, it ***might*** change us slightly. Obviously, it is ***we***, the readers, who must do the changing. The text doesn't do it for us. When we read that tonight's game is away, instead of at home, we have to change our plans to let us get to the other school. We have to take in the information and do something with it. If we don't, if we show up at the home field despite what we have read, the reading will have been pointless, a waste of time. And the evening will be wasted, as well. We have to pay attention to the book — what's on the page, and to our heads — what we thought before we read and what we now think. And we have to take it to heart — that is to say, we have to act on what we now know and think.

Other reading, however, might enable us to change more significantly. We might change our thinking about an important problem, or we might change our attitude about an important issue. We can't tell you which text will do that for you or how you might grow and change as a result of reading it. That's much too individual. It's hard to predict unless you know the reader well and know some of the texts that might matter to him or her:

- Some of us might read about child labor in foreign countries and change our minds about what we will buy and what we will boycott.
- You might read *To Kill a Mockingbird*, and change your thinking about race relations.
- You might read about climate change and wonder what you can do to help preserve the earth.

We can't know exactly what book will be powerful for which reader. But we can safely predict that if you don't notice what the text offers, think about it, and take what matters to you into your head and heart, then the reading probably won't mean much to you.

We're going to urge you to pay attention to three elements as you read:

- **The Book.** Or whatever text you have in your hand, whether it is a book, an article, a poem, or something else. We are going to urge you to listen carefully to what it tells you, and we're going to give you some strategies that we hope will make that easy for you to do.
- **Your Head.** We're going to ask you also to pay attention to your own thoughts. If it's an article you're reading, then keep in mind what you thought about the topic before you began, and then think seriously about how you might have changed your thinking as a result of what you've read. If it's a story or a poem or a movie, then think about what thoughts or feelings it brought to mind and how they might have shaped your reaction to the text.
- **Your Heart.** Finally, we encourage you to ask yourself what you want to carry away from the reading. What matters to you? How might you change your thinking? How might you have shifted your attitudes about something, even if only slightly? What do you take to heart?

It all begins with noticing.

But there's a lot in a book to notice, so it might help to keep in mind just a few things that you will probably see in almost any text (unless it is very short). We call these elements "signposts" because they serve readers just as signposts or street signs serve drivers — they alert them to something significant. The careless driver, who doesn't pay attention and misses a stop sign or a hairpin-curve sign, is likely to end up in trouble. The lazy reader, who doesn't notice the signposts, won't end up in trouble — he just isn't likely to know what's going on in the text.

THE FICTION SIGNPOSTS

We want to share 6 signposts that help you when reading fiction.

CONTRASTS AND CONTRADICTIONS

Without a contrast or a contradiction, everything is just the same, just the usual, just what you would have expected. Boring.

But when some event occurs that contrasts vividly with what you would have expected, then you are likely — if you're paying attention — to notice it.

When a friend's behavior suddenly changes and contrasts with what you would expect, you will notice it and ask yourself why. Similarly, when a character in a story does something drastically different from what he has usually done, you should pause and wonder why. Or, when a writer gives you an idea that contradicts the thoughts you have always held, again you might slow down and ask yourself, "Is she right or am I? Should I accept those thoughts or reject them? Is the answer somewhere in between what I have read and what I used to think?" Keep in mind the general question "Why is the character doing or saying that?" and it will lead you to other questions you might ask about the moment of contrast and contradiction, that moment when you bump into something unexpected.

In Neil Gaiman's "Chivalry," a student has noted a CONTRAST AND CONTRADICTION and asked this question: Why would the character act and feel this way?

Then she walked into her parlor and looked at the mantelpiece: at the little china basset hound, and the Holy Grail, and the photograph of her late husband Henry, shirtless, smiling and eating an ice cream in black and white, almost forty years away.	Mrs. Whitaker looks closely at the photograph of her late husband when he was young, as if she's thinking about him.
She went back into the kitchen. The kettle had begun to whistle. She poured a little steaming water into the teapot, swirled it around, and poured it out. Then she added two spoonfuls of tea and one for the pot and poured in the rest of the water. All this she did in silence. She turned to Galaad then, and she looked at him. "Put that apple away," she told Galaad, firmly. "You shouldn't offer things like that to old ladies. It isn't proper."	Perhaps she refuses to take the apple, which could have restored her youth, because she misses him. Galaad's offer may not be "proper" because Mrs. Whitaker doesn't want to betray the memory of her husband.

AHA MOMENT

Sometimes too many days go by without one of those moments when you suddenly understand something. But when you have such a moment you recognize that it's important and you stop and think about it. One day you might suddenly say to yourself "I'm echoing everything my friends say, but I don't really believe any of it." That's an important moment that may lead to a change in what you do, or at least to some hard thinking about the choices you have made. You've had an insight — an Aha — and you have to ask yourself what it means.

In the same way, the character in the story will almost always come to some insight into his situation, some "Aha" moment in which he realizes, perhaps suddenly, something about himself, his situation, or his life. When you come to such a moment, ask yourself "How will this change things?" Because it almost always will. Aha Moments are usually indicated with phrases such as "I knew," "I understood," "He figured it out," "She slowly realized," or "She nodded, knowing what she had to do . . ."

In Katherine Mansfield's "A Cup of Tea," a student has noted an AHA MOMENT and asked this question: How might this change things?

"Pretty?" Rosemary was so surprised that she blushed. "Do you think so? I—I hadn't thought about it."	Rosemary blushes, an Aha Moment, when she realizes that her husband thinks "Miss Smith" is pretty.
"Good Lord!" Philip struck a match. "She's absolutely lovely. Look again, my child. I was bowled over when I came into your room just now. However . . . I think you're making a ghastly mistake. Sorry, darling, if I'm crude and all that. But let me know if Miss Smith is going to dine with us in time for me to look up *The Milliner's Gazette*."	Then he says the girl is "absolutely lovely" and wonders if she's going to eat dinner with them.
"You absurd creature!" said Rosemary, and she went out of the library, but not back to her bedroom. She went to her writing-room and sat down at her desk. Pretty! Absolutely lovely! Bowled over! Her heart beat like a heavy bell. Pretty! Lovely!	I'll bet Rosemary's attitude changes. She sounds jealous enough to quit pitying the girl, and she might even try to keep her away from Philip.

TOUGH QUESTIONS

"Do you want pizza or spaghetti for dinner?" really isn't a tough question, even if you can't make up your mind. Your answer isn't going to change much of anything, and tomorrow you probably won't even remember that you made a choice. You aren't going to think about it for very long or very hard, and no one will ever write a book about the choice between pizza and spaghetti. If they do, we won't read it.

A tough question is one we struggle with, one that might change the course of our lives — one, at least, that will have some serious consequences for us. "Should I play football, as the coach wants me to, or should I join the band, as I want to?" "Should I follow the crowd, as everyone is pressing me to do, or should I respect my own thoughts and let the crowd condemn me for it?" These are tough questions, and how we might answer them will shape the days to come.

Often a story, even an entire book, is built around the tough question. If we ask ourselves "What does this make me wonder about?" we will probably be led into exploring the same issue the character or the writer is exploring. The writer probably wanted to see what would happen if his character answered the question in a certain way. If you notice the tough question, and ask yourself about it, you will probably be looking at the main issue of the book.

In Geoffrey Chaucer's "**The Wife of Bath's Tale,**" a student has noted a **TOUGH QUESTION** and asked this: What does this question make me wonder about?

"You have two choices; which one will you try? To have me old and ugly till I die, But still a loyal, true, and humble wife That never will displease you all her life, Or would you rather I were young and pretty And chance your arm what happens in a city Where friends will visit you because of me, Yes, and in other places too, maybe. Which would you have? The choice is all your own."	I wonder how I'd answer the same Tough Question. What leads to lasting happiness in a relationship? How important is appearance? Is it possible to ignore appearance, even if you know you'll be loved and supported forever?

WORDS OF THE WISER

You may think that you have heard too many of these in your own life.

You probably think there is always someone around who wants to offer you advice, teach you how things are, and tell you what to do and how to think. Sometimes these wise words are right, truly wise, and sometimes they are wrong. But they are almost always an effort to guide you, or the character, to teach something about living in the world.

In a story, we usually hear Words of the Wiser in a quiet moment, when two characters are in a serious conversation about a problem or a decision. Usually the one who is — or thinks she is — wiser, will offer a serious lesson about life. The story will be about the character struggling along, unwilling to learn that lesson until the end; or about the character accepting the lesson and following it to whatever adventures it leads; or perhaps, in rare cases, about the words of the wiser not being wise after all.

In any case, when you notice Words of the Wiser in the story you should ask the same question you are likely to ask in your own life — "What is the lesson, and how will it affect the character (or me)?"

In William Shakespeare's *The Tragedy of Hamlet*, a student has noted WORDS OF THE WISER and asked this question: What is the life lesson, and how might this affect the character?

Ophelia. No more but so? **Laertes.** Think it no more. For nature, crescent, does not grow alone In thews and bulk, but, as this temple waxes, The inward service of the mind and soul Grows wide withal. Perhaps he loves you now, And now no soil nor cautel doth besmirch The virtue of his will; but you must fear, His greatness weighed, his will is not his own, For he himself is subject to his birth. He may not, as unvalued persons do, Carve for himself, for on his choice depends The safety and the health of this whole state. And therefore must his choice be circumscribed Unto the voice and yielding of that body Whereof he is the head.	Laertes is trying to convince Ophelia that she shouldn't love Hamlet, no matter how they currently feel about each other. His Words of the Wiser suggest that Hamlet will always do what's best for Denmark, even if it means marrying someone else. Ophelia might reject Hamlet or pretend not to love him, despite her feelings.

AGAIN AND AGAIN

One teacher I had always called on the second or third person to raise a hand, or perhaps on some student who was looking out the window — never on the first hand in the sky.

It happened again and again. Until, of course, I got clever and decided to shoot my hand up quickly even though I didn't have the foggiest notion what the answer was. That must have been the day that the teacher recognized the lesson of Again and Again, and realized that he had established a pattern. Or perhaps he had been planning the switch all along. In any case, it was the day I shot my hand up first that he decided to change his routine. At my expense. . . .

Something that happens over and over, again and again, establishes a pattern. If we pay attention, we'll notice that pattern and ask ourselves, "Why does this happen over and over, again and again?" In our lives, the again and again moment probably teaches us something about our friends, or our teachers, or, perhaps, about the way the world works. And sometimes it alerts us to something that is likely to change.

In any case, whenever we notice something happening again and again, we should take note of it, and ask ourselves "Why does this keep happening repeatedly?" Our answer may be that it teaches us some consistent pattern that we can rely on. Or it may be that it is setting up expectations that we can predict will suddenly not be met. It may be leading us into a surprising Contrast and Contradiction. That, after all is what my teacher did to me. If I had thought more carefully about the Again and Again, and asked myself why he was always avoiding the first hand that waved, I might have guessed that he was preparing a trick and that one day he would call on that first hand.

In Sir Thomas Malory's *Le Morte D'Arthur*, a student has noted an instance of AGAIN AND AGAIN and asked this question: Why might the author bring this up again and again?

For three weeks, while Sir Gawain was recovering, the siege was relaxed and both sides skirmished only halfheartedly. But once recovered, Sir Gawain rode up to the castle walls and challenged Sir Launcelot again: "Sir Launcelot, traitor! Come forth, it is Sir Gawain who challenges you." "Sir Gawain, why these insults? I have the measure of your strength and you can do me but little harm." "Come forth, traitor, and this time I shall make good my revenge!" Sir Gawain shouted. "Sir Gawain, I have once spared your life; should you not beware of meddling with me again?"	Launcelot has been trying to end the conflict with Arthur, but Sir Gawain has resisted Again and Again, insisting that the kingdom's honor is at stake. Malory might be bringing up Gawain's repeated attacks to show how a sense of lasting dishonor can prevent peace.

MEMORY MOMENT

Sometimes, in a reflective moment, a memory will surprise you. You won't have been trying to remember that day, or that person, or that event. It will just pop up like an almost forgotten old friend who knocks at your door and surprises you.

But something called that memory up at that moment. Something that was happening right now reached into your distant past and pulled that memory into your thoughts. Figuring out why that happened will probably tell you something important. It may explain why you are feeling the way you are feeling. It may even explain why you are acting as you are at the moment.

In a story, the Memory Moment is an author's creation. She has decided to reach back into the past for something that she thinks you, as a reader, need to know. It's easy to skip over these moments. After all, you want to go forwards, not backwards, and the Memory Moment steps back into the past. But it's probably important to ask yourself "Why is this moment important?" Because you can assume that if the writer is any good at all, she thinks you should notice it and take note of it.

In the epic poem *Beowulf*, a student has noted a MEMORY MOMENT and asked this question: Why might this memory be important?

Hrothgar, the helmet of Shieldings, spoke: "Beowulf, my friend, you have travelled here to favour us with help and to fight for us. There was a feud one time, begun by your father. With his own hands he had killed Heatholaf, who was a Wulfing; so war was looming and his people, in fear of it, forced him to leave. He came away then over rolling waves to the South-Danes here, the sons of honour. I was then in the first flush of kingship, establishing my sway over all the rich strongholds of this heroic land. Heorogar, my older brother and the better man, also a son of Halfdane's, had died. Finally I healed the feud by paying: I shipped a treasure-trove to the Wulfings and Ecgtheow acknowledged me with oaths of allegiance."	Hrothgar relates the memory of his favor to Ecgtheow, explaining that Ecgtheow had sworn "oaths of allegiance" to him. This Memory Moment explains why Beowulf feels obliged to assist the Danes in their fight: his family owes Hrothgar a debt for having ended the feud with the Wulfings.

NONFICTION SIGNPOSTS

Nonfiction has text clues as well. Just as in fiction, they invite you to stop and think about what's happening. These clues will help you focus on author's purpose — a critical issue to keep in mind when reading nonfiction. More importantly, these signposts will help you as you keep in mind what we call the Three Big Questions. These questions ought to guide all the reading we do, but especially the nonfiction reading. As you read, just keep asking yourself:

- What surprised me?
- What did the author think I already knew?
- What changed, challenged, or confirmed my thinking?

That first one will keep you thinking about the text. Just look for those parts that make you think, "Really!?!" and put an exclamation point there. The second one will be helpful when the language is tough, or the author is writing about something you don't know much about. Mark those points with a question mark and decide if you need more information. That final question, well, that question is why we read. Reading ought to change us. It ought to challenge our thinking. And sometimes it will confirm it. When you find those parts, just put a "C" in the margin. When you review your notes, you will decide if your thinking was changed, challenged, or confirmed.

As you're looking at what surprised you, or thinking about what is challenging you, or perhaps even as you find a part where it seems the author thinks you know something that you don't, you might discover that one of the following signposts appears right at that moment. So, these signposts help you think about the Three Big Questions. We have found five useful signposts for nonfiction.

CONTRASTS AND CONTRADICTIONS

The world is full of contrasts and contradictions — if it weren't, it would be a pretty dull place to live.

This is the same Contrast and Contradiction that you are familiar with from fiction. It's that moment when you encounter something you didn't expect, something that surprises you. It may be a fact that you find startling, a perspective that you had never heard before, or perhaps an argument that is new to you. We should welcome those moments, even though they may be disconcerting. They give us the opportunity to change our minds about things, to sharpen our thinking. The last person we want to become is that reader who reads only to confirm what he has already decided. That reader is committed to not learning, not growing, and standing absolutely still intellectually.

In Marah's *My Syrian Diary*, a student has noted CONTRASTS AND CONTRADICTIONS and asked this question: What is the difference, and why does it matter?

My city was once magnificent. In spring, it bloomed. We used to wake up to the sound of birds chirping and to the fragrant scent of flowers. Today, spring is here again. But what kind of spring is this? We now wake up to the sound of falling bombs.	Marah contrasts the past with current life in the city, which drives the point home: sights, sounds, and scents have been transformed by the conflict.
Every day, we open our eyes to our bleak reality: to the mortar shells that bring fear, death, disease and destruction. It has robbed us of our loved ones, destroyed our special places, hurt our close friends. Take my neighbor's daughter. At just seven years old, she has lost the ability to speak after a rocket landed close to our street.	The beauties of spring and the city's magnificence have been lost.

EXTREME AND ABSOLUTE LANGUAGE

We are all guilty of overstatement all the time.

Well, that's an overstatement. We aren't all guilty, and those of us who are probably aren't guilty all of the time. When we hear "all," or "none," or "always," or "never," we can be absolutely certain — let's make that "almost certain" — that we are hearing absolute language. All it takes is one exception to make the claim false.

But we do tend to exaggerate and occasionally overstate our claims. Absolute language is easy to spot, and it's often harmless over-statement. Extreme language approaches absolute language but usually stops short. Much of the time, it's harmless, too. When you tell your buddy you're starving, you probably aren't. Or when you say you just heard the funniest joke in the world, even though that's probably not true, your comment causes no real harm.

Sometimes, however, an extreme statement is potentially dangerous. If, for example, someone in authority were to say something like, "I am 100% certain that the airline crash was caused by terrorists," and we had not yet even found the black box that would explain the cause of the accident, then gullible listeners might believe and form opinions based on that statement, even though the phrase "100% certain" shows us clearly that it is an extreme statement. After all, no one ever claims to be 100% certain unless he isn't. So the question becomes, "How certain is he?" 80%? 40%? 20%?

When we spot absolute or extreme language, we should ask ourselves "Why did the author say it this way?" Sometimes the answer will be revealing.

In the Paston Family's *The Paston Letters*, a student has noted EXTREME AND ABSOLUTE LANGUAGE and asked this question: Why did the author use this language?

The duke's men ransacked the church, and carried off all the goods that were left there, both ours and the tenants, and left little behind; they stood on the high altar and ransacked the images, and took away everything they could find. They shut the parson out of the church until they had finished, and ransacked everyone's house in the town five or six times. The ringleaders in the thefts were the bailiff of Eye and the bailiff of Stradbroke, Thomas Slyford. And Slyford was the leader in robbing the church and, after the bailiff of Eye, it is he who has most of the proceeds of the robbery. As for the lead, brass, pewter, iron, doors, gates, and other household stuff, men from Costessey and Cawston have got it, and what they could not carry they hacked up in the most spiteful fashion. If possible, I would like some reputable men to be sent for from the king, to see how things are both there and at the lodge, before any snows come, so that they can report the truth. . . .	Throughout her letter, Paston uses both Extreme and Absolute Language. Not only does her use of language stress the injustice of the attacks, but it also communicates how widespread and serious the attacks have been. Paston's language emphasizes a distinct message to her husband: you need to come home, and you should bring help from the king when you do.

NUMBERS AND STATS

"If I've told you once, I've told you a million times. . . ."

Those are numbers — 1 (once) and 1,000,000 — though we prefer to see that as Extreme and Absolute Language. Still, it allows us to make the point, which is that numbers are used to make a point. In this case, they reveal that the speaker is annoyed at how often he has to repeat himself for you to get the message. You barely have to ask the anchor question "Why did the writer or speaker use those numbers or amounts?"

But that's the question you should ask when numbers or stats or amounts appear in something you are reading. Writers include them because they think those numbers, which look like hard, objective, indisputable data, will be persuasive. The questions are, "What are they trying to persuade you to think or believe?" And, "Are the numbers reliable?"

When a writer tells you, for instance, that 97–98% of scientists who have studied the issue think that humans are affecting the environment in damaging ways, we probably want to ask what those figures tell us, both about the situation and the writer's purpose. Our answer will probably be that the writer believes the scientists have reached a consensus that we are endangering the planet. The writer might have said "most of the scientists agree," but "most" is vague. It could mean anything from slightly more than half to almost all. But "97–98%" is much more precise. And it's very close to 100%, so it should be persuasive. Numbers and stats help us visualize what the author is trying to show; it's up to you to decide if there's more you need to know.

In George Osborne's speech "Budget 2016," a student has noted NUMBERS AND STATS and asked this question: Why did the author use these numbers or amounts?

Mr. Deputy Speaker, you cannot have a long term plan for the country unless you have a long term plan for our children's health care. Here are the facts we know. • Five-year-old children are consuming their body weight in sugar every year. • Experts predict that within a generation, over half of all boys and 70% of girls could be overweight or obese. Here's another fact that we all know. Obesity drives disease. It increases the risk of cancer, diabetes and heart disease—and it costs our economy £27 billion a year. . . .	Osborne includes these startling Numbers and Stats because they clearly communicate a significant threat to children's health in the long term. They also suggest that the extraordinary cost of obesity-related diseases will continue to rise, if children's health care is not addressed.

QUOTED WORDS

American writer Ambrose Bierce said that quotation is "The act of repeating erroneously the words of another." When writers use quotations they are probably doing one of two things. They may be giving you an individual example so that you can see what some person thought or felt about a certain situation, event, or idea. In that case, the writer is probably trying to help you see the human impact of what otherwise might be an abstract idea, difficult to imagine. A writer might, for instance, tell you about the massive damage Hurricane Harvey brought to the coast of Texas. A description of the widespread destruction will give you a picture of what happened; but the quoted words of someone who heard the hundred-mile-an-hour winds for hours when the storm came ashore or whose house was flooded by the rising waters will give you a feel for the impact of the storm on a real person.

Writers also use quoted words to lend authority to a claim they are making. Quoting the authority adds some credibility to the situation. The Houston meteorologist who has studied the data and reports, "Harvey dumped more water in a shorter period of time on Houston than any other storm in Houston's history" ought to be believed more than the guy on the street corner who announces, "This is the worst storm ever."

In Langdon Winner's "Frankenstein: Giving Voice to the Monster," a student has noted QUOTED WORDS and asked this question: Why is this person quoted or cited, and what did this add?

In a BBC interview last year, Stephen Hawking warned, "The development of full artificial intelligence could spell the end of the human race. . . . Humans, limited by slow biological evolution, couldn't compete and would be superseded by AI. . . . One can imagine such technology outsmarting financial markets, out-inventing human researchers, out-manipulating human leaders, and developing weapons we cannot even understand. Whereas the short-term impact of AI depends on who controls it, the long-term impact depends on whether it can be controlled at all."	I had no idea that a scientist as famous as the late Stephen Hawking saw danger in the development of artificial intelligence! Winner includes Hawking's Quoted Words because Hawking is a trusted authority who poses concerns similar to those of Mary Shelley, supporting Winner's purpose.

WORD GAPS

Unless we read such simple texts that we know everything there is to know about the subject, we will almost inevitably stumble into the gap between the writer's vocabulary and ours. Although that's occasionally frustrating, we might see it as an opportunity to sharpen our understanding. We might either learn a new word or learn how a word we already know might be used in a new way.

If we are in a hurry (and reading in a hurry is probably a bad idea because it doesn't give us time to think), then when we encounter a new word our first question might be, "Can I get by without knowing this word?" If you can, maybe you should make what sense you can of the sentence and move on. When we do that we lose the opportunity to learn something, but occasionally we just don't have the time. At the very least, you might jot down the word on the blank pages at the back of the book as a reminder to look it up later, so that the opportunity won't be completely lost.

A better way to approach the problem of the unknown word, however, might be to strategically ask several questions. Obviously the first step is to see if the word is at least partially explained by the context. For instance, if you read "hard, objective, indisputable data," and you don't know what "indisputable" means, you can easily figure out that it is something close to "hard" or "objective." Perhaps it means "definite," "not arguable," or something similar. Close enough. If you can get that far you can probably go on without losing much. You may want to ask someone later what the word "indisputable" means, or look it up in the dictionary, but at the moment you will be able to read on.

If that easy fix doesn't work, however, you might start with "Do I know this word from somewhere else?" If you do, then you have a place to begin. What the word meant in the context with which you are familiar might be a clue to what it means in this new context. For instance, you know what it means when someone says, "I'm depositing my paycheck in the bank." But then you hear your friend say, "You can bank on me." You know your friend isn't becoming a financial lending institution. But, if you'll give yourself a moment to think about what you know about banks, then you might be able to figure out that this means you can count on your friend.

Sometimes, the word is a technical word, a term used primarily by experts in the field, and if you don't know the language of that field, you'll simply need to look it up.

In Dr. Steven Hatch's *Inferno: A Doctor's Ebola Story*, a student has noted a WORD GAP and asked this question: Can I find clues in the sentence to help me understand the word?

But what was he concerned about? He was, after all, cured, possessing Ebola-specific antibodies and lymphocytes, which now made him immune to a repeat infection. But . . . did he know that? As I spoke with him, I sat there puzzling this over. Surely he knew at some intuitive level that he was not at risk of getting sick again while he spent day after day convalescing, although maybe he had thought a reset button had been pressed when he emerged from the decontamination shower. But how to explain a concept like acquired immunity to someone who probably had no formal education beyond grade school?	"Lymphocytes" is a technical word, but the sentence provides clues to its meaning. The word is related to curing George and to making him "immune to repeat infection."

READING AND WRITING ACROSS GENRES

by Carol Jago

Reading is a first-class ticket around the world. Not only can you explore other lands and cultures, but you can also travel to the past and future. That journey is sometimes a wild ride. Other books can feel like comfort food, enveloping you in an imaginative landscape full of friends and good times. Making time for reading is making time for life.

Genre

One of the first things readers do when we pick up something to read is notice its genre. You might not think of it exactly in those terms, but consider how you approach a word problem in math class compared to how you read a science fiction story. Readers go to different kinds of text for different purposes. When you need to know how to do or make something, you want a reliable, trusted source of information. When you're in the mood to spend some time in a world of fantasy, you happily suspend your normal disbelief in dragons.

In every unit of *Into Literature,* you'll find a diverse mix of genres all connected by a common theme, allowing you to explore a topic from many different angles.

GENRE: INFORMATIONAL TEXT

GENRE: SHORT STORY

GENRE: LITERARY NONFICTION

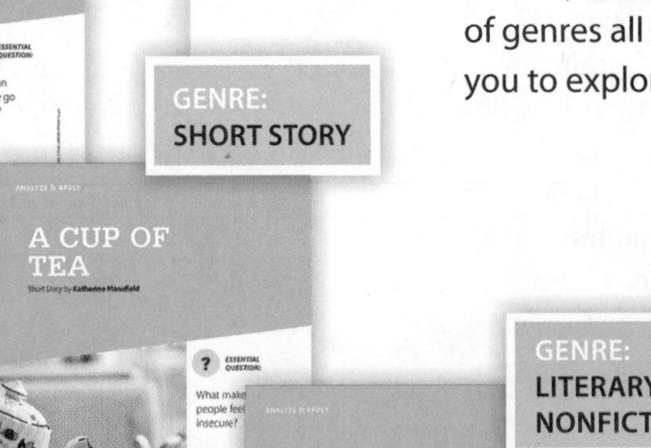

GENRE: POETRY

Writer's Craft

Learning how writers use genre to inform, to explain, to entertain, or to surprise readers will help you better understand—as well as enjoy—your reading. Imitating how professional writers employ the tools of their craft—descriptive language, repetition, sensory images, sentence structure, and a variety of other features—will give you many ideas for making your own writing more lively.

GENRE ELEMENTS: SHORT STORY
- is a work of short fiction that centers on a single idea and can be read in one sitting
- usually includes one main conflict that involves the characters and keeps [...] moving
- includes the basic ele[...] of fiction—plot, chara[...] setting, and theme
- may be based on real [...] and historical events

GENRE ELEMENTS: INFORMATIONAL TEXT
- provides factual information
- includes evidence to support ideas
- contains text features
- includes many forms, such as news articles and essays

GENRE ELEMENTS: LITERARY NONFICTION
- shares factual information, ideas, or experiences
- develops a key insight about the topic that goes beyond the facts
- uses literary techn[...] as figurative langu[...] narration
- reflects a persona[...] involvement in th[...]

GENRE ELEMENTS: POETRY
- may use figurative language, including personification
- often includes imagery that appeals to the five senses
- expresses a theme, or a "big idea" message about life

Into Literature provides you with the tools you need to understand the elements of all the critical genres and advice on how to learn from professional texts to improve your own writing in those genres.

Reading with Independence

Finding a good book can sometimes be a challenge. Like every other reader, you have probably experienced "book desert" when nothing you pick up seems to have what you are looking for (not that it's easy to explain exactly what you are looking for, but whatever it is, "this" isn't it). If you find yourself in this kind of reading funk, bored by everything you pick up, give yourself permission to range more widely, exploring graphic novels, contemporary biographies, books of poetry, historical fiction. And remember that long doesn't necessarily mean boring. My favorite kind of book is one that I never want to end.

Take control over your own reading with *Into Literature's* Reader's Choice selections and the HMH Digital Library. And don't forget: your teacher, librarian, and friends can offer you many more suggestions.

UNIT 4

EMOTION AND EXPERIMENTATION

THE FLOWERING OF ROMANTICISM

"I will not Reason and Compare; my business is to Create."

—William Blake

Discuss the **Essential Questions** with your whole class or in small groups. As you read Emotion and Experimentation, consider how the selections explore these questions.

? ***ESSENTIAL QUESTION:***

What can nature offer us?

As the 19th century dawned, England's cities underwent tremendous growth. Urban life had advantages, but some observers worried about the negative consequences of so many people leaving the countryside and losing contact with the natural world. Today, the idea of going outside and "back to nature" holds great appeal for many. Why are people drawn to nature? What does nature offer that we cannot find anywhere else?

? ***ESSENTIAL QUESTION:***

How do you define beauty?

Beauty was a topic of great interest during the Romantic period. Writers, artists, and others sought to discover beauty not only in such conventional places as nature, the arts, and the human form, but also in such abstract concepts as emotions, ideals, and the human spirit. Some writers even explored the idea of beauty in failure and tragedy. What does it mean for something to be described as beautiful? How do definitions of beauty vary from person to person and from culture to culture?

? ***ESSENTIAL QUESTION:***

How can science go wrong?

The Enlightenment ushered in a new era of scientific progress and confidence in the power of humanity over the natural world. With advances, however, came new responsibilities and new dilemmas, many of which still concern scientists and society today. What happens when scientific discoveries or experiments result in harm or get out of control? When do the risks of pursuing scientific advancement outweigh the benefits to society? Who gets to define ethical scientific practices?

? ***ESSENTIAL QUESTION:***

What shapes your outlook on life?

One hallmark of Romanticism was its focus on individual feelings and personal experiences. As humans, we are often shaped by our most emotionally intense experiences. Still, it is not experience alone that molds perspective. Two people can live through the same event and come away from it with completely different perspectives, based on their outlooks on life or how they view and interact with the world. If experience cannot account for all of the differences in perspective, what can?

THE FLOWERING OF ROMANTICISM

The literary movement known as Romanticism developed in reaction to many social influences: the unrest of the French Revolution, the economic excesses of the Industrial Revolution, and the widespread poverty and oppression of workers.

A Time of Revolution During the American Revolution and, later, the French Revolution, George III ruled Britain. He was not a very capable king, and many blamed the loss of the American colonies chiefly on his inflexible attitude toward the colonists. In 1788, the year before the French Revolution began, George III suffered a major attack of mental illness; in 1811 he was declared permanently insane. His son George ruled as prince regent until the king's death in 1820.

Initially, many British citizens, including most of the early Romantic writers and poets, felt sympathy for the French Revolution and its ideals of liberty, equality, and brotherhood. The Romantics saw the revolution as a turning point in human history, a move toward an ideal civilized society in which those who had previously struggled under oppression would find relief. When the revolution turned radical and violent, however, British sympathy dissipated, and the Romantics turned elsewhere for inspiration.

During the Reign of Terror, radical revolutionaries persecuted and massacred thousands of French aristocrats and middle-class citizens. The British upper and middle classes were all too aware that England's lower classes faced many of the same social ills as the French lower classes. The British ruling classes were afraid that any efforts at reform could lead to anarchy as it had in France. As a result, British leaders grew more conservative, suppressing reform and outlawing writing or speech that was critical of the government.

War with France In 1793 Britain entered into a war with France that would last for more than 25 years. It was during this conflict that General Napoleon Bonaparte took control of France's government, made himself emperor, and then proceeded to conquer much of continental Europe. Britain was continually threatened with invasion until the British fleet destroyed the French navy in 1805. After that, Britain was able to loosen Napoleon's hold on Europe, and Napoleon was finally defeated at Waterloo in 1815.

COLLABORATIVE DISCUSSION

In a small group, discuss how the events on the timeline influenced British society. Was this influence mainly direct or indirect?

1780

1789
The French Revolution begins.

1793
The French Revolution gives way to the Reign of Terror; war begins between Britain and France.

1794
William Blake publishes *Songs of Innocence and of Experience.*

The Downside of Industry During this period, England was an industrial as well as an agricultural country. The Industrial Revolution and improvements in farming brought increased prosperity to the middle and upper classes, but brought degrading poverty to the families employed in the factories and mills. Living and working conditions were appalling. There were no laws to regulate work safety, hours, wages, or child labor. At the time, Britain operated under the doctrine of *laissez-faire* economics, which means that an economy works best without government intervention.

Shortly after George III's son took control as regent, an economic depression resulted in the loss of many factory jobs. Advances in technology caused even more job losses, as fewer workers were needed to run textile mills. In the ensuing Luddite Riots, unemployed mill workers rioted, smashing the machines they blamed for taking their jobs. Frightened by the violence, Parliament, instead of working to solve the root causes of the violence, passed laws that made the rioters' actions punishable by death. Labor unions were illegal, and workers had little power in Parliament. Some workers organized anyway, but were quickly put down by the government.

The Romantics Romantic writers often sympathized with the oppressed lower classes and wrote about their plight. Lord Byron, a Romantic poet

RESEARCH
What about this historical period interests you? Choose a topic, event, or person to learn more about. Then add your own entry to the timeline.

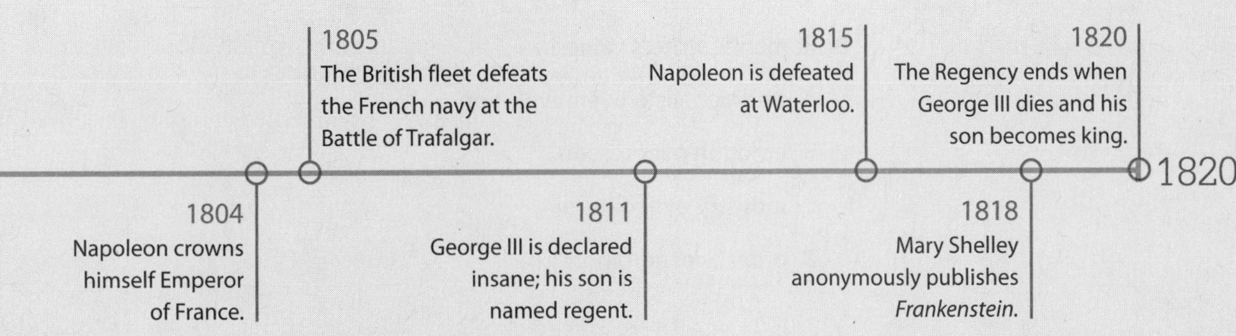

and a member of Parliament, openly expressed his sympathy for the poor to other members of the British government. In fact, he was one of only three members of Parliament to vote against the law punishing the Luddite rioters with death.

Such political efforts, however, yielded few results. Many of the Romantic writers reacted to the harsh realities of industrialization by turning to nature for truth and beauty. They revolted against the order, propriety, and traditionalism of the Age of Reason and rejected the classical tradition that venerated the achievements of ancient Greece and Rome. The Romantics were influenced by the same forces that gave rise to the American and French revolutions and by the agitation for political, social, and economic change taking place in their own country. For the Romantics, emotion became more important than reason. Thus, they preferred styles of writing that allowed self-expression, like lyric poetry, which came to dominate English literature during this time.

CHECK YOUR UNDERSTANDING

Choose the best answer to each question.

1 Which event caused many British citizens to lose sympathy for the French Revolution?

A Britain's loss of the American colonies in an earlier revolution

B The takeover of the French government by Napoleon Bonaparte

C The execution of French aristocrats during the Reign of Terror

D The defeat of the French navy by the British fleet

2 Which factor contributed most directly to the Luddite Riots?

F Instigation by Romantic writers like Lord Byron

G Appointment of George III's son as regent in his father's place

H Discontent over the outlawed status of labor unions

J Loss of factory jobs due to advances in technology

3 Romantic writers valued —

A traditionalism over revolution

B emotion over reason

C industry over nature

D order over agitation

ACADEMIC VOCABULARY

Academic Vocabulary words are words you use when you discuss and write about texts. In this unit, you will learn the following five words:

☑ **appreciate** ❑ **insight** ❑ **intensity** ❑ **invoke** ❑ **radical**

Study the Word Network to learn more about the word **appreciate.**

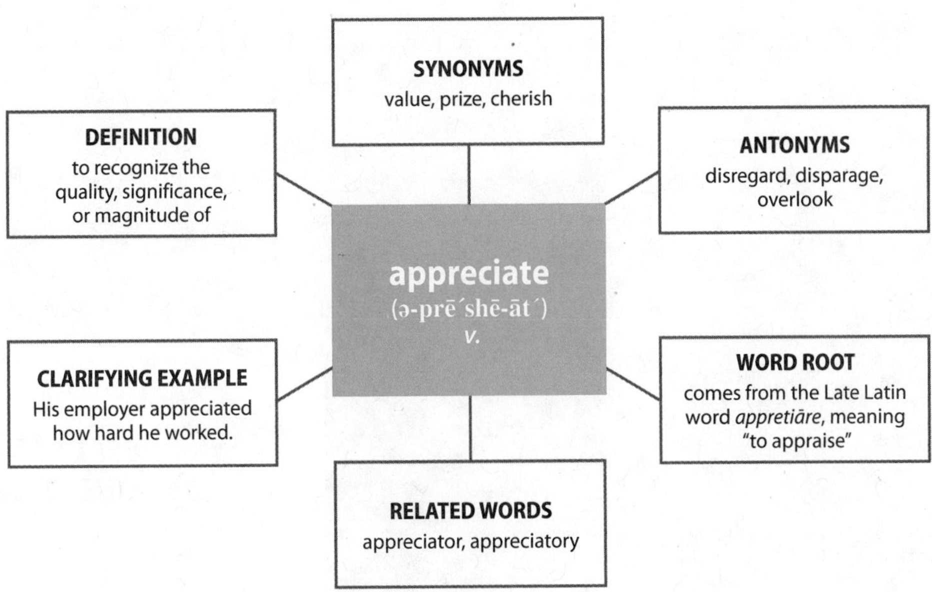

Write and Discuss Discuss your completed Word Network with a partner, making sure to talk through all of the boxes until you both understand the word, its synonyms, antonyms, and related forms. Then fill out a Word Network for the remaining four words. Use a dictionary or online resource to help you complete the activity.

Go online to access the Word Networks.

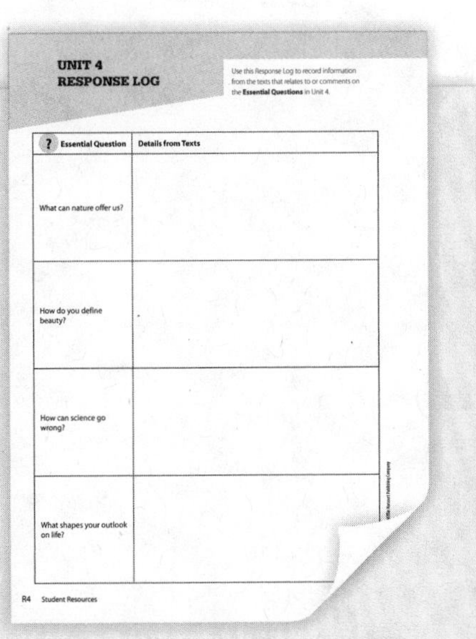

RESPOND TO THE ESSENTIAL QUESTIONS

In this unit, you will explore four different **Essential Questions** about Emotion and Experimentation. As you read each selection, you will gather your ideas about one of these questions and write about it in the **Response Log** that appears on page R4. At the end of the unit, you will have the opportunity to write an **explanatory essay** related to one of the Essential Questions. Filling out the Response Log after you read each text will help you prepare for this writing task.

You can also go online to access the Response Log.

POEMS BY WILLIAM WORDSWORTH

? ESSENTIAL QUESTION:

What can nature offer us?

QUICK START

Think about a time you were in nature and were fully absorbed in the present moment. What do you remember seeing, hearing, and smelling? How did it make you feel?

ANALYZE ROMANTIC POETRY

Romanticism was a literary movement that flourished in Britain and Europe in the 19th century. Unlike the neoclassical poets who preceded them, the Romantics emphasized the importance of the individual's subjective experiences rather than issues that concerned society as a whole. Their philosophy valued emotion, spontaneity, and imagination over reason, analysis, and orderliness.

Romantic poets wrote about personal experiences, often using simple, unadorned language. Many Romantic poems celebrate the beauty and grandeur of the natural world. The Romantics rejected the forces of industrialization that were beginning to transform Europe and tended to idealize the distant past. They looked to nature for inspiration and also for insight into their creative processes.

You are about to read three poems by William Wordsworth, one of the key figures of the Romantic movement. As you read, use a chart such as this one to note details that display the characteristics of Romantic poetry.

GENRE ELEMENTS: LYRIC POETRY

- usually written in the first person
- expresses the feelings and thoughts of the speaker
- uses sound devices such as rhythm and repetition to create a musical quality
- often deals with intense emotions surrounding events like death, love, or loss

DETAILS FROM THE POEMS	CHARACTERISTICS OF ROMANTIC POETRY

GET READY

ANALYZE IMAGERY

Imagery is language that creates vivid sensory experiences for the reader. Visual imagery, which appeals to the sense of sight, is the most common form of imagery used in literature, but writers also use words and phrases to appeal to the senses of hearing, touch, smell, and taste to deepen their readers' understanding of and connection to their works. For example, in "Lines Composed a Few Miles Above Tintern Abbey," Wordsworth refers to the "soft inland murmur" of the Wye River. This auditory image describes the sound of the moving water and also suggests its calming effect.

As you read Wordsworth's poems, look for sensory language and create mental images of the sights and sounds of the landscapes and experiences the poet describes. Also notice how Wordsworth develops the subject, mood, and theme of each poem through imagery. Consider the following lines from "Lines Composed a Few Miles Above Tintern Abbey":

Therefore let the moon
Shine on thee in thy solitary walk;
And let the misty mountain winds be free
To blow against thee:

The visual image of the moon shining and the tactile image of the misty winds blowing against his sister as she walks alone help develop the solemn, reverent mood of the poem. This imagery also reflects the poet's ideas related to the spiritual nourishment that the natural world can provide and the importance of the individual's unique experience.

ANNOTATION MODEL

NOTICE & NOTE

As you read, note passages in the poems that reflect characteristics of Romanticism, and examine how Wordsworth uses imagery to develop ideas about nature and the experiences of individuals. This model shows one reader's notes about "Lines Composed a Few Miles Above Tintern Abbey."

Five years have passed; five summers, with the length
Of five long winters! and again I hear
These waters, rolling from their mountain-springs
With a soft inland murmur. Once again
Do I behold these steep and lofty cliffs,
That on a wild secluded scene impress
Thoughts of more deep seclusion; and connect
The landscape with the quiet of the sky.

These images suggest the grandeur of the wilderness near Tintern Abbey.

The speaker draws a connection between the landscape and the turning inward of his thoughts.

BACKGROUND

William Wordsworth *(1770–1850) helped launch the Romantic movement in England. Rebelling against the formal diction and lofty writings of many poets of the time, Wordsworth used simple language to celebrate subjects drawn mostly from nature and everyday life.*

As a child, Wordsworth happily explored the countryside near his home. When he was seven, his mother died, and he was sent to boarding school. Fortunately, he was able to continue spending time outdoors there, developing his deep love for the natural world and writing poetry. He went to Cambridge University, graduating in 1791.

POEMS BY WILLIAM WORDSWORTH

A walking tour of France in 1790 interested Wordsworth in the political changes happening as a result of the French Revolution. In 1791 Wordsworth returned to France and fell in love with a French woman, Annette Vallon. Lacking money, he returned to England in 1792, but when war broke out between France and England he was prevented from reuniting with Annette and their newborn baby.

In 1795 Wordsworth and his sister set up a home together in a rural area in Dorset. There they befriended the poet Samuel Taylor Coleridge. Wordsworth and Coleridge collaborated on a book of poetry, Lyrical Ballads *(1798), that ushered in the Romantic movement.*

In many of his poems, Wordsworth describes specific natural settings and often shares his thoughts and feelings about them. In "Lines Composed a Few Miles Above Tintern Abbey," Wordsworth reflects on his memories of the beauty of the Wye River Valley in Wales, an area he hiked through extensively. Near this valley are the ruins of Tintern Abbey, a medieval monastery that captivated public imagination with its picturesque decay.

In 1802 Wordsworth married childhood friend Mary Hutchinson. Over the next two decades, he struggled to find readers and critical acceptance for his work. In the 1820s his reputation gradually improved, and by the 1830s he was hugely popular. In 1843 his immense achievement as a poet was recognized when he was named England's poet laureate.

Notice & Note

Use the side margins to notice and note signposts in the text.

9 repose: lie at rest.

14 copses (kŏp´sĭz): thickets of small trees.

16 pastoral (păs´tər-əl): rural and serene.

20 vagrant: wandering.

ANALYZE ROMANTIC POETRY

Annotate: Mark words and phrases in lines 27–49 that describe the speaker's feelings about the landscape.

Analyze: Why are these feelings important for the speaker?

SETTING A PURPOSE

As you read, pay attention to the ideas expressed in the poems about how people are affected by nature and by city life. Also notice how Wordsworth uses imagery to appeal to the reader's senses.

Lines Composed a Few Miles Above Tintern Abbey

Five years have passed; five summers, with the length
Of five long winters! and again I hear
These waters, rolling from their mountain-springs
With a soft inland murmur. Once again
Do I behold these steep and lofty cliffs,
That on a wild secluded scene impress
Thoughts of more deep seclusion; and connect
The landscape with the quiet of the sky.
The day is come when I again repose
Here, under this dark sycamore, and view
These plots of cottage ground, these orchard tufts,
Which at this season, with their unripe fruits,
Are clad in one green hue, and lose themselves
'Mid groves and copses. Once again I see
These hedgerows, hardly hedgerows, little lines
Of sportive wood run wild; these pastoral farms,
Green to the very door; and wreaths of smoke
Sent up, in silence, from among the trees!
With some uncertain notice, as might seem
Of vagrant dwellers in the houseless woods,
Or of some Hermit's cave, where by his fire
The Hermit sits alone.

These beauteous forms,
Through a long absence, have not been to me
As is a landscape to a blind man's eye;
But oft, in lonely rooms, and 'mid the din
Of towns and cities, I have owed to them,
In hours of weariness, sensations sweet,
Felt in the blood, and felt along the heart;
And passing even into my purer mind,
With tranquil restoration—feelings too
Of unremembered pleasure; such, perhaps,
As have no slight or trivial influence
On that best portion of a good man's life,
His little, nameless, unremembered, acts
Of kindness and of love. Nor less, I trust,
To them I may have owed another gift,

Of aspect more sublime; that blessed mood,
In which the burthen of the mystery,
In which the heavy and the weary weight
Of all this unintelligible world,
Is lightened—that serene and blessed mood,
In which the affections gently lead us on—
Until, the breath of this corporeal frame
And even the motion of our human blood
Almost suspended, we are laid asleep
In body, and become a living soul;
While with an eye made quiet by the power
Of harmony, and the deep power of joy,
We see into the life of things.

If this
Be but a vain belief, yet, oh! how oft—
In darkness and amid the many shapes
Of joyless daylight; when the fretful stir
Unprofitable, and the fever of the world,
Have hung upon the beatings of my heart—
How oft, in spirit, have I turned to thee,
O sylvan Wye! thou wanderer through the woods,
How often has my spirit turned to thee!

And now, with gleams of half-extinguished thought
With many recognitions dim and faint,
And somewhat of a sad perplexity,
The picture of the mind revives again;
While here I stand, not only with the sense
Of present pleasure, but with pleasing thoughts
That in this moment there is life and food
For future years. And so I dare to hope,
Though changed, no doubt, from what I was when first
I came among these hills; when like a roe
I bounded o'er the mountains, by the sides
Of the deep rivers, and the lonely streams,
Wherever nature led—more like a man
Flying from something that he dreads than one
Who sought the thing he loved. For nature then
(The coarser pleasures of my boyish days,
And their glad animal movements all gone by)
To me was all in all.—I cannot paint
What then I was. The sounding cataract
Haunted me like a passion; the tall rock,
The mountain, and the deep and gloomy wood,
Their colors and their forms, were then to me

38 burthen: burden.

43 corporeal (kôr-pôr´ē-əl): bodily.

56 sylvan: located in a wood or forest; **Wye:** a river near Tintern Abbey.

67 roe: deer.

76 cataract (kăt´ə-răkt): waterfall.

ANALYZE IMAGERY

Annotate: Mark the auditory and visual imagery in lines 76–78.

Analyze: How does this imagery affect the reader's understanding of the speaker's experience?

NOTICE & NOTE

86 Faint I: I lose heart.

88 recompense (rĕk´əm-pĕns): compensation.

93 chasten (chā´sən): scold; make modest.

An appetite; a feeling and a love,
That had no need of a remoter charm,
By thought supplied, nor any interest
Unborrowed from the eye.—That time is past,
And all its aching joys are now no more,
And all its dizzy raptures. Not for this
Faint I, nor mourn nor murmur; other gifts
Have followed; for such loss, I would believe,
Abundant recompense. For I have learned
To look on nature, not as in the hour
Of thoughtless youth; but hearing oftentimes
The still, sad music of humanity,
Nor harsh nor grating, though of ample power
To chasten and subdue. And I have felt
A presence that disturbs me with the joy
Of elevated thoughts; a sense sublime
Of something far more deeply interfused,
Whose dwelling is the light of setting suns,
And the round ocean and the living air,

NOTICE & NOTE 

And the blue sky, and in the mind of man:
A motion and a spirit, that impels
All thinking things, all objects of all thought,
And rolls through all things. Therefore am I still
A lover of the meadows and the woods,
And mountains; and of all that we behold
From this green earth; of all the mighty world
Of eye, and ear—both what they half create,
And what perceive; well pleased to recognize
In nature and the language of the sense
The anchor of my purest thoughts, the nurse,
The guide, the guardian of my heart, and soul
Of all my moral being.

Nor perchance,
If I were not thus taught, should I the more
Suffer my genial spirits to decay:
For thou art with me here upon the banks
Of this fair river; thou my dearest Friend,

ANALYZE IMAGERY

Annotate: Mark images of nature in lines 93–102.

Analyze: How do these images support the speaker's idea about a force that affects all things?

111 perchance: by chance; perhaps.

113 genial (jēn´yəl): relating to genius; creative.

115 thou my dearest Friend: Wordsworth´s sister, Dorothy.

NOTICE & NOTE

My dear, dear Friend; and in thy voice I catch
The language of my former heart, and read
My former pleasures in the shooting lights
Of thy wild eyes. Oh! yet a little while
May I behold in thee what I was once,
My dear, dear Sister! and this prayer I make,
Knowing that Nature never did betray
The heart that loved her; 'tis her privilege,
Through all the years of this our life, to lead
From joy to joy: for she can so inform
The mind that is within us, so impress
With quietness and beauty, and so feed
With lofty thoughts, that neither evil tongues,
Rash judgments, nor the sneers of selfish men,
Nor greetings where no kindness is, nor all
The dreary intercourse of daily life,
Shall e'er prevail against us, or disturb
Our cheerful faith, that all which we behold
Is full of blessings. Therefore let the moon
Shine on thee in thy solitary walk;
And let the misty mountain winds be free
To blow against thee: and, in after years,
When these wild ecstasies shall be matured
Into a sober pleasure; when thy mind
Shall be a mansion for all lovely forms,
Thy memory be as a dwelling place
For all sweet sounds and harmonies; oh! then,
If solitude, or fear, or pain, or grief
Should be thy portion, with what healing thoughts
Of tender joy wilt thou remember me,
And these my exhortations! Nor, perchance—
If I should be where I no more can hear
Thy voice, nor catch from thy wild eyes these gleams
Of past existence—wilt thou then forget
That on the banks of this delightful stream
We stood together; and that I, so long
A worshiper of Nature, hither came
Unwearied in that service; rather say
With warmer love—oh! with far deeper zeal
Of holier love. Nor wilt thou then forget,
That after many wanderings, many years
Of absence, these steep woods and lofty cliffs,
And this green pastoral landscape, were to me
More dear, both for themselves and for thy sake!

ANALYZE ROMANTIC POETRY

Annotate: Mark the verbs used in lines 123–134 to describe nature's actions.

Analyze: What romantic idea does Wordsworth express in this passage?

146 exhortations: words of encouraging advice.

149 past existence: the speaker's own past experience five years before (see lines 116–119).

CHECK YOUR UNDERSTANDING

Answer these questions about "Lines Composed a Few Miles Above Tintern Abbey" before moving on to the next selection.

1 How did the speaker's memories of the valley affect him during the past five years?

A They tormented him.

B They restored his spirit.

C They made him resent city life.

D They caused him to avoid nature.

2 What has the speaker lost since he last visited the valley?

F His ability to run up the mountains

G His memory of where the ruined abbey stood

H His career in the city

J His passionate reaction to nature

3 What does the speaker observe in his sister?

A She responds to nature the same way he used to.

B She fears hurting herself in the valley.

C She shares his memories of the valley.

D She behaves recklessly on their hike.

Composed upon Westminster Bridge, September 3, 1802

Earth has not anything to show more fair:
Dull would he be of soul who could pass by
A sight so touching in its majesty;
This City now doth, like a garment, wear
The beauty of the morning; silent, bare,
Ships, towers, domes, theaters, and temples lie
Open unto the fields, and to the sky;
All bright and glittering in the smokeless air.
Never did sun more beautifully steep
In his first splendor, valley, rock, or hill;
Ne'er saw I, never felt, a calm so deep!
The river glideth at his own sweet will:
Dear God! the very houses seem asleep;
And all that mighty heart is lying still!

ANALYZE ROMANTIC POETRY

Annotate: Mark language in lines 9–14 that conveys the emotions of the speaker.

Analyze: What emotions does this language convey?

9 steep: soak; saturate.

12 The river: Westminster Bridge spans the Thames (tĕmz)—the principal river in London.

13 houses: possibly a pun on the Houses of Parliament, near Westminster Bridge.

CHECK YOUR UNDERSTANDING

Answer these questions about "Composed upon Westminster Bridge, September 3, 1802" before moving on to the next selection.

1 What time of day does "Composed upon Westminster Bridge, September 3, 1802" describe?

A Dawn

B Dusk

C Midnight

D Midday

2 Which of the following best describes the speaker's meaning in lines 2 and 3?

F He prefers being in the city to being in nature.

G He believes people should stop to appreciate the world around them.

H He thinks his soul is better than the souls of other people.

J He feels saddened by the majestic view.

3 How does the scene he describes in the poem make the speaker feel?

A Excited

B Melancholy

C Peaceful

D Disappointed

NOTICE & NOTE

I Wandered Lonely As a Cloud

I wandered lonely as a cloud
That floats on high o'er vales and hills,
When all at once I saw a crowd,
A host, of golden daffodils;
Beside the lake, beneath the trees,
Fluttering and dancing in the breeze.

Continuous as the stars that shine
And twinkle on the milky way,
They stretched in never-ending line
Along the margin of a bay:
Ten thousand saw I at a glance,
Tossing their heads in sprightly dance.

The waves beside them danced; but they
Outdid the sparkling waves in glee;
A poet could not but be gay,
In such a jocund company;
I gazed—and gazed—but little thought
What wealth the show to me had brought:

2 vales: valleys.

ANALYZE IMAGERY

Annotate: Mark the imagery that describes nature in lines 1–12.

Analyze: How do these images help the reader understand the speaker's experience?

16 jocund (jŏk´ənd): merry.

For oft, when on my couch I lie
In vacant or in pensive mood,
They flash upon that inward eye
Which is the bliss of solitude;
And then my heart with pleasure fills,
And dances with the daffodils.

CHECK YOUR UNDERSTANDING

Answer these questions before moving on to the **Analyze the Texts** section on the following page.

1 What sight captures the speaker's attention in "I Wandered Lonely As a Cloud"?

A Clouds

B Daffodils

C Dancers

D Waves

2 The tone of the poem is best described as —

F lonely

G joyful

H solemn

J humorous

3 What does Wordsworth mean in line 21 when he says that the daffodils "flash upon that inward eye"?

A They remind him that he is alone.

B They keep him awake at night.

C They make him feel pensive.

D They appear in his imagination.

ANALYZE THE TEXTS

Support your responses with evidence from the texts. NOTEBOOK

1. **Analyze** What details in lines 1–22 of "Lines Composed a Few Miles Above Tintern Abbey" suggest that Wordsworth preferred to celebrate the individual in his work rather than society?
2. **Draw Conclusions** In "Lines Composed a Few Miles Above Tintern Abbey," how has the speaker's relationship with nature changed over time?
3. **Analyze** How does Wordsworth use imagery in "Composed upon Westminster Bridge, September 3, 1802" to support the mood and theme of the poem?
4. **Interpret** Reread lines 17–24 of "I Wandered Lonely As a Cloud." What is the "wealth" that the speaker doesn't initially appreciate when he sees the daffodils?
5. **Synthesize** Which characteristics of Romanticism do all three of these poems share?

RESEARCH

RESEARCH TIP
Before you begin researching, identify key words from the research prompt to help start your online search.

Tintern Abbey and Westminster Bridge are real places in England. With a partner, research these places to find out more about them.

- Read some background information about the history of these places.
- Search for images so you can see what each place looks like.
- Do a map search so you can see where the locations are in reference to the rest of England.

Use a chart like the one below to record the results of your research.

PLACE	HISTORY	APPEARANCE	LOCATION
Tintern Abbey			
Westminster Bridge			

Extend The poem "I Wandered Lonely As a Cloud" describes the scenery of the Lake District, another real place in England. Research the Lake District, add a row to your chart, and record information about its history, appearance, and location.

CREATE AND DISCUSS

Write a Summary Write a summary of "Lines Composed a Few Miles Above Tintern Abbey." To do this, you will briefly retell the events and experiences described in the poem in your own words.

- ❑ Introduce the speaker and the other people mentioned in the poem.
- ❑ Describe the setting of the poem, and explain the effect it has on the speaker.
- ❑ Explain how the imagery in the poem engages the reader's senses and conveys meaning.
- ❑ Include a statement of the poem's theme, or central message.

Discuss Consider the ideas Wordsworth expresses in his poetry about nature and the comfort it can provide. With a partner, discuss any of your own experiences in nature that you've found meaningful or helpful in your life.

- ❑ Listen thoughtfully as your partner tells you about his or her experiences.
- ❑ Ask questions about any ideas or details that are unclear or need elaboration.
- ❑ Brainstorm to come up with ideas as to how you and your partner might seek out additional meaningful experiences in nature.

Go to **Participating in Collaborative Discussions** in the **Speaking and Listening Studio** for more help.

RESPOND TO THE ESSENTIAL QUESTION

What can nature offer us?

Gather Information Review your annotations and notes on the poems by William Wordsworth. Then, add relevant information to your Response Log. As you determine which information to include, think about:

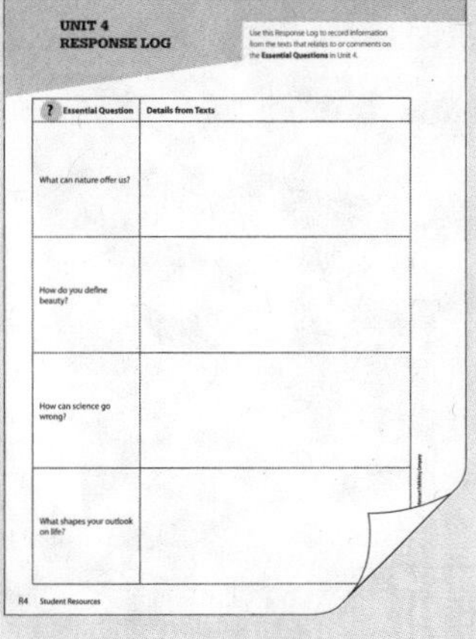

UNIT 4
RESPONSE LOG

Use this Response Log to record information from the texts that relates to or comments on the **Essential Questions** in Unit 4.

? Essential Question	Details from Texts
What can nature offer us?	
How do you define beauty?	
How can science go wrong?	
What shapes your outlook on life?	

R4 Student Resources

- the mental and emotional solace Wordsworth finds in nature
- the role of memory in Wordsworth's poems
- what you value about your own memories of experiences with nature

ACADEMIC VOCABULARY

As you write and discuss what you learned from the poems, be sure to use the Academic Vocabulary words. Check off each of the words that you use.

- ❑ **appreciate**
- ❑ **insight**
- ❑ **intensity**
- ❑ **invoke**
- ❑ **radical**

ODE ON A GRECIAN URN

Poem by **John Keats**

? ESSENTIAL QUESTION:

How do you define beauty?

QUICK START

Write a description of your favorite artwork or a prized possession. Discuss the feelings you associate with this object and why you find it so appealing. Include at least four sensory details in your description.

ANALYZE STANZA STRUCTURE

A **stanza** is a group of lines that form a unit in a poem. In traditional poetic forms, stanzas often contain the same number of lines and have the same rhyme scheme and meter. Stanzas often function like paragraphs in prose, each presenting a discrete idea.

Although odes can vary in structure, the five stanzas of "Ode on a Grecian Urn" have a regular structure of ten lines of **iambic pentameter,** a metrical pattern of five feet, or units. Each iambic foot consists of two syllables, the first unstressed and the second stressed.

Thou stíll unrávish'd bríde of quíetnéss,

Thou fóster-chíld of sílence ánd slow tíme,

Keats sometimes varies the meter to emphasize certain words and to keep the poem from sounding monotonous. You can gain insight into the meaning of the poem by reading it aloud and noticing which words are stressed. As you read, also notice the main idea expressed in each stanza.

ANALYZE RHYME SCHEME

The **rhyme scheme** of a poem is the pattern of **end rhyme** that helps establish the structure and unity of a stanza and adds to the poem's musicality. A rhyme scheme is described using letters, such as *abab* or *aabb*, where lines that rhyme are given the same letter. Certain poetic forms, such as the various types of sonnets, follow a set rhyme scheme.

Keats's "Ode on a Grecian Urn" has a complex rhyme scheme. The first four lines of each stanza rhyme *abab*. The next six lines follow one of these patterns: *cdedce, cdeced,* or *cdecde*. Because of these variations, the rhyming becomes subtler and more unexpected as you move farther along in a stanza. While reading the poem, notice how the rhyme scheme appeals to your sense of hearing.

GENRE ELEMENTS: ODE

- lyric poem that develops a single theme
- has a serious tone
- appeals to both the imagination and the intellect
- may commemorate an event or praise people or nature's beauty

GET READY

ANALYZE APOSTROPHE

Apostrophe is a figure of speech in which the speaker addresses an object, abstract concept, or absent or imaginary person as if present and able to understand. Poets often use apostrophe to express strong emotions. This device was especially popular among the Romantic poets. In "Ode on a Grecian Urn," Keats uses apostrophe to address both the urn itself and the figures portrayed on it.

> **O Attic shape! Fair attitude! with brede**
> **Of marble men and maidens overwrought,**

Here the speaker addresses the urn as one might speak to an admired person, heightening the reader's sense of his emotional response to seeing the urn. As you read the poem, pay attention to the shifting focus of the apostrophe.

ANNOTATION MODEL

NOTICE & NOTE 

As you read, note words and phrases that convey ideas about the artwork discussed in the poem. Also notice how the rhyme scheme and meter emphasize important words. In the model, you can see one reader's notes about the opening lines of "Ode on a Grecian Urn."

Thou still unravish'd bride of quietness,
Thou foster-child of silence and slow time,
Sylvan historian, who canst thus express
A flowery tale more sweetly than our rhyme:
What leaf-fring'd legend haunts about thy shape
Of deities or mortals, or of both,
In Tempe or the dales of Arcady?
What men or gods are these? What maidens loath?
What mad pursuit? What struggle to escape?
What pipes and timbrels? What wild ecstasy?

The speaker uses phrases that compare the urn to specific types of people. This helps give the impression that he is addressing something that can understand him.

NOTICE & NOTE

BACKGROUND

__John Keats__ (1795–1821) only lived to age 25, yet he produced some of the most famous poems in the English language. Keats's life was marred by illness and tragedy. His father died in a riding accident when he was young. Later, both his mother and brother died of tuberculosis, and Keats himself became ill with the disease at 22. His poor health prevented him from marrying his sweetheart, Fanny Brawne. It was during his illness, however, that he produced some of his greatest work. "Ode on a Grecian Urn" was probably inspired by ancient Greek urns that Keats saw at the British Museum. Such urns were often painted with mythological scenes, as described in this poem.

ODE ON A GRECIAN URN

Poem by John Keats

SETTING A PURPOSE

As you read, notice the ideas that the speaker associates with images on the urn.

Thou still unravish'd bride of quietness,
  Thou foster-child of silence and slow time,
Sylvan historian, who canst thus express
  A flowery tale more sweetly than our rhyme:
What leaf-fring'd legend haunts about thy shape
  Of deities or mortals, or of both,
    In Tempe or the dales of Arcady?
  What men or gods are these? What maidens loath?
What mad pursuit? What struggle to escape?
    What pipes and timbrels? What wild ecstasy?

Heard melodies are sweet, but those unheard
  Are sweeter; therefore, ye soft pipes, play on;
Not to the sensual ear, but, more endear'd,
  Pipe to the spirit ditties of no tone:
Fair youth, beneath the trees, thou canst not leave
  Thy song, nor ever can those trees be bare;

Notice & Note

Use the side margins to notice and note signposts in the text.

3 Sylvan: pertaining to trees or woods.

5 haunts about: surrounds.

7 Tempe (tĕm´pē) **. . . Arcady** (är´kə-dē): two places in Greece that became traditional literary settings for an idealized rustic life. Tempe is a beautiful valley; Arcady (Arcadia) is a mountainous region.

8 loath: unwilling; reluctant.

10 timbrels: tambourines.

NOTICE & NOTE

ANALYZE RHYME SCHEME

Annotate: Mark the end rhymes in lines 11–20.

Analyze: What is the rhyme scheme in this stanza?

29 cloy'd: having had too much of something; oversatisfied.

ANALYZE APOSTROPHE

Annotate: In lines 32–40, mark the two images that the author addresses.

Interpret: What emotions does the author express about each of these images?

41 Attic: pure and classical; in the style of Attica, the part of Greece where Athens is located; **brede** (brēd): interwoven design.

45 Pastoral (păs´tər-əl): an artistic work that portrays rural life in an idealized way.

ANALYZE STANZA STRUCTURE

Annotate: In lines 41–45, mark the syllables that are stressed.

Identify: Where in the passage does Keats vary the metrical pattern to emphasize certain words?

Bold lover, never, never canst thou kiss,
Though winning near the goal—yet, do not grieve;
She cannot fade, though thou hast not thy bliss,
For ever wilt thou love, and she be fair!

Ah, happy, happy boughs! that cannot shed
Your leaves, nor ever bid the spring adieu;
And, happy melodist, unweariéd,
For ever piping songs for ever new;
More happy love! more happy, happy love!
For ever warm and still to be enjoyed,
For ever panting, and for ever young;
All breathing human passion far above,
That leaves a heart high-sorrowful and cloy'd,
A burning forehead, and a parching tongue.

Who are these coming to the sacrifice?
To what green altar, O mysterious priest,
Lead'st thou that heifer lowing at the skies,
And all her silken flanks with garlands drest?
What little town by river or sea shore,
Or mountain-built with peaceful citadel,
Is emptied of this folk, this pious morn?
And, little town, thy streets for evermore
Will silent be; and not a soul to tell
Why thou art desolate, can e'er return.

O Attic shape! Fair attitude! with brede
Of marble men and maidens overwrought,
With forest branches and the trodden weed;
Thou, silent form, dost tease us out of thought
As doth eternity: Cold Pastoral!
When old age shall this generation waste,
Thou shalt remain, in midst of other woe
Than ours, a friend to man, to whom thou say'st,
"Beauty is truth, truth beauty,"—that is all
Ye know on earth, and all ye need to know.

CHECK YOUR UNDERSTANDING

Answer these questions before moving on to the **Analyze the Text** section on the following page.

1 In line 3, the phrase "Sylvan historian" refers to —

A a Greek writer

B a man pictured on the urn

C the reader of the poem

D the Grecian urn

2 In line 20, why does the author say, "For ever wilt thou love, and she be fair"?

F True love is everlasting.

G Their images are frozen in time.

H They exist only in each other's memories.

J Their love is immortalized in song.

3 What is the urn's message, delivered in its last two lines?

A Beauty and truth are unable to stand the test of time.

B Beauty and truth are equivalent and eternal.

C Beauty and truth both are important.

D Beauty and truth are often confused.

RESPOND

ANALYZE THE TEXT

Support your responses with evidence from the text. NOTEBOOK

1. **Analyze** In lines 1–4, Keats addresses the urn as an "unravish'd bride" and a "Sylvan historian." What characteristics of the urn do these phrases in the apostrophe convey?
2. **Interpret** Reread lines 11–14. How do you interpret the statement, "Heard melodies are sweet, but those unheard / Are sweeter"?
3. **Identify Patterns** What words are repeated in stanza 3? What idea does this repetition help develop in the stanza?
4. **Draw Conclusions** Why might Keats have chosen to vary the rhyme scheme in the last six lines of the stanzas?
5. **Connect** How might Keats's personal circumstances have contributed to the sentiments expressed in the poem?

RESEARCH

Like most educated people of his era, Keats studied classical literature. He was also inspired by Greek art and philosophy. With a partner, research Keats's connections to ancient Greece. Use what you learn to answer these questions.

RESEARCH TIP

When looking for information in an online source or digital document, use Ctrl + F to do a search of the page. Put phrases in quotation marks to search only for that exact phrase.

QUESTION	ANSWER
What artworks in the British Museum probably inspired "Ode on a Grecian Urn"?	
What characteristics of the Greek goddess Psyche does Keats emphasize in his poem "Ode to Psyche"?	
In the poem "On First Looking into Chapman's Homer," what does Keats admire about the translation of the Greek epics referred to in the title?	

Extend Read "Ode to Psyche." With a partner, discuss the poem's ideas and also its formal qualities, such as stanza structure and rhyme scheme. Compare the poem with "Ode on a Grecian Urn."

CREATE AND PRESENT

Write a Poem Using Apostrophe Is there an inanimate object or abstract idea that you have strong feelings about? Perhaps you love winter or are upset about the closing of a local restaurant. Write a poem addressing that inanimate object or abstract idea to express your feelings.

- ❑ Address the object or idea directly. Use apostrophe to express strong emotion.
- ❑ Include several stanzas. Decide whether you will use regular patterns of rhyme and meter or if you'll write in free verse, with no regular patterns.
- ❑ Use sensory details to create a vivid experience for your reader.

Present Your Poem Give a dramatic reading of your poem for a group or the whole class.

- ❑ Practice your dramatic reading and revise the text as necessary for dramatic effectiveness and ease of speech.
- ❑ Make notations to remind yourself to emphasize certain words or phrases.
- ❑ When giving your presentation, use voice inflection, facial expressions, gestures, and eye contact.

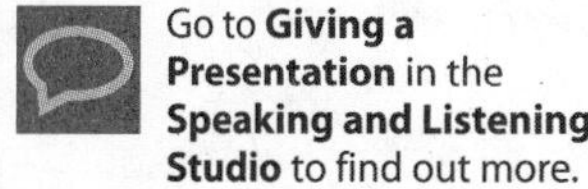

Go to **Giving a Presentation** in the **Speaking and Listening Studio** to find out more.

RESPOND TO THE ESSENTIAL QUESTION

? How do you define beauty?

Gather Information Review your annotations and notes on "Ode on a Grecian Urn." Then, add relevant information to your Response Log. As you determine which information to include, think about:

- whether beauty is subjective or objective
- what emotions beauty inspires
- whether your experiences change how you perceive beauty

ACADEMIC VOCABULARY

As you write and discuss what you learned from the poem, be sure to use the Academic Vocabulary words. Check off each of the words that you use.

- ❑ **appreciate**
- ❑ **insight**
- ❑ **intensity**
- ❑ **invoke**
- ❑ **radical**

ANALYZE & APPLY

from FRANKENSTEIN

Novel by **Mary Shelley**

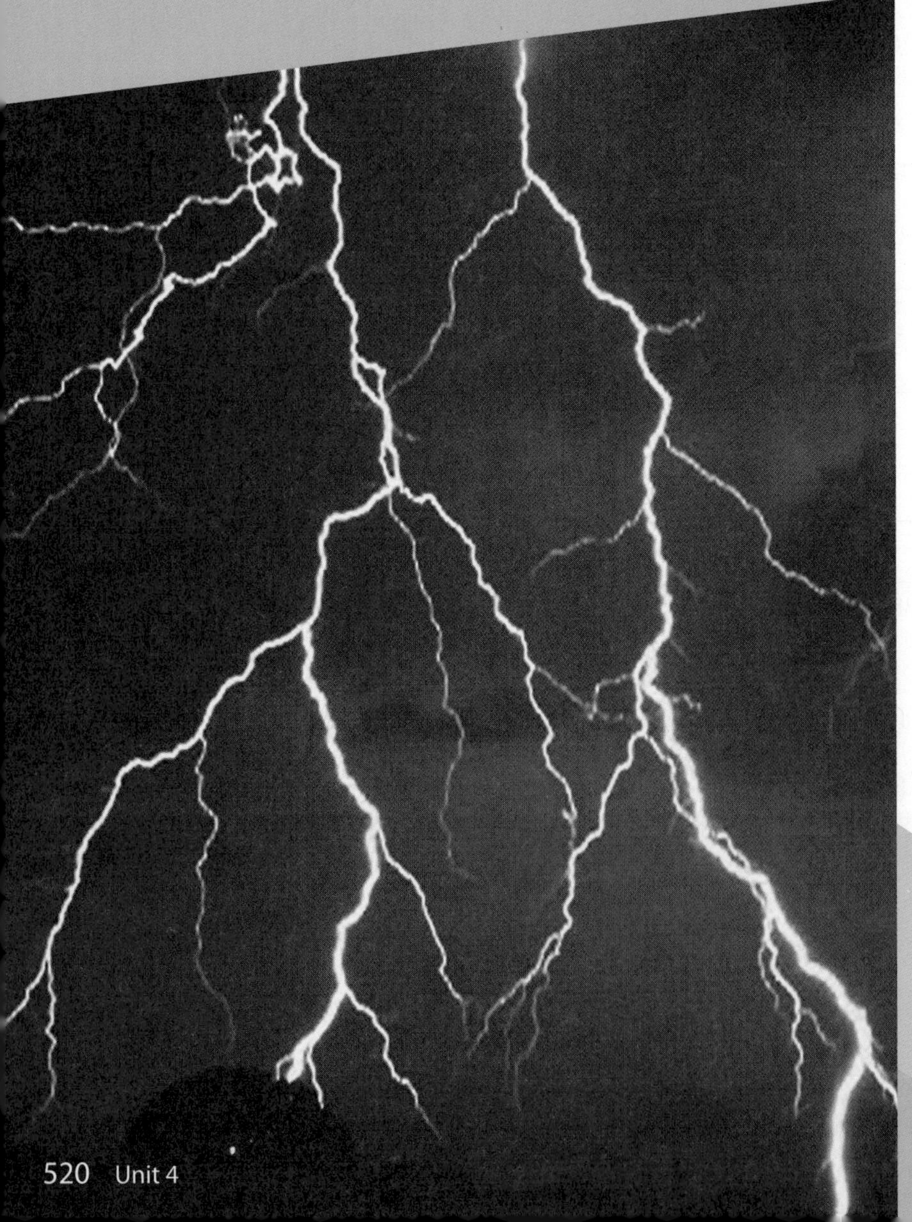

ESSENTIAL QUESTION:

How can science go wrong?

QUICK START

The name *Frankenstein* is often used to describe scientific research that has gotten out of control. To what extent should scientists be held accountable for the results of their discoveries? Discuss this question with a partner.

ANALYZE SCIENCE FICTION

Frankenstein is a work of gothic horror that is also considered one of the first science fiction novels. **Science fiction** is a literary genre based on imagined scientific or technological developments, such as time travel or encounters with extraterrestrial life. Mary Shelley said that the idea for the book came to her in a dream after spending several stormy nights discussing ghost stories and medical experiments with a group of friends. She wrote a story about a scientist who creates a man from human remains, which she later expanded into the novel *Frankenstein*.

As you read, use a chart like the one below to note how imaginary advances in science or medicine influence important elements of the novel.

Elements of Science Fiction in *Frankenstein*	
Plot	
Characters	
Theme	

GENRE ELEMENTS: NOVEL

- a long fictional prose narrative
- includes the same fictional elements as a short story
- usually has a more complex plot and a wider range of characters than a short story
- may be written in subgenres such as science fiction, historical fiction, or mystery

ANALYZE MOTIVATION

Motivation is the stated or implied reason behind a fictional character's behavior. Sometimes motivation is directly expressed in a story, but usually readers must infer a character's motivation from dialogue, thoughts, and actions. Characters' motivations often influence the plot and theme of a work, so careful readers look closely for relationships among these elements.

In Shelley's novel, Victor Frankenstein struggles with the moral dilemma of whether to accept or abandon the creature he has created. As you read, analyze the motivations that contribute toward this dilemma. Also, analyze the motivations underlying the creature's behavior toward Frankenstein.

GET READY

CRITICAL VOCABULARY

infuse	**ardor**	**inarticulate**	**precipice**
inanimate	**tumult**	**misdeed**	**odious**

To see how many Critical Vocabulary words you already know, use them to complete the sentences.

1. Because of his __________ for his experiment, he would stop at nothing to discover how to make the __________ creature come to life.
2. Frankenstein's mind was in a __________ about what he had created, and he felt that he was standing at the edge of a terrifying __________ in the history of science.
3. Though at first the creature was __________, he later learned to speak and even to __________ his speech with the tones and cadences used in real human conversation.
4. The __________ creature, cast out from human society, was determined to find his creator and deny that he had committed any __________.

LANGUAGE CONVENTIONS

Sensory Language In this lesson, you will examine how sensory language is used to help re-create sensory experiences for the reader. Sensory language includes descriptive words or phrases that appeal to one or more of the five senses: sight, hearing, smell, taste, and touch.

In this sentence from *Frankenstein*, Mary Shelley uses sensory language that helps the reader feel the cold wind that the narrator experiences in the novel:

> **I was troubled: a mist came over my eyes, and I felt a faintness seize me; but I was quickly restored by the cold gale of the mountains.**

As you read the excerpt from *Frankenstein*, note places where the author uses sensory language.

ANNOTATION MODEL

NOTICE & NOTE

As you read, make note of any elements of horror and science fiction. In the model, you can see one reader's notes on a passage from *Frankenstein*.

It was on a dreary night of November that I beheld the accomplishment of my toils. With an anxiety that almost amounted to agony, I collected the instruments of life around me, that I might infuse a spark of being into the lifeless thing that lay at my feet.

Shelley opens with a classic horror story phrase to describe the setting.

The details about bringing something dead to life ("the instruments of life" and "might infuse a spark of being") tell me this is a science fiction story.

NOTICE & NOTE 

BACKGROUND

Mary Shelley *(1797–1851) was the daughter of two famous writers, the early feminist Mary Wollstonecraft and the philosopher William Godwin. Shelley's education benefited from access to her father's vast library and the many scientific and literary people she encountered during her upbringing. When she was 19, she married the poet Percy Bysshe Shelley. Although her literary reputation was long overshadowed by those of her parents and husband, in recent decades Shelley has gained increased recognition as an important writer. Written in 1818,* Frankenstein *was first published anonymously, then later under Shelley's name.*

FRANKENSTEIN

Novel by Mary Shelley

SETTING A PURPOSE

As you read, pay attention to Victor Frankenstein's reactions to the creature he created, and consider whether his reactions are out of proportion based on the creature's words and behavior.

Notice & Note

Use the side margins to notice and note signposts in the text.

A young Swiss scientist named Victor Frankenstein sets out to learn the secret of creating life. For two years he devotes himself to studying chemistry and human anatomy. Finally, after assembling a creature from human remains, he prepares to use an electrical charge to bring it to life.

1 It was on a dreary night of November that I beheld the accomplishment of my toils. With an anxiety that almost amounted to agony, I collected the instruments of life around me, that I might **infuse** a spark of being into the lifeless thing that lay at my feet. It was already one in the morning; the rain pattered dismally against the panes, and my candle was nearly burnt out, when, by the glimmer of the half-extinguished light, I saw the dull yellow eye of the creature open; it breathed hard, and a convulsive motion agitated its limbs.

ANALYZE SCIENCE FICTION

Annotate: In paragraph 1, mark the words and phrases that suggest scientific endeavors.

Explain: How do these details support the categorization of *Frankenstein* as one of the first works of science fiction?

infuse
(ĭn-fyōōz´) *v.* to fill or cause to be filled with something.

NOTICE & NOTE

ANALYZE MOTIVATION

Annotate: In paragraph 2, mark the words or phrases that demonstrate the great care Frankenstein took in building his creation.

Analyze: Why would Frankenstein have taken such pains to make his creation?

inanimate
(ĭn-ăn´ə-mĭt) *adj.* not having the qualities associated with active, living organisms.

ardor
(är´dər) *n.* intensity of emotion, especially strong desire, enthusiasm, or devotion.

tumult
(to͞o´mŭlt) *n.* a state of agitation of the mind or emotions.

inarticulate
(ĭn-är-tĭk´yə-lĭt) *adj.* uttered without the use of normal words or syllables; incomprehensible as speech or language.

2 How can I describe my emotions at this catastrophe, or how delineate the wretch whom, with such infinite pains and care, I had endeavored to form? His limbs were in proportion, and I had selected his features as beautiful. Beautiful! Great God! His yellow skin scarcely covered the work of muscles and arteries beneath; his hair was of a lustrous black, and flowing; his teeth of a pearly whiteness; but these luxuriances only formed a more horrid contrast with his watery eyes, that seemed almost of the same color as the dun white sockets in which they were set, his shriveled complexion, and straight black lips.

3 The different accidents of life are not so changeable as the feelings of human nature. I had worked hard for nearly two years, for the sole purpose of infusing life into an **inanimate** body. For this I had deprived myself of rest and health. I had desired it with an **ardor** that far exceeded moderation; but now that I had finished, the beauty of the dream vanished, and breathless horror and disgust filled my heart. Unable to endure the aspect of the being I had created, I rushed out of the room, and continued a long time traversing my bed-chamber, unable to compose my mind to sleep. At length lassitude succeeded to the **tumult** I had before endured; and I threw myself on the bed in my clothes, endeavoring to seek a few moments of forgetfulness. But it was in vain: I slept indeed, but I was disturbed by the wildest dreams. I thought I saw Elizabeth, in the bloom of health, walking in the streets of Ingolstadt. Delighted and surprised, I embraced her; but as I imprinted the first kiss on her lips, they became livid with the hue of death; her features appeared to change, and I thought that I held the corpse of my dead mother in my arms; a shroud enveloped her form, and I saw the grave-worms crawling in the folds of the flannel. I started from my sleep with horror; a cold dew covered my forehead, my teeth chattered, and every limb became convulsed; when, by the dim and yellow light of the moon, as it forced its way through the window-shutters, I beheld the wretch, the miserable monster whom I had created. He held up the curtain of the bed; and his eyes, if eyes they may be called, were fixed on me. His jaws opened, and he muttered some **inarticulate** sounds, while a grin wrinkled his cheeks.

4 He might have spoken, but I did not hear; one hand was stretched out, seemingly to detain me, but I escaped, and rushed downstairs. I took refuge in the courtyard belonging to the house which I inhabited; where I remained during the rest of the night, walking up and down in the greatest agitation, listening attentively, catching and fearing each sound as if it were to announce the approach of the demoniacal corpse to which I had so miserably given life. . . .

After fleeing from his creation, Victor Frankenstein falls seriously ill and is cared for by a friend. He learns that the creature has killed his younger brother, William, and framed a family servant for the murder. Frankenstein returns home, but he is unable to save the servant from execution for William's murder. Tormented by guilt, he sets out for a hike in the Swiss Alps, hoping to relieve his despair.

5 It was nearly noon when I arrived at the top of the ascent. For some time I sat upon the rock that overlooks the sea of ice. A mist covered both that and the surrounding mountains. Presently a breeze dissipated the cloud, and I descended upon the glacier. The surface is very uneven, rising like the waves of a troubled sea, descending low, and interspersed by rifts that sink deep. The field of ice is almost a league in width, but I spent nearly two hours in crossing it. The opposite mountain is a bare perpendicular rock. From the side where I now stood Montanvert was exactly opposite, at the distance of a league; and above it rose Mont Blanc, in awful majesty. I remained in a recess of the rock, gazing on this wonderful and stupendous scene. The sea, or rather the vast river of ice, wound among its dependent mountains, whose aerial summits hung over its recesses. Their icy and glittering peaks shone in the sunlight over the clouds. My heart, which was before sorrowful, now swelled with something like joy; I exclaimed — "Wandering spirits, if ye indeed wander, and do not rest in your narrow beds, allow me this faint happiness, or take me as your companion, away from the joys of life."

LANGUAGE CONVENTIONS

Annotate: Mark the language that evokes the senses in paragraph 5.

Infer: What impression of the setting does the sensory language help convey?

6 As I said this, I suddenly beheld the figure of a man, at some distance, advancing towards me with superhuman speed. He bounded over the crevices of the ice, among which I had walked with caution; his stature also, as he approached, seemed to exceed that of man.

7 I was troubled: a mist came over my eyes, and I felt a faintness seize me; but I was quickly restored by the cold gale of the mountains. I perceived, as the shape came nearer (sight tremendous and abhorred!), that it was the wretch whom I had created. I trembled with rage and horror, resolving to wait his approach, and then close with him in mortal combat. He approached; his countenance bespoke bitter anguish, combined with disdain and malignity, while its unearthly ugliness rendered it almost too horrible for human eyes. But I scarcely observed this; anger and hatred had at first deprived me of utterance, and I recovered only to overwhelm him with words expressive of furious detestation and contempt.

ANALYZE MOTIVATION

Annotate: Mark words in paragraph 7 that show how Frankenstein feels about his creation and what he plans to do to it.

Infer: Why might Frankenstein feel this way and resolve to take this action?

NOTICE & NOTE

ANALYZE MOTIVATION

Annotate: Mark the words or phrases in paragraph 9 that show what the creature asks of Frankenstein.

Draw Conclusions: What does the creature ask for, and what motivates his request?

misdeed
(mĭs-dēd´) *n.* a wrong or illegal deed; a wrongdoing.

8 "Devil!" I exclaimed, "do you dare approach me? and do you not fear the fierce vengeance of my arm wreaked on your miserable head? Begone, vile insect! or rather stay, that I may trample you to dust! and, oh, that I could, with the extinction of your miserable existence, restore those victims whom you have so diabolically murdered!"

9 "I expected this reception," said the demon. "All men hate the wretched; how then must I be hated, who am miserable beyond all living things! Yet you, my creator, detest and spurn me, thy creature, to whom thou art bound by ties only dissoluble by the annihilation of one of us. You purpose to kill me. How dare you sport thus with life? Do your duty towards me, and I will do mine towards you and the rest of mankind. If you will comply with my conditions, I will leave them and you at peace; but if you refuse, I will glut the maw of death, until it be satisfied with the blood of your remaining friends."

10 "Abhorred monster! fiend that thou art! the tortures of hell are too mild a vengeance for thy crimes. Wretched devil! you reproach me with your creation; come on then, that I may extinguish the spark which I so negligently bestowed."

11 My rage was without bounds; I sprang on him, impelled by all the feelings which can arm one being against the existence of another.

He easily eluded me, and said, —

12 "Be calm! I entreat you to hear me, before you give vent to your hatred on my devoted head. Have I not suffered enough, that you seek to increase my misery? Life, although it may only be an accumulation of anguish, is dear to me, and I will defend it. Remember, thou hast made me more powerful than thyself; my height is superior to thine; my joints more supple. But I will not be tempted to set myself in opposition to thee. I am thy creature, and I will be even mild and docile to my natural lord and king, if thou wilt also perform thy part, the which thou owest me. Oh, Frankenstein, be not equitable to every other, and trample upon me alone, to whom thy justice, and even thy clemency and affection, is most due. Remember, that I am thy creature: I ought to be thy Adam; but I am rather the fallen angel, whom thou drivest from joy for no **misdeed**. Everywhere I see bliss, from which I alone am irrevocably excluded. I was benevolent and good; misery made me a fiend. Make me happy, and I shall again be virtuous."

13 "Begone! I will not hear you. There can be no community between you and me; we are enemies. Begone, or let us try our strength in a fight, in which one must fall."

14 "How can I move thee? Will no entreaties cause thee to turn a favorable eye upon thy creature, who implores thy goodness and compassion? Believe me, Frankenstein: I was benevolent; my soul glowed with love and humanity: but am I not alone, miserably alone?

You, my creator, abhor me; what hope can I gather from your fellow-creatures, who owe me nothing? They spurn and hate me. The desert mountains and dreary glaciers are my refuge. I have wandered here many days; the caves of ice, which I only do not fear, are a dwelling to me, and the only one which man does not grudge. These bleak skies I hail, for they are kinder to me than your fellow-beings. If the multitude of mankind knew of my existence, they would do as you do, and arm themselves for my destruction. Shall I not then hate them who abhor me? I will keep no terms with my enemies. I am miserable, and they shall share my wretchedness. Yet it is in your power to recompense me, and deliver them from an evil which it only remains for you to make so great, that not only you and your family, but thousands of others, shall be swallowed up in the whirlwinds of its rage. Let your compassion be moved, and do not disdain me. Listen to my tale: when you have heard that, abandon or commiserate me, as you shall judge that I deserve. But hear me. The guilty are allowed, by human laws, bloody as they may be, to speak in their own defense, before they are condemned. Listen to me, Frankenstein. You accuse me of murder; and yet you would, with a satisfied conscience, destroy your own creature. Oh, praise the eternal justice of man! Yet I ask you not to spare me: listen to me; and then, if you can, and if you will, destroy the work of your hands."

15 "Why do you call to my remembrance circumstances of which I shudder to reflect that I have been the miserable origin and author? Cursed be the day, abhorred devil, in which you first saw light! Cursed (although I curse myself) be the hands that formed you! You have made me wretched beyond expression. You have left me no power to consider whether I am just to you or not. Begone! relieve me from the sight of your detested form."

16 "Thus I relieve thee, my creator," he said, and placed his hated hand before my eyes, which I flung from me with violence; "thus I take from thee a sight which you abhor. Still thou canst listen to me, and grant me thy compassion. By the virtues that I once possessed, I demand this from you. Hear my tale; it is long and strange, and the temperature of this place is not fitting to your fine sensations; come to the hut upon the mountain. The sun is yet high in the heavens; before it descends to hide itself behind yon snowy **precipices**, and illuminate another world, you will have heard my story, and can decide. On you it rests, whether I quit forever the neighborhood of man, and lead a harmless life, or become a scourge to your fellow-creatures, and the author of your own speedy ruin."

ANALYZE SCIENCE FICTION

Annotate: In paragraph 14, mark the words or phrases that show that the creature believes he should be treated the same as all humans.

Evaluate: Do you find the creature's argument convincing? Why or why not?

precipice
(prĕs´ə-pĭs) *n.* an overhanging or extremely steep mass of rock; the brink of a dangerous or disastrous situation.

NOTICE & NOTE

AHA MOMENT

Notice & Note: What does Frankenstein realize for the first time in paragraph 17? Mark the sentence where he expresses this thought.

Evaluate: Is Frankenstein partly responsible for the creature's behavior? Why or why not?

17 As he said this, he led the way across the ice: I followed. My heart was full, and I did not answer him; but, as I proceeded, I weighed the various arguments that he had used, and determined at least to listen to his tale. I was partly urged by curiosity, and compassion confirmed my resolution. I had hitherto supposed him to be the murderer of my brother, and I eagerly sought a confirmation or denial of this opinion. For the first time, also, I felt what the duties of a creator towards his creature were, and that I ought to render him happy before I complained of his wickedness. These motives urged me to comply with his demand. We crossed the ice, therefore, and ascended the opposite rock. The air was cold, and the rain again began to descend: we entered the hut, the fiend with an air of exultation, I with a heavy heart and depressed spirits. But I consented to listen; and, seating myself by the fire which my **odious** companion had lighted, he thus began his tale.

odious
(ō´dē-əs) *adj.* extremely unpleasant; repulsive.

CHECK YOUR UNDERSTANDING

Answer these questions before moving on to the **Analyze the Text** section on the following page.

1 Why does Frankenstein feel disgusted by the creature soon after bringing him to life?

A The creature acts violently.

B The creature chases him.

C The creature has an ugly appearance.

D The creature is physically weak.

2 How does Frankenstein react when the creature finds him in the Swiss Alps?

F He is afraid of the creature.

G He tries to run away.

H He feels guilty for creating the creature.

J He wants to kill the creature.

3 The creature demands that Frankenstein —

A listen to his story

B protect him from his enemies

C be his companion

D improve his appearance

RESPOND

ANALYZE THE TEXT

Support your responses with evidence from the text. NOTEBOOK

1. **Interpret** In paragraph 3, Frankenstein dreams that Elizabeth, a woman he loves, turns into a corpse after he kisses her. How does this dream reflect his experience in the previous paragraph?
2. **Draw Conclusions** Why does the creature think that he should be forgiven for his crimes? Cite evidence for your conclusion.
3. **Analyze** What moral dilemma does Frankenstein experience in the Swiss Alps? What actions and motivations have contributed to this dilemma?
4. **Critique** Did Shelley choose an effective setting for the confrontation between Frankenstein and the creature? Explain why or why not.
5. **Notice & Note** In paragraph 17, Frankenstein says, "For the first time, also, I felt what the duties of a creator towards his creature were." How does this realization relate to scientific and technological developments today?

RESEARCH

RESEARCH TIP
When researching a subject at a specific time period, use specific search terms like "science early 19th century" or "science and *Frankenstein*." Using specific search terms makes it easier to find relevant information quickly.

Scientific understanding was much different during Mary Shelley's time than it is today. With a partner, research scientific and medical knowledge in the early 19th century. Use the following questions to guide your research.

QUESTION	ANSWER
What did scientists know about electricity by the early 19th century?	
What methods did scientists use to generate electricity?	
What ideas did scientists have about the relationship between electricity and life?	

Extend With a small group, discuss how the information you learned about early 19th-century science relates to *Frankenstein*.

CREATE AND DISCUSS

Write a Science Fiction Story Write a short science fiction story that addresses a moral or ethical issue. The story can be set in the present and involve an imagined scientific or technological development, or it can be set in the future.

- ❏ Identify an imagined scientific or technological advance or invention and evaluate the moral and ethical dilemmas involved with this innovation.
- ❏ Consider the motivations of your characters as you develop the story.
- ❏ Use details to develop the characters and the setting of your story.
- ❏ Think about ways you can use sensory language to give your readers a vivid experience.

Go to **Writing Narratives** in the **Writing Studio** for more about writing short stories.

Discuss Have a discussion about the possible negative effects and dangers of the rapid advancement of science, medicine, and technology.

- ❏ Discuss possible ways in which people might respond to and address the issues brought on by major advancements in science, medicine, and technology.
- ❏ Listen carefully to your classmates, ask questions, and comment respectfully on others' ideas.
- ❏ As a group, summarize the key points of the discussion and identify points of agreement.

Go to **Participating in Collaborative Discussions** in the **Speaking and Listening Studio** for more help with having a discussion.

RESPOND TO THE ESSENTIAL QUESTION

How can science go wrong?

Gather Information Review your annotations and notes on the excerpt from *Frankenstein*. Then, add relevant information to your Response Log. As you determine which information to include, think about:

- how scientific and medical technologies require ethical consideration
- how science fiction can reflect human nature
- how science can be used for both good and bad purposes

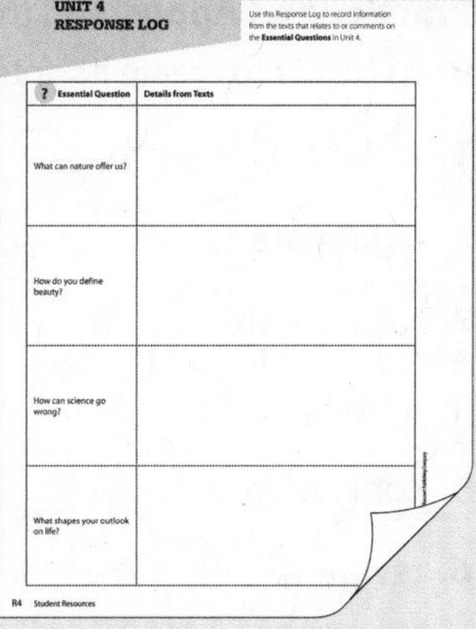

UNIT 4 RESPONSE LOG

Use this Response Log to record information from the texts that relates to or comments on the **Essential Questions** in Unit 4.

? Essential Question	Details from Texts
What can nature offer us?	
How do you define beauty?	
How can science go wrong?	
What shapes your outlook on life?	

R4 Student Resources

ACADEMIC VOCABULARY

As you write and discuss what you learned from the novel, be sure to use the Academic Vocabulary words. Check off each of the words that you use.

- ❏ **appreciate**
- ❏ **insight**
- ❏ **intensity**
- ❏ **invoke**
- ❏ **radical**

RESPOND

WORD BANK

infuse	**inarticulate**
inanimate	**misdeed**
ardor	**precipice**
tumult	**odious**

CRITICAL VOCABULARY

Practice and Apply Use your understanding of the Critical Vocabulary words to answer each question.

1. If a person is **inarticulate,** would that person make an excellent or a poor public speaker?
2. If someone feels **ardor** toward another person, does that person hate or love the other?
3. Would an **odious** meal be one you look forward to eating or one you refuse to eat?
4. If tea is **infused** with lemons, does that mean it is made of lemons or it contains lemons?
5. Which is an **inanimate** object, a rock or a bird?
6. Would a **misdeed** be more likely to be punished or celebrated?
7. If you were afraid of heights, would you be likely to stand near a **precipice**?
8. Which would be more likely to cause a **tumult,** going on a vacation or moving to a new city?

VOCABULARY STRATEGY: Antonyms

Go to **Synonyms and Antonyms** in the **Vocabulary Studio** for more on antonyms.

An **antonym** is a word with a meaning opposite that of another word. Some antonyms are formed by adding a prefix that means "not" to a word to create one with the opposite meaning. For example, the word *inanimate* is formed by adding the prefix *in-* to the adjective *animate,* which means "living."

Practice and Apply Add the prefix *dis-, il-, im-, in-, ir-, non-,* or *un-* to each word below to create its antonym.

1. violent
2. legitimate
3. responsible
4. mobile
5. conclusive
6. reverent
7. orderly
8. intelligible

LANGUAGE CONVENTIONS: Sensory Language

Sensory language includes descriptive words and phrases that appeal to one or more of the reader's senses, creating a more vivid experience for the reader. In *Frankenstein*, Mary Shelley often uses sensory words and phrases to provide descriptions that elicit feelings of horror in the reader. For instance, read the following sentence from the novel.

> **It was already one in the morning; the rain pattered dismally against the panes, and my candle was nearly burnt out, when, by the glimmer of the half-extinguished light, I saw the dull yellow eye of the creature open; it breathed hard, and a convulsive motion agitated its limbs.**

Notice that in this sentence, Shelley appeals to the senses of sight ("dull yellow eye") and hearing ("rain pattered dismally"). Now compare that sentence to the following paraphrased version.

> **It was already one in the morning. Rain was falling, and my candle was nearly burnt out. I saw the creature's eye open. It breathed hard and moved its limbs.**

Which version is more effective at establishing a mood and bringing the reader into the story? Why?

Practice and Apply Revisit the science fiction story you wrote. Identify settings, characters, and events in the story that lack vivid description. Look for opportunities to enhance your reader's experience by using sensory language. Revise your story to help bring your reader into the action of the story by adding details that appeal to the senses. Share your revisions with a partner.

Go to the **Writing Studio: Writing Narratives** for more on the language of narratives.

FRANKENSTEIN: GIVING VOICE TO THE MONSTER

Essay by **Langdon Winner**

? ***ESSENTIAL QUESTION:***

How can science go wrong?

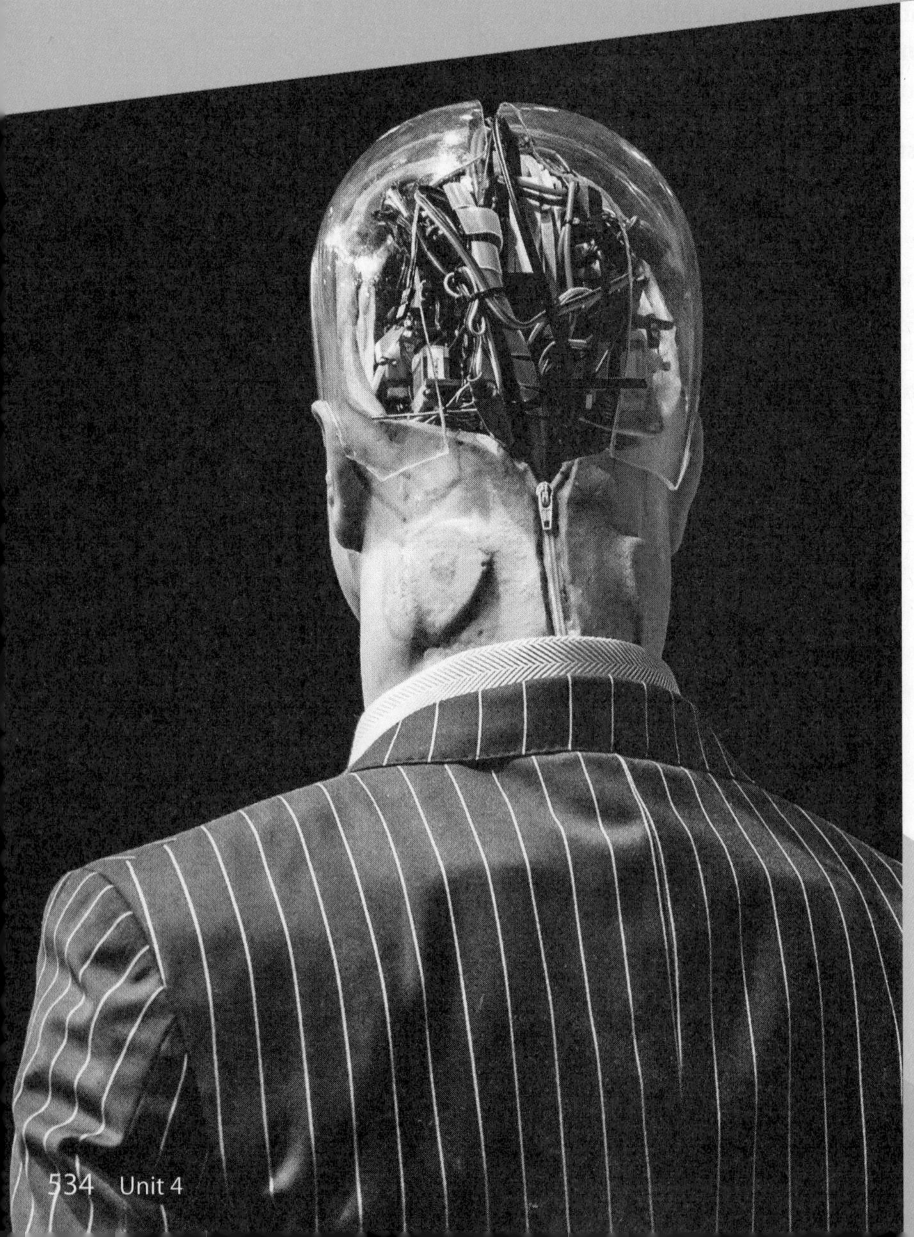

QUICK START

Imagine a world in which robots do all of the work. Would such a development make life better? Might there be disadvantages to a fully automated society? Would there be possible dangers to consider? Discuss these questions with a partner.

EVALUATE AN ESSAY

An essay is a brief work of nonfiction that offers an opinion on a subject. A **formal essay** is well organized and has a clear main idea. Formal essays are usually serious and impersonal in tone. Most formal essays are written to inform or persuade or to express ideas. An **informal essay** may be more loosely structured; the tone is conversational, reflecting the personality of the author. The purpose of an informal essay is often to express ideas and feelings or to entertain.

In "Frankenstein: Giving Voice to the Monster," Langdon Winner offers an interesting perspective on the relevance of Mary Shelley's novel today. As you read his essay, notice how he uses his analysis of the novel to support his ideas about science and technology.

GENRE ELEMENTS: ESSAY

- is a short piece of nonfiction
- offers an opinion on a subject
- formal essays have a serious and impersonal tone
- informal essays are loosely structured and have a conversational tone

MONITOR COMPREHENSION

Some texts are more difficult than others due to their complex ideas, writing style, or unfamiliar content. When you **monitor comprehension,** you check to make sure that you understand what you are reading. One method is to ask questions about a text before, during, and after reading. The following types of questions can help clarify and deepen your understanding:

- **Literal questions** can be answered directly from statements in the text. You might also ask literal questions before you start reading; for example, you might ask yourself what you already know about the topic of an essay or what your purpose is in reading it.
- **Inferential questions** have answers that are not directly stated in the text. Readers make inferences and draw conclusions based on details in a text and their own knowledge and experience.
- **Evaluative questions** are generally asked after reading a text. You might ask whether you agree with ideas in an essay or how effectively you think the author presented them.

As you read this essay, mark up statements that you have trouble understanding, and make note of any questions you have about the content. Review and try to answer your questions after you finish reading.

GET READY

CRITICAL VOCABULARY

sentient	**recoil**	**ominous**	**domain**
artifice	**succinct**	**calamity**	**prescient**

To see how many Critical Vocabulary words you already know, use them to complete the sentences.

1. The magician used __________ to trick all of the __________ beings in the room.
2. A(n) __________ mood filled the room as the seer used his __________ powers to direct the detectives to the missing child.
3. The nauseated medical student fought the urge to __________ in horror at the sight of the bloody __________.
4. "Welcome to my __________," said the teacher. "Please keep your comments __________ as I dislike long, rambling explanations."

LANGUAGE CONVENTIONS

Parallel Structure In this lesson, you'll learn about parallel structure—the use of similar grammatical constructions to express ideas that are related or equal in importance. Notice the parallel phrases in this example:

> **Mary Shelley's insights on these matters were . . . some of the most ominous hazards and most ghastly calamities. . . .**

The repeated grammatical construction of the adjective *most* plus a second adjective and a noun emphasizes that the two phrases are related and equally important. As you read Winner's essay, notice other uses of parallelism.

ANNOTATION MODEL

NOTICE & NOTE

As you read the essay, practice monitoring your comprehension by taking notes, marking the text, and asking questions. The model below shows one reader's notes in response to the text.

The possibility that artificial creatures, products of human hands, might achieve sentience and take on an active role in society is an age-old conception in world cultures, the subject of myths, stories, moral fables, and philosophical speculation.

In Greek mythology one finds the tale of Pygmalion who carves a statue named Galatea with whom he falls in love and who eventually comes to life.

What does this word mean?

Why has this been a common theme in literature? What does this say about humans? Does it reflect the need to create?

The writer uses this detail to support his point in the sentence above.

BACKGROUND

Langdon Winner *(1944–present) is a professor and political theorist. He has taught in colleges and universities and lectured on several continents. He currently serves as the humanities and social sciences department chair at Rensselaer Polytechnic Institute in Troy, New York. His essay "Frankenstein: Giving Voice to the Monster" was presented in Geneva in 2016 at the "Frankenstein's Shadow" conference, honoring the 200th anniversary of the writing of Mary Shelley's novel.*

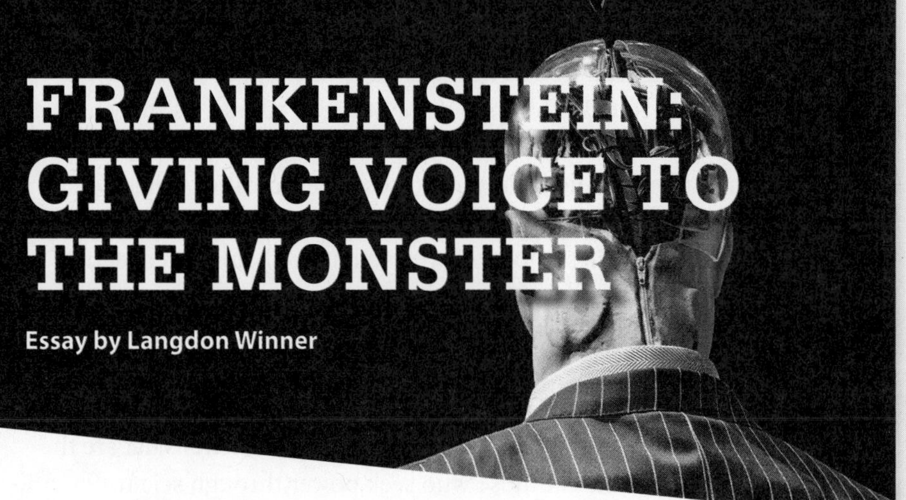

FRANKENSTEIN: GIVING VOICE TO THE MONSTER

Essay by Langdon Winner

SETTING A PURPOSE

As you read, note Winner's ideas about the novel Frankenstein *and how he connects those ideas to society today.*

Notice & Note

Use the side margins to notice and note signposts in the text.

1 The possibility that artificial creatures, products of human hands, might achieve sentience and take on an active role in society is an age-old conception in world cultures, the subject of myths, stories, moral fables, and philosophical speculation.

2 In Greek mythology one finds the tale of Pygmalion who carves a statue named Galatea with whom he falls in love and who eventually comes to life. In Jewish folklore there are stories of the Golem, an artificial creature animated with surprising results. Norse legends include reports of clay giants able to move on their own accord. An ancient Chinese text describes the work of Yan Shi who in the 10th century B.C. crafted a humanoid figure with lifelike qualities.

EVALUATE AN ESSAY

Annotate: Reread paragraph 2. Mark the examples of myths and legends.

Analyze: What is the author's purpose for listing these examples?

3 Both Plato and Aristotle draw upon the myth of the statues of Daedalus[1], mythical creations that could move, perform certain

[1] **Daedalus** (dĕd´l-əs): Greek Mythology; A renowned craftsman, sculptor, and inventor and builder of the Labyrinth. He fashioned the wings with which he and his son Icarus escaped from Crete after their imprisonment by Minos.

NOTICE & NOTE

kinds of work and would wander off on their own unless tied down by a rope. In the *Politics* Aristotle uses the metaphor in his defense of slavery: ". . . if every tool could perform its own work when ordered, or by seeing what to do in advance, like the statues of Daedalus in the story . . . master-craftsmen would have no need of assistants and masters no need of slaves."

4 World literature, not to mention modern science fiction, contains a great many stories of this kind, ones that are often used to shed light upon basic questions about what it means to be alive, what it means to be conscious, what it means to be human, what membership in society entails.

MONITOR COMPREHENSION

Annotate: Mark the reference to technology in the last sentence of paragraph 5.

Infer: What inferential question can you develop in response to this statement? How would you answer it?

5 Within this tradition of thought Mary Shelley's *Frankenstein* plays a pivotal role. Within popular culture, of course, its story has spawned an astonishing range of novels, stories, movies, television programs, advertisements, toys, and costumes, most of which center upon images of monstrosity, horror and the mad scientist. Beyond these familiar manifestations, however, the novel offers a collection of deeply unsettling reflections upon the human condition, ones brought to focus by modern dreams of creating **sentient**, artificial, humanoid beings.

sentient
(sĕn´shənt) *adj.* having sense perception; conscious.

6 In direct, provocative ways the book asks: What is the relationship between the creator and the thing created? What are the larger responsibilities of those who seek power through scientific knowledge and technological accomplishment? What happens when those responsibilities are not recognized or otherwise left unattended?

7 Questions of this kind concern particular projects that involve attempts to create artificial devices that exhibit features and abilities similar to or even superior to ones associated with human beings. In a larger sense, however, the problems posed by the novel point to situations in which scientific technologies introduced into nature and society seem to run out of control, to achieve a certain autonomy, taking on a life of their own beyond the plans and intentions of the persons involved in their creation.

8 As she addresses issues of this kind, the genius of Mary Shelley is to give voice not only to Victor Frankenstein, his family, friends and acquaintances, but to the creature that sprang from his work and after a time learns to speak, read and form his thoughts, eager to speak his mind about his situation. I do not know whether this is the first time in world literature that one finds a serious dialogue between an artificial creation and its creator. But first instance or not, it is a literary device that Shelley uses with stunning effectiveness.

artifice
(är´tə-fĭs) *n.* cleverness or ingenuity in making or doing something.

9 At their climatic meeting high in the Alps, the creature's observations and arguments painfully articulate the perils of unfinished, imperfect, carelessly prepared **artifice**, suddenly released

into the world, emphasizing the obligations of the creator as well as the consequences of insensitivity and neglect.

> I am thy creature, and I will be even mild and docile to my natural lord and king if thou wilt also perform thy part, that which thou owest me.
>
> You propose to kill me. How dare you sport thus with life? Do your duty towards me, and I will do mine toward you and the rest of mankind. If you will comply with my conditions I will leave them and you at peace; but if you refuse, I will glut the maw of death, until it be satiated with the blood of your remaining friends.

10 The creature goes on to explain that his greatest desire is to be made part of the human community, something that has been strongly, even brutally, denied him to that point. His stern admonition to Victor is to recognize that the invention of something powerful, ingenious, even marvelous cannot be the end of the work at hand. Thoughtful care must be given to its place in the sphere of human relationships.

11 At first Victor **recoils** and bitterly denounces the creature's demands that he recognize, affirm and fulfill his obligations. But as the threat of violent revenge becomes clear, Victor finally yields to the validity of the argument. "For the first time," he admits, "I felt what the duties of a creator towards his creature were, and that I ought to render him happy before I complained of his wickedness."

12 Following that flash of recognition the story careens toward a disastrous conclusion. Within the wreckage that envelops both Victor and his creature, the book reveals crucial insight, one before its time and with profound implications for similar projects in the future. It can be stated **succinctly** as follows: The quest for power through scientific technology often tends to override and obscure the recognition of the profound responsibilities that the possession of such power entails.

13 Put even more simply: The impulse to power and control typically comes first, while the recognition of personal and collective moral obligation arrives later, if ever at all. Within that unfortunate gap—between aspirations to power through science and belated recognitions of responsibility—arise generations of monstrosity.

14 Mary Shelley's insights on these matters were well ahead of their time and foreshadow some of the most **ominous** hazards and most ghastly **calamities** found along the path to modernity from the early 19th century up to the present day. . . .

15 One could offer a great many historical and contemporary illustrations of what I would call "Frankenstein's problem." An

EVALUATE AN ESSAY

Annotate: Reread the author's analysis of a passage from *Frankenstein* in paragraphs 10–12. Mark words and phrases with strong connotations.

Evaluate: Identify the author's tone. How does his choice of words contribute to the persuasiveness of his essay?

recoil
(rĭ-koil´) *v.* to shrink back, as in fear or repugnance.

succinct
(sək-sĭngkt´) *adj.* characterized by clear, precise expression in few words; concise and terse.

LANGUAGE CONVENTIONS

Annotate: Mark the author's use of parallel structure in the first sentence of paragraph 13.

Evaluate: How does parallelism strengthen the connection between ideas here?

ominous
(ŏm´ə-nəs) *adj.* menacing; threatening.

calamity
(kə-lăm´ĭ-tē) *n.* an event that brings terrible loss, lasting distress, or severe affliction; a disaster.

NOTICE & NOTE

domain
(dō-mān′) *n.* a sphere of activity, influence, or knowledge.

appropriate, highly practical, obviously troubling set of developments at present are found within a particular **domain** of scientific inquiry and application, a zone of works not all that dissimilar from the one the fictional Victor Frankenstein explored—today's realm of advanced computerization, smart algorithms, artificial intelligence (AI) and robotics. . . . During the past several years, notable scientists, engineers and luminaries in the technology business sector have stepped forward to express distress at what they see as dire risks that research in AI presents to the human species overall.

QUOTED WORDS

Notice & Note: Mark the names of notable people the author quotes in paragraphs 16–18.

Critique: Do these quotations provide effective support for the author's opinion about artificial intelligence? Why or why not?

16 In a BBC interview last year, Stephen Hawking warned, "The development of full artificial intelligence could spell the end of the human race. . . . Humans, limited by slow biological evolution, couldn't compete and would be superseded by AI. . . . One can imagine such technology outsmarting financial markets, out-inventing human researchers, out-manipulating human leaders, and developing weapons we cannot even understand. Whereas the short-term impact of AI depends on who controls it, the long-term impact depends on whether it can be controlled at all."

17 In a live exchange on the internet, Microsoft cofounder Bill Gates offered similar views. "I am in the camp that is concerned about super intelligence," Gates wrote. "First the machines will do a lot of jobs for us and not be super intelligent. . . . A few decades after that though the intelligence is strong enough to be a concern."

18 In the same vein, British inventor Clive Sinclair recently told the BBC, "Once you start to make machines that are rivaling and surpassing humans with intelligence, it's going to be very difficult for us to survive. It's just an inevitability." . . .

19 Studies of and speculation about issues of this kind has inspired the creation of a collection of new research centers at leading universities. Among them are the Cambridge Center for the Study of Existential Risk and The Future of Life Institute at MIT. Taken together the shelf of books on AI and Robots, the systematic studies of the future of automation and employment, and the excited warnings about artificial devices superseding human beings as the key actors on the stage of world history are, in my view, a contemporary realization of the **prescient** concerns and warnings at the heart of Mary Shelley's book—concerns and warnings about the headlong flight from responsibility.

prescient
(prĕsh′ənt) *adj.* of or relating to prescience—which means knowledge of actions or events before they occur.

CHECK YOUR UNDERSTANDING

Answer these questions before moving on to the **Analyze the Text** section on the following page.

1 According to the author, the genius of Shelley is in —

A setting the climactic meeting place in the Alps

B giving a voice to Frankenstein's creature

C anticipating the novel's effect on popular culture

D introducing the concept of a mad scientist

2 What is one of the deeper questions posed by Shelley's novel?

F Who should participate in scientific development?

G What is the relationship between nature and society?

H What scientific projects should never be attempted?

J What responsibilities accompany scientific development?

3 The attitude that Gates, Hawking, and Sinclair share about the future of artificial intelligence is one of —

A concern and caution

B hope and excitement

C annoyance and dismay

D doubt and negativity

ANALYZE THE TEXT

Support your responses with evidence from the text. NOTEBOOK

1. **Identify** What is the main idea of this essay?
2. **Evaluate** Does the author provide sufficient support for his opinion that Shelley's genius was to "give voice to the monster"? Why or why not?
3. **Critique** How effective is the author's conclusion to the essay? Explain.
4. **Question** Review your markups and notes on "Frankenstein: Giving Voice to the Monster." What questions do you have after reading this essay? What kind of research or investigation might help you answer these questions?
5. **Notice and Note** Reread paragraphs 16–18. Do you think that the author should have included a quotation from someone with a different view of the future of artificial intelligence? Explain why or why not.

RESEARCH TIP
Look for sources that include up-to-date research and provide evidence in the form of facts, statistics, and logical reasoning.

RESEARCH

Winner suggests that some problems resulting from the development of artificial intelligence might be related to the "future of automation and employment." He quotes Bill Gates, who also mentions the issue of machines doing many of our jobs. Research these concerns. What jobs are currently being replaced by machines? What jobs are in danger of being replaced in the future? Use the chart below to record your findings.

JOBS ALREADY REPLACED OR ARE BEING REPLACED	JOBS IN DANGER OF BEING REPLACED IN THE NEAR FUTURE	JOBS PROBABLY NOT IN DANGER OF BEING REPLACED

Extend Use the information you found to think about your own plans for a future career. Write a brief paragraph explaining how the research might influence your planning for the future.

CREATE AND DISCUSS

Write a Reflective Essay Respond to Winner's essay with a **reflective essay** in which you make connections between the text and yourself. Use your own point of view to express your personal reaction to the ideas presented in the essay.

- ❑ Record your personal reactions to the text. Use the annotations and notes you made while reading. How does the text relate to your life?
- ❑ Use a topical outline or a chart to organize your thoughts.
- ❑ Begin your essay with a hook, such as an anecdote or an interesting example.
- ❑ As you write, stay organized. Maintain a personal tone appropriate to your purpose and audience, using academic vocabulary as applicable.
- ❑ Conclude by sharing what you discovered about yourself, important insights you gained, or a decision you made as a result of your reflection upon the essay.

Discuss Your Essay Use your reflective essay to generate discussion in a small group.

- ❑ Read your essay to the members of your group.
- ❑ Ask each member of the group to give a brief oral response to your essay.
- ❑ Encourage the group to discuss ideas and questions raised in your essay.
- ❑ Listen and respond appropriately as other group members read their essays.

Go to the **Writing Studio: Writing as a Process** for help with writing your reflective essay.

Go to **Participating in Collaborative Discussions** in the **Speaking and Listening Studio** to find out more.

RESPOND TO THE ESSENTIAL QUESTION

How can science go wrong?

Gather Information Review your annotations and notes on "Frankenstein: Giving Voice to the Monster." Then, add relevant information to your Response Log. As you determine which information to include, think about:

- possible dangers and problems related to the development of artificial intelligence
- society's responsibility in controlling scientific developments
- how Shelley's novel relates to Winner's ideas

UNIT 4 RESPONSE LOG

Essential Question	Details from Texts
What can nature offer us?	
How do you define beauty?	
How can science go wrong?	
What shapes your outlook on life?	

ACADEMIC VOCABULARY

As you write and discuss what you learned from the essay, be sure to use the Academic Vocabulary words. Check off each of the words that you use.

- ❑ **appreciate**
- ❑ **insight**
- ❑ **intensity**
- ❑ **invoke**
- ❑ **radical**

RESPOND

CRITICAL VOCABULARY

WORD BANK

sentient	**ominous**
artifice	**calamity**
recoil	**domain**
succinct	**prescient**

Practice and Apply Choose the word that completes the sentence.

1. The politician used __________ to make it appear as if he wanted to enrich the people when, in fact, he wanted only to enrich himself.
   a. artifice **b.** sentient

2. Despite the __________ clouds on the near horizon, the skipper pressed onward toward the stricken vessel.
   a. prescient **b.** ominous

3. When the dam broke above the village, __________ ensued.
   a. calamity **b.** recoil

4. The professor delivered a __________ lecture that ended well before the class period was over.
   a. succinct **b.** domain

VOCABULARY STRATEGY: Latin Roots

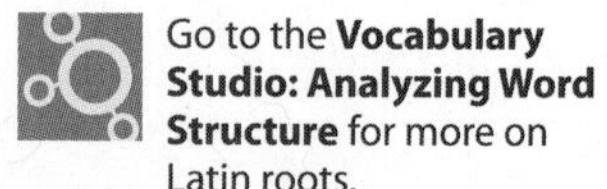

Go to the **Vocabulary Studio: Analyzing Word Structure** for more on Latin roots.

Knowing Latin roots can give you clues to the meanings of unfamiliar words. For example, knowing that the Latin root *sent* means "to feel" could help you figure out the meaning of *sentient*, which means "capable of feeling." When the author speaks of sentient beings, you know that he means beings that are aware of their surroundings and capable of emotions. Another word in the essay with the same root is *sentience,* which refers to the state of being sentient.

Practice and Apply The following words are all based on a Latin root. Write the root for each word and then the meaning of the root. Use a dictionary to help you. Notice how the definition of the word is related to its root. Can you think of other words that might be based on each root?

1. artifice
2. domain
3. prescient
4. ominous

LANGUAGE CONVENTIONS: Parallel Structure

Parallel structure, or parallelism, is the use of similar grammatical constructions to express ideas that are closely related or equal in importance. The grammatical constructions may include phrases, clauses, or sentences. Parallel structure helps writers organize, clarify, and emphasize their thoughts. It can also affect the meaning and tone of a sentence or passage. Read this sentence from Langdon Winner's essay:

> **World literature, . . . contains a great many stories of this kind, ones that are often used to shed light upon basic questions about what it means to be alive, what it means to be conscious, what it means to be human, what membership in society entails.**

Winner uses a series of noun clauses beginning with *what* that are the objects of the preposition *about*. The repetition of this grammatical construction gives equal weight to the "basic questions" he identifies in world literature. The parallelism also gives the sentence a pleasing rhythm that makes it more memorable. Consider that he could have written the sentence like this:

> **World literature, . . . contains a great many stories of this kind, ones that are often used to shed light upon basic questions about what it means to be alive, conscious, and human, and what membership in society entails.**

In this sentence without parallel structure, the relationship between the questions is less clear. The sentence is also less memorable because it lacks a strong rhythm.

Writers can use parallel structure not only within sentences but also in groups of sentences. For example, Winner starts the first two sentences in paragraph 2 with "In Greek mythology" and "In Jewish folklore," using parallelism to tie together examples from different cultural traditions to support his idea.

Practice and Apply Underline the parallel structures in the sentences below. Then, use each sentence as a model to write two sentences of your own with the same parallel structures.

1. "One can imagine such technology outsmarting financial markets, out-inventing human researchers, out-manipulating human leaders, and developing weapons we cannot even understand."
2. "Whereas the short-term impact of AI depends on who controls it, the long-term impact depends on whether it can be controlled at all."

COLLABORATE & COMPARE

POEM

ODE TO THE WEST WIND

by **Percy Bysshe Shelley**

pages 549–552

COMPARE THEMES

As you read, notice how both poets describe the effects of the wind in autumn. What can you infer about the poems' themes based on their imagery, figurative language, diction, and other elements? Once you have read both poems, you will collaborate with a small group on a research project.

ESSENTIAL QUESTION:

What shapes your outlook on life?

POEM

SONG OF A THATCHED HUT DAMAGED IN AUTUMN WIND

by **Du Fu**

pages 554–555

QUICK START

People constantly learn from nature. Think about a lesson you have learned by observing some aspect of nature, such as a seasonal change. With a partner, discuss the lesson you learned and why it is important.

ANALYZE FORM

In poetry, **form** refers to the arrangement of words into structural patterns, including the length of a poem's lines and their grouping into stanzas. Form can also refer to a poem's rhyme scheme, meter, or its traditional poetic type, such as sonnet or ode. The form of a poem helps support its mood and theme.

Prior to the 20th century, poets usually relied on traditional forms to express their ideas and feelings. One popular form that you have already encountered is the **sonnet,** which has 14 lines and a regular rhyme scheme. Another traditional form is the **ode,** a complex lyric that develops a serious theme. Odes typically have a dignified or reflective tone, and they often commemorate events or praise people, ideas, or elements of nature. Shelley's "Ode to the West Wind," a famous example, employs a complex rhyme scheme and regular meter.

During the 20th century, poets increasingly turned away from traditional forms, often producing **free verse**—poems that do not have regular patterns of rhyme and meter. This form usually gives their poems a rhythm closer to that of everyday speech. Instead of following a fixed structure, lines are organized according to a plan developed by the poet. The poet Du Fu wrote "Song of a Thatched Hut Damaged in Autumn Wind" in a traditional Chinese form; however, the translation you are about to read is composed in free verse.

As you read the two poems, notice these characteristics of their forms:

"Ode to the West Wind"	• Follows a regular meter • Written in terza rima, a series of three-line stanzas linked by rhyme • Highly melodic with a dignified tone
"Song of a Thatched Hut Damaged in Autumn Wind"	• Free verse translation • Lines not grouped in stanzas • Rhythms approximate speech • Includes alliteration, figurative language, and other poetic devices

GENRE ELEMENTS: LYRIC POETRY

- expresses the personal thoughts and feelings of a single speaker
- has a musical quality
- is marked by imagination and evocative language
- creates a strong, unified impression
- can be in a variety of forms covering many subjects

GET READY

ANALYZE DICTION

Careful control of language is especially important in poetry. To shape the perception of readers, poets must choose appropriate **diction,** a term that refers to both word choice and **syntax,** the order or arrangement of words. Traditionally, poets used a special diction, **inverted syntax,** which reverses the expected order of words. Inverted syntax can help maintain patterns of rhyme and meter. Poets also tended to choose elevated and vivid vocabulary. In contrast, the syntax of modern poetry is usually closer to natural speech, though poets still rely on concrete, vivid words, and distinct poetic elements to appeal to readers' senses.

Use the following questions to help guide your analysis of diction:

- Does the poet use plain or elevated vocabulary?
- Does the poet choose mostly concrete words, which name specific things, or abstract words that identify concepts?
- Does the poet select words with strong connotations, or associated feelings?
- Is the writer's syntax formal or informal? inverted or natural?

NOTICE & NOTE 

ANNOTATION MODEL

As you read, note elements of each poem's form and mark distinctive examples of the poet's diction. In the model, you can see one reader's notes about lines 1–6 of "Ode to the West Wind."

O wild West Wind, thou breath of Autumn's being,
Thou, from whose unseen presence the leaves dead
Are driven, like ghosts from an enchanter fleeing,

Yellow, and black, and pale, and hectic red,
Pestilence-stricken multitudes: O thou,
Who chariotest to their dark wintry bed

The poem includes elevated and abstract vocabulary.

The syntax is formal. The phrase "the leaves dead" is an example of inverted syntax.

Words like "dead" and "hectic" and "Pestilence-stricken" have strong, serious connotations.

NOTICE & NOTE

BACKGROUND

Percy Bysshe Shelley *(1792–1822) led a turbulent life. As an adolescent, he embraced radical political and social views, which alienated him from his aristocratic relatives. Shelley wrote "Ode to the West Wind" in the autumn of 1819 when he and his family were living in Florence, Italy. Earlier that year, English workers demonstrating for reform were killed by soldiers in the Peterloo Massacre. This event outraged Shelley, who opposed all injustice and dreamed of changing the world through poetry. In 1822, shortly before he would have turned 30, he drowned when his sailboat sank in a storm off the coast of Italy.*

ODE TO THE WEST WIND

Poem by Percy Bysshe Shelley

PREPARE TO COMPARE

As you read, note the ways in which the poet describes and personifies the autumn wind. Think about what this suggests about the poet's view of nature and how these details contribute to the theme of the poem.

I

O wild West Wind, thou breath of Autumn's being,
Thou, from whose unseen presence the leaves dead
Are driven, like ghosts from an enchanter fleeing,

Yellow, and black, and pale, and hectic red,
Pestilence-stricken multitudes: O thou,
Who chariotest to their dark wintry bed

The wingéd seeds, where they lie cold and low,
Each like a corpse within its grave, until
Thine azure sister of the Spring shall blow

Notice & Note

Use the side margins to notice and note signposts in the text.

ANALYZE FORM

Annotate: Use letters to mark the patterns of end rhyme in lines 1–14.

Analyze: What is the rhyme scheme? How does rhyme link each stanza to the next?

4 hectic: feverish.

9 sister . . . Spring: the reviving south wind of spring.

Her clarion o'er the dreaming earth, and fill
(Driving sweet buds like flocks to feed in air)
With living hues and odors plain and hill:

Wild Spirit, which art moving everywhere;
Destroyer and preserver; hear, oh, hear!

II

Thou on whose stream, mid the steep sky's commotion,
Loose clouds like earth's decaying leaves are shed,
Shook from the tangled bough of Heaven and Ocean,

Angels of rain and lightning: there are spread
On the blue surface of thine aëry surge,
Like the bright hair uplifted from the head

Of some fierce Maenad, even from the dim verge
Of the horizon to the zenith's height,
The locks of the approaching storm. Thou dirge

Of the dying year, to which this closing night
Will be the dome of a vast sepulcher,
Vaulted with all thy congregated might

Of vapors, from whose solid atmosphere
Black rain, and fire, and hail will burst: oh, hear!

III

Thou who didst waken from his summer dreams
The blue Mediterranean, where he lay,
Lulled by the coil of his crystálline streams,

Beside a pumice isle in Baiae's bay,
And saw in sleep old palaces and towers
Quivering within the wave's intenser day,

All overgrown with azure moss and flowers
So sweet, the sense faints picturing them! Thou
For whose path the Atlantic's level powers

Cleave themselves into chasms, while far below
The sea-blooms and the oozy woods which wear
The sapless foliage of the ocean, know

Thy voice, and suddenly grow gray with fear,
And tremble and despoil themselves: oh, hear!

NOTICE & NOTE

10 clarion: a trumpet with a clear, ringing tone.

ANALYZE DICTION

Annotate: Mark words and phrases in lines 15–28 that are examples of elevated language.

Analyze: How does Shelley's use of elevated language in this description shape your impression of the wind?

18 Angels: messengers.

19 aëry: airy.

20–22 Like . . . height: The clouds lie in streaks from the horizon upward, looking like the streaming hair of a maenad (mē´năd)—a wildly dancing female worshiper of Dionysus, the Greek god of wine.

23 dirge: funeral song.

25 sepulcher (sĕp´əl-kər): tomb.

31 crystálline (krĭs´tə-lĭn) **streams:** the different-colored currents of the Mediterranean Sea.

32 pumice (pŭm´ĭs): a light volcanic rock; **Baiae's** (bī´ēz´) **bay:** the Bay of Naples, site of the ancient Roman resort of Baiae.

37 level powers: surface.

NOTICE & NOTE

ANALYZE FORM

Annotate: A couplet is two lines of verse that rhyme and form a unit. Mark the words that rhyme at the end of the couplet in section IV.

Analyze: What idea does Shelley emphasize with the rhymed words in this couplet?

50 skyey (skī´ē) **speed:** the swiftness of clouds moving across the sky.

51 vision: something impossible to achieve.

57 lyre: a reference to the Aeolian harp; an instrument whose strings make musical sounds when the wind blows over them.

62 impetuous (ĭm-pĕch´o͞o-əs): violently forceful; impulsive.

65 incantation: recitation, as of a magic spell.

IV

If I were a dead leaf thou mightest bear;
If I were a swift cloud to fly with thee;
A wave to pant beneath thy power, and share

The impulse of thy strength, only less free
Than thou, O uncontrollable! If even
I were as in my boyhood, and could be

The comrade of thy wanderings over Heaven,
As then, when to outstrip thy skyey speed
Scarce seemed a vision; I would ne'er have striven

As thus with thee in prayer in my sore need.
Oh, lift me as a wave, a leaf, a cloud!
I fall upon the thorns of life! I bleed!

A heavy weight of hours has chained and bowed
One too like thee: tameless, and swift, and proud.

V

Make me thy lyre, even as the forest is:
What if my leaves are falling like its own!
The tumult of thy mighty harmonies

Will take from both a deep, autumnal tone,
Sweet though in sadness. Be thou, Spirit fierce,
My spirit! Be thou me, impetuous one!

Drive my dead thoughts over the universe
Like withered leaves to quicken a new birth!
And, by the incantation of this verse,

Scatter, as from an unextinguished hearth
Ashes and sparks, my words among mankind!
Be through my lips to unawakened earth

The trumpet of a prophecy! O Wind,
If Winter comes, can Spring be far behind?

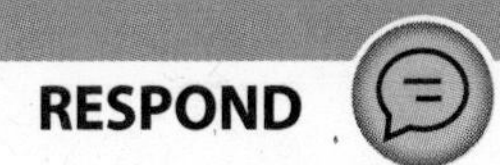

CREATE AND PRESENT

Create a Visual Representation In both selections, the wind is personified in different ways—that is, it is given some human characteristics. Develop a visual representation of the wind in each poem.

- ❑ Think about the similarities and differences in the two poems. How does each poet describe the wind?
- ❑ Identify the human characteristics ascribed to the wind in each selection. Are these descriptions positive or negative?
- ❑ Think about how you can represent these characteristics visually.

Present Your Image Pair up with a partner, and take turns presenting your visual representations.

- ❑ Identify two elements of your visual representation that you would like to present.
- ❑ Present your visual to your partner, and explain two of your choices in creating it. For instance, explain why you chose a certain color or style.
- ❑ Take turns giving each other feedback. If it makes sense, incorporate your partner's feedback into your visual representation.

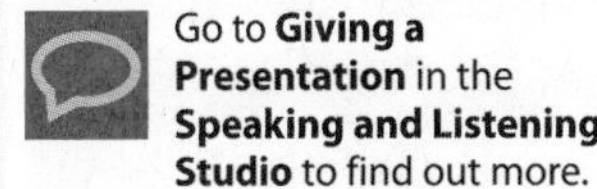

Go to **Giving a Presentation** in the **Speaking and Listening Studio** to find out more.

RESPOND TO THE ESSENTIAL QUESTION

? What shapes your outlook on life?

Gather Information Review your annotations and notes on "Ode to the West Wind" and "Song of a Thatched Hut Damaged in Autumn Wind." Then, add relevant information to your Response Log. As you determine which information to include, think about:

- how nature affects the way you perceive the world
- the experiences that have shaped the way you relate to people and the world around you
- the relationship between the natural world and human society

ACADEMIC VOCABULARY

As you write and discuss what you learned from the poems, be sure to use the Academic Vocabulary words. Check off each of the words that you use.

- ❑ **appreciate**
- ❑ **insight**
- ❑ **intensity**
- ❑ **invoke**
- ❑ **radical**

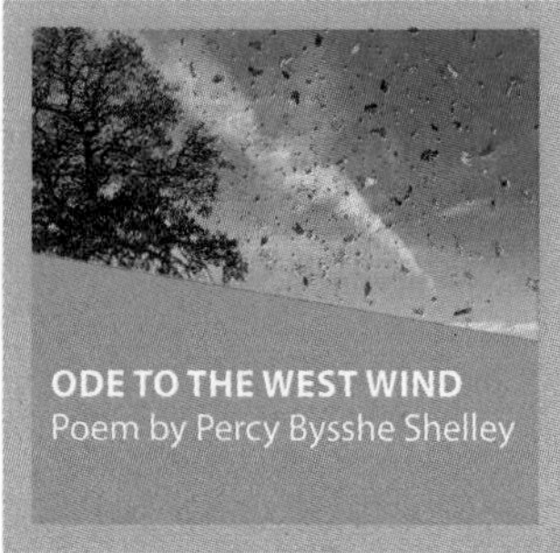

ODE TO THE WEST WIND
Poem by Percy Bysshe Shelley

SONG OF A THATCHED HUT DAMAGED IN AUTUMN WIND
Poem by Du Fu

Collaborate & Compare

COMPARE THEMES

"Ode to the West Wind" and "Song of a Thatched Hut Damaged in Autumn Wind" share a topic—the effects of the wind in autumn. However, the two poems may express different **themes,** or messages about life or human nature.

Poets usually do not state their themes directly. It is up to readers to infer a theme based on a poem's imagery, figurative language, diction, and other elements. Some poems may have multiple themes.

To begin gathering details with which to make inferences about themes, complete the following chart.

	"ODE TO THE WEST WIND"	"SONG OF A THATCHED HUT DAMAGED IN AUTUMN WIND"
Form		
Imagery		
Figurative Language		
Diction		
Other Elements		

ANALYZE THE TEXTS

Discuss these questions in your group.

1. **Compare** With your group, review the imagery that you cited in your chart. How are the images in the two poems similar? How do they differ?
2. **Interpret** Both poems describe some of the ways we relate to nature. Discuss each poem's treatment of nature. Cite evidence in your discussion.
3. **Evaluate** In "Ode to the West Wind," Shelley uses elevated language and formal diction; however, in "Song of a Thatched Hut Damaged in Autumn Wind," Du Fu does the opposite. Which approach do you find most effective, and why?
4. **Draw Conclusions** According to the two poems, what insights about life or human nature can we gain by considering the wind and other elements of the natural world?

COLLABORATE AND PRESENT

With your group, continue exploring the ideas in the poems by identifying and comparing their themes. Follow these steps:

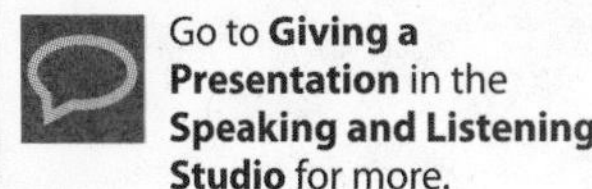

Go to **Giving a Presentation** in the **Speaking and Listening Studio** for more.

1. **Make inferences about themes.** Review your charts as a group, considering details, imagery, figurative language, diction, and other elements from both poems. Then, work together to infer possible themes for each poem.

2. **Agree on a theme.** Determine a theme statement for each poem. You may use a chart like the one below to track the themes and supporting details your group identifies.

	THEME STATEMENT	SUPPORTING DETAILS
"Ode to the West Wind"		
"Song of a Thatched Hut Damaged in Autumn Wind"		

3. **Present to the class.** Organize your ideas, and choose a spokesperson to present them to the class. Include clear statements of the theme for each poem, and explain similarities or differences in the two themes. Be sure to introduce your ideas, to include transitions from idea to idea in the body of your presentation, and to conclude your presentation effectively. You may add visuals or diagrams to help convey information to the class.

PRESENTATION TIPS

When giving a presentation, be sure to pace yourself and enunciate all of your words so your audience can understand you. Also, be sure to make eye contact and address one topic at a time so you don't lose your audience.

COLLABORATE & COMPARE

POEMS

from SONGS OF INNOCENCE

by **William Blake**

pages 563–566

ESSENTIAL QUESTION:

What shapes your outlook on life?

COMPARE POEMS

As you read, pay attention to the ways in which William Blake describes the two contrasting states of being—innocence and experience. How are the details in the poems similar or different, and how do they contribute to the themes described?

POEMS

from SONGS OF EXPERIENCE

by **William Blake**

pages 568–570

QUICK START

What comes to mind when you think of innocence and experience? Write down a list of at least three ideas or images for each state.

INNOCENCE	EXPERIENCE

ANALYZE SYMBOLS

A **symbol** is a person, place, object, or action that has a concrete meaning in itself and also stands for something beyond itself, such as an idea or feeling. For example, a dove is widely known as a symbol of peace. In literature, symbols often take their meaning from the context in which they appear, and the symbolic meaning may be interpreted in different ways.

Symbols play an important role in Blake's poetry. Although at first glance the poems in *Songs of Innocence* and *Songs of Experience* seem simple and straightforward, Blake uses symbols to convey complex spiritual and social themes. As you read these poems, look for clues to help you interpret the symbols. Use this chart to jot down your interpretations.

PERSON, PLACE, OR OBJECT	CONCRETE MEANING	SYMBOLIC IDEA OR FEELING

GENRE ELEMENTS: LYRIC POETRY

- expresses personal thoughts or feelings
- written from a first-person perspective
- has a musical quality
- marked by imagination and evocative language

GET READY

UNDERSTAND HISTORICAL BACKGROUND

Background information on historical, social, cultural, and economic issues may be important for understanding a poem's theme. William Blake sometimes used his poetry to comment on child labor, slavery, science, and other social and cultural issues. In *Songs of Innocence* and *Songs of Experience,* for example, Blake describes the plight of chimney sweepers, boys from poor families who were apprenticed to chimney sweeps and used to clean chimneys in London and other British cities.

During the Romantic period, most fireplaces in England burned coal for fuel, creating sticky soot that had to be brushed or scraped away. Children crawled up narrow chimneys to perform this work. Sometimes their masters would light fires underneath them to make sure they moved quickly. People who worked as sweepers rarely lived past middle age due to respiratory illnesses, cancer, and other diseases.

As early as 1788, legislation was enacted to prohibit children younger than eight from working as sweeps' apprentices. Subsequent legislation raised the minimum age again, but these laws were unenforced and ineffective. In 1834 Parliament passed the Chimney Sweeps Act; however, this too was largely ignored. It was not until 1875 that sweeps were required to be licensed and police were given the power to enforce legislation, bringing an end to the practice of child labor. As you read Blake's poems about chimney sweepers, make connections between this historical information and details of the poems.

ANNOTATION MODEL

NOTICE & NOTE 

As you read, note clues to the meaning of symbols in Blake's poems. Also note any details about social conditions in Britain. This model shows one reader's notes about lines 1–6 of "The Lamb."

Little Lamb, who made thee? Dost thou know who made thee? Gave thee life & bid thee feed, By the stream & o'er the mead; Gave thee clothing of delight, Softest clothing wooly bright;	The rhythm and sweet tone remind me of a nursery rhyme. Details emphasize that the lamb is small and soft. This suggests it is a symbol of gentleness and innocence.

NOTICE & NOTE

BACKGROUND

William Blake *(1757–1827) was born into a modest family in London. He learned to read and write at home, while studying the Bible and the works of John Milton. When he was 10, his father sent him to a drawing school. Blake began writing poetry when he was 12. However, the cost of the school was high, so four years later his parents apprenticed him to a master engraver.*

After setting up shop as an engraver, Blake developed a technique that allowed him to print pages of text and illustration from the same plate, which he then hand colored. Blake used this time-consuming process, called illuminated printing, to publish most of his works.

from SONGS OF INNOCENCE

Poems by William Blake

In 1782 Blake married Catherine Boucher. She was illiterate when they met, but Blake taught her how to read, write, and paint. She was an assistant in his work and became a skilled draftsperson.

In 1789 Blake completed his first illuminated book, Songs of Innocence, *featuring poems written for children that also depicted the innocent nature of childhood. Blake's later works were written on a grand scale, marked by prophetic and mythic visions. Imaginatively illustrated and difficult to understand, these complex works were largely ignored by his contemporaries. More than100 years passed before people began to recognize Blake's stunning achievements as a poet and artist.*

In this selection, you will read two poems from Blake's first collection. The second collection, Songs of Experience, *which you will read next, includes poems that expand on similar themes, with contrasting perspectives. Two such poems, "The Lamb" and "The Tyger," are an example of companion poems that are in separate volumes.*

PREPARE TO COMPARE

As you read, think about how each poem expresses ideas about innocence or experience.

Notice & Note

Use the side margins to notice and note signposts in the text.

NOTICE & NOTE

4 **mead:** meadow.

8 **vales:** valleys.

ANALYZE SYMBOLS

Annotate: Mark references to the lamb's creator in lines 11–18.

Interpret: How does this passage develop the symbolic meaning of the lamb?

13–14 He . . . Lamb: In the New Testament, Jesus is sometimes called the Lamb of God.

The Lamb

Little Lamb, who made thee?
Dost thou know who made thee?
Gave thee life & bid thee feed,
By the stream & o'er the mead;
Gave thee clothing of delight,
Softest clothing wooly bright;
Gave thee such a tender voice,
Making all the vales rejoice!
Little Lamb who made thee?
Dost thou know who made thee?

Little Lamb I'll tell thee,
Little Lamb I'll tell thee!
He is callèd by thy name,
For he calls himself a Lamb:
He is meek & he is mild,
He became a little child:
I a child & thou a lamb,
We are callèd by his name.
Little Lamb God bless thee.
Little Lamb God bless thee.

CHECK YOUR UNDERSTANDING

Answer these questions about "The Lamb" before moving on to the next selection.

1 In "The Lamb," the speaker begins by asking —

A whether the lamb is lost

B how old the lamb is

C who created the lamb

D what is the lamb's name

2 Blake reveals that the poem's speaker is —

F the lamb

G a child

H Jesus Christ

J Blake himself

3 Which of God's characteristics does Blake emphasize in "The Lamb"?

A Gentleness

B Power

C Beauty

D Creativity

3 **´weep! ´weep!:** the child´s attempt to say "Sweep! Sweep!" —a chimney sweeper's street cry.

UNDERSTAND HISTORICAL BACKGROUND

Annotate: Mark details in lines 1–14 that relate to the historical context of the poem.

Infer: What can you infer from these details about social conditions in late 18th century Britain?

18 **sport:** play or frolic.

20 **want:** lack.

The Chimney Sweeper

When my mother died I was very young,
And my father sold me while yet my tongue
Could scarcely cry "'weep! 'weep! 'weep! 'weep!"
So your chimneys I sweep & in soot I sleep.

There's little Tom Dacre, who cried when his head
That curl'd like a lamb's back, was shav'd, so I said,
"Hush, Tom! never mind it, for when your head's bare,
You know that the soot cannot spoil your white hair."

And so he was quiet, & that very night,
As Tom was a-sleeping he had such a sight!
That thousands of sweepers, Dick, Joe, Ned, & Jack,
Were all of them lock'd up in coffins of black;

And by came an Angel who had a bright key,
And he open'd the coffins & set them all free;
Then down a green plain, leaping, laughing they run,
And wash in a river and shine in the Sun.

Then naked & white, all their bags left behind,
They rise upon clouds, and sport in the wind.
And the Angel told Tom, if he'd be a good boy,
He'd have God for his father & never want joy.

And so Tom awoke; and we rose in the dark
And got with our bags & our brushes to work.
Tho' the morning was cold, Tom was happy & warm;
So if all do their duty, they need not fear harm.

CHECK YOUR UNDERSTANDING

Answer these questions about "The Chimney Sweeper" before moving on to the next selection.

1 In "The Chimney Sweeper," the speaker knows Tom Dacre because —

A they go to the same school

B they are brothers

C they work together

D Tom appeared in a dream

2 Why does Tom cry in "The Chimney Sweeper"?

F His hair is shaved off.

G His hair becomes dirty.

H His father sells him.

J He sees boys in coffins.

3 Tom is "happy & warm" in the morning because he —

A had a good night's sleep

B worked over a warm fireplace

C was allowed to miss work

D dreamed of an angel comforting him

NOTICE & NOTE

BACKGROUND

William Blake *(1757–1827) published* Songs of Experience *in 1794 as a companion volume to* Songs of Innocence. *He said his purpose in putting them together was to show "the two contrary states of the human soul." The contrast between the collections lies in the perspectives of the speakers rather than the subjects of the poems. Much darker in mood and tone,* Songs of Experience *includes poems that link to poems in the earlier volume, including some with matching titles.*

Notice & Note

Use the side margins to notice and note signposts in the text.

The Tyger

Tyger! Tyger! burning bright
In the forests of the night,
What immortal hand or eye
Could frame thy fearful symmetry?

In what distant deeps or skies
Burnt the fire of thine eyes?
On what wings dare he aspire?
What the hand dare seize the fire?

And what shoulder, & what art,
Could twist the sinews of thy heart?
And when thy heart began to beat,
What dread hand? & what dread feet?

What the hammer? what the chain?
In what furnace was thy brain?
What the anvil? what dread grasp
Dare its deadly terrors clasp?

4 symmetry (sĭm´ĭ-trē): balance or beauty of form.

7 he: the tiger's creator.

ANALYZE SYMBOLS

Annotate: Mark details in lines 1–12 that describe the tiger.

Analyze: What symbolic meaning is suggested by these details?

15 anvil (ăn´vĭl): iron block on which metal objects are hammered into shape.

When the stars threw down their spears
And watered heaven with their tears,
Did he smile his work to see?
Did he who made the Lamb make thee?

Tyger! Tyger! burning bright
In the forests of the night,
What immortal hand or eye
Dare frame thy fearful symmetry?

NOTICE & NOTE 

TOUGH QUESTIONS

Notice & Note: Mark each question in the poem.

Draw Conclusions: Why does the poem consist of so many questions?

CHECK YOUR UNDERSTANDING

Answer these questions about "The Tyger" before moving on to the next selection.

1 What does the "immortal hand or eye" in "The Tyger" refer to?

A God

B Death

C Mankind

D Nature

2 Which aspect of nature does Blake associate with the tiger?

F Wind

G Air

H Water

J Fire

3 The lines "What the anvil? what dread grasp / Dare its deadly terrors clasp" express —

A pity for the animals devoured by the tiger

B fear that the tiger cannot be controlled

C awe for the creator of such a terrifying creature

D suspicion that the tiger is not real

NOTICE & NOTE

The Chimney Sweeper

A little black thing among the snow
Crying "'weep, 'weep," in notes of woe!
"Where are thy father & mother? say?"
"They are both gone up to the church to pray.

"Because I was happy upon the heath,
And smil'd among the winter's snow;
They clothed me in the clothes of death,
And taught me to sing the notes of woe.

"And because I am happy, & dance & sing,
They think they have done me no injury,
And are gone to praise God & his Priest & King,
Who make up a heaven of our misery."

2 'weep, 'weep: the child's attempt to say "Sweep, Sweep"—a chimney sweeper's street cry.

5 heath: a tract of open land that cannot be farmed.

UNDERSTAND HISTORICAL BACKGROUND

Annotate: Mark details in lines 5–12 that help create the tone of "The Chimney Sweeper."

Infer: Identify the tone of this poem. What does it suggest about British society?

CHECK YOUR UNDERSTANDING

Answer these questions before moving on to the **Analyze the Texts** section on the following page.

1 What is the "black thing" Blake refers to in "The Chimney Sweeper"?

A A child

B A piece of coal

C A chimney

D Soot-coated snow

2 Why don't the parents of the chimney sweeper see that he is being harmed by his work?

F He lies to them.

G He keeps up a cheerful appearance.

H He has run away from them.

J He praises God for his job.

3 In "The Chimney Sweeper," what does the phrase "make up a heaven of our misery" suggest?

A The church and the king profit from his sweeping.

B The priest and the king also suffer.

C His parents will be rewarded in heaven.

D His parents' religion glorifies suffering.

RESPOND

ANALYZE THE TEXTS

Support your responses with evidence from the texts. NOTEBOOK

1. **Identify** Notice the words, phrases, and lines that Blake repeats in "The Lamb." What mood does this repetition help create?
2. **Interpret** In "The Tyger," the speaker describes the animal as "fearful" and "deadly." Do the negative connotations of this language suggest that the tiger should never have been created? Explain.
3. **Draw Conclusions** In "The Tyger," Blake uses words such as *art, hammer, furnace,* and *anvil* to describe the tiger's creation, as if the animal were a metal sculpture. What does this symbolic meaning of the tiger suggest about Blake's view of art?
4. **Analyze** Describe Blake's use of the colors white and black in "The Chimney Sweeper" poems. What do these colors symbolize?
5. **Notice & Note** In "The Chimney Sweeper" poems, the speakers have two sharply contrasting perspectives on religion. Considered together, what do both poems suggest about Blake's view of the religious establishment of his time? Explain.

RESEARCH

RESEARCH TIP
When researching social, historical, or political events, consider referring to an encyclopedia. Encyclopedias are useful because they tend to be organized according to a specific subject or domain. You may, for instance, refer to an encyclopedia of history.

As you've read, poets sometimes draw inspiration from social, historical, and political events. "The Chimney Sweeper" poems, for example, express social commentary on the use and abuse of young boys to clean chimneys before child labor laws were implemented. Research another William Blake poem that addresses a social, historical, or political issue or event. Use the graphic organizer below to explain the poem's social, historical, or political connection.

TITLE OF POEM	SOCIAL, HISTORICAL, OR POLITICAL CONNECTION

Extend Research another poet who writes about social, historical, or political events. What are some similarities and differences between this poet and William Blake? Consider organizing your findings in a Venn diagram.

RESPOND

CREATE AND DISCUSS

Write an Essay Choose a social issue that is considered one of the compelling concerns of contemporary times. Write a short problem-solution essay to explore the issue and possible remedies.

- ❑ Focus on a problem that directly affects your community.
- ❑ If you are working actively to confront this social problem, share your firsthand knowledge.
- ❑ Ask yourself questions about the problem as a way to explore ways it might be solved. Your essay might include more than one approach.
- ❑ Identify a symbol that could meaningfully convey your message.

Make a Podcast Form a small group to plan a podcast. Identify the key ideas in your essay and organize them into discussion points. Then record a "talk" on these discussion points to create your podcast.

- ❑ Use your problem-solution essays as well as other research to support your views.
- ❑ Assign a host to keep the conversation flowing. Exchange ideas in a lively manner and try to avoid "talking-down" to your audience.
- ❑ Uphold the basic goal to leave your listeners motivated.

Go to **Writing Informative Texts** in the **Writing Studio** for more help.

Go to **Participating in Collaborative Discussions** in the **Speaking and Listening Studio** for help.

RESPOND TO THE ESSENTIAL QUESTION

What shapes your outlook on life?

Gather Information Review your annotations and notes on poems from *Songs of Innocence* and *Songs of Experience*. Then, add relevant information to your Response Log. As you determine which information to include, think about:

- the experiences and characteristics of children and of adults—how they are similar and different
- how nature has influenced the way you think about life
- the tension between opposites, like innocence and experience, and how exploring such opposites helps us understand our world

ACADEMIC VOCABULARY

As you write and discuss what you learned from the poems, be sure to use the Academic Vocabulary words. Check off each of the words that you use.

- ❑ **appreciate**
- ❑ **insight**
- ❑ **intensity**
- ❑ **invoke**
- ❑ **radical**

RESPOND

from
SONGS OF INNOCENCE
Poems by William Blake

Collaborate & Compare

COMPARE POEMS

Compare and contrast the perspectives of the poems from *Songs of Innocence* and *Songs of Experience,* using the following criteria:

- **Word choice:** Look for descriptive words and note how they are used to emphasize characteristics of a subject.
- **Ideas:** Identify common or contrasting ideas expressed in the poems.
- **Tone:** Notice the speaker's attitude toward the subject.

As you read, you may use a chart like this one to record similarities and differences between each linked pair of poems.

	"THE LAMB"	"THE TYGER"
Word Choice		
Ideas		
Tone		

ANALYZE THE TEXTS

Discuss these questions in your group.

1. **Compare** "The Lamb" and "The Tyger" develop around questions posed at the beginning of each poem. How do the speakers' different responses to these questions reflect the contrast between innocence and experience?

2. **Critique** Does Blake use symbols effectively to help convey his themes? Why or why not?

3. **Interpret** Is Blake's view of innocence and experience essentially the same as the idea of good versus evil? Explain your response.

4. **Draw Conclusions** Do these poems suggest that innocence is better than experience? Explain your response.

COLLABORATE AND PRESENT

With your group, continue exploring the ideas in the poems by identifying and comparing word choice, symbols, and themes. Follow these steps:

1. **Decide on the most important details with your group.** Review your chart to identify the most important details from each poem. What words or phrases stood out the most to you? Come to a consensus with your group.

2. **Come up with a message.** Determine a message for each poem based on the details, diction, ideas, and symbols. You may use a chart to keep track of the themes your group members come up with.

	DETAILS	MESSAGE
Songs of Innocence		
Songs of Experience		

3. **Compare ideas.** Compare ideas with your group and discuss whether the messages are similar or different. Listen actively to the members of your group and ask them to clarify any points you do not understand.

4. **Present to the class.** Next, present your ideas to the class. Be sure to include clear statements on the theme for each poem. Discuss whether the messages are similar or different.

Go to **Participating in a Collaborative Discussion** in the **Speaking and Listening Studio** to support group discussion.

COLLABORATION TIP

When discussing your ideas in a group, be sure to listen attentively. Give your peers an opportunity to share their ideas and respect their views. If you disagree with an idea, present evidence from the selections to support your ideas. Give all group members an opportunity to have a turn.

INDEPENDENT READING

ESSENTIAL QUESTIONS

Review the four Essential Questions for this unit on page 491.

Reader's Choice

Setting a Purpose Select one or more of these options from your eBook to continue your exploration of the Essential Questions.

- Read the descriptions to see which text attracts your interest.
- Think about which genres you enjoy reading.

Notice & Note

In this unit, you practiced noticing and noting the signposts and asking big questions about nonfiction. As you read independently, these signposts and others will aid your understanding. Below are the key questions to ask when you read literature and nonfiction.

Reading Literature: Stories, Poems, and Plays	
Signpost	**Key Question**
Contrasts and Contradictions	Why did the character act that way?
Aha Moment	How might this change things?
Tough Questions	What does this make me wonder about?
Words of the Wiser	What's the lesson for the character?
Again and Again	Why might the author keep bringing this up?
Memory Moment	Why is this memory important?

Reading Nonfiction: Essays, Articles, and Arguments	
Signpost	**Key Question(s)**
Big Questions	What surprised me? What did the author think I already knew? What challenged, changed, or confirmed what I already knew?
Contrasts and Contradictions	What is the difference, and why does it matter?
Extreme or Absolute Language	Why did the author use this language?
Numbers and Stats	Why did the author use these numbers or amounts?
Quoted Words	Why was this person quoted or cited, and what did this citation add?
Word Gaps	Do I know this word from someplace else? Does it seem like technical talk for this topic? Do clues in the sentence help me understand the word?

INDEPENDENT READING

You can preview these texts in Unit 4 of your eBook.

Then check off the text or texts that you select to read on your own.

☐ EXPLANATORY ESSAY

William Blake: Visions and Verses
Rachel Galvin

Why was William Blake considered eccentric during his life but is now praised as a creative visionary?

☐ POEM

Frost at Midnight
Samuel Taylor Coleridge

How do the poet's memories of his childhood affect what he wants for his son?

☐ PERSONAL NARRATIVE

Walking with Wordsworth
Bruce Stutz

A naturalist describes continuity as well as change in the landscapes that Wordsworth held dear.

☐ EXPLANATORY ESSAY

***from* A Defense of Poetry**
Percy Bysshe Shelley

Why does Shelley believe that poetry is the foundation of society as well as a source of beauty?

☐ POEM

The Skylark
John Clare

Clare contrasts young boys' fanciful view of flight with the skylark's awareness of nature's risks and dangers.

Collaborate and Share With a partner, discuss what you learned from at least one of your independent readings.

- Give a brief synopsis or summary of the text.
- Describe any signposts that you noticed in the text and explain what they revealed to you.
- Describe what you most enjoyed or found most challenging about the text. Give specific examples.
- Decide if you would recommend the text to others. Why or why not?

Go to the **Reading Studio** for more resources on **Notice & Note.**

Write an Explanatory Essay

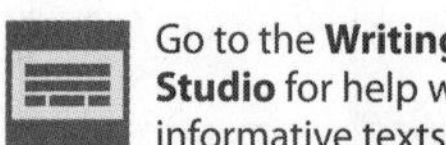

Go to the **Writing Studio** for help writing informative texts.

In this unit, you have read literature from the Romantic period. Many Romantic writers celebrated nature in their works. Others warned of the dangers of tampering with nature. For your next writing task, you will write an explanatory essay on the relationship between humans and nature, using your readings as sources to support your own ideas. The article "Frankenstein: Giving Voice to the Monster" is an explanatory essay that discusses the concept of the human creation of life using Mary Shelley's *Frankenstein* as a source. You will use this essay as a mentor text as you plan and draft your own essay.

As you write your explanatory essay, you can use the notes from your Response Log which you filled out after reading the texts in this unit.

Writing Prompt

Read the information in the box below.

This is the topic or context for your explanatory essay.

> **The human relationship with the natural world is a major topic of literature, including fiction, poetry, and literary essays.**

Think carefully about the following question.

How might this Essential Question relate to an explanatory essay?

> **What can nature offer us?**

How might an experience of nature relate to an explanatory essay?

Write an explanatory essay about how experiencing the natural world can alter a person's state of mind.

Be sure to—

Review these points as you write and again when you finish. Make any needed changes.

- ❑ have a "big idea" that your essay develops
- ❑ organize your essay into paragraphs that present a key idea, such as an opinion, an observation, or a claim
- ❑ support your key ideas with such evidence as facts, quotations from texts, expert opinions, or evidence
- ❑ write an opening that catches your reader's attention while introducing your topic
- ❑ write a conclusion that wraps up your ideas and leaves the reader with some "food for thought"

1 Plan

Before you begin planning your essay, go through your notes on the texts and look for anything you might use, such as something an author said about nature that you found particularly striking or true, or a thought you had in response. Think about your own experiences with the natural world and how they have affected you.

To generate more ideas for your essay, try these strategies:

- word mapping
- free writing
- group discussion

Review your notes and mark the ones that are most important. Then reflect and come up with your "big idea." You may need to do some more free writing. As E.M. Forster said, "How can I know what I think until I see what I say?"

Use a chart like the one below to plan your essay.

Explanatory Essay Planning Table	
Genre	Explanatory essay
Topic	Human relationship with nature
Details and ideas from texts	
Ideas from word mapping and/or free writing	
Ideas from group discussion	
Ideas from my personal experiences	
My "big idea"	

Background Reading Review the notes you have made in your Response Log that relate to the question "What can nature offer us?" Texts in this unit provide background reading that will help you formulate your "big idea" and your key ideas.

Go to **Writing Informative Texts: Developing a Topic** for help planning your explanatory essay.

Notice & Note

From Reading to Writing

As you plan your explanatory essay, apply what you've learned about signposts to your own writing. Remember that writers use common features called signposts to help convey their message to readers.

Think how you can incorporate **Quoted Words** into your essay.

Go to the **Reading Studio** for more resources on **Notice & Note.**

Use the notes from your Response Log as you plan your explanatory essay.

UNIT 4 RESPONSE LOG

Use this Response Log to record information from the texts that relates to or comments on the **Essential Questions** in Unit 4.

? Essential Question	Details from Texts
What can nature offer us?	
How do you define beauty?	
How can science go wrong?	
What shapes your outlook on life?	

R4 Student Resources

WRITING TASK

Go to **Writing Informative Texts: Organizing Ideas** for help organizing your explanatory essay.

Organize Your Ideas After you have gathered ideas from your planning activities, you need to organize them in a way that will help you draft your explanatory essay. You can use the chart below to help you organize the elements of your essay.

Topic: Human relationship with nature		
Big Idea:		
Key Idea	**Key Idea**	**Key Idea**
Supporting Details	**Supporting Details**	**Supporting Details**
Final Reflection/"Food for Thought"		

2 Develop a Draft

You might prefer to draft your explanatory essay online.

Once you have completed your planning activities, you will be ready to begin drafting your explanatory essay. Refer to the elements of an explanatory essay and your organizing chart as well as any notes you took as you studied the texts in this unit. These will provide a kind of map for you to follow as you write. Using a word processor or online writing application makes it easier to make changes or move sentences around later when you are ready to revise your first draft.

Use the Mentor Text

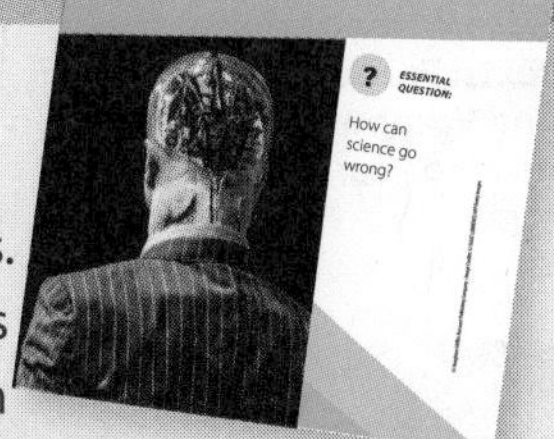

Author's Craft

Your explanatory essay should include several key ideas supported by details. A key idea can be your opinion, an observation, or a claim; supporting details will include facts, quotes from background readings, or short anecdotes from your experiences or those of others. Each key idea and its supporting details should be organized together in a paragraph, but if a paragraph is very long, you should break it into two or more paragraphs.

The possibility that artificial creatures, products of human hands, might achieve sentience and take on an active role in society is an age-old conception in world cultures. . . .

The first sentence presents an observation.

In Greek mythology one finds the tale of Pygmalion who carves a statue named Galatea with whom he falls in love and who eventually comes to life. In Jewish folklore there are stories of the Golem, an artificial creature animated with surprising results.

These details are facts that support the observation.

Apply What You've Learned To develop a key idea, state an opinion, an observation, or a claim related to your big idea and then provide details that support it. Make sure all of the details you provide are relevant to this key idea.

Genre Characteristics

Bringing in background reading will enrich your essay. When you quote a text, make sure you introduce it by giving the author and the name of the text, as well as some information about the quote's relevance.

In a live exchange on the internet, Microsoft cofounder Bill Gates offered similar views. "I am in the camp that is concerned about super intelligence," Gates wrote. "First the machines will do a lot of jobs for us and not be super intelligent. . . . A few decades after that though the intelligence is strong enough to be a concern."

Winner identifies where the quote came from, "live exchange on the internet," the author of the quote, Bill Gates, and states that Gates holds "similar views."

Apply What You've Learned Include quotes from your background readings to support your key ideas. For each quote, tell the reader where the quote is from and give some explanation of how it relates to one of your key ideas.

3 Revise

Go to **Writing Informative Texts: Precise Language and Vocabulary** for help revising your explanatory essay.

On Your Own Once you have written your draft, you'll want to go back and look for ways to improve your explanatory essay. As you reread and revise, think about whether you have achieved your purpose. The Revision Guide will help you focus on specific elements to make your writing stronger.

Revision Guide		
Ask Yourself	**Tips**	**Revision Techniques**
1. Does my first paragraph engage the reader and introduce the topic and my big idea?	**Circle** the part that will grab the reader's interest and **underline** the sentences that introduce the topic and the big idea.	**Add** a surprising detail or vivid image. **Reword** or add a sentence to introduce the topic and big idea more clearly.
2. Do I present a few key ideas that support my big idea?	**Underline** the sentences that state your key ideas.	**Review** your planning notes and **look for** more key ideas to include.
3. Do I provide details that support my key ideas?	**Circle** the first word of each sentence that provides a supporting detail to see if each paragraph has more than one.	**Add** details from your notes or quotes from your background readings.
4. Do I provide smooth transitions between ideas and paragraphs?	**Underline** the transition words and phrases in your essay.	**Add** transition words and phrases to connect ideas.
5. Does my final reflection summarize my big idea?	**Underline** the sentence that summarizes your big idea.	**Look back** at your key ideas to see what conclusions you can draw from all of them.
6. Do I leave my reader with "food for thought"?	**Circle** your "food for thought" statement or question.	**Add** a sentence that invites the reader to consider a question not answered in your essay.

ACADEMIC VOCABULARY

As you conduct your **peer review,** be sure to use these words.

- ❑ **appreciate**
- ❑ **insight**
- ❑ **intensity**
- ❑ **invoke**
- ❑ **radical**

With a Partner Once you and your partner have worked through the Revision Guide on your own, exchange explanatory essays and evaluate each other's draft in a **peer review.** Focus on providing revision suggestions for at least three of the items mentioned in the chart. Explain why you think your partner's draft should be revised and what your specific suggestions are.

When receiving feedback from your partner, listen attentively and ask questions to make sure you fully understand the revision suggestions.

4 Edit

Look closely at your essay to make sure you do not have fragments or run-on sentences, that you have used punctuation correctly, and that you have subject-verb agreement. Cut unnecessary words and break up long sentences.

Language Conventions

Sensory Language Sensory language includes descriptive words and phrases that appeal to the reader's senses. This language helps readers imagine they are seeing, hearing, tasting, touching, or smelling what the writer describes in the text.

Here is an example of text revised to make use of sensory language. Note the underlined sensory words and phrases in the revised text.

Original	Revised
The hiking trail near my house is nice in the springtime. There are a lot of wildflowers and pretty insects.	In the springtime, the hiking trail near my house turns balmy in the afternoon, when wildflowers release their sweet scent and the air buzzes with insects whose wings flash with color.

In this example, the writer has revised the text to use words and phrases that appeal to the senses. *Balmy* appeals to the sense of touch, *sweet scent* appeals to the sense of smell, *buzzes* appeals to the sense of hearing, and *flash with color* appeals to the sense of sight. Notice how the use of these words and phrases brings the writing to life for the reader and helps the reader to imagine the hiking trail in detail.

Look back at your writing to find places where you can add detail through sensory language. Try to incorporate all five senses.

5 Publish

Finalize your explanatory essay and choose a way to share it with your audience. Consider these options:

- Record your essay as a podcast.
- Compile the class's essays into an eBook.

WRITING TASK

Use the scoring guide to evaluate your essay.

Writing Task Scoring Guide: Explanatory Essay

	Organization/Progression	Development of Ideas	Use of Language and Conventions
4	• The introduction engages the reader and establishes the topic. • Every part of the paper supports the big idea. • Key ideas in the essay are organized in a logical manner. • There is a conclusion that summarizes the big idea and leaves the reader with "food for thought."	• Key ideas are presented in a way that clearly supports the big idea. • Details in each paragraph are relevant to the key idea.	• The writer's word choice and language are clear, concise, and appropriate to the expository writing task. • The writer shows consistent command of grammar with only minor errors in punctuation or spelling.
3	• The opening presents the topic but is only somewhat engaging to the reader. • The big idea of the essay is fairly clear but is presented in a formulaic manner. • Key ideas in the essay are mostly logical, although the organizational structure of the paper is weak at some points. • There is a conclusion but it does not fully summarize the big idea.	• Most key ideas are supported by details. • Details presented are mostly relevant to the key ideas, but some seem unnecessary or off topic.	• The writer's word choice and language are mostly clear and unambiguous, and the tone of the paper is appropriate. • The writer shows adequate command of grammar with occasional errors in spelling and punctuation.
2	• The opening does not clearly introduce the topic and does not engage the reader. • The paper contains a big idea, but it is not clearly defined or focused. • The key ideas are not presented in a logical manner, and the organizational structure of the paper is often confused.	• Either the key ideas are not well supported by details, or the details given are irrelevant to the key idea. • Many details are irrelevant or off topic.	• The writing is formulaic and simple, and the tone is not appropriate to expository writing. • The writer shows only moderate command of grammar, spelling, and punctuation, but key ideas are still clear.
1	• The big idea of the paper is not clear at all, and the paper often wanders from the topic. • There is no organizational structure in the presentation of the key ideas.	• Either no details are given, or the details that are provided are irrelevant and do not support key ideas.	• The writing is vague and confusing. Sentences are simple and awkward. • The writer shows little or no command of grammar, spelling, and punctuation, which causes key ideas to be unclear.

Reflect on the Unit

By completing your explanatory essay, you have created a writing product that pulls together and expresses your thoughts about the reading you have done in this unit. Now is a good time to reflect on what you have learned.

Reflect on the Essential Questions

- Review the four Essential Questions on page 491. How have your answers to these questions changed in response to the texts you've read in this unit?
- What are some examples from the texts you've read that show human beings' relationship with the natural world?

Reflect on Your Reading

- Which selections were the most interesting or surprising to you?
- From which selection did you learn the most about human beings' relationship with the natural world?

Reflect on the Writing Task

- What difficulties did you encounter while working on your explanatory essay? How might you avoid them next time?
- Which parts of the essay were the easiest to write? The hardest to write? Why?
- What improvements did you make to your essay as you were revising?

UNIT 4 SELECTIONS

- **"Lines Composed a Few Miles Above Tintern Abbey"**
- **"Composed upon Westminster Bridge, September 3, 1802"**
- **"I Wandered Lonely As a Cloud"**
- **"Ode on a Grecian Urn"**
- **from *Frankenstein***
- **"Frankenstein: Giving Voice to the Monster"**
- **"Ode to the West Wind"**
- **"Song of a Thatched Hut Damaged in Autumn Wind"**
- **from *Songs of Innocence***
- **from *Songs of Experience***

UNIT 5

AN ERA OF RAPID CHANGE

THE VICTORIANS

> "The history of England is emphatically the history of progress."
>
> —Thomas Babington Macaulay

Discuss the **Essential Questions** with your whole class or in small groups. As you read An Era of Rapid Change, consider how the selections explore these questions.

? ***ESSENTIAL QUESTION:***

What is a true benefactor?

In 19th-century Great Britain, there was a wide gap between the impoverished many and the wealthy few. Occasionally, well-to-do members of the middle and upper classes would become benefactors, providing financial or other material assistance to those who were less fortunate. How did benefactors determine who would receive their help? What made a person a good benefactor in Victorian Britain? Was the role ever abused? What role do benefactors play in modern society?

? ***ESSENTIAL QUESTION:***

How do you view the world?

The 19th century was a time not only of changing technology, but also of changing ideas. As society evolved, so did people's thinking about such topics as religion, science, social structures, and their own place in the world. Some viewed progress with optimism for the future while others noted that progress brought its own set of challenges. When you look at the world around you today, what do you see?

? ***ESSENTIAL QUESTION:***

What brings out cruelty in people?

Although the Victorian Era was a time of improvement in the quality of life for many, not all benefited equally. As is the case today, the daily life of some people was marked by needless cruelty. Who are the perpetrators and the victims of cruelty? What might motivate someone to treat another human or an animal cruelly? What roles do society and social structures play in promoting and/or preventing cruelty?

? ***ESSENTIAL QUESTION:***

Which invention has had the greatest impact on your life?

The Victorian Era was a time of remarkable technological advancement. Great Britain led the Industrial Revolution, and the strength and influence of the British Empire ensured that British industry and inventions soon spread around the world. Many modern conveniences that we take for granted today were invented, or were in the early stages of development, during that period. Which inventions do you use most in your everyday life? How would your life be different without them?

THE VICTORIANS

"The sun never sets on the British Empire," boasted the Victorians, and it was true: with holdings around the globe, from Africa to India, from New Zealand to Canada, it was always daytime in some part of the vast territory ruled by Great Britain. The phrase also captured the attitude of the era. During the reign of Queen Victoria, Britain was a nation in motion at the height of its power, both politically and economically. Abroad, Britain dominated world politics. At home, the Industrial Revolution was in full swing. For those with wealth and influence, Victoria's reign was a time not only of change but of prosperity. Yet, large segments of the population suffered greatly during this period, leading many writers to criticize the rapid pace and materialism of the age and the injustices that resulted.

The New Monarchy Queen Victoria, for whom the period is named, was just 18 years old when she came to the throne in 1837. She went on to rule for more than 60 years, longer than any English ruler before her. Victoria's devotion to hard work and duty, her insistence on proper behavior, and her support of British imperialism became the hallmarks of the Victorian period.

Victoria knew that previous monarchs had clashed with Parliament, and she realized that the role of royalty had to change. She accepted the concept of a constitutional monarchy in which she gave advice rather than orders, and yielded control of day-to-day governmental affairs to a series of very talented prime ministers. When the queen withdrew from politics and went into mourning in 1861, after the death of her beloved husband Prince Albert, the position of prime minister became even more important.

Progress, Problems, and Reform The Industrial Revolution had already transformed Britain into a modern industrial state by the time Victoria took the throne. By 1850 England boasted 18,000 cotton mills and produced half of the world's iron. Progress also brought new inventions, such as the telephone, light bulb, radio, and automobile, and advances in science and medicine, like the work of British surgeon Joseph Lister. Building on the ideas of Louis Pasteur, Lister developed standards for keeping hospitals clean and germ-free, vastly increasing the survival rates of his patients.

Some writers expressed enthusiasm for the material advantages afforded by the industrial age. Others were appalled by the materialism of the

COLLABORATIVE DISCUSSION
In a small group, review the timeline and discuss which events would have had the greatest effects on everyday life for people in Victorian Britain.

1835

1837 Victoria becomes Queen of Great Britain.

1842 Britain gains control of Hong Kong.

1844 Samuel Morse sends the first long-distance telegraph message.

1845 The Irish Potato Famine begins.

1847 Charlotte Brontë publishes *Jane Eyre*; Emily Brontë publishes *Wuthering Heights*.

1859 Charles Darwin publishes *On the Origin of Species.*

1860 Charles Dickens publishes the first magazine installment of *Great Expectations*.

1861 Prince Albert dies.

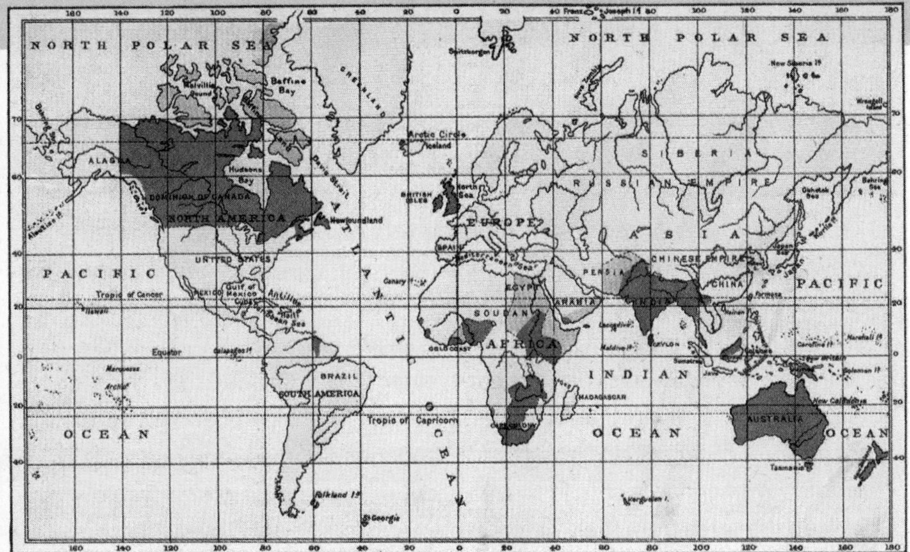

The British Empire, 1880

Victorian upper and middle classes—an attitude they considered tasteless, joyless, and destructive of community.

While the middle class grew more prosperous, conditions for the poor became intolerable. Factory workers, including many children, spent long hours toiling for low wages under harsh and dangerous conditions. In the 1840s, unemployment soared in England and the Great Famine devastated Ireland. Families without income and starving Irish immigrants crowded into England's already squalid slums.

Though Parliament enacted many important reforms during this period, change came slowly. The Great Reform Act of 1832 expanded suffrage, or the right to vote, to wealthy middle-class men. Before this law, only about 5 percent of Britain's population had the right to vote. In 1833 slavery was abolished in the British Empire, and the first laws restricting child labor were enacted. In decades that followed, laws were passed establishing public schools, improving sanitation and housing, legalizing trade unions, easing harsh factory conditions, and giving working-class men the right to vote.

Victorian Poetry Confronted with the harsh realities of the Victorian world, many poets followed the lead of the Romantics, focusing on idealized love and the awe-inspiring beauty of nature. But some poets, especially later in the century, addressed contemporary issues such as spiritual doubt and the loss of old customs, traditions, and values due to the pressures of industrialization and scientific discoveries.

RESEARCH
What about this historical period interests you? Choose a topic, event, or person to learn more about. Then, add your own entry to the timeline.

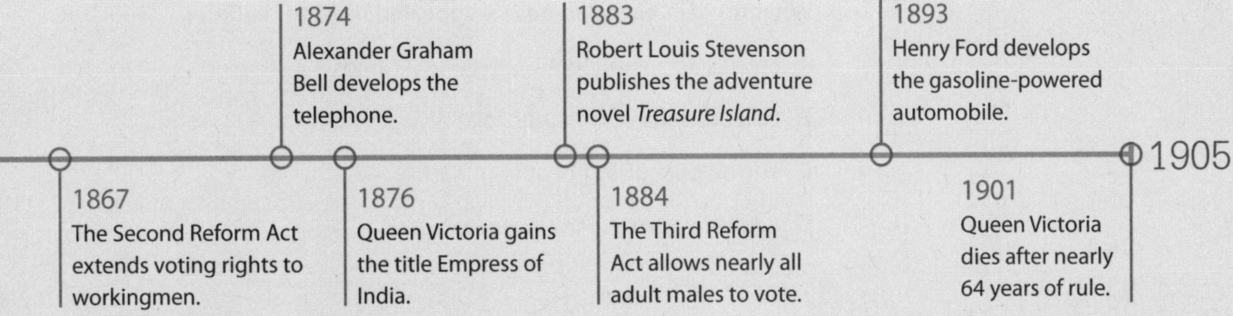

Realism While many poets retreated from modern life, novelists embraced the issues of the age. Victorian novels were weighty affairs, quite literally—so weighty that they typically had to be divided into three volumes. Keen-eyed, sharp-witted writers probed every corner of society—from the drawing room to the slums, exposing problems and pretensions. Victorian readers craved this realism. They wanted to meet characters like themselves and the people they knew; they wanted to learn more about their rapidly changing world. Families often spent evenings reading aloud to each other, laughing at the adventures of Charles Dickens's Mr. Pickwick and his oddball friends or sighing over Heathcliff and Catherine's doomed romance in Emily Brontë's *Wuthering Heights*. In the next century, modernist writers would pick up the torch from their Victorian predecessors and grapple with issues the Victorians could not have imagined.

CHECK YOUR UNDERSTANDING

Choose the best answer to each question.

1 Which **best** describes the British government during the Victorian Era?

A Conflicts between Victoria and Parliament led to the weakening of the monarchy.

B Victoria and Parliament agreed to give primary authority to the prime minister.

C Victoria modified the role of the monarch and strengthened the position of the prime minster.

D Parliament took Victoria's retirement from politics as an opportunity to establish a constitutional monarchy.

2 The reforms enacted by Parliament primarily affected the lower classes by —

F increasing the oppression faced by factory workers

G slowly improving living and working conditions

H addressing the unemployment crisis that arose in the 1840s

J contributing to the development of slums

3 What topic in Victorian novels appealed most to readers?

A Stories about ancient myths and legends

B Celebrations of romantic love

C The awe-inspiring beauty of nature

D Realistic portrayals of everyday people

ACADEMIC VOCABULARY

Academic Vocabulary words are words you use when you discuss and write about texts. In this unit, you will learn the following five words:

☑ **abandon** ☐ **confine** ☐ **conform** ☐ **depress** ☐ **reluctance**

Study the Word Network to learn more about the word **abandon**.

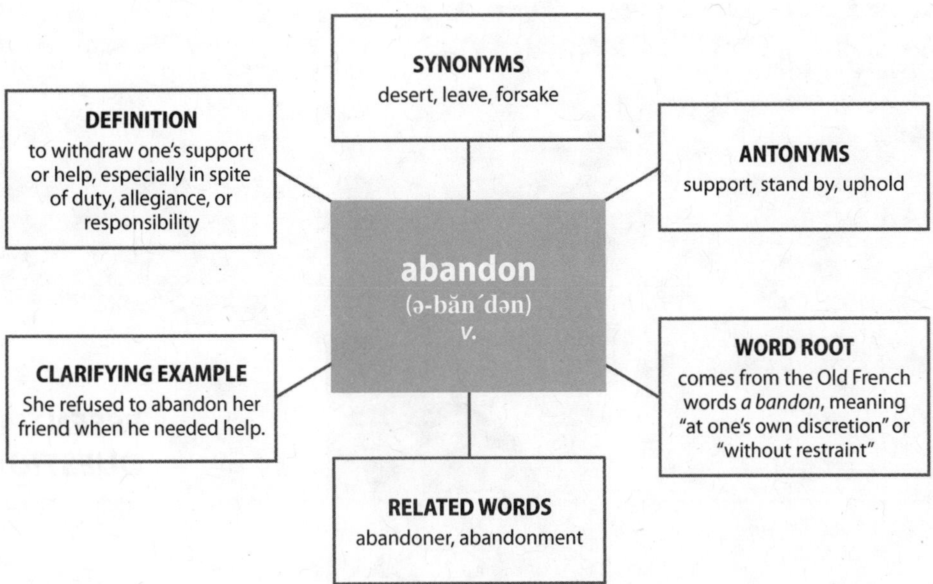

Write and Discuss Discuss your completed Word Network with a partner, making sure to talk through all of the boxes until you both understand the word, its synonyms, antonyms, and related forms. Then, fill out a Word Network for the remaining four words. Use a dictionary or online resource to help you complete the activity.

Go online to access the Word Networks.

RESPOND TO THE ESSENTIAL QUESTION

In this unit, you will explore four different **Essential Questions** about literature of the Victorian Era. As you read each selection, you will gather your ideas about one of these questions and write about it in the **Response Log** that appears on page R5. At the end of the unit, you will have the opportunity to write a **research report** related to one of the essential questions. Filling out the Response Log after you read each text will help you prepare for this writing task.

You can also go online to access the Response Log.

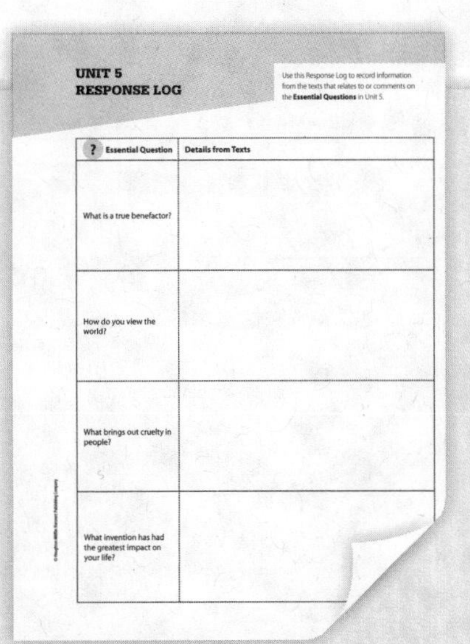

UNIT 5 RESPONSE LOG

Use this Response Log to record information from the texts that relates to or comments on the **Essential Questions** in Unit 5.

? Essential Question	Details from Texts
What is a true benefactor?	
How do you view the world?	
What brings out cruelty in people?	
What invention has had the greatest impact on your life?	

from JANE EYRE

Novel by **Charlotte Brontë**

ESSENTIAL QUESTION:

What is a true benefactor?

QUICK START

Think about a time of transition in your life, perhaps moving to a new neighborhood or changing schools. What were some of the obstacles you faced? What helped you adjust to your new circumstances? Discuss your experience with a partner.

ANALYZE FIRST-PERSON POINT OF VIEW

Stories are told from a narrative perspective, or **point of view.** In *Jane Eyre*, the story is narrated in the first-person point of view. The narrator is the character Jane, who uses the personal pronouns *I, me,* and *my*. Readers experience everything through her eyes. Jane's thoughts and commentary convey the intensity of her feelings about the Lowood boarding school and its occupants.

As you read, notice how Charlotte Brontë's use of the first-person point of view affects what you learn about the novel's characters, events, setting, and themes.

GENRE ELEMENTS: NOVEL

- is a long work of fiction
- is usually written in the first- or third-person point of view
- can develop characters and conflict more thoroughly than a short story
- often develops complex plot structures, including subplots

ANALYZE SETTING

The **setting** of a novel is the time and place in which the action occurs. This excerpt from *Jane Eyre* is set in a boarding school for girls. During the Victorian period, hundreds of charity schools were established in Britain to provide free education, clothing, lodging, and meals for orphans and poor children. They were funded by contributions from wealthy donors. Some of the people who ran these schools were very idealistic and treated students well. However, many schools were led by harsh disciplinarians and offered only the most basic education. Schools for the poorest children were called "ragged schools," a name inspired by the children's shabby clothing.

As you read, notice how the setting is connected to the novel's plot, characterization, and themes. Use a chart like this one to record details that reveal the historical, economic, and social context of the setting.

SETTING DETAILS	HISTORICAL, ECONOMIC, AND SOCIAL CONTEXT

GET READY

CRITICAL VOCABULARY

ruddy **dismay** **morose** **vogue** **commence** **verandah**

To see how many Critical Vocabulary words you already know, identify which underlined word in each sentence is used incorrectly.

1. They commenced the meeting to the verandah after the office air conditioner broke down.
   a. commenced **b.** verandah

2. Her morose face showed how much she appreciated the in-vogue garments presented at the fashion show.
   a. morose **b.** vogue

3. She was quite dismayed at his ruddy complexion, and asked if he ever got outdoors to enjoy the sunshine.
   a. dismayed **b.** ruddy

LANGUAGE CONVENTIONS

Gerunds and Gerund Phrases In this lesson, you will learn about gerunds and gerund phrases. A **gerund** is a verb ending in *-ing* that is used as a noun. You can add modifiers and complements to a gerund to make it a **gerund phrase.** Writers use gerunds and gerund phrases to effectively combine short sentences into one.

As you read the excerpt, notice the author's use of gerunds and gerund phrases.

ANNOTATION MODEL

NOTICE & NOTE

As you read, note the details that Brontë provides about the setting and how the narrator reacts to the treatment she receives from different people at the school. In the model, you can see one reader's notes about the excerpt from *Jane Eyre*.

The refectory was a great, low-ceiled, gloomy room; on two long tables smoked basins of something hot, which, however, to my dismay, sent forth an odor far from inviting. I saw a universal manifestation of discontent when the fumes of the repast met the nostrils of those destined to swallow it . . .

The room itself seems like it would make you lose your appetite. The narrator uses a formal, restrained tone to describe the food's awful smell, which suggests she's describing it when she's older.

BACKGROUND

Charlotte Brontë *(1816–1855) grew up in a rural area of England, the daughter of a clergyman and a mother who died when she was five. She worked as a governess and teacher before beginning her writing career. Her first book was a collection of poetry that she wrote with two of her sisters, Emily and Anne.* Jane Eyre*, originally published under a pseudonym, was her first novel. It blended the suspense and moody atmosphere of a Gothic novel with a realistic portrayal of the moral, social, and economic pressures faced by a Victorian woman who lacked family support.*

from JANE EYRE

Novel by Charlotte Brontë

SETTING A PURPOSE

As you read, pay attention to how Jane reacts to conditions at the school and to the people she meets there.

Orphaned as a young child, Jane Eyre has spent most of her childhood at Gateshead, the home of her wealthy yet heartless aunt, Mrs. Reed. At Gateshead, Jane is tormented by her cousins and repeatedly reminded of her low economic and social status. After a fight with one of her cousins, Jane's aunt decides to send her away to boarding school when she is 10 years old. As this excerpt begins, Jane has left Gateshead and is traveling by coach to the Lowood Institution, a boarding school for orphans and poor girls.

1 The afternoon came on wet and somewhat misty: as it waned into dusk, I began to feel that we were getting very far indeed from Gateshead: we ceased to pass through towns; the country changed; great grey hills heaved up round the horizon: as twilight deepened, we descended a valley, dark with wood, and long after night had overclouded the prospect, I heard a wild wind rushing amongst trees.

Notice & Note

Use the side margins to notice and note signposts in the text.

NOTICE & NOTE

2 Lulled by the sound, I at last dropped asleep: I had not long slumbered when the sudden cessation of motion awoke me; the coach-door was open, and a person like a servant was standing at it: I saw her face and dress by the light of the lamps.

3 "Is there a little girl called Jane Eyre here?" she asked. I answered "Yes," and was then lifted out; my trunk was handed down, and the coach instantly drove away.

ANALYZE FIRST-PERSON POINT OF VIEW

Annotate: In paragraph 4, mark details about what Jane sees after being lifted from the coach.

Analyze: How does this description give the impression that we see everything through Jane's eyes?

4 I was stiff with long sitting, and bewildered with the noise and motion of the coach: gathering my faculties, I looked about me. Rain, wind, and darkness filled the air; nevertheless, I dimly discerned a wall before me and a door open in it. Through this door I passed with my new guide: she shut and locked it behind her. There was now visible a house or houses—for the building spread far—with many windows, and lights burning in some; we went up a broad pebbly path, splashing wet, and were admitted at a door; then the servant led me through a passage into a room with a fire, where she left me alone.

5 I stood and warmed my numbed fingers over the blaze, then looked round; there was no candle, but the uncertain light from the hearth showed, by intervals, papered walls, carpet, curtains, shining mahogany furniture: it was a parlor, not so spacious or splendid as the drawing-room at Gateshead, but comfortable enough. I was puzzling to make out the subject of a picture on the wall, when the door opened, and an individual carrying a light entered; another followed close behind.

6 The first was a tall lady with dark hair, dark eyes, and a pale and large forehead; her figure was partly enveloped in a shawl, her countenance was grave, her bearing erect.

7 "The child is very young to be sent alone," said she, putting her candle down on the table. She considered me attentively for a minute or two, then further added—

8 "She had better be put to bed soon; she looks tired: are you tired?" she asked, placing her hand on my shoulder.

9 "A little, ma'am."

10 "And hungry too, no doubt: let her have some supper before she goes to bed, Miss Miller. Is this the first time you have left your parents to come to school, my little girl?"

11 I explained to her that I had no parents. She inquired how long they had been dead; then how old I was, what was my name, whether I could read, write, and sew a little: then she touched my cheek gently with her forefinger, and saying,

12 "She hoped I should be a good child," dismissed me along with Miss Miller.

13 The lady I had left might be about twenty-nine; the one who went with me appeared some years younger: the first impressed me by her voice, look, and air. Miss Miller was more ordinary; **ruddy** in complexion, though of a careworn countenance; hurried in gait and

ruddy
(rŭd′ē) *adj.* having a healthy, reddish glow.

action, like one who had always a multiplicity of tasks on hand: she looked, indeed, what I afterwards found she really was, an under-teacher. Led by her, I passed from compartment to compartment, from passage to passage, of a large and irregular building; till, emerging from the total and somewhat dreary silence pervading that portion of the house we had traversed, we came upon the hum of many voices, and presently entered a wide, long room, with great deal tables, two at each end, on each of which burnt a pair of candles, and seated all round on benches, a congregation of girls of every age, from nine or ten to twenty. Seen by the dim light of the dips, their number to me appeared countless, though not in reality exceeding eighty; they were uniformly dressed in brown stuff frocks of quaint fashion, and long holland pinafores. It was the hour of study; they were engaged in conning[1] over their tomorrow's task, and the hum I had heard was the combined result of their whispered repetitions.

14 Miss Miller signed to me to sit on a bench near the door, then walking up to the top of the long room, she cried out—

15 "Monitors, collect the lesson-books and put them away!"

16 Four tall girls arose from different tables, and going round, gathered the books and removed them. Miss Miller again gave the word of command—

17 "Monitors, fetch the supper-trays!"

18 The tall girls went out and returned presently, each bearing a tray, with portions of something, I knew not what, arranged thereon, and a pitcher of water and mug in the middle of each tray. The portions were handed round; those who liked took a draught of the water, the mug being common to all. When it came to my turn, I drank, for I was thirsty, but did not touch the food, excitement and fatigue rendering me incapable of eating: I now saw, however, that it was a thin oaten cake, shared into fragments.

ANALYZE SETTING

Annotate: Mark details in paragraph 18 about the girls' supper.

Draw Conclusions: What does this description suggest about living conditions at Lowood?

19 The meal over, prayers were read by Miss Miller, and the classes filed off, two and two, upstairs. Overpowered by this time with weariness, I scarcely noticed what sort of a place the bedroom was; except that, like the schoolroom, I saw it was very long. Tonight I was to be Miss Miller's bed-fellow; she helped me to undress: when laid down I glanced at the long rows of beds, each of which was quickly filled with two occupants; in ten minutes the single light was extinguished; amid silence and complete darkness, I fell asleep.

20 The night passed rapidly: I was too tired even to dream; I only once awoke to hear the wind rave in furious gusts, and the rain fall in torrents, and to be sensible that Miss Miller had taken her place by my side. When I again unclosed my eyes, a loud bell was ringing: the girls were up and dressing; day had not yet begun to dawn, and a rushlight or two burnt in the room. I too rose reluctantly; it was bitter

[1] **conning:** examining or studying.

cold, and I dressed as well as I could for shivering, and washed when there was a basin at liberty, which did not occur soon, as there was but one basin to six girls, on the stands down the middle of the room. Again the bell rang: all formed in file, two and two, and in that order descended the stairs and entered the cold and dimly-lit schoolroom: here prayers were read by Miss Miller; afterwards she called out—

21 "Form classes!"

22 A great tumult succeeded for some minutes, during which Miss Miller repeatedly exclaimed, "Silence!" and "Order!" When it subsided, I saw them all drawn up in four semi-circles, before four chairs, placed at the four tables; all held books in their hands, and a great book, like a Bible, lay on each table, before the vacant seat. A pause of some seconds succeeded, filled up by the low, vague hum of numbers; Miss Miller walked from class to class, hushing this indefinite sound.

ANALYZE SETTING

Annotate: Mark details about books and reading in paragraphs 22–25.

Analyze: What does this passage reveal about education at Victorian charity schools?

23 A distant bell tinkled: immediately three ladies entered the room, each walked to a table and took her seat; Miss Miller assumed the fourth vacant chair, which was that nearest the door, and around which the smallest of the children were assembled: to this inferior class I was called, and placed at the bottom of it.

24 Business now began: the day's Collect was repeated, then certain texts of Scripture were said, and to these succeeded a protracted reading of chapters in the Bible, which lasted an hour. By the time that exercise was terminated, day had fully dawned. The indefatigable bell now sounded for the fourth time: the classes were marshalled and marched into another room to breakfast: how glad I was to behold a prospect of getting something to eat! I was now nearly sick from inanition, having taken so little the day before.

25 The refectory[2] was a great, low-ceiled, gloomy room; on two long tables smoked basins of something hot, which, however, to my **dismay**, sent forth an odor far from inviting. I saw a universal manifestation of discontent when the fumes of the repast met the nostrils of those destined to swallow it; from the van of the procession, the tall girls of the first class, rose the whispered words—

dismay
(dĭs-mā´) *v.* to upset or distress.

26 "Disgusting! The porridge is burnt again!"

27 "Silence!" ejaculated a voice; not that of Miss Miller, but one of the upper teachers, a little and dark personage, smartly dressed, but of somewhat **morose** aspect who installed herself at the top of one table, while a more buxom lady presided at the other. I looked in vain for her I had first seen the night before; she was not visible: Miss Miller occupied the foot of the table where I sat, and a strange, foreign looking, elderly lady, the French teacher, as I afterwards found, took the corresponding seat at the other board. A long grace was said and

morose
(mə-rōs´, mô-) *adj.* sullen or gloomy.

[2] **refectory:** a room where meals are served in a school or institution.

a hymn sung; then a servant brought in some tea for the teachers, and the meal began.

28 Ravenous, and now very faint, I devoured a spoonful or two of my portion without thinking of its taste; but the first edge of hunger blunted, I perceived I had got in hand a nauseous mess: burnt porridge is almost as bad as rotten potatoes; famine itself soon sickens over it. The spoons were moved slowly: I saw each girl taste her food and try to swallow it; but in most cases the effort was soon relinquished. Breakfast was over, and none had breakfasted. Thanks being returned for what we had not got, and a second hymn chanted, the refectory was evacuated for the schoolroom. I was one of the last to go out, and in passing the tables, I saw one teacher take a basin of the porridge and taste it; she looked at the others; all their countenances expressed displeasure, and one of them, the stout one, whispered—

CONTRASTS AND CONTRADICTIONS

Notice & Note: Mark two statements that express contradictory ideas in paragraph 28.

Infer: What do these statements suggest about how girls are treated at the school?

29 "Abominable stuff! How shameful!"

30 A quarter of an hour passed before lessons again began, during which the schoolroom was in a glorious tumult; for that space of time, it seemed to be permitted to talk loud and more freely, and they used their privilege. The whole conversation ran on the breakfast, which one and all abused roundly. Poor things! it was the sole consolation they had. Miss Miller was now the only teacher in the room: a group of great girls standing about her, spoke with serious and sullen gestures. I heard the name of Mr. Brocklehurst pronounced by some lips; at which Miss Miller shook her head disapprovingly; but she made no great effort to check the general wrath: doubtless she shared in it.

31 A clock in the schoolroom struck nine; Miss Miller left her circle, and standing in the middle of the room, cried—

32 "Silence! To your seats!"

33 Discipline prevailed: in five minutes the confused throng was resolved into order, and comparative silence quelled the Babel clamour of tongues. The upper teachers now punctually resumed their posts: but still, all seemed to wait. Ranged on benches down the sides of the room, the eighty girls sat motionless and erect: a quaint assemblage they appeared, all with plain locks combed from their faces, not a curl visible; in brown dresses, made high and surrounded by a narrow tucker about the throat, with little pockets of holland (shaped something like a Highlander's purse) tied in front of their frocks, and designed to serve the purpose of a work-bag: all too wearing woollen stockings and country-made shoes, fastened with brass buckles. Above twenty of those clad in this costume were full-grown girls, or rather young women; it suited them ill, and gave an air of oddity even to the prettiest.

34 I was still looking at them, and also at intervals examining the teachers—none of whom precisely pleased me; for the stout one was

a little coarse, the dark one not a little fierce, the foreigner harsh and grotesque, and Miss Miller, poor thing! looked purple, weather-beaten, and over-worked—when, as my eye wandered from face to face, the whole school rose simultaneously, as if moved by a common spring.

35 What was the matter? I had heard no order given: I was puzzled. Ere I had gathered my wits, the classes were again seated: but as all eyes were now turned to one point, mine followed the general direction, and encountered the personage who had received me last night. She stood at the bottom of the long room, on the hearth; for there was a fire at each end: she surveyed the two rows of girls silently and gravely. Miss Miller approaching, seemed to ask her a question, and having received her answer, went back to her place, and said aloud—

36 "Monitor of the first class, fetch the globes!"

37 While the direction was being executed, the lady consulted moved slowly up the room. I suppose I have a considerable organ of Veneration, for I retain yet the sense of admiring awe with which my eyes traced her steps. Seen now, in broad daylight, she looked tall, fair, and shapely; brown eyes, with a benignant light in their irids,

ANALYZE FIRST-PERSON POINT OF VIEW

Annotate: Mark words and phrases in paragraph 37 that express Jane's admiration for Miss Temple.

Analyze: Which details reveal that Jane has spent time in fashionable society?

and a fine penciling of long lashes round, relieved the whiteness of her large front; on each of her temples her hair, of a very dark brown, was clustered in round curls, according to the fashion of those times, when neither smooth bands nor long ringlets were in **vogue**; her dress, also in the mode of the day, was of purple cloth, relieved by a sort of Spanish trimming of black velvet; a gold watch (watches were not so common then as now) shone at her girdle. Let the reader add, to complete the picture, refined features; a complexion, if pale, clear; and a stately air and carriage, and he will have, at least, as clearly as words can give it, a correct idea of the exterior of Miss Temple—Maria Temple, as I afterwards saw the name written in a prayer-book entrusted to me to carry to church.

vogue
(vōg) *n.* the prevailing fashion, practice, or style.

38 The superintendent of Lowood (for such was this lady) having taken her seat before a pair of globes placed on one of the tables, summoned the first class round her, and **commenced** giving a lesson in geography; the lower classes were called by the teachers: repetitions in history, grammar, etc., went on for an hour; writing and arithmetic succeeded, and music lessons were given by Miss Temple to some of the elder girls. The duration of each lesson was measured by the clock, which at last struck twelve. The superintendent rose—

commence
(kə-mĕns´) *v.* to begin or start.

39 "I have a word to address to the pupils," said she.

40 The tumult of cessation from lessons was already breaking forth, but it sank at her voice. She went on—

41 "You had this morning a breakfast which you could not eat; you must be hungry—I have ordered that a lunch of bread and cheese shall be served to all."

42 The teachers looked at her with a sort of surprise.

43 "It is to be done on my responsibility," she added, in an explanatory tone to them, and immediately afterwards left the room.

44 The bread and cheese was presently brought in and distributed, to the high delight and refreshment of the whole school. The order was now given "To the garden!" Each put on a coarse straw bonnet, with strings of colored calico, and a cloak of grey frieze. I was similarly equipped, and, following the stream, I made my way into the open air.

45 The garden was a wide enclosure, surrounded with walls so high as to exclude every glimpse of prospect: a covered **verandah** ran down one side, and broad walks bordered a middle space divided into scores of little beds: these beds were assigned as gardens for the pupils to cultivate, and each bed had an owner. When full of flowers they would doubtless look pretty; but now, at the latter end of January, all was wintry blight and brown decay. I shuddered as I stood and looked round me: it was an inclement day for outdoor exercise; not positively rainy, but darkened by a drizzling yellow fog; all underfoot was still soaking wet with the floods of yesterday. The stronger among the girls ran about and engaged in active games, but sundry pale and thin

verandah
(və-răn´də) *n.* a porch or balcony.

ANALYZE SETTING

Annotate: Mark details in paragraph 45 showing how the girls feel about their exercise period.

Analyze: What does this description suggest about the school's attitude toward the girls' well-being?

NOTICE & NOTE

LANGUAGE CONVENTIONS

Annotate: Mark the sentence that contains gerunds in paragraph 46.

Evaluate: What do these gerunds emphasize about Jane's character?

ones herded together for shelter and warmth in the verandah; and amongst these, as the dense mist penetrated to their shivering frames, I heard frequently the sound of a hollow cough.

46 As yet I had spoken to no one, nor did anybody seem to take notice of me; I stood lonely enough: but to that feeling of isolation I was accustomed; it did not oppress me much. I leant against a pillar of the verandah, drew my grey mantle close about me, and, trying to forget the cold which nipped me without, and the unsatisfied hunger which gnawed me within, delivered myself up to the employment of watching and thinking. My reflections were too undefined and fragmentary to merit record: I hardly yet knew where I was; Gateshead and my past life seemed floated away to an immeasurable distance; the present was vague and strange, and of the future I could form no conjecture. I looked round the convent-like garden, and then up at the house; a large building, half of which seemed grey and old, the other half quite new. The new part, containing the schoolroom and dormitory, was lit by mullioned and latticed windows, which gave it a church-like aspect; a stone tablet over the door, bore this inscription—

47 "Lowood Institution.—This portion was rebuilt A.D.—, by Naomi Brocklehurst, of Brocklehurst Hall, in this county."

48 "Let your light so shine before men that they may see your good works, and glorify your Father which is in heaven."— St. Matt. v. 16.

49 I read these words over and over again: I felt that an explanation belonged to them, and was unable fully to penetrate their import. I was still pondering the signification of "Institution," and endeavoring to make out a connection between the first words and the verse of Scripture, when the sound of a cough close behind me, made me turn my head. I saw a girl sitting on a stone bench near; she had bent over a book, on the perusal of which she seemed intent: from where I stood I could see the title—it was "Rasselas;" a name that struck me as strange, and consequently attractive. In turning a leaf she happened to look up, and I said to her directly—

50 "Is your book interesting?" I had already formed the intention of asking her to lend it to me some day.

51 "I like it," she answered, after a pause of a second or two, during which she examined me.

52 "What is it about?" I continued, I hardly know where I found the hardihood thus to open a conversation with a stranger; the step was contrary to my nature and habits: but I think her occupation touched a chord of sympathy somewhere; for I too liked reading, though of a frivolous and childish kind; I could not digest or comprehend the serious or substantial.

53 "You may look at it," replied the girl, offering me the book.

54 I did so; a brief examination convinced me that the contents were less taking than the title: "Rasselas" looked dull to my trifling taste; I saw nothing about fairies, nothing about genii; no bright variety seemed spread over the closely-printed pages. I returned it to her; she received it quietly, and without saying anything she was about to relapse into her former studious mood: again I ventured to disturb her—

55 "Can you tell me what the writing on that stone over the door means? What is Lowood Institution?"

56 "This house where you are come to live."

57 "And why do they call it Institution? Is it in any way different from other schools?"

58 "It is partly a charity-school: you and I, and all the rest of us, are charity-children. I suppose you are an orphan: are not either your father or your mother dead?"

59 "Both died before I can remember."

60 "Well, all the girls here have lost either one or both parents, and this is called an institution for educating orphans."

61 "Do we pay no money? Do they keep us for nothing?"

62 "We pay, or our friends pay, fifteen pounds a year for each."

63 "Then why do they call us charity-children?"

64 "Because fifteen pounds is not enough for board and teaching, and the deficiency is supplied by subscription."

65 "Who subscribes?"

66 "Different benevolent-minded ladies and gentlemen in this neighborhood and in London."

67 "Who was Naomi Brocklehurst?"

68 "The lady who built the new part of this house as that tablet records, and whose son overlooks and directs everything here."

69 "Why?"

70 "Because he is treasurer and manager of the establishment."

71 "Then this house does not belong to that tall lady who wears a watch, and who said we were to have some bread and cheese."

72 "To Miss Temple? Oh, no! I wish it did: she has to answer to Mr. Brocklehurst for all she does. Mr. Brocklehurst buys all our food and all our clothes."

73 "Does he live here?"

74 "No—two miles off, at a large hall."

75 "Is he a good man?"

76 "He is a clergyman, and is said to do a great deal of good."

77 "Did you say that tall lady was called Miss Temple? "

78 "Yes."

79 "And what are the other teachers called?"

80 "The one with red cheeks is called Miss Smith; she attends to the work, and cuts out—for we make our own clothes, our frocks, and pelisses, and every thing; the little one with black hair is Miss

ANALYZE FIRST-PERSON POINT OF VIEW

Annotate: Mark paragraph 57.

Analyze: Why does Jane ask these questions? What do they indicate about the type of person she is?

NOTICE & NOTE

ANALYZE FIRST-PERSON POINT OF VIEW

Annotate: Mark the girl's response to Jane's question about Miss Temple.

Compare: How does the girl's response contrast with Jane's reasons for admiring Miss Temple?

Scatcherd; she teaches history and grammar, and hears the second class repetitions; and the one who wears a shawl, and has a pocket-handkerchief tied to her side with a yellow riband, is Madame Pierrot: she comes from Lisle, in France, and teaches French."

81 "Do you like the teachers?"

82 "Well enough."

83 "Do you like the little black one, and the Madame—?—I cannot pronounce her name as you do."

84 "Miss Scatcherd is hasty—you must take care not to offend her; Madame Pierrot is not a bad sort of person."

85 "But Miss Temple is the best—isn't she?"

86 "Miss Temple is very good, and very clever; she is above the rest, because she knows far more than they do."

87 "Have you been long here?"

88 "Two years."

89 "Are you an orphan?"

90 "My mother is dead."

91 "Are you happy here?"

92 "You ask rather too many questions. I have given you answers enough for the present: now I want to read."

93 But at that moment the summons sounded for dinner: all reentered the house. The odor which now filled the refectory was scarcely more appetizing than that which had regaled our nostrils at breakfast: the dinner was served in two huge tin-plated vessels, whence rose a strong steam redolent of rancid fat. I found the mess to consist of indifferent potatoes and strange shreds of rusty meat, mixed and cooked together. Of this preparation a tolerably abundant plateful was apportioned to each pupil. I ate what I could, and wondered within myself whether every day's fare would be like this.

94 After dinner, we immediately adjourned to the schoolroom: lessons recommenced, and were continued till five o'clock.

95 The only marked event of the afternoon was, that I saw the girl with whom I had conversed in the verandah, dismissed in disgrace, by Miss Scatcherd, from a history class, and sent to stand in the middle of the large schoolroom. The punishment seemed to me in a high degree ignominious, especially for so great a girl—she looked thirteen or upwards. I expected she would show signs of great distress and shame; but to my surprise she neither wept nor blushed: composed, though grave, she stood, the central mark of all eyes. "How can she bear it so quietly—so firmly?" I asked of myself. "Were I in her place, it seems to me I should wish the earth to open and swallow me up. She looks as if she were thinking of something beyond her punishment—beyond her situation: of something not round nor before her. I have heard of daydreams—is she in a daydream now? Her eyes are fixed on the floor, but I am sure they do not see it—her sight seems turned in, gone down into her heart:

she is looking at what she can remember, I believe; not at what is really present. I wonder what sort of a girl she is—whether good or naughty."

96 Soon after five P.M. we had another meal, consisting of a small mug of coffee and half a slice of brown bread. I devoured my bread and drank my coffee with relish; but I should have been glad of as much more—I was still hungry. Half an hour's recreation succeeded, then study; then the glass of water and the piece of oat-cake, prayers, and bed. Such was my first day at Lowood.

CHECK YOUR UNDERSTANDING

Answer these questions before moving on to the **Analyze the Text** section on the following page.

1 What is Miss Temple's reaction when she first meets Jane?

A She is annoyed that Jane has arrived so late.

B She expresses sympathy and concern for Jane.

C She thinks Jane is too young for the school.

D She fears that Jane will misbehave.

2 Why does Miss Temple order bread and cheese to be served on Jane's first day at Lowood?

F She wants to celebrate Jane's arrival.

G Mr. Brocklehurst is coming for a visit.

H The students could not eat their breakfast.

J The school has run out of other food.

3 Who makes the decisions about how Lowood is run?

A Miss Temple

B Miss Miller

C Miss Scatcherd

D Mr. Brocklehurst

ANALYZE THE TEXT

Support your responses with evidence from the text. NOTEBOOK

1. **Compare** Reread the introductory note below Setting a Purpose on page 595. How does Jane's experience at Lowood compare with the life she led at Gateshead?

2. **Evaluate** England did not have government-funded schools in the period covered by the novel; because the children at Lowood are poor, they must rely on charity for their education. Based on Jane's descriptions of the setting, how well does this system serve the needs of students? Explain.

3. **Draw Conclusions** What does the excerpt hint about Mr. Brocklehurst's character?

4. **Critique** Is the first-person narration of *Jane Eyre* effective, or should Brontë have used the third-person point of view to tell the story? Give reasons for your opinion.

5. **Notice & Note** Jane is surprised that the older girl shows no emotion when Miss Scatcherd makes her stand in the middle of the room as punishment. What does this incident reveal about Jane's personality?

RESEARCH TIP

When researching a specific part of a particular time period, it is best to use search strings that include all elements, starting with the most important. For example, for this research, the search string "ragged schools Victorian England" would be most likely to yield useful results.

RESEARCH

Research "ragged schools" and other charitable education institutions in England during the Victorian era. Why did these schools exist? Who did they serve? What impact did they have on pupils? Use the following chart to record your findings.

PURPOSE	POPULATION SERVED	IMPACT ON POPULATION

Extend Use the information found in your research to explain how Charlotte Brontë utilized details about education in her writing. Write a brief paragraph analyzing the effectiveness of the author's use of such details.

CREATE AND PRESENT

Write a Comparison Obtain a filmed adaptation of *Jane Eyre* to view the scenes described in the novel excerpt. Focus on how effectively the film version captures the setting and overall atmosphere of the classic.

- ❑ Isolate a few striking descriptions of setting from the novel excerpt. Find and view similar scenes from film. Pause occasionally to examine shots.
- ❑ Make a chart, if you wish, to compare details from the novel excerpt and film.
- ❑ Consider how closely the filmed setting matches the novel excerpt. Think about any deliberate changes the director might have made.
- ❑ You may include other aspects for comparison, such as character portrayals. Cover how these elements are presented in both versions.

Present Your Comparison Now that you've written a comparison, present it to the group. If possible, play segments of the film version to illustrate your points.

- ❑ Read your comparison aloud or refer to it as you present your views.
- ❑ Encourage your listeners to react to your view and offer their own. Ask your listeners how well they followed your points, and if they can add ideas that might strengthen the comparison.

Go to **Writing Informative Texts** in the **Writing Studio** to organize ideas for the comparison.

Go to **Using Media in a Presentation** in the **Speaking and Listening Studio** to learn more.

RESPOND TO THE ESSENTIAL QUESTION

What is a true benefactor?

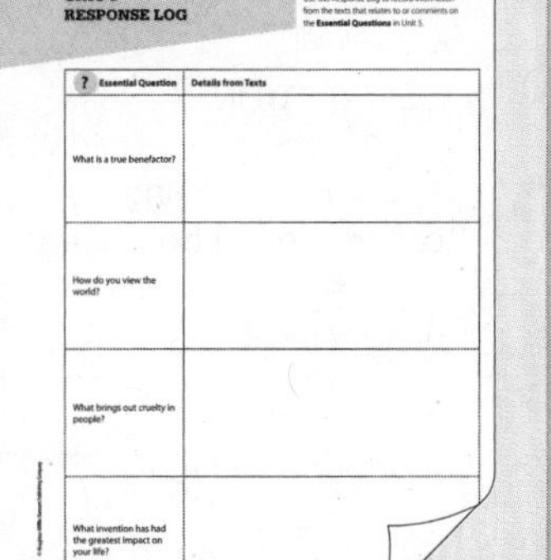

UNIT 5
RESPONSE LOG

Use this Response Log to record information from the texts that relate to or comment on the **Essential Questions** in Unit 5.

? Essential Question	Details from Texts
What is a true benefactor?	
How do you view the world?	
What brings out cruelty in people?	
What invention has had the greatest impact on your life?	

Gather Information Review your annotations and notes on the excerpt from *Jane Eyre*. Then, add relevant information to your Response Log. As you determine which information to include, think about:

- what a benefactor, or supporter, should provide to someone in need
- how a benefactor would act toward someone he or she was helping
- how a benefactor might try to help, but fail to provide the support a person truly needs

ACADEMIC VOCABULARY

As you write and discuss what you learned from *Jane Eyre*, be sure to use the Academic Vocabulary words. Check off each of the words that you use.

- ❑ **abandon**
- ❑ **confine**
- ❑ **conform**
- ❑ **depress**
- ❑ **reluctance**

RESPOND

CRITICAL VOCABULARY

WORD BANK
ruddy
dismay
morose
vogue
commence
verandah

Practice and Apply Choose the situation that best fits with the Critical Vocabulary word.

1. If you're drinking tea on the **verandah,** are you indoors or outside?
2. If your complexion is **ruddy,** have you been exposed to the sun or covered up?
3. If a movie were described as **morose,** would it be sad or funny?
4. If a class is **commencing,** is it beginning or ending?
5. If you are feeling **dismayed,** are you happy or unhappy?
6. If a woman's outfit is said to be in **vogue,** is it in style or out of style?

VOCABULARY STRATEGY: Foreign Words or Phrases

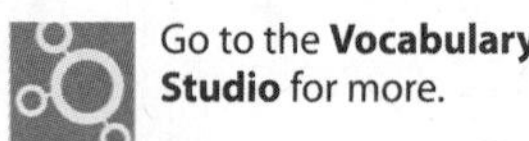

Go to the **Vocabulary Studio** for more.

Foreign words or phrases are often incorporated into English language usage. Typically, the meaning is similar to the way the word is used in the original language, but not always. Additionally, these words and phrases can be categorized based on use. For example, many German terms used in English refer to philosophy or sociology, while many Latin words deal with the law. French words, like the term *vogue* used in *Jane Eyre*, often refer to food or social class.

In the novel, Jane describes Miss Temple's appearance, including her physical form and how she presents herself through dress and style. The word *vogue* is not only descriptive of the woman's appearance but is also indicative of her social standing, indicating she is above those she is charged with teaching.

WORD BANK
agenda
genre
café
kindergarten

Practice and Apply Read each of the clues to identify the foreign word or phrase commonly used in English.

DESCRIPTION	ORIGIN	WORD OR PHRASE
A restaurant serving coffee or other beverages along with baked goods or light meals	French	
A category or type	French	
A program or class for children aged four to six	German	
A program of things to be done or considered, or an unstated underlying motive	Latin	

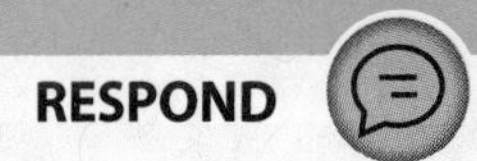

LANGUAGE CONVENTIONS: Gerunds and Gerund Phrases

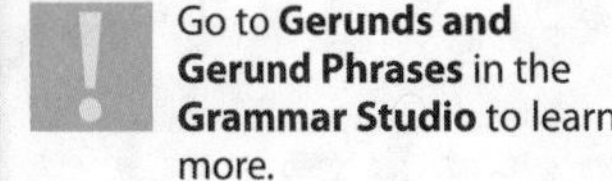

Go to **Gerunds and Gerund Phrases** in the **Grammar Studio** to learn more.

A **gerund** is a verb form ending in *-ing* that functions as a noun. **Gerund phrases** include the gerund plus its modifiers and complements. Gerunds and gerund phrases may perform any function that a noun performs and can appear in any part of a sentence where a noun could be used. Gerunds can add a sense of motion or action to a sentence.

PART OF THE SENTENCE	EXAMPLE
subject	**Having little food** was a way of life at Lowood.
direct object	The girls finished **gardening.**
indirect object	They gave **working** their full attention.
subject complement	Her best skill is **coping with hardship.**
object of the preposition	She came home weary from **working all day.**

Practice and Apply Write your own sentences with gerunds or gerund phrases using the sentences above as models.

MEDIA

FACTORY REFORM

Documentary by **Timelines.tv**

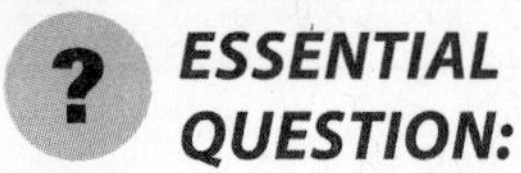

ESSENTIAL QUESTION:

What is a true benefactor?

QUICK START

Write a paragraph about any incident in which an individual took a stand or made efforts on behalf of others. Share your paragraph with a partner.

EVALUATE DOCUMENTARIES

A **documentary** is a nonfiction film about social, political, or historical subject matter. A historical documentary usually focuses on a particular time period, person, or event and informs viewers by taking a detailed look at the subject. Documentary filmmakers often rely on visual and sound elements to immerse viewers in the subject and to convey certain viewpoints.

VISUAL AND SOUND ELEMENTS	• **Footage** is recorded material used to reveal information about a subject. It can include photos, film clips, even reenactments. • **Illustrations** can be used to help create a storyline by portraying important people and incidents. • **Music** and **sound effects** can be used to set a mood or to capture viewers' attention.
STRATEGIES FOR VIEWING	• Consider the viewpoint of the documentary. Is it **objective,** based strictly on the facts? Or does it make its points in a **subjective** way by sharing only certain views? • Note images used to help you connect ideas. • Think about what the creators emphasize and what impressions they might want to convey.

GENRE ELEMENTS: DOCUMENTARY

- informational
- covers a specific person, place, event, or idea
- should rely on facts, but may also express opinions
- uses visual and sound elements
- conveys information through a narrator (or voice-over narration)

Go to the **Speaking and Listening Studio: Using Media in a Presentation** to find out about visual and sound elements.

BACKGROUND

"Factory Reform" is an excerpt from the documentary History of Britain—Changing Lives *on the website Timelines.tv. It depicts manufacturer Titus Salt's advocacy for Britain's lower-class factory workers. In the Industrial Revolution, business owners became quite wealthy, while average citizens lived in poverty. Workers—men, women, and children—sometimes worked more than 14 hours per day and made very little money. Many were killed or severely injured; accidents ranging from falls to explosions were common in Victorian factories.*

SETTING A PURPOSE

Pay attention to the visual and sound elements in the film. Listen for sounds and words in the narration that help to connect viewers to the conditions in Victorian factories. Also, note visual elements that may persuade you to take a certain viewpoint about the subject. **NOTEBOOK**

To view the video, log in online and select "**FACTORY REFORM**" from the unit menu.

As needed, pause the documentary to make notes about what impresses you or about ideas you might want to talk about later. Replay or rewind so you can clarify anything you do not understand.

RESPOND

ANALYZE MEDIA

Support your responses with evidence from the documentary. NOTEBOOK

1. **Identify** At the start of the documentary, what sounds do you hear as the presenter gives background information? What mental images do these sounds conjure up?

2. **Analyze** How does footage of the community of Saltaire help to convey the risk Titus Salt took by moving his factory and investing in living quarters for his workers?

3. **Analyze** What does the appearance of a narrator, as well as the use of his voice-over, contribute to the documentary?

4. **Compare** "Factory Reform" repeatedly shows illustrations in a notebook that depict life in Victorian factories. How are workers depicted compared to images of the wealthy factory owners?

5. **Summarize** According to the documentary, how did Salt's factory influence future factory owners?

RESEARCH

RESEARCH TIP

When choosing sources for your research, look for keywords and synonyms from the class video or text. Use an online dictionary to define unfamiliar words, especially if they make it challenging for you to understand a source.

"Factory Reform" portrays how Titus Salt demonstrated his social concerns, which led to great changes in factories and the lives of working families. The Industrial Revolution in Britain influenced an Industrial Revolution in America. Now that you're familiar with conditions in Victorian factories, research the history of conditions in American factories and the lives of American workers.

	VICTORIAN FACTORIES	AMERICAN FACTORIES
Conditions	Men in Bradford made less than fifty cents per day. Women and children earned half of that. Workers struggled with health and nutrition.	
Child labor	Young children were used because of their low salaries. Boys were even fired once they reached adulthood.	
Risks	Workers were forced to work in dark coal mines and around dangerous machinery. Many lost their eyesight, limbs, and/or their lives while working.	

Connect Recall the visual and sound elements in the documentary. If you were a director, how would you present examples of factory conditions? With a partner, write a description of visual and sound elements you would use to present the subject. You might choose to present your ideas in the form of a storyboard—a pictorial outline that shows a series of scenes.

CREATE AND PRESENT

Write a Short Story Depict a time you received support from someone you might call a benefactor. The short story may be based on a real event or from your imagination.

- ❑ Determine where and when the story takes place.
- ❑ Create events in order to establish the conflict you faced and follow through to a clear resolution. To ensure a solid beginning, middle, and end, use a story map to plan the details of the plot.
- ❑ Use vivid language to paint clear pictures in readers' or listeners' minds.
- ❑ Reread and edit your narrative. Add more details as needed.

Go to the **Writing Studio: Writing Narratives** for more help.

Present Your Story Read your short story aloud to a small group. Before you present:

- ❑ Create simple sketches to illustrate your narrative.
- ❑ Change your voice to match the changing events of your story. For example, let your tone convey curiosity, uncertainty, or excitement.

Go to the **Speaking and Listening Studio: Giving a Presentation** to learn more.

RESPOND TO THE ESSENTIAL QUESTION

What is a true benefactor?

Gather Information Review your notes on "Factory Reform." Then, add relevant information to your Response Log. As you determine which information to include, think about:

- the purpose of the documentary
- the use of visual and sound elements to influence viewers
- the conditions endured by Victorian factory workers
- the ways factory workers' lives were altered over time

ACADEMIC VOCABULARY

As you write and discuss what you learned from the documentary, be sure to use the Academic Vocabulary words. Check off each of the words that you use.

- ❑ **abandon**
- ❑ **confine**
- ❑ **conform**
- ❑ **depress**
- ❑ **reluctance**

THE LADY OF SHALOTT

Narrative Poem by **Alfred, Lord Tennyson**

? ESSENTIAL QUESTION:

How do you view the world?

QUICK START

Many legends and fairy tales depict a character who is confined to a place and shut off from the world. Imagine what it would be like to experience such isolation. How do you think it would affect you? What risks might you take to gain freedom and live among other people? Write a paragraph in response to these questions. Then, exchange paragraphs with a partner and discuss your thoughts.

ANALYZE ALLEGORY

An **allegory** is a story with two levels of meaning—a literal one and a symbolic one. In allegorical fiction and poetry, characters represent abstract qualities or ideas. Allegory is closely tied to symbolism. These forms of figurative language both use one thing to stand for another, and they allow writers to represent ideas in nontraditional ways. As in a fable or parable, the purpose of an allegory may be to convey truths about life, to teach religious or moral lessons, or to criticize social institutions.

Some critics of *The Lady of Shalott* argue that the poem is an allegory for the life of an artist, while others believe the poem represents the plight of women in Victorian society. As you read *The Lady of Shalott,* use a chart like this one to help you analyze symbolic elements that contribute to the poem's allegorical meaning.

SYMBOLIC ELEMENT	POSSIBLE MEANING	SUPPORTING DETAILS
The island of Shalott		
Camelot		
The loom and the web		
The mirror		
Sir Lancelot		
The boat ride		

GENRE ELEMENTS: NARRATIVE POETRY

- tells a story
- uses elements of fiction, such as character, setting, and plot
- is written in poetic form using lines and stanzas
- may be written with regular patterns of rhyme and meter, or in free verse without a regular structure

GET READY

ANALYZE MOOD

Mood is the feeling or atmosphere that a writer creates for the reader. Some examples of words describing mood are *mysterious, somber*, and *joyful*. A poem's mood may change as a poem progresses. Elements that help create a poem's mood include diction, imagery, line length, stanza structure, and sound devices, such as repetition and rhyme.

Read these lines from the beginning of *The Lady of Shalott*:

On either side the river lie
Long fields of barley and of rye,
That clothe the wold and meet the sky;
And through the field the road runs by
To many-towered Camelot;

Each line in this passage contains four iambic feet, consisting of an unstressed syllable followed by a stressed syllable. The strong, regular pattern of this meter, the rhyme scheme, and the imagery of King Arthur's mythical realm of Camelot contribute to a tranquil and orderly mood early in the poem. As you read, think about how these elements combine to create that mood or other moods that arise throughout Tennyson's poem.

ANNOTATION MODEL

NOTICE & NOTE 

As you read, note the use of vivid imagery and how this contributes to the overall mood of the poem. You can also mark up other places you find symbols or striking images. In the model you can see one reader's notes about *The Lady of Shalott*.

Willows whiten, aspens quiver,
Little breezes dusk and shiver
Through the wave that runs forever
By the island in the river
Flowing down to Camelot.
Four gray walls, and four gray towers,
Overlook a space of flowers,
And the silent isle imbowers
The Lady of Shalott.

Word choices like whiten, quiver, dusk, and shiver give this stanza a mood of coldness and isolation.

The images of the trees and wind, a wave that runs forever, gray walls and towers, and a silent isle also contribute to the somber mood.

The phrase "space of flowers" adds a tiny element of hope.

BACKGROUND

Alfred, Lord Tennyson *(1809–1892) experienced misfortune early in life, but he became the most celebrated poet of his age. He left Cambridge University without completing his degree due to lack of funds, and soon afterward the death of his closest friend devastated him. Although he struggled financially and professionally for many years, his fortunes turned in 1850 when Queen Victoria named him poet laureate. Decades later, the rank of baron and title of "Lord" were bestowed upon him.* The Lady of Shalott, *an early work, was inspired by the legends of King Arthur.*

THE LADY OF SHALOTT

Narrative Poem by Alfred, Lord Tennyson

SETTING A PURPOSE

As you read, consider the situation in which the Lady of Shalott finds herself, and imagine what it would be like to see the world from her perspective.

Part I

On either side the river lie
Long fields of barley and of rye,
That clothe the wold and meet the sky;
And through the field the road runs by
    To many-towered Camelot;
And up and down the people go,
Gazing where the lilies blow
Round an island there below,
    The island of Shalott.

Notice & Note

Use the side margins to notice and note signposts in the text.

ANALYZE MOOD

Annotate: Mark the words or phrases that establish the moods of the first and second stanzas.

Analyze: How does the mood change from the first to the second stanza?

3 wold: rolling plain.

7 blow: bloom.

17 imbowers: encloses; surrounds.

ANALYZE ALLEGORY

Annotate: In lines 19–27, mark details that suggest the Lady of Shalott is invisible or unknown to the citizens of Camelot.

Interpret: How might these details relate to the allegorical meaning of the poem?

22 shallop (shăl´əp): a small open boat.

25 casement: a hinged window that opens outward.

Willows whiten, aspens quiver,
Little breezes dusk and shiver
Through the wave that runs forever
By the island in the river
        Flowing down to Camelot.
Four gray walls, and four gray towers,
Overlook a space of flowers,
And the silent isle imbowers
        The Lady of Shalott.

By the margin, willow-veiled,
Slide the heavy barges trailed
By slow horses; and unhailed
The shallop flitteth silken-sailed
        Skimming down to Camelot:
But who hath seen her wave her hand?
Or at the casement seen her stand?
Or is she known in all the land,
        The Lady of Shalott?

Only reapers, reaping early
In among the bearded barley,
Hear a song that echoes cheerly
From the river winding clearly,
        Down to towered Camelot;
And by the moon the reaper weary,
Piling sheaves in uplands airy,
Listening, whispers "'Tis the fairy
        Lady of Shalott."

Part II

There she weaves by night and day
A magic web with colors gay.
She has heard a whisper say,
A curse is on her if she stay
        To look down to Camelot.
She knows not what the curse may be,
And so she weaveth steadily,
And little other care hath she,
        The Lady of Shalott.

And moving through a mirror clear
That hangs before her all the year,
Shadows of the world appear.
There she sees the highway near
Winding down to Camelot;
There the river eddy whirls,
And there the surly village churls,
And the red cloaks of market girls,
Pass onward from Shalott.

Sometimes a troop of damsels glad,
An abbot on an ambling pad,
Sometimes a curly shepherd lad,
Or long-haired page in crimson clad,
Goes by to towered Camelot;
And sometimes through the mirror blue
The knights come riding two and two:
She hath no loyal knight and true,
The Lady of Shalott.

But in her web she still delights
To weave the mirror's magic sights,
For often through the silent nights
A funeral, with plumes and lights
And music, went to Camelot;
Or when the moon was overhead,
Came two young lovers lately wed:
"I am half sick of shadows," said
The Lady of Shalott.

Part III

A bowshot from her bower eaves,
He rode between the barley sheaves,
The sun came dazzling through the leaves,
And flamed upon the brazen greaves
Of bold Sir Lancelot.
A red-cross knight forever kneeled
To a lady in his shield,
That sparkled on the yellow field,
Beside remote Shalott.

NOTICE & NOTE

46–48 Weavers often used mirrors while working from the back of a tapestry to view the tapestry's appearance, but this one is used to view the outside world.

52 surly village churls: rude members of the lower class in a village.

55 damsels: young, unmarried women.

56 abbot . . . pad: the head monk in a monastery on a slow-moving horse.

58 page: a boy in training to be a knight.

ANALYZE ALLEGORY

Annotate: In lines 64–72, mark the words or phrases that represent the isolation experienced by the main character.

Infer: What does the Lady's statement in line 71 suggest about her character?

73 bowshot: the distance an arrow can be shot; **bower** (bou′ər) **eaves:** the part of the roof that extends above the Lady's private room.

76 brazen greaves: metal armor for protecting the legs below the knees.

78–79 A red-cross . . . shield: His shield showed a knight wearing a red cross and kneeling to honor a lady. The red cross was a symbol worn by knights who had fought in the Crusades.

NOTICE & NOTE

82 gemmy: studded with gems.

87 blazoned (blā´zənd) **baldric:** a decorated leather belt worn across the chest to support a sword or, as in this case, a bugle.

The gemmy bridle glittered free,
Like to some branch of stars we see
Hung in the golden Galaxy.
The bridle bells rang merrily
    As he rode down to Camelot;
And from his blazoned baldric slung
A mighty silver bugle hung,
And as he rode his armor rung,
    Beside remote Shalott.

All in the blue unclouded weather
Thick-jeweled shone the saddle leather,
The helmet and the helmet-feather
Burned like one burning flame together,
    As he rode down to Camelot;
As often through the purple night,
Below the starry clusters bright,
Some bearded meteor, trailing light,
    Moves over still Shalott.

His broad clear brow in sunlight glowed;
On burnished hooves his war horse trode;
From underneath his helmet flowed
His coal-black curls as on he rode,
    As he rode down to Camelot.
From the bank and from the river
He flashed into the crystal mirror,
"Tirra lirra," by the river
    Sang Sir Lancelot.

AGAIN AND AGAIN

Notice & Note: In lines 109–113, mark the repeated words.

Infer: What effect does this repetition have on the stanza?

She left the web, she left the loom,
She made three paces through the room,
She saw the water lily bloom,
She saw the helmet and the plume,
    She looked down to Camelot.
Out flew the web and floated wide;
The mirror cracked from side to side;
"The curse is come upon me," cried
    The Lady of Shalott.

NOTICE & NOTE 

Part IV

In the stormy east wind straining,
The pale yellow woods were waning,
The broad stream in his banks complaining,
Heavily the low sky raining
    Over towered Camelot;
Down she came and found a boat
Beneath a willow left afloat,
And round about the prow she wrote
    The Lady of Shalott.

And down the river's dim expanse
Like some bold seër in a trance,
Seeing all his own mischance—
With a glassy countenance
    Did she look to Camelot.

ANALYZE MOOD

Annotate: In lines 118–153, mark instances of imagery and sound devices.

Analyze: How do these images and sound devices help convey a tragic mood?

128 seër (sē´ər): someone who can see into the future; a prophet.

129 mischance: misfortune; bad luck.

NOTICE & NOTE

And at the closing of the day
She loosed the chain, and down she lay;
The broad stream bore her far away,
The Lady of Shalott.

Lying, robed in snowy white
That loosely flew to left and right—
The leaves upon her falling light—
Through the noises of the night
She floated down to Camelot;
And as the boat-head wound along
The willowy hills and fields among,
They heard her singing her last song,
The Lady of Shalott.

ANALYZE ALLEGORY

Annotate: Mark details about the Lady of Shalott's death in lines 145–153.

Interpret: What idea might be suggested by her death?

150 ere (âr): before.

Heard a carol, mournful, holy,
Chanted loudly, chanted lowly,
Till her blood was frozen slowly,
And her eyes were darkened wholly,
Turned to towered Camelot.
For ere she reached upon the tide
The first house by the waterside,
Singing in her song she died,
The Lady of Shalott.

Under tower and balcony,
By garden wall and gallery,
A gleaming shape she floated by,
Dead-pale between the houses high,
Silent into Camelot.
Out upon the wharfs they came,
Knight and burgher, lord and dame,
And round the prow they read her name,
The Lady of Shalott.

160 burgher: a middle-class citizen of a town.

Who is this? and what is here?
And in the lighted palace near
Died the sound of royal cheer;
And they crossed themselves for fear,
All the knights at Camelot:
But Lancelot mused a little space;
He said, "She has a lovely face;
God in his mercy lend her grace,
The Lady of Shalott."

CHECK YOUR UNDERSTANDING

Answer these questions before moving on to the **Analyze the Text** section on the following page.

1 What will set off the Lady of Shalott's curse?

A Viewing the world without looking through her mirror

B Falling in love with a loyal knight

C Asking forbidden questions

D Taking a break from weaving her tapestry

2 Before Lancelot appears in her mirror, the Lady of Shalott —

F feels tormented by her isolation

G enjoys spending her time weaving

H tries to undo the curse placed on her

J yearns to live in Camelot

3 Lines 73–90 show that Lancelot's life is different from the Lady's by —

A contrasting his boldness with her shyness

B contrasting the way people react to him with the way they react to her

C contrasting his freedom with her confinement

D contrasting the appearance of his armor with the appearance of her gown

RESPOND

ANALYZE THE TEXT

Support your responses with evidence from the text. NOTEBOOK

1. **Infer** Why does the Lady of Shalott decide to look down upon Camelot?
2. **Draw Conclusions** Is it likely that the Lady's actions would be different if she knew more about the curse? Why or why not?
3. **Analyze** Identify the rhyme scheme of the poem. What effect does this rhyme scheme create?
4. **Interpret** Which images, objects, or ideas in *The Lady of Shalott* can be seen as symbols that suggest the poem is an allegory for the experience of women in Victorian society?
5. **Notice & Note** Consider the pattern of repetition of words in the fifth and ninth lines of each stanza. Also note that these lines are indented and usually shorter than the other lines in the stanza. How do these repeating patterns affect the mood of the poem?

RESEARCH

RESEARCH TIP

When researching the laws and rights of a group of people from history, it's best to use reliable sources that focus specifically on that time period. For this research, you should look for a resource that concentrates on the Victorian Era.

The Victorian Era was a difficult one for women. With a partner, research what life was like for women in England during this period (1832–1901).

QUESTION	ANSWER
How were women viewed during the Victorian Era?	
What rights did women have during this time period?	

Extend If, as some critics say, this poem is an allegory for women's life in the Victorian Era, what kinds of allegories could represent what life is like for women in today's society? With a partner, discuss stories, poems, songs, or other forms of media that could be considered allegories for women's lives in today's world.

CREATE AND RECITE

Illustrate a Narrative Poem Create an illustration—such as a painting, drawing, or collage—to depict the characters, setting, and/or events of the story told in *The Lady of Shalott.*

- ❑ Decide what kind of illustration you will create.
- ❑ Reread the poem and form mental images of the characters, setting, and events in the poem.
- ❑ Choose the subject of your illustration by determining which aspect(s) of the story you relate to most strongly.
- ❑ Present your illustration to the class. Explain what inspired you or why you chose to focus on the subject of your illustration.

Recite a Poem With a group, recite part of *The Lady of Shalott* aloud for the class.

Go to **Giving a Presentation: Delivering Your Presentation** in the **Speaking and Listening Studio** to find out more.

- ❑ Work with your group to select at least one stanza of the poem.
- ❑ Discuss how you will recite the section of the poem you've chosen. Will you recite it together as a choral reading? Will each member of your group speak a different part? Will you sing it like a song?
- ❑ Memorize your lines and rehearse them a few times with your group.
- ❑ Present the poem to the class, using appropriate volume, enunciation, and gestures.

RESPOND TO THE ESSENTIAL QUESTION

How do you view the world?

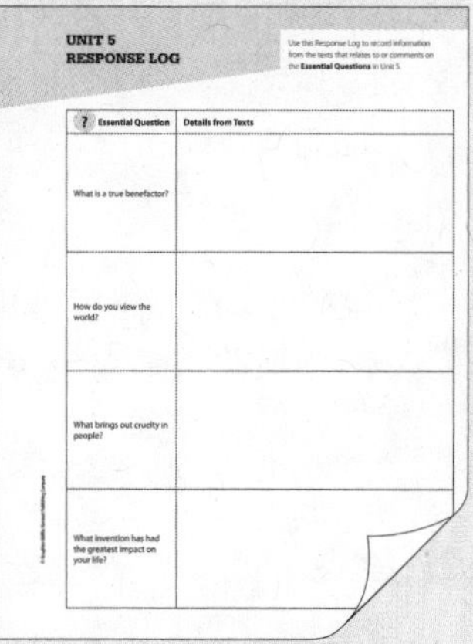

UNIT 5
RESPONSE LOG

Use this Response Log to record information from the texts that relates to or comments on the **Essential Questions** in Unit 5.

? Essential Question	Details from Texts
What is a true benefactor?	
How do you view the world?	
What brings out cruelty in people?	
What invention has had the greatest impact on your life?	

Gather Information Review your annotations and notes on *The Lady of Shalott*. Then, add relevant information to your Response Log. As you determine which information to include, think about:

- how you view your world compared to how others might view your world
- how your mood can affect how you view the world around you
- how something such as an animal or the weather can represent something entirely unrelated

ACADEMIC VOCABULARY

As you write and discuss what you learned from the poem, be sure to use the Academic Vocabulary words. Check off each of the words that you use.

- ❑ **abandon**
- ❑ **confine**
- ❑ **confirm**
- ❑ **depress**
- ❑ **reluctance**

from GREAT EXPECTATIONS

Novel by **Charles Dickens**

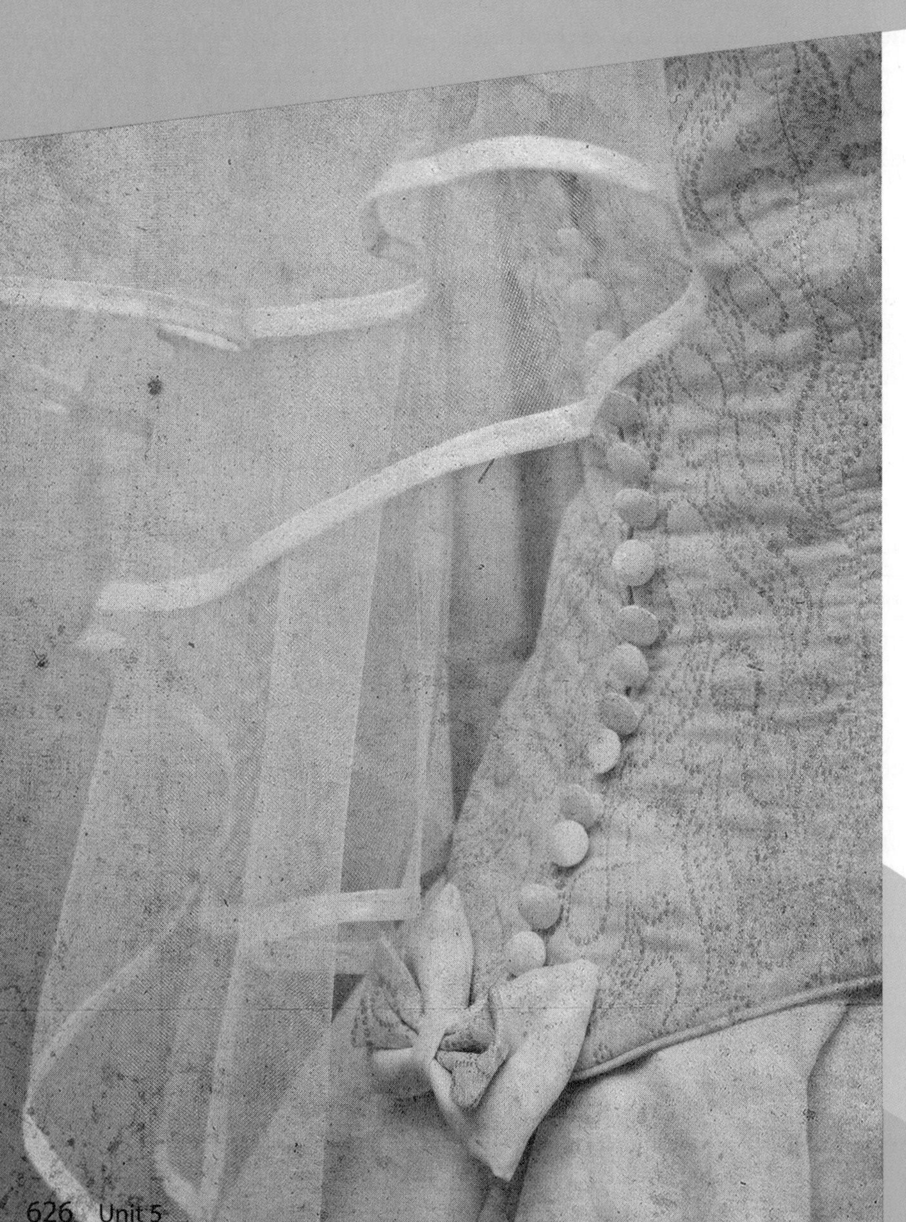

? *ESSENTIAL QUESTION:*

What brings out cruelty in people?

QUICK START

Think about the most unusual or eccentric person you've ever met. What was this person like, and what made him or her unique? Use the chart to note interesting details about the person.

PERSON	CHARACTERISTICS

ANALYZE PLOT

Great Expectations is set in Victorian England following the Industrial Revolution. This social and historical context has an important influence on the **plot**—the series of events that occur in a literary work. During this time, class differences became more pronounced as the middle class grew wealthier while the poor sank deeper into poverty. In the excerpt you are about to read, the main character, Pip, visits the mansion of a wealthy old woman. He feels intimidated in her presence, especially when a girl who lives with her comments negatively about his lower-class background.

A **subplot** is an additional, or secondary, plot in a story. Subplots often concern the backstories of particular characters. The excerpt you will read has a subplot that relates to Miss Havisham, which is revealed in part by the old, yellowing wedding dress she wears. As you read, consider what this detail suggests about Miss Havisham's past and look for other ways the subplot is developed.

GENRE ELEMENTS: NOVEL

- is a long work of fiction
- is usually written in the first- or third-person point of view
- can develop characters and conflict more thoroughly than a short story
- often develops complex plot structures, including subplots

ANALYZE CHARACTERIZATION

Characterization is the way a writer creates and develops characters. There are four basic methods of characterization:

- The narrator may comment directly about a character, including discussion of the character's personality, social class, and economic status.
- The writer may describe the character's physical appearance.
- The writer may present the character's own thoughts, speech, and actions.
- The writer may develop the character through the thoughts, speech, and actions of other characters.

Characterization is often affected by the point of view from which a story is told, and it can have important connections to the theme, setting, and plot. As you read the excerpt from *Great Expectations*, pay attention to the way Dickens portrays the characters in the selection. Also consider how these characterizations relate to the theme, setting, and plot of the story.

GET READY

CRITICAL VOCABULARY

self-possessed	**trinket**	**aversion**
gilded	**dogged**	**brooding**

To see how many Critical Vocabulary words you already know, use them to complete the sentences.

1. Eva's favorite __________ was the necklace her grandmother gave her.
2. Overcome with __________ determination to complete the race, Andre made it to the finish line in record time.
3. After getting a bad stomach virus, Sarah developed a(n) __________ to strawberries.
4. Although Mary was very upset by the decision made, she was quite ______ at the meeting.
5. The featured exhibit at the museum was a collection of __________ sculptures.
6. When he heard the trip was canceled, he stormed off and sat __________ in the corner of the room.

LANGUAGE CONVENTIONS

Imagery To describe a scene or convey a mood, Dickens uses **imagery**—words and phrases that create vivid sensory experiences for the reader. Dickens frequently creates this imagery through effective use of precise adjectives and other descriptive words. As you read this selection from *Great Expectations*, pay attention to how these descriptions appeal to your senses and help you better understand the characters and setting of the story.

ANNOTATION MODEL

NOTICE & NOTE 

As you read, mark adjectives that help to characterize Miss Havisham, Mr. Pumblechook, and others in the novel. The model shows one reader's notes about how Estella is characterized.

She seemed much older than I, of course, being a girl, and beautiful and self-possessed; and she was as scornful of me as if she had been one-and-twenty, and a queen.

These descriptions characterize Estella as someone who is both self-assured and a bit snobby.

BACKGROUND

Charles Dickens *(1812–1870) was born into a middle-class family in England. After his father went to prison, Dickens had to withdraw from school and work in a factory, an experience that deeply influenced his writing.* Great Expectations *is considered one of his finest works. The main character, Pip, is an orphan raised by his sister. In this excerpt, a relative named Mr. Pumblechook takes him to play at the house of Miss Havisham, a wealthy and eccentric old woman.*

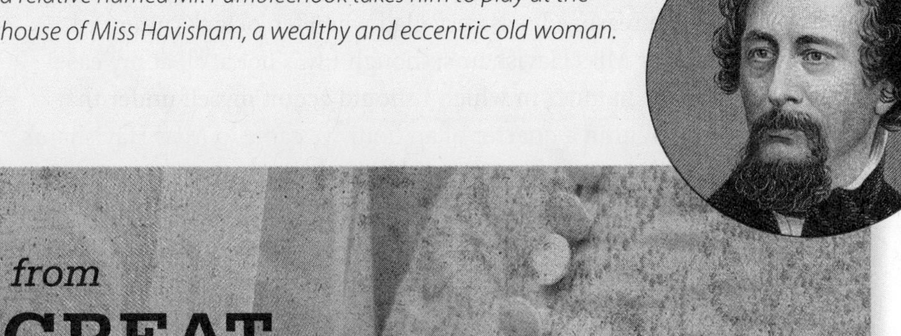

from

GREAT EXPECTATIONS

Novel by Charles Dickens

SETTING A PURPOSE

As you read, allow yourself to visualize each of the scenes and characters as they are described. Consider how the author's characterization of the people in the story relates to the plot and theme of the selection.

1 Mr. Pumblechook and I breakfasted at eight o'clock in the parlor behind the shop, while the shopman took his mug of tea and hunch of bread-and-butter on a sack of peas in the front premises. I considered Mr. Pumblechook wretched company. Besides being possessed by my sister's idea that a mortifying and penitential character ought to be imparted to my diet—besides giving me as much crumb as possible in combination with as little butter, and putting such a quantity of warm water into my milk that it would have been more candid to have left the milk out altogether—his conversation consisted of nothing but arithmetic. On my politely bidding him Good morning, he said, pompously, "Seven times nine, boy?" And how should *I* be able to answer, dodged in that way, in a strange place, on an empty stomach! I was hungry, but before I had swallowed a morsel, he began a running sum that lasted all through the breakfast.

Notice & Note

Use the side margins to notice and note signposts in the text.

ANALYZE CHARACTERIZATION

Annotate: Mark details in paragraph 1 that reveal aspects of Mr. Pumblechook's character.

Analyze: Which methods of characterization does Dickens use to portray him?

NOTICE & NOTE

“Seven?” “And four?” “And eight?” “And six?” “And two?” “And ten?” And so on. And after each figure was disposed of, it was as much as I could do to get a bite or a sup, before the next came; while he sat at his ease guessing nothing, and eating bacon and hot roll, in (if I may be allowed the expression) a gorging and gormandising manner.

2 For such reasons I was very glad when ten o'clock came and we started for Miss Havisham's; though I was not at all at my ease regarding the manner in which I should acquit myself under that lady's roof. Within a quarter of an hour we came to Miss Havisham's house, which was of old brick, and dismal, and had a great many iron bars to it. Some of the windows had been walled up; of those that remained, all the lower were rustily barred. There was a courtyard in front, and that was barred; so, we had to wait, after ringing the bell, until some one should come to open it. While we waited at the gate, I peeped in (even then Mr. Pumblechook said, “And fourteen?” but I pretended not to hear him), and saw that at the side of the house there was a large brewery. No brewing was going on in it, and none seemed to have gone on for a long time.

3 A window was raised, and a clear voice demanded “What name?” To which my conductor replied, “Pumblechook.” The voice returned, “Quite right,” and the window was shut again, and a young lady came across the courtyard, with keys in her hand.

4 “This,” said Mr. Pumblechook, “is Pip.”

5 “This is Pip, is it?” returned the young lady, who was very pretty and seemed very proud; “come in, Pip.”

6 Mr. Pumblechook was coming in also, when she stopped him with the gate.

7 “Oh!” she said. “Did you wish to see Miss Havisham?”

8 “If Miss Havisham wished to see me,” returned Mr. Pumblechook, discomfited.

9 “Ah!” said the girl; “but you see she don't.”

10 She said it so finally, and in such an undiscussible way, that Mr. Pumblechook, though in a condition of ruffled dignity, could not protest. But he eyed me severely—as if *I* had done anything to him!—and departed with the words reproachfully delivered: “Boy! Let your behavior here be a credit unto them which brought you up by hand!” I was not free from apprehension that he would come back to propound through the gate, “And sixteen?” But he didn't.

11 My young conductress locked the gate, and we went across the courtyard. It was paved and clean, but grass was growing in every crevice. The brewery buildings had a little lane of communication with it; and the wooden gates of that lane stood open, and all the brewery beyond stood open, away to the high enclosing wall; and all was empty and disused. The cold wind seemed to blow colder there, than outside the gate; and it made a shrill noise in howling in and out

LANGUAGE CONVENTIONS

Annotate: Mark Dickens's use of imagery to describe the courtyard and buildings in paragraph 11.

Analyze: What mood does this imagery help create?

at the open sides of the brewery, like the noise of wind in the rigging of a ship at sea.

12 She saw me looking at it, and she said, "You could drink without hurt all the strong beer that's brewed there now, boy."

13 "I should think I could, miss," said I, in a shy way.

14 "Better not try to brew beer there now, or it would turn out sour, boy, don't you think so?"

15 "It looks like it, miss."

16 "Not that anybody means to try," she added, "for that's all done with, and the place will stand as idle as it is, till it falls. As to strong beer, there's enough of it in the cellars already, to drown the Manor House."

17 "Is that the name of this house, miss ?"

18 "One of its names, boy."

19 "It has more than one, then, miss ?"

20 "One more. Its other name was Satis; which is Greek, or Latin, or Hebrew, or all three—or all one to me—for enough."

21 "Enough House!" said I: "that's a curious name, miss."

22 "Yes," she replied; "but it meant more than it said. It meant, when it was given, that whoever had this house, could want nothing else. They must have been easily satisfied in those days, I should think. But don't loiter, boy."

23 Though she called me "boy" so often, and with a carelessness that was far from complimentary, she was of about my own age. She seemed much older than I, of course, being a girl, and beautiful and **self-possessed**; and she was as scornful of me as if she had been one-and-twenty, and a queen.

24 We went into the house by a side door—the great front entrance had two chains across it outside—and the first thing I noticed was, that the passages were all dark, and that she had left a candle burning there. She took it up, and we went through more passages and up a staircase, and still it was all dark, and only the candle lighted us.

25 At last we came to the door of a room, and she said, "Go in."

26 I answered, more in shyness than politeness, "After you, miss,"

27 To this, she returned: "Don't be ridiculous, boy; I am not going in." And scornfully walked away, and—what was worse—took the candle with her.

28 This was very uncomfortable, and I was half afraid. However, the only thing to be done being to knock at the door, I knocked, and was told from within to enter. I entered, therefore, and found myself in a pretty large room, well lighted with wax candles. No glimpse of daylight was to be seen in it. It was a dressing-room, as I supposed from the furniture, though much of it was of forms and uses then quite unknown to me. But prominent in it was a draped table with a **gilded** looking-glass, and that I made out at first sight to be a fine lady's dressing-table.

ANALYZE CHARACTERIZATION

Annotate: Mark details in paragraphs 12–23 that characterize the girl.

Draw Conclusions: What does this passage suggest about her personality?

self-possessed
(sĕlf´pə-zĕst´) *adj.* having calm and self-assured command of one's faculties, feelings, and behavior.

gilded
(gĭl´dĭd) *adj.* covered with or having the appearance of being covered with a thin layer of gold.

29 Whether I should have made out this object so soon, if there had been no fine lady sitting at it, I cannot say. In an arm-chair, with an elbow resting on the table and her head leaning on that hand, sat the strangest lady I have ever seen, or shall ever see.

30 She was dressed in rich materials—satins, and lace, and silks—all of white. Her shoes were white. And she had a long white veil dependent from her hair, and she had bridal flowers in her hair, but her hair was white. Some bright jewels sparkled on her neck and on her hands, and some other jewels lay sparkling on the table. Dresses, less splendid than the dress she wore, and half-packed trunks, were scattered about. She had not quite finished dressing, for she had but one shoe on—the other was on the table near her hand—her veil was but half arranged, her watch and chain were not put on, and some lace for her bosom lay with those **trinkets**, and with her handkerchief, and gloves, and some flowers, and a Prayer-book, all confusedly heaped about the looking-glass.

31 It was not in the first few moments that I saw all these things, though I saw more of them in the first moments than might be supposed. But, I saw that everything within my view which ought to be white, had been white long ago, and had lost its luster and was faded and yellow. I saw that the bride within the bridal dress had withered like the dress, and like the flowers, and had no brightness left but the brightness of her sunken eyes. I saw that the dress had been put upon the rounded figure of a young woman, and that the figure upon which it now hung loose, had shrunk to skin and bone. Once, I had been taken to see some ghastly waxwork at the Fair, representing I know not what impossible personage lying in state. Once, I had been taken to one of our old marsh churches to see a skeleton in the ashes of a rich dress, that had been dug out of a vault under the church pavement. Now, waxwork and skeleton seemed to have dark eyes that moved and looked at me. I should have cried out, if I could.

32 "Who is it?" said the lady at the table.

33 "Pip, ma'am."

34 "Pip?"

35 "Mr. Pumblechook's boy, ma'am. Come—to play."

36 "Come nearer; let me look at you. Come close."

37 It was when I stood before her, avoiding her eyes, that I took note of the surrounding objects in detail, and saw that her watch had stopped at twenty minutes to nine, and that a clock in the room had stopped at twenty minutes to nine.

38 "Look at me," said Miss Havisham. " You are not afraid of a woman who has never seen the sun since you were born?"

39 I regret to state that I was not afraid of telling the enormous lie comprehended in the answer "No."

ANALYZE CHARACTERIZATION

Annotate: In paragraphs 30 and 31, mark repeated words used to describe Miss Havisham and her dress.

Analyze: What does Dickens emphasize through the use of repetition in this description?

trinket
(trĭng´kĭt) *n.* a small ornament, such as a piece of jewelry.

40 "Do you know what I touch here?" she said, laying her hands, one upon the other, on her left side.

41 "Yes, ma'am." (It made me think of the young man.)

42 "What do I touch?"

43 "Your heart."

44 "Broken!"

ANALYZE PLOT

Annotate: Mark details in paragraph 45 that describe how Miss Havisham delivers her remark about her heart.

Predict: Based on this remark and the way Miss Havisham is dressed, what do you predict the novel will reveal about her past?

45 She uttered the word with an eager look, and with strong emphasis, and with a weird smile that had a kind of boast in it. Afterwards, she kept her hands there for a little while, and slowly took them away as if they were heavy.

46 "I am tired," said Miss Havisham. "I want diversion, and I have done with men and women. Play."

47 I think it will be conceded by my most disputatious reader, that she could hardly have directed an unfortunate boy to do anything in the wide world more difficult to be done under the circumstances.

48 "I sometimes have sick fancies," she went on, "and I have a sick fancy that I want to see some play. There, there!" with an impatient movement of the fingers of her right hand; "play, play, play!"

dogged
(dô´gĭd, dŏg´ĭd) *adj.* stubbornly persevering; tenacious.

49 For a moment, with the fear of my sister's working me before my eyes, I had a desperate idea of starting round the room in the assumed character of Mr. Pumblechook's chaise-cart. But, I felt myself so unequal to the performance that I gave it up, and stood looking at Miss Havisham in what I suppose she took for a **dogged** manner, inasmuch as she said, when we had taken a good look at each other:

50 "Are you sullen and obstinate?"

51 "No, ma'am, I am very sorry for you, and very sorry I can't play just now. If you complain of me I shall get into trouble with my sister, so I would do it if I could; but it's so new here, and so strange, and so fine—and melancholy—" I stopped, fearing I might say too much, or had already said it, and we took another look at each other.

52 Before she spoke again, she turned her eyes from me, and looked at the dress she wore, and at the dressing-table, and finally at herself in the looking-glass.

53 "So new to him," she muttered, "so old to me; so strange to him, so familiar to me; so melancholy to both of us! Call Estella."

54 As she was still looking at the reflection of herself, I thought she was still talking to herself, and kept quiet.

55 "Call Estella," she repeated, flashing a look at me. "You can do that. Call Estella. At the door."

56 To stand in the dark in a mysterious passage of an unknown house, bawling Estella to a scornful young lady neither visible nor responsive, and feeling it a dreadful liberty so to roar out her name, was almost as bad as playing to order. But, she answered at last, and her light came along the dark passage like a star.

57 Miss Havisham beckoned her to come close, and took up a jewel from the table, and tried its effect upon her fair young bosom and

against her pretty brown hair. "Your own, one day, my dear, and you will use it well. Let me see you play cards with this boy."

58 "With this boy! Why, he is a common laboring-boy!"

59 I thought I overheard Miss Havisham answer—only it seemed so unlikely—"Well? You can break his heart."

60 "What do you play, boy?" asked Estella of myself, with the greatest disdain.

61 "Nothing but beggar my neighbor, Miss."

62 "Beggar him," said Miss Havisham to Estella. So we sat down to cards.

63 It was then I began to understand that everything in the room had stopped, like the watch and the clock, a long time ago. I noticed that Miss Havisham put down the jewel exactly on the spot from which she had taken it up. As Estella dealt the cards, I glanced at the dressing-table again, and saw that the shoe upon it, once white, now yellow, had never been worn. I glanced down at the foot from which the shoe was absent, and saw that the silk stocking on it, once white, now yellow, had been trodden ragged. Without this arrest of everything, this standing still of all the pale decayed objects, not even the withered bridal dress on the collapsed form could have looked so like grave-clothes, or the long veil so like a shroud.

64 So she sat, corpse-like, as we played at cards; the frillings and trimmings on her bridal dress, looking like earthy paper. I knew nothing then of the discoveries that are occasionally made of bodies buried in ancient times, which fall to powder in the moment of being distinctly seen; but, I have often thought since, that she must have looked as if the admission of the natural light of day would have struck her to dust.

65 "He calls the knaves, Jacks, this boy!" said Estella with disdain, before our first game was out. "And what coarse hands he has! And what thick boots!"

66 I had never thought of being ashamed of my hands before; but I began to consider them a very indifferent pair. Her contempt for me was so strong, that it became infectious, and I caught it.

67 She won the game, and I dealt. I misdealt, as was only natural, when I knew she was lying in wait for me to do wrong; and she denounced me for a stupid, clumsy laboring-boy.

68 "You say nothing of her," remarked Miss Havisham to me, as she looked on. "She says many hard things of you, yet you say nothing of her. What do you think of her?"

69 "I don't like to say," I stammered.

70 "Tell me in my ear," said Miss Havisham, bending down.

71 "I think she is very proud," I replied, in a whisper.

72 "Anything else?"

73 "I think she is very pretty."

74 "Anything else?"

AHA MOMENT

Notice & Note: Underline the sentence in paragraph 63 that expresses Pip's realization.

Draw Conclusions: What does this realization help us understand about the subplot involving Miss Havisham?

NOTICE & NOTE

aversion
(ə-vûr´zhən) *n.* a fixed, intense dislike; repugnance.

ANALYZE PLOT

Annotate: Reread paragraphs 68–80. Mark Miss Havisham's questions to Pip.

Infer: Why do you think Miss Havisham wants to know how Pip feels about Estella?

brooding
(brōō´dĭng) *adj.* thinking about something moodily.

75 "I think she is very insulting." (She was looking at me then with a look of supreme **aversion.**)

76 "Anything else?"

77 "I think I should like to go home."

78 "And never see her again, though she is so pretty?"

79 "I am not sure that I shouldn't like to see her again, but I should like to go home now."

80 "You shall go soon," said Miss Havisham aloud. "Play the game out."

81 Saving for the one weird smile at first, I should have felt almost sure that Miss Havisham's face could not smile. It had dropped into a watchful and **brooding** expression—most likely when all the things about her had become transfixed— and it looked as if nothing could ever lift it up again. Her chest had dropped, so that she stooped; and her voice had dropped, so that she spoke low, and with a dead lull upon her; altogether, she had the appearance of having dropped, body and soul, within and without, under the weight of a crushing blow.

82 I played the game to an end with Estella, and she beggared me. She threw the cards down on the table when she had won them all, as if she despised them for having been won of me.

83 "When shall I have you here again?" said Miss Havisham. "Let me think."

84 I was beginning to remind her that today was Wednesday, when she checked me with her former impatient movement of the fingers of her right hand.

85 "There, there! I know nothing of days of the week; I know nothing of weeks of the year. Come again after six days. You hear?"

86 "Yes, ma'am."

87 "Estella, take him down. Let him have something to eat, and let him roam and look about him while he eats. Go, Pip."

88 I followed the candle down, as I had followed the candle up, and she stood it in the place where we had found it. Until she opened the side entrance, I had fancied, without thinking about it, that it must necessarily be nighttime. The rush of the daylight quite confounded me, and made me feel as if I had been in the candlelight of the strange room many hours.

89 "You are to wait here, you boy," said Estella; and disappeared and closed the door.

CHECK YOUR UNDERSTANDING

Answer these questions before moving on to the **Analyze the Text** section on the following page.

1 What surprises Mr. Pumblechook when he arrives with Pip at Miss Havisham's house?

A Pip shows poor manners when Estella greets them.

B Estella doesn't want him to come inside the house.

C Miss Havisham doesn't come down to say hello.

D Estella is not how he remembers her.

2 What does Pip find most strange about Miss Havisham when he meets her?

F She is very thin.

G She is only wearing one shoe.

H She is dressed in a wedding gown.

J She doesn't seem to recognize him.

3 Why is Estella scornful toward Pip?

A He is unable to play by himself.

B He stares too much at Miss Havisham.

C He is very shy and quiet.

D He comes from a lower-class family.

ANALYZE THE TEXT

Support your responses with evidence from the text. NOTEBOOK

1. **Interpret** In paragraph 10, Mr. Pumblechook says to Pip, "Let your behavior here be a credit unto them which brought you up by hand!" What does this remark suggest about why Pip's family agreed to send him to visit Miss Havisham?

2. **Evaluate** What method of characterization does Dickens rely on most in his characterization of Miss Havisham? Is his use of this method effective? Explain why or why not.

3. **Draw Conclusions** Dickens introduces the subplot involving Miss Havisham's past through clues such as the yellowed wedding dress and her comment about her broken heart. How might this subplot relate to the events of this excerpt? Cite details in your response.

4. **Predict** Miss Havisham tells Pip to return in six days. What do you predict will happen on his future visits to her house?

5. **Notice & Note** In paragraph 66, Pip says that for the first time he feels ashamed of his hands. What has his experience in this wealthy household made him realize about himself?

RESEARCH

RESEARCH TIP

As you research, pay attention whenever you notice that sources disagree on certain points. Try to find out why they disagree and which source, if any, has the most accurate information.

Class differences are an important theme of *Great Expectations*. Conduct research on the class structure of Victorian England and note how this aligns with the excerpt you read from the novel. Use a chart like the one below to make your notes.

CLASS IN VICTORIAN ENGLAND	EXAMPLES FROM THE TEXT

Extend Research some of Charles Dickens's other books, paying special attention to themes that are commonly explored in his writing. How might this information help you better understand the selection from *Great Expectations*?

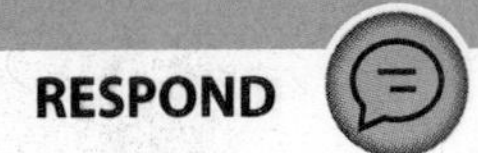

CREATE AND DISCUSS

Write a Story Write a short story about the most unusual person you've ever met. Use characterization to help your readers understand why this person is unusual.

- ❑ Describe what he or she looks like.
- ❑ Describe several of the person's most prominent personality traits.
- ❑ Use dialogue to bring the characters in your story to life.
- ❑ Include imagery to help your readers imagine the people, places, and events in the story.

Discuss People are often considered unusual when they behave in ways that fall outside of social norms or expectations. In a small group, discuss what kinds of behavior fall outside of the social norms of today's society. As you discuss, think about how Miss Havisham's behavior would be considered outside of the social norms of her day.

- ❑ Think about fashions that are accepted as normal in current society.
- ❑ Discuss what defines "normal" behavior. Make sure each member of your group has a chance to share his or her thoughts.
- ❑ Consider how the definition of "normal" changes over time, and discuss both the positive and negative results of living a life that others might believe to be strange or unique.

Go to **Writing Narratives** in the **Writing Studio** for more help writing a short story.

Go to **Participating in Collaborative Discussions** in the **Speaking and Listening Studio** for more help.

RESPOND TO THE ESSENTIAL QUESTION

What brings out cruelty in people?

Gather Information Review your annotations and notes on *Great Expectations*. Then, add relevant information to your Response Log. As you determine which information to include, think about:

- a person's history and how this affects their decisions
- the times you have been cruel or been tempted to be cruel and what motivated you
- the times when someone has been cruel to you and what might have motivated that person

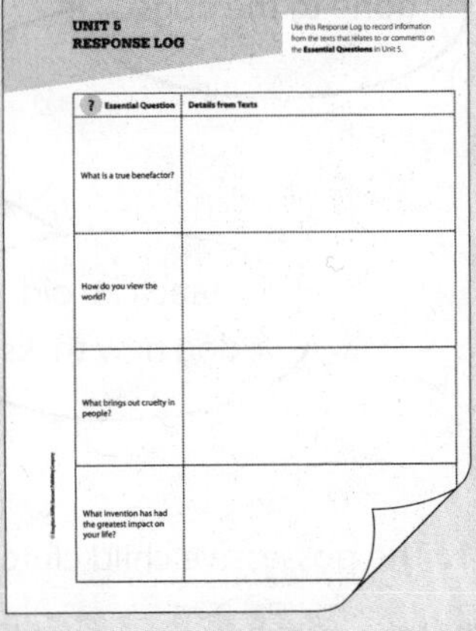

UNIT 5 RESPONSE LOG

Use this Response Log to record information from the texts that relates to or comments on the **Essential Questions** in Unit 5.

? Essential Question	Details from Texts
What is a true benefactor?	
How do you view the world?	
What brings out cruelty in people?	
What invention has had the greatest impact on your life?	

ACADEMIC VOCABULARY

As you write and discuss what you learned from *Great Expectations*, be sure to use the Academic Vocabulary words. Check off each of the words that you use.

- ❑ **abandon**
- ❑ **confine**
- ❑ **conform**
- ❑ **depress**
- ❑ **reluctance**

RESPOND

WORD BANK
self-possessed
gilded
trinket
dogged
aversion
brooding

CRITICAL VOCABULARY

Practice and Apply Select the word that correctly finishes the sentence.

1. At Laura's church, the ceilings were __________.
   a. gilded **b.** dogged

2. James found a(n) __________ at the antique store.
   a. aversion **b.** trinket

3. When Janine met Eric, he was __________ over a book in the library.
   a. self-possessed **b.** brooding

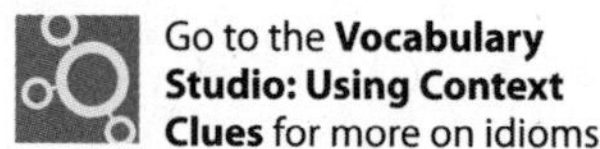

Go to the **Vocabulary Studio: Using Context Clues** for more on idioms.

VOCABULARY STRATEGY: Idioms

An **idiom** is a common figure of speech whose meaning is different from the literal meaning of its words. For example, the phrase "raining cats and dogs" means that it is raining heavily, not that animals are falling from the sky. A **specialized dictionary** may list common idioms and explain their origins.

Practice and Apply Complete each sentence with the idiom in the diagram that makes the most sense. Use context and your knowledge of dog behavior to help you choose the correct idiom. When you are finished, try to explain the meaning of each idiom you used.

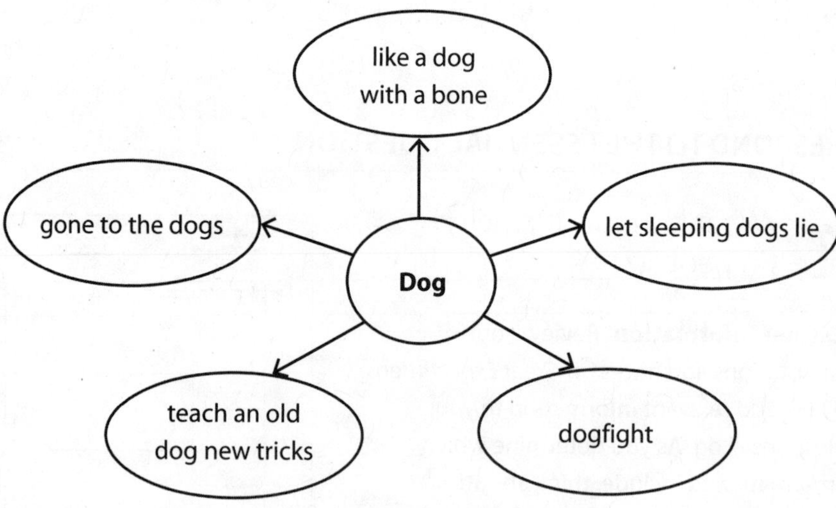

1. The possessive child clutched the toy __________.
2. I tried showing my grandfather a different way to fold his shirts, but you can't __________.
3. The combat flyer had a __________ with an enemy pilot.
4. The service wasn't great here last time, but now it has really __________.
5. Stop raking up the past; it's better to __________.

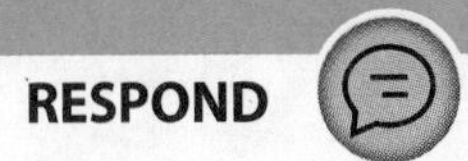

LANGUAGE CONVENTIONS: Imagery

Dickens carefully chose precise adjectives and other descriptive words and phrases to create vivid **imagery** in his stories. The majority of imagery in literature is visual, but imagery may also appeal to the readers' senses of smell, hearing, taste, and touch. In addition, images may re-create sensations of heat, movement, or bodily tension. Often the most effective imagery appeals to more than one sense simultaneously. The chart shows several kinds of imagery and provides examples.

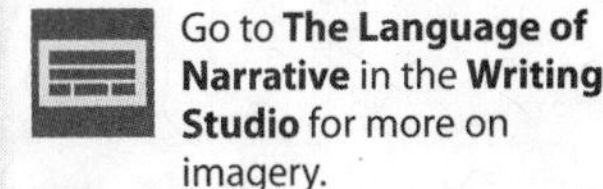
Go to **The Language of Narrative** in the **Writing Studio** for more on imagery.

KIND OF IMAGERY	SENSE TO WHICH IT APPEALS	EXAMPLE
Visual	Sight	faded, yellow clothes
Olfactory	Smell	a musty chamber
Auditory	Hearing	a shrill howling of the wind
Gustatory	Taste	sour milk
Tactile	Touch	coarse hands

Practice and Apply Read each of the following lines from *Great Expectations*. Identify the adjectives and verbs in each sentence that create imagery, and then write your own sentence using similar elements to appeal to the senses.

1. **It was paved and clean, but grass was growing in every crevice.** (paragraph 11)
2. **I entered, therefore, and found myself in a pretty large room, well lighted with wax candles.** (paragraph 28)
3. **I glanced down at the foot from which the shoe was absent, and saw that the silk stocking on it, once white, now yellow, had been trodden ragged.** (paragraph 63)

THE VICTORIANS HAD THE SAME CONCERNS ABOUT TECHNOLOGY AS WE DO

Essay by **Melissa Dickson**

? ***ESSENTIAL QUESTION:***

Which invention has had the greatest impact on your life?

QUICK START

Think about and write down the number of times per day that you use technology (e.g., smartphone, social media, Internet, mobile apps, tablets). Imagine a day without these tools. How would you describe that day? List the descriptions in your notebook and share with a partner.

ANALYZE COMPARE AND CONTRAST ESSAY

A **thesis** is an expression of the main idea or purpose of an essay. In this essay, the thesis is articulated in the title. To convince readers to accept this thesis, Melissa Dickson structures her essay as a **point-by-point comparison** of the similarities between Victorian and contemporary concerns about technology. She compares both historical periods one point at a time, instead of discussing the Victorian period first and then the contemporary period. As you read, use a chart like the one below to keep track of the main points presented and Dickson's supporting details related to both the Victorian and current perspectives on this issue.

POINT #1	POINT #2
Victorian:	Victorian:
Current:	Current:

Evaluate the essay's organizational pattern and consider whether this structure effectively serves the author's intended purpose.

EVALUATE MULTIMODAL TEXTS

A **multimodal text** strategically employs two or more modes of communication—words and visuals, for instance—to help the reader construct meaning about the content. Graphic features—such as images, charts, and maps—can play an important role in communicating an author's meaning.

Melissa Dickson reproduces two Victorian Era images in her essay, commenting directly on one of them. As you read, think about how effectively Dickson uses these images to support her ideas.

GENRE ELEMENTS: ESSAY

- has an introduction that includes the broader subject as well as a specific topic, hooks the audience, and briefly describes how the topic will be developed
- contains a thesis statement that offers some original insight on the topic
- contains well-developed body paragraphs, each with a main idea related to the writer's thesis statement or position, and tangible evidence that supports those ideas
- has a conclusion that often neatly summarizes the topic and leaves the audience with something to think about

GET READY

CRITICAL VOCABULARY

forebear	**pervasive**	**sea change**	**immersion**
underpin	**cacophony**	**posit**	**Luddite**

To see how many Critical Vocabulary words you already know, use them to complete the sentences.

1. Mr. Keller's __________ position on the use of online platforms in the classroom conflicted with the school's plan to engage students by offering complete __________ in new technology.

2. Amid the __________ of fireworks and the cheering crowd, he thought of his __________ who had fought for his country's independence long ago.

3. Some researchers believe a(n) __________ is taking place in the minds of young people because they have allowed social media to have a(n) __________ influence on their ideas and behaviors.

4. Ample moisture and nutrients, the scientists __________, will __________ the bacteria's ability to multiply quickly.

LANGUAGE CONVENTIONS

Sentence Structure Writers use a variety of sentence structures to express ideas clearly. Simple sentences have one main clause, while other structures include more than one clause. These clauses are connected by commas and conjunctions or by semicolons. As you read, take note of the different kinds of sentences the author uses to convey her ideas.

ANNOTATION MODEL

NOTICE & NOTE

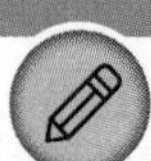

As you read, notice the parallels between the use of, and attitudes toward, technology in Victorian society and today's culture. Look for details that highlight similarities and differences between the two. In the model, you can see one reader's notes about the text.

Many of us struggle with the bombardment of information we receive and experience anxiety as a result of new media, which we feel threaten our relationships and "usual" modes of human interaction.

Though the technologies may change, these fears actually have a very long history: more than a century ago our forebears had the same concerns.

These details show that people in both Victorian society and today's culture are concerned with how distracting technology can be and the impact it has on relationships.

BACKGROUND

__Melissa Dickson__ completed her PhD at King's College in London in 2013. In her doctoral thesis, she wrote about the tales of the Arabian Nights, *exploring how these Middle Eastern folktales influenced British drama, fiction, poetry, travel writing, and children's literature. "The Victorians Had the Same Concerns About Technology as We Do" grew out of her involvement in a project called "Diseases of Modern Life," which investigates 19th-century cultural, literary, and medical understandings of stress, overwork, and other disorders.*

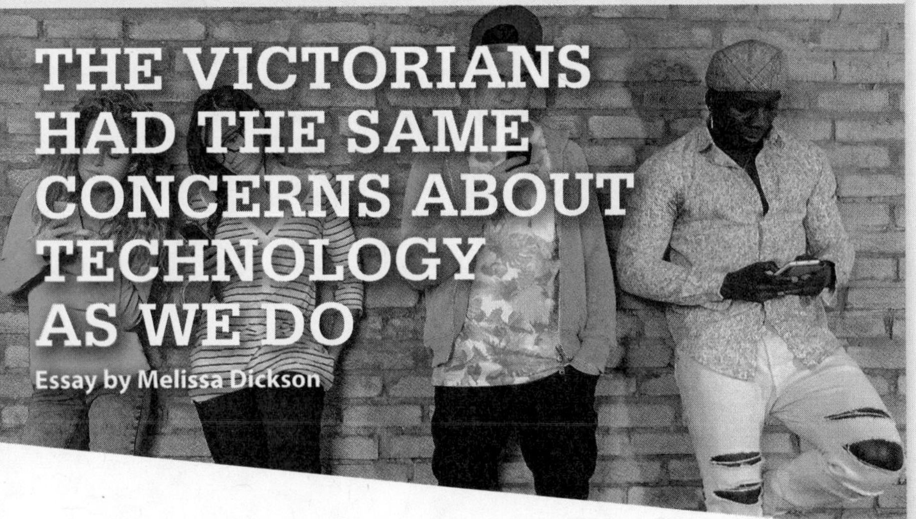

THE VICTORIANS HAD THE SAME CONCERNS ABOUT TECHNOLOGY AS WE DO

Essay by Melissa Dickson

SETTING A PURPOSE

As you read, make note of the author's thesis and the supporting details she uses to develop her main ideas.

1 We live, we are so often told, in an information age. It is an era obsessed with space, time and speed, in which social media inculcates[1] virtual lives that run parallel to our "real" lives and in which communications technologies collapse distances around the globe. Many of us struggle with the bombardment of information we receive and experience anxiety as a result of new media, which we feel threaten our relationships and "usual" modes of human interaction.

2 Though the technologies may change, these fears actually have a very long history: more than a century ago our **forebears** had the same concerns. Literary, medical and cultural responses in the Victorian age to the perceived problems of stress and overwork anticipate many of the preoccupations of our own era to an extent that is perhaps surprising.

[1] **inculcate:** to impress (something) upon the mind of another by frequent instruction or repetition; instill.

Notice & Note

Use the side margins to notice and note signposts in the text.

ANALYZE COMPARE AND CONTRAST ESSAY

Annotate: Mark details in paragraph 2 about Victorian issues that also concern people today.

Connect: What are some recent complaints about the harmful effects of new technology that you have heard about?

forebear
(fôr′bâr) *n.* a person from whom one is descended; an ancestor.

3 This parallel is well illustrated by the following 1906 cartoon from *Punch*, a satirical British weekly magazine:

Worrying trends, 1906.

EVALUATE MULTIMODAL TEXTS

Annotate: Mark details in paragraphs 4 and 5 that support the idea presented in the cartoon.

Analyze: Which details in the cartoon support the author's thesis?

4 The caption reads: "These two figures are not communicating with one another. The lady receives an amatory[2] message, and the gentleman some racing results." The development of the "wireless telegraph" is portrayed as an overwhelmingly isolating technology.

5 Replace these strange contraptions with smartphones, and we are reminded of numerous contemporary complaints regarding the stunted social and emotional development of young people, who no longer hang out in person, but in virtual environments, often at great physical distance. Different technology, same statement. And it's **underpinned** by the same anxiety that "real" human interaction is increasingly under threat from technological innovations that we have, consciously or unconsciously, assimilated into daily life. By using such devices, so the popular paranoia would have it, we are somehow damaging ourselves.

underpin (ŭn-dər-pĭn´) *tr.v.* to give support or substance to.

Cacophony of voices

6 The 19th century witnessed the rapid expansion of the printing industry. New techniques and mass publishing formats gave rise to a far more **pervasive** periodical press, reaching a wider readership

pervasive (pər-vā´sĭv,-zĭv) *adj.* having the quality or tendency to pervade or permeate.

[2] **amatory:** of, relating to, or expressive of love, especially romantic love.

than ever before. Many celebrated the possibility of instant news and greater communication. But concerns were raised about the overwhelmed middle-class reader who, it was thought, lacked the discernment to judge the new mass of information critically, and so read everything in a superficial, erratic manner.

7 The philosopher and essayist Thomas Carlyle, for example, lamented the new lack of direct contact with society and nature caused by the intervention of machinery in every aspect of life. Print publications were fast becoming the principal medium of public debate and influence, and they were shaping and, in Carlyle's view, distorting human learning and communications.

EVALUATE MULTIMODAL TEXTS

Annotate: Mark details in paragraphs 7 and 8 that are expressed visually in the illustration called *A London Street Scene.*

Analyze: What is the significance of this illustration?

John Orlando Parry, *A London Street Scene,* 1835. © Alfred Dunhill Collection

NOTICE & NOTE

cacophony
(kə-kŏf′ə-nē) *n.* jarring, discordant sound; dissonance.

QUOTED WORDS

Notice & Note: Mark the quoted words in paragraph 8.

Evaluate: The author could have paraphrased John Stuart Mill's ideas, or restated the ideas in her own words. What is the effect of including Mill's exact words?

ANALYZE COMPARE AND CONTRAST ESSAY

Annotate: Mark the concern expressed in paragraph 11 about how technology changes the way we read.

Connect: How does this concern relate to a Victorian concern about technology?

sea change
(sē chānj) *n.* a marked transformation.

posit
(pŏz′ĭt) *tr.v.* to assume or put forward, as for consideration or the basis of argument.

immersion
(ĭ-mûr′zhən, -shən) *n.* the act or instance of engaging in something wholly or deeply.

8 The philosopher and economist John Stuart Mill heartily agreed, expressing his fears in an essay entitled "Civilisation". He thought that the **cacophony** of voices supposedly overwhelming the general public was creating:

> *A state of society where any voice, not pitched in an exaggerated key, is lost in the hubbub. Success in so crowded a field depends not upon what a person is, but upon what he seems: mere marketable qualities become the object instead of substantial ones, and a man's capital and labor are expended less in doing anything than in persuading other people that he has done it. Our own age has seen this evil brought to its consummation.*

9 Individual authors and writers were becoming disempowered, lost in a glutted marketplace of ideas, opinions, adverts and quacks.

Old complaints

10 The parallels with the concerns of our own society are striking. Arguments along not at all dissimilar lines have been advanced against contemporary means of acquiring information, such as Twitter, Facebook, and our constant access to the internet in general.

11 In his 2008 article, "Is Google Making Us Stupid?", journalist Nicolas Carr speculated that "we may well be in the midst of a **sea change** in the way we read and think". Reading online, he **posits**, discourages long and thoughtful **immersion** in texts in favor of a form of skipping, scanning and digressing via hyperlinks that will ultimately diminish our capacity for concentration and contemplation.

12 Writers, too, have shared Carr's anxieties. Philip Roth and Will Self, for example, have both prophesied these trends as contributing to the death of the novel, arguing that people are increasingly unused to and ill-equipped to engage with its characteristically long, linear form.

13 Of course, all old technologies were once new. People were at one point genuinely concerned about things we take for granted as perfectly harmless now. In the later decades of the 19th century it was thought that the telephone would induce deafness and that sulphurous vapors were asphyxiating passengers on the London Underground. These then-new advancements were replacing older still technologies that had themselves occasioned similar anxieties on their introduction. Plato, as his oral culture began to transition to a literary one, was gravely worried that writing itself would erode the memory.

14 While we cannot draw too strict a line of comparison between 19th-century attitudes to such technologies as the telegraph, train, telephone, and newspaper and our own responses as a culture to the advent of the internet and the mobile phone, there are parallels that almost argue against the **Luddite** position. As dramatically as technology changes, we, at least in the way we regard it, remain surprisingly unchanged.

NOTICE & NOTE

LANGUAGE CONVENTIONS

Annotate: Mark how the clauses of sentences in paragraph 14 are joined.

Evaluate: How do these complex sentences contribute to the author's style and tone?

Luddite
(lŭd´īt) *n.* one who opposes technical or technological change.

CHECK YOUR UNDERSTANDING

Answer these questions before moving on to the **Analyze the Text** section on the following page.

1 The role of the graphic features in the essay is to —

A Emphasize the ideas expressed by the author

B Illustrate how distracted people can be

C Show how pervasive technology is today

D Suggest that technology has always been in the news

2 Based on the details in the essay, the 21st century is often referred to as the Information Age because people —

F Always share information

G Are continually distracted by new information

H Have access to overwhelming amounts of information

J Are unsure which information is accurate

3 The author refers to Plato in paragraph 13 to —

A Suggest that he believed technology should be banned

B Show that he had concerns about technology

C Dismiss the opinions of those who fear technology

D Contrast ancient ideas about technology with current ones

RESPOND

ANALYZE THE TEXT

Support your responses with evidence from the text. NOTEBOOK

1. **Infer** Reread paragraph 1. Does Dickson agree with the contemporary concerns she summarizes here, or does she seem skeptical of them? Cite details from anywhere in the essay to support your response.
2. **Evaluate** Is point-by-point comparison an effective format for the essay, or should Dickson have discussed the Victorian elements first and then discussed contemporary elements? Explain your response.
3. **Evaluate** Do the images Dickson chose provide good support for her essay? Why or why not?
4. **Critique** Reread paragraph 14. Does Dickson's comparison of Victorian and contemporary fears offer a convincing reason not to worry about current technological changes? Explain your opinion.
5. **Notice & Note** How does the quotation from Nicholas Carr in paragraph 11 support the author's ideas?

RESEARCH

Go online and find editorials and other arguments on the topic of how teenagers are affected by using smartphones and social media. Analyze how authors reach similar and different conclusions on this topic, and list your findings in the chart below.

RESEARCH TIP
The four main ways to conduct an online search for an editorial or news article are searching by keywords, subject, title, and author. A keyword search retrieves the most results because it searches for the word(s) throughout the entire catalog or database. A subject search is more focused because it looks for the word in a specific field. If you know the name of an important author or the title of an article in your area of interest, you can search specifically for them.

AUTHOR'S NAME	TITLE OF WORK	AUTHOR'S POSITION

Connect Think about how social media and other digital tools impact your life. Create a list of pros and cons associated with your access to technology. Share your lists with a partner.

CREATE AND DISCUSS

Write an Op-Ed Analyze the different authors' perspectives and ideas from the research you previously conducted. Then, write a brief opinion editorial that conveys your position on the topic of the impact social media and smartphones have on teenagers.

- ❑ Identify a clear thesis statement. What is your position on the topic?
- ❑ Who is your audience? Will your reader understand your argument?
- ❑ Is your argument organized in a way that effectively engages the reader?
- ❑ What evidence and details have you included to support your ideas?

Go to **Writing Arguments** in the **Writing Studio** for more help with writing an op-ed.

Analyze and Discuss Your Ideas Find a partner and take turns reading your opinion editorials to each other. Analyze each other's conclusions and discuss whether or not you agree with each other's positions.

- ❑ Does your partner have a compelling argument?
- ❑ What evidence can you point to in your partner's writing that supports his or her thesis?
- ❑ Are your partner's introduction and conclusion clear and effective?

Go to **Participating in Collaborative Discussions** in the **Speaking and Listening Studio** for more help.

RESPOND TO THE ESSENTIAL QUESTION

Which invention has had the greatest impact on your life?

Gather Information Review your annotations and notes on the essay. Then, add relevant information to your Response Log. As you determine which information to include, think about:

- how technology has impacted your life
- how often you access social media or your smartphone
- how your life would be different if certain technological advances had not been made

ACADEMIC VOCABULARY

As you write and discuss what you learned from the essay, be sure to use the Academic Vocabulary words. Check off each of the words that you use.

- ❑ **abandon**
- ❑ **confine**
- ❑ **conform**
- ❑ **depress**
- ❑ **reluctance**

RESPOND

WORD BANK
forebear
underpin
pervasive
cacophony
sea change
posit
immersion
Luddite

CRITICAL VOCABULARY

Practice and Apply Fill in the blanks with the correct words.

1. Micah's concentration was often interrupted by a(n) __________ of voices and laughter coming from downstairs.
2. Brenda considered her grandfather a(n) __________; her __________ always complained about technology.
3. Your lack of studying is likely to __________ poor scores in math class.
4. The author __________ that the __________ use of social media would ultimately cause people to feel less connected to others.
5. Some people believe video gaming will go through a(n) __________ because we will soon be able to create total __________ in virtual reality environments.

VOCABULARY STRATEGY: Synonyms and Antonyms

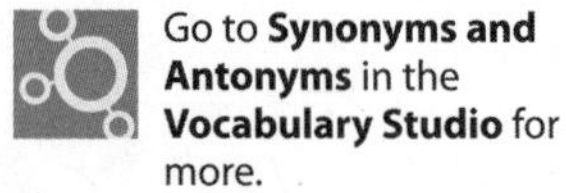

Go to **Synonyms and Antonyms** in the **Vocabulary Studio** for more.

Reference tools help writers understand the precise meaning of words so they can use them correctly. The thesaurus, for example, is used to find **synonyms,** or words with similar meaning, and **antonyms,** words that have opposite meaning. Take a look at this example of a thesaurus entry for the Critical Vocabulary word *pervasive.*

> **pervasive** *adjective*
> **synonyms:** *prevalent, permeating, extensive, ubiquitous*
> **antonyms:** *limited, narrow, restricted*

Practice and Apply For each Critical Vocabulary word, follow these steps:

1. Look up each word in a print or digital thesaurus, identify the synonyms appropriate to the meaning of each term as it is used in the selection.
2. Write a sample sentence using each word.
3. In each sentence, replace the vocabulary word with one of your synonyms. Make sure that the sentences make sense by having a partner check your work.

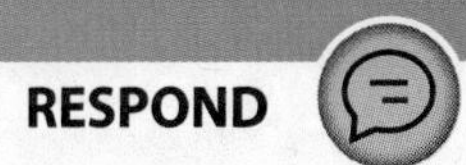

LANGUAGE CONVENTIONS: Sentence Structure

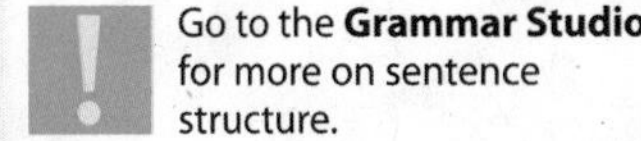

Go to the **Grammar Studio** for more on sentence structure.

Good writers use a variety of sentence structures to avoid monotony and to effectively articulate their ideas. The simplest structure has one **clause,** a group of words that contains a subject and a verb. More complex sentence structures include more than one clause. Study the examples in the chart.

SENTENCE STRUCTURE	EXAMPLE
A **simple sentence** has one independent clause and no subordinate clauses.	We live in the Information Age.
A **compound sentence** has two or more independent clauses joined by a comma and a coordinating conjunction, such as *and*, *or*, or *but*.	People love using social media, but some worry about how it will affect our relationships in the long run.
A **complex sentence** has an independent clause and one or more subordinate clauses. The subordinate clause begins with a subordinating conjunction, such as *when*, *as*, *after*, *because*, or *while*.	After comparing the concerns people had in the 19th century to those of people in the present day, the author concluded that humans will always be fearful of technology.
A **compound-complex sentence** has two or more independent clauses and at least one subordinate clause.	Teenagers are constantly bombarded by information, but they understand the need to think critically when it comes to online sources.

Notice how the conjunctions in the example sentences connect the ideas in the clauses. Without the conjunctions, each sentence would be a **run-on,** or multiple sentences written as if they were one. The writer's meaning would also be less clear without conjunctions.

Run-on example: Teenagers are constantly bombarded by information they understand the need to think critically it comes to online sources.

Practice and Apply Write a paragraph about an invention you believe you cannot live without. Then, go back and review the paragraph, making sure to scan for simple sentences and repeated subjects or verbs in different sentences. Combine these sentences to form complex sentences by compounding verbs and using subordinate clauses to show the relationships among your ideas.

POEM

DOVER BEACH

by **Matthew Arnold**

pages 657–658

COMPARE THEMES

As you read, notice how the speakers in these poems use observations of nature as a springboard to discussing their feelings about the times they live in. Think about how the themes of these poems relate to each other. After you read both poems, you will collaborate with a small group on a final product.

ESSENTIAL QUESTION:

How do you view the world?

POEM

THE DARKLING THRUSH

by **Thomas Hardy**

pages 660–661

QUICK START

Our personal perspectives have a strong influence on how we react to things. Identify three important issues that affect your community, the country, or the world. Then, work with a partner to describe the different ways an optimist and a pessimist might view these issues. Use this chart to record your ideas.

OPTIMISTIC VIEW	PESSIMISTIC VIEW

ANALYZE EXTENDED METAPHORS

Like any metaphor, an **extended metaphor** is a comparison between two essentially unlike things that nevertheless have something in common. In an extended metaphor, however, the figurative comparison is made at length and in various ways throughout a stanza, a paragraph, or an entire literary work. An extended metaphor is similar to a metaphysical conceit, but the comparison is not as surprising.

Both of the poems you will read in this lesson contain extended metaphors. In "Dover Beach," for example, Matthew Arnold develops a metaphor comparing the sea to traditional religious faith. The poet first offers some specific observations about the sea, then connects these details to his ideas about faith.

As you read each poem, consider how the extended metaphor helps to convey a theme about the period when the poem was written.

GENRE ELEMENTS: LYRIC POETRY

- expresses strong feelings or thoughts
- has a musical quality
- deals with intense emotions surrounding events like death, love, or loss
- includes forms such as ode, elegy, and sonnet

GET READY

ANALYZE SOUND DEVICES

The earliest poetry was composed to be sung in performance. Poets still use sound devices to create musical effects and to help unify lines and stanzas. The most common sound devices are rhyme and meter. Here are some other types of sound devices.

- **Alliteration**—the repetition of a consonant sound at the beginning of words (*His crypt the cloudy canopy*)
- **Assonance**—the repetition of a vowel sound in two or more stressed syllables that do not end with the same consonant (*The tide is full, the moon lies fair*)
- **Consonance**—the repetition of consonant sounds within and at the end of words (*Like strings of broken lyres*)
- **Onomatopoeia**—the use of words whose sounds echo their meanings (*grating*)

After you read these poems the first time, read them again aloud and notice how the sound devices appeal to your sense of hearing. Also, consider how sound devices support each poem's subject, mood, and theme.

NOTICE & NOTE

ANNOTATION MODEL

As you read, notice how each poet uses nature imagery to appeal to the reader's senses and to develop an extended metaphor. Mark up examples of sound devices. In the model, you can see one reader's notes about the beginning of "Dover Beach."

The sea is calm tonight.
The tide is full, the moon lies fair
Upon the straits – on the French coast the light
Gleams and is gone; the cliffs of England stand,
Glimmering and vast, out in the tranquil bay.
Come to the window, sweet is the night air!

The imagery suggests nature's vastness and establishes a peaceful mood at the beginning. Alliteration of the "g" sound contributes to this mood.

The sixth line tells us the speaker is addressing someone in the same room.

BACKGROUND

***Matthew Arnold** (1822–1888) was one of the leading poets and essayists of the Victorian era. In his youth, he struggled to live up to the expectations of his father, a famous headmaster of Rugby School. Arnold attended Rugby and then Oxford University; he later held teaching positions at both schools. While at Oxford, he began to gain recognition for his poetry. Arnold's poems are contemplative, often addressing serious themes of isolation and religious doubt.*

DOVER BEACH

Poem by Matthew Arnold

PREPARE TO COMPARE

As you read, note the imagery in the speaker's description of the natural world and the sound devices in his description. Consider the thoughts and feelings the speaker associates with the sea.

The sea is calm tonight.
The tide is full, the moon lies fair
Upon the straits—on the French coast the light
Gleams and is gone; the cliffs of England stand,
Glimmering and vast, out in the tranquil bay.
Come to the window, sweet is the night air!
Only, from the long line of spray
Where the sea meets the moon-blanched land,
Listen! you hear the grating roar
Of pebbles which the waves draw back, and fling,
At their return, up the high strand,
Begin, and cease, and then again begin,
With tremulous cadence slow, and bring
The eternal note of sadness in.

Notice & Note

Use the side margins to notice and note signposts in the text.

3 straits: the Strait of Dover, a narrow channel separating England and France, located at the northern end of the English Channel.

8 moon-blanched: shining palely in the moonlight.

13 tremulous cadence (trĕm´yə-ləs kād´ns): trembling rhythm.

NOTICE & NOTE

15 Sophocles (sŏf´ə-klēz): an ancient Greek writer of tragic plays.

16 Aegean (ĭ-jē´ən): the Aegean Sea, the portion of the Mediterranean Sea between Greece and Turkey.

17 turbid: in a state of turmoil; muddled.

21 Sea of Faith: traditional religious beliefs about God and the world, long viewed as true and unshakable.

23 girdle: a belt or sash worn around the waist.

27 drear: dreary.

28 shingles: pebbly beaches.

ANALYZE SOUND DEVICES

Annotate: Read lines 29–37 aloud. Mark sound devices you notice.

Analyze: What mood do the sound devices help create?

Sophocles long ago
Heard it on the Aegean, and it brought
Into his mind the turbid ebb and flow
Of human misery; we
Find also in the sound a thought,
Hearing it by this distant northern sea.

The Sea of Faith
Was once, too, at the full, and round earth's shore
Lay like the folds of a bright girdle furled.
But now I only hear
Its melancholy, long, withdrawing roar,
Retreating, to the breath
Of the night wind, down the vast edges drear
And naked shingles of the world.

Ah, love, let us be true
To one another! for the world, which seems
To lie before us like a land of dreams,
So various, so beautiful, so new,
Hath really neither joy, nor love, nor light,
Nor certitude, nor peace, nor help for pain;
And we are here as on a darkling plain
Swept with confused alarms of struggle and flight,
Where ignorant armies clash by night.

CHECK YOUR UNDERSTANDING

Answer these questions about "Dover Beach" before moving on to the next selection.

1 In the poem, the speaker is —

A looking out to sea from the English coast

B sailing on a ship in the English Channel

C swimming in the Aegean Sea

D fighting in a war in France

2 What does the speaker compare to waves pulling back from the shore?

F Armed conflict

G Ships sailing into the channel

H Loss of religious faith

J Lovers parting

3 The speaker takes comfort in —

A his spirituality

B nature's beauty

C social progress

D personal relationships

NOTICE & NOTE

BACKGROUND

Thomas Hardy *(1840–1928) was born in a small village in southwestern England, the setting of many of his novels and poems. As a young man, he wrote poems and stories in his spare time while working as an architect. Hardy became famous for his novels, although their pessimism and controversial subject matter were often criticized. He published "The Darkling Thrush" just a few days before the end of the 19th century.*

THE DARKLING THRUSH

Poem by Thomas Hardy

PREPARE TO COMPARE

As you read, notice the poet's word choices in describing a landscape.

I leant upon a coppice gate
When Frost was specter-gray,
And Winter's dregs made desolate
The weakening eye of day.

The tangled bine-stems scored the sky
Like strings of broken lyres,
And all mankind that haunted nigh
Had sought their household fires.

The land's sharp features seemed to be
The Century's corpse outleant,
His crypt the cloudy canopy,
The wind his death-lament.
The ancient pulse of germ and birth
Was shrunken hard and dry,
And every spirit upon earth
Seem'd fervorless as I.

At once a voice arose among
The bleak twigs overhead
In a full-hearted evensong

Notice & Note

Use the side margins to notice and note signposts in the text.

1 coppice (kŏp´ĭs) **gate:** a gate leading to a coppice, a small wood or thicket.

2 specter-gray: ghost-gray.

5 bine-stems scored: twining stems cut across.

6 lyres: harp-like musical instruments.

7 nigh: near.

10 outleant: outstretched.

13 germ: seed; bud.

19 evensong: evening song.

Of joy illimited;
An aged thrush, frail, gaunt, and small,
In blast-beruffled plume,
Had chosen thus to fling his soul
Upon the growing gloom.

So little cause for carollings
Of such ecstatic sound
Was written on terrestrial things
Afar or nigh around,
That I could think there trembled through
His happy good-night air
Some blessed Hope, whereof he knew
And I was unaware.

NOTICE & NOTE

20 illimited: unlimited.

22 blast-beruffled plume: wind-ruffled feathers.

ANALYZE EXTENDED METAPHORS

Annotate: Underline words that describe natural features in lines 9–16. Circle words that describe the century as it is compared to nature.

Analyze: What idea does this extended metaphor express?

CHECK YOUR UNDERSTANDING

Answer these questions before moving on to the **Analyze the Texts** section on the following page.

1 What is the poem's setting?

A Sunrise on a mountain slope

B An open snowy field

C A lake's frozen shore

D The edge of the woods in winter

2 The lines "Had chosen thus to fling his soul / Upon the growing gloom" suggest that the thrush —

F shares the speaker's sense of hopelessness

G is defying the grimness of its surroundings

H probably won't live much longer

J has flown down from the tree branch

3 The speaker says in lines 29–32 that —

A the thrush may have some unknown reason to be happy

B he understands why the thrush sings joyfully

C he mistook the thrush's singing as a sign of hope

D the singing has plunged him even deeper into despair

RESPOND

ANALYZE THE TEXTS

Support your responses with evidence from the texts. NOTEBOOK

1. **Analyze** In "Dover Beach," how does Arnold use details about the sea to develop his extended metaphor about faith?
2. **Infer** Arnold refers to Sophocles in lines 15–20 of "Dover Beach." What idea does he suggest through this allusion to the ancient Greek playwright?
3. **Interpret** Reread lines 29–37 of "Dover Beach." How does the speaker's description of the world connect to his plea that he and his love "be true / To one another"?
4. **Analyze** How does Hardy's use of alliteration and assonance in lines 1–4 of "The Darkling Thrush" support the subject and theme of the poem?
5. **Draw Conclusions** In "The Darkling Thrush," why did Hardy choose to describe the bird as an "aged thrush, frail, gaunt, and small"?

RESEARCH

Both of these poems reflect the poets' feelings about changes that occurred during their lifetimes. With a partner, research historical developments during the Victorian era. Use what you learn to answer the following questions.

QUESTION	ANSWER
What challenges to traditional religious beliefs occurred during the Victorian era?	
How did industrialization affect rural life in Britain during this period?	

RESEARCH TIP
When researching an aspect of a particular time period, it is easiest to find the answers you're looking for by using specific search strings. In this case, you might use strings like "Victorian + religion" or "how industrialization affected British rural life."

Extend Although the Victorian era is often characterized as a period of optimism and progress, some of its finest writers expressed a pessimistic outlook. Find other poems by Arnold and Hardy that address subjects such as loss and disillusionment. With a partner, discuss how they compare with the poems you read in this lesson.

CREATE AND DISCUSS

Create a List Select an aspect of nature, such as a season, a type of landscape, or a particular animal. Create a list of words and phrases that describe this aspect of nature, and then list thoughts or feelings that you associate with them. Include at least 20 words or phrases in your list. Review your analysis and interpretation of the two poems to see examples from Arnold and Hardy.

- ❑ Identify an aspect of nature that is representative of how you view the world.
- ❑ Review examples of how poets have used nature to represent ideas.
- ❑ Brainstorm and construct a list of words and phrases.

Discuss Your List People can react to the same sights and experiences in strikingly different ways. Share and discuss your list with a small group.

- ❑ Review each descriptive word or phrase with your group.
- ❑ Then, discuss the thoughts and feelings you associated with these details. Ask every group member to explain how their reactions compare with yours.
- ❑ Make sure to respect everyone's responses. If you are confused by a response, ask the student to clarify it.

RESPOND TO THE ESSENTIAL QUESTION

How do you view the world?

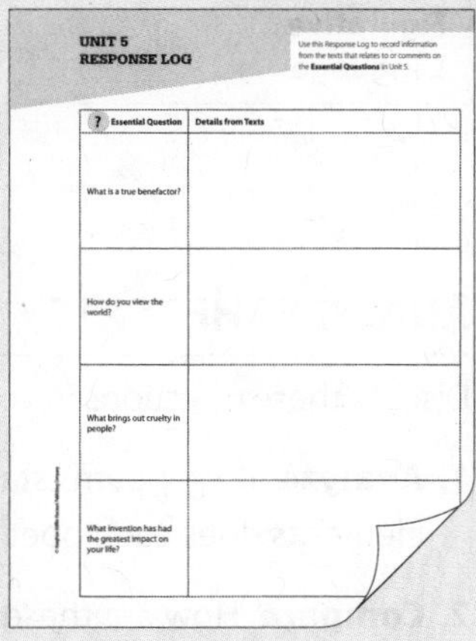

UNIT 5 RESPONSE LOG

Use this Response Log to record information from the texts that relates to or comments on the **Essential Questions** in Unit 5.

? Essential Question	Details from Texts
What is a true benefactor?	
How do you view the world?	
What brings out cruelty in people?	
What invention has had the greatest impact on your life?	

Gather Information Review your annotations and notes on "Dover Beach" and "The Darkling Thrush." Then, add relevant details to your Response Log. As you determine which information to include, think about:

- how poets describe the natural world in different ways
- how you experience the world around you
- how similar elements can be used to express opposite ideas

ACADEMIC VOCABULARY

As you write and discuss what you learned from the lyric poems, be sure to use the Academic Vocabulary words. Check off each of the words that you use.

- ❑ **abandon**
- ❑ **confine**
- ❑ **conform**
- ❑ **depress**
- ❑ **reluctance**

Collaborate & Compare

DOVER BEACH
Poem by Matthew Arnold

THE DARKLING THRUSH
Poem by Thomas Hardy

COMPARE THEMES

A poem's **theme** is the message the author conveys to the reader. Although even a short poem may express several ideas, the theme is the major idea that the poet communicates. Themes are developed through word choice, imagery, figurative language, and other elements.

In both "Dover Beach" and "The Darkling Thrush," the poets use their descriptions of nature to express themes about disillusionment and hopelessness.

Poets seldom directly state their themes, so you must infer them from a close reading of a poem. As you read to understand each poem's message, consider:

- **Key statements**—made by the speaker
- **Imagery**—details that appeal to the reader's senses
- **Figurative language**—language that communicates ideas beyond the literal meaning of the words.

With your group, complete the chart with details from both poems.

	"DOVER BEACH"	"THE DARKLING THRUSH"
Key Statements		
Imagery		
Figurative Language		

ANALYZE THE TEXTS

Discuss these questions in your group:

1. **Analyze** Both poems start out with descriptions of nature. What literary elements does each poet rely on to develop his description?

2. **Compare** How are these two poems similar or different in mood?

3. **Draw Conclusions** Which poem expresses a more hopeful view of the world? Explain.

4. **Analyze** Both poems include extended metaphors comparing something in nature with an abstract idea. How does this technique help the poets develop their poems?

RESPOND

COLLABORATE AND PRESENT

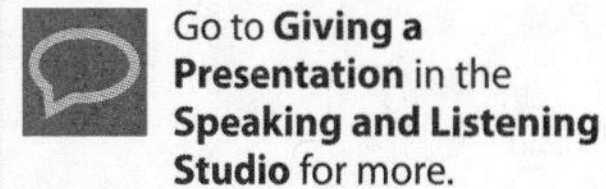
Go to **Giving a Presentation** in the **Speaking and Listening Studio** for more.

Now, with your group, continue exploring the ideas in the poems by identifying and comparing their themes. Follow these steps:

1. **Decide on the most important details** With your group, review your chart to identify the most important details from each poem. Identify points on which you agree, and resolve disagreements by identifying evidence from the poems that support your ideas.
2. **Determine a theme** Based on the word choices, figurative language, sound devices, and feelings evoked from each poem, determine a theme for each. You may use a chart to keep track of the themes your group members suggest.

	DETAILS	THEME
"DOVER BEACH"		
"THE DARKLING THRUSH"		

3. **Compare themes** Compare themes with your group and discuss whether the themes are similar or different. Listen actively to the members of your group and ask them to clarify any points you do not understand.
4. **Present to the class** Next, present your ideas to the class. Be sure to include clear statements on the theme for each poem. Discuss whether the themes are similar or different. You may add other visuals or diagrams to help convey information to the class.

POEM

MY LAST DUCHESS

by **Robert Browning**

pages 669–670

ESSENTIAL QUESTION:

What brings out cruelty in people?

COMPARE THEMES

As you read "My Last Duchess" and "Confession," take note of how each poem addresses the imperfections of human character. After you read both poems, you will collaborate with a small group to create a final presentation comparing their themes.

POEM

CONFESSION

by **Linh Dinh**

page 672

QUICK START

You probably know someone who tends to criticize other people. What is the danger of being overly critical in your interactions with others? Discuss this question with a small group of classmates.

DRAW CONCLUSIONS ABOUT SPEAKERS

The **speaker** of a poem is the voice that talks to the reader. In many poems, the speaker expresses the poet's own thoughts and feelings. However, you should not assume that the speaker is the same as the poet, even if he or she uses the pronouns *I* and *me*.

Some poems have a fictional character, or **persona,** as the speaker. *Persona* is a Latin word meaning "actor's mask." A persona allows the poet to pretend to be someone with a different personality or situation. For example, in "Confession," Linh Dinh uses the persona of a painter to explore an idea about the visual arts.

A **dramatic monologue** is a type of persona poem in which the speaker addresses a silent or absent listener during an intense or emotionally complex moment. Dramatic monologues require readers to make inferences: the speakers reveal themselves by dropping clues that the reader must piece together. Browning's "My Last Duchess," a famous monologue, is set in 16th-century Italy. The speaker is a duke negotiating with an agent to marry a count's daughter. Notice how Browning begins the poem in the middle of their conversation:

> **That's my last Duchess painted on the wall,**
> **Looking as if she were alive.**

As you read, use a chart like the one below to gather evidence and draw conclusions about the character and circumstances of each poem's speaker.

	HOW SPEAKER VIEWS HIMSELF	HOW SPEAKER VIEWS OTHERS
"My Last Duchess"		
"Confession"		

GENRE ELEMENTS: LYRIC POETRY

- usually written in the first person
- expresses the feelings and thoughts of the speaker, who may be a fictional character
- uses sound devices, such as rhythm and repetition, to create a musical quality
- often deals with intense emotions surrounding events like death, love, or loss

GET READY

ANALYZE IMAGERY

Imagery refers to words and phrases that create vivid sensory experiences for the reader. Most imagery is visual, but imagery can also appeal to the senses of smell, hearing, taste, and touch. Imagery appears in all literary forms, but it is especially important in poetry for establishing a mood, expressing emotions, and conveying ideas.

The two poems in this lesson focus on a painting or the act of painting. Because of this subject, they are both rich in visual imagery. As you read, notice how each poet uses an image or group of images to support the poem's theme. Use a chart like this one to help you analyze ideas and feelings associated with the imagery.

EXAMPLE OF IMAGERY	IDEAS OR FEELINGS LINKED TO IMAGE

ANNOTATION MODEL

NOTICE & NOTE 

As you read, draw conclusions about each poem's speaker. Also, note how the imagery in each poem helps create a mood or express a theme. In the model you can see one reader's notes about "My Last Duchess."

That's my last Duchess painted on the wall,
Looking as if she were alive. I call
That piece a wonder, now: Frà Pandolf 's hands
Worked busily a day, and there she stands.
Will't please you sit and look at her?

The Duke uses the term "last Duchess," which is a cold way to refer to his late wife.

He emphasizes how realistic the painting is, like he's describing a real person. The painting seems to have special importance to him.

BACKGROUND

Robert Browning *(1812–1889) showed intellectual brilliance at a young age. When his first book of poetry was harshly criticized for its personal content, he decided to write poems about people and characters other than himself. Browning married the poet Elizabeth Barrett in 1846; they lived happily together in Italy until her death 15 years later. After decades of obscurity, Browning began to gain recognition during the 1860s for his dramatic monologues. He is widely considered one of the most important poets of the Victorian Era.*

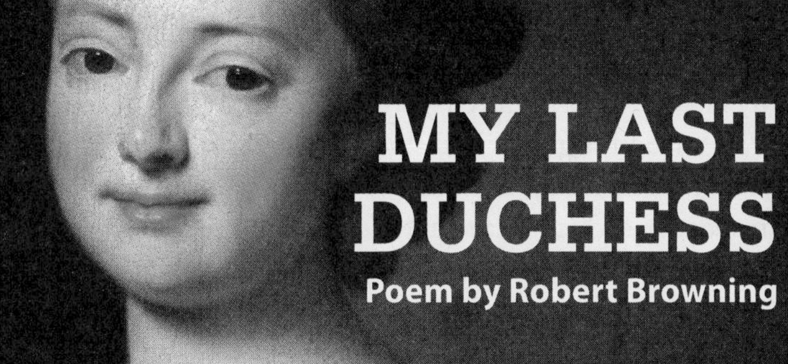

MY LAST DUCHESS

Poem by Robert Browning

PREPARE TO COMPARE

As you read, note what the speaker reveals about himself through the course of the poem. Pay close attention to his word choices and the imagery that helps describe his behaviors and feelings for his wife.

That's my last Duchess painted on the wall,
Looking as if she were alive. I call
That piece a wonder, now: Frà Pandolf's hands
Worked busily a day, and there she stands.
Will't please you sit and look at her? I said
"Frà Pandolf" by design, for never read
Strangers like you that pictured countenance,
The depth and passion of its earnest glance,
But to myself they turned (since none puts by
The curtain I have drawn for you, but I)
And seemed as they would ask me, if they durst,
How such a glance came there; so, not the first
Are you to turn and ask thus. Sir, 'twas not
Her husband's presence only, called that spot
Of joy into the Duchess' cheek: perhaps
Frà Pandolf chanced to say "Her mantle laps

Notice & Note

Use the side margins to notice and note signposts in the text.

3 Frà Pandolf's: of Brother Pandolf, a fictitious friar-painter.

DRAW CONCLUSIONS ABOUT SPEAKERS

Annotate: Mark the phrases in lines 5–13 that hint at the character of the speaker.

Infer: What can you infer about the duke? What details support your inference?

11 durst: dared.

16 mantle: cloak.

ANALYZE IMAGERY

Annotate: Mark details in lines 22–34 that describe what the duchess was like.

Compare: How does her character differ from that of the duke?

27 officious: offering unwanted services; meddling.

35 trifling: actions of little importance.

41 forsooth: in truth; indeed.

49 munificence (myo͞o-nĭf′ĭ-səns): generosity.

50 just pretense: legitimate claim.

51 dowry (dou′rə): payment given to a groom by the bride's father.

54 Neptune: in Roman mythology, the god of the sea.

DRAW CONCLUSIONS ABOUT SPEAKERS

Annotate: Mark the words in lines 44–56 that reveal the duke's sense of his own authority and power.

Interpret: What is the duke's motivation for telling the listener the story of his late wife? Has he revealed more than he intended? Explain.

Over my lady's wrist too much," or "Paint
Must never hope to reproduce the faint
Half-flush that dies along her throat": such stuff
Was courtesy, she thought, and cause enough
For calling up that spot of joy. She had
A heart—how shall I say?—too soon made glad,
Too easily impressed; she liked whate'er
She looked on, and her looks went everywhere.
Sir, 'twas all one! My favor at her breast,
The dropping of the daylight in the West,
The bough of cherries some officious fool
Broke in the orchard for her, the white mule
She rode with round the terrace—all and each
Would draw from her alike the approving speech,
Or blush, at least. She thanked men—good! but thanked
Somehow—I know not how—as if she ranked
My gift of a nine-hundred-years-old name
With anybody's gift. Who'd stoop to blame
This sort of trifling? Even had you skill
In speech—(which I have not)—to make your will
Quite clear to such an one, and say, "Just this
Or that in you disgusts me; here you miss,
Or there exceed the mark"—and if she let
Herself be lessoned so, nor plainly set
Her wits to yours, forsooth, and made excuse
—E'en then would be some stooping; and I choose
Never to stoop. Oh sir, she smiled, no doubt,
Whene'er I passed her; but who passed without
Much the same smile? This grew; I gave commands;
Then all smiles stopped together. There she stands
As if alive. Will't please you rise? We'll meet
The company below, then. I repeat,
The Count your master's known munificence
Is ample warrant that no just pretense
Of mine for dowry will be disallowed;
Though his fair daughter's self, as I avowed
At starting, is my object. Nay, we'll go
Together down, sir. Notice Neptune, though,
Taming a sea horse, thought a rarity,
Which Claus of Innsbruck cast in bronze for me!

CHECK YOUR UNDERSTANDING

Answer these questions about "My Last Duchess" before moving on to the next selection.

1 In the discussion of the duchess's portrait, the duke focuses on the —

A value of the painting

B style of the painter

C duchess's beauty

D expression on her face

2 The duke thinks that he should be admired because of his —

F social status

G intelligence

H appearance

J eloquence

3 Why didn't the duke tell his late wife that she was offending him?

A He was worried she would leave him.

B He was too proud to complain.

C He wanted her to figure it out on her own.

D He knew she would die soon.

NOTICE & NOTE

BACKGROUND

Linh Dinh *(1963–) is a contemporary poet from Vietnam. He has authored two collections of stories, a novel, and several poetry collections. He is best known for* Postcards from the End of America, *a book of photographs and text documenting life in America. To create that work, he crisscrossed the country by bus, train, and foot, encountering people from all walks of life, including those living on the margins of society. His portrait of the nation underscores the strength it takes to overcome hardship.*

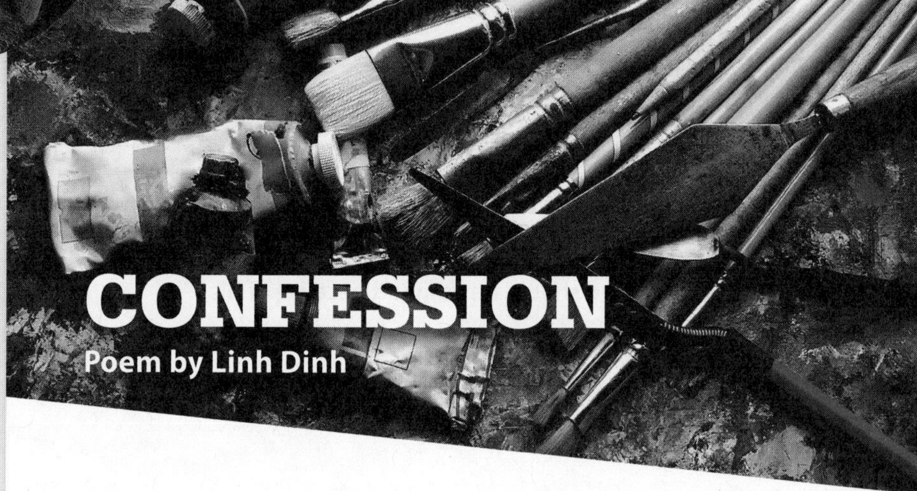

CONFESSION

Poem by Linh Dinh

Notice & Note

Use the side margins to notice and note signposts in the text.

PREPARE TO COMPARE

As you read this poem, note how the character of its speaker differs from that of the speaker in "My Last Duchess." Consider the ways that both poems express themes about the negative side of human nature.

Perhaps I'm a cruel artist. I always depict
In great details, lovingly, all the defects
On the faces and bodies of my models.
I use my eyes and brushes to thread
The jagged gaps of their stiff smiles. I pamper
Each pimple, hump, massage each incrustation.

I cajole my models into poses that are awkward,
Dangerous, unhygienic, sometimes mortifying.
I don't care to paint smooth, poreless skin but collect
All manners of rashes and eruptions. Inspired,
I've forced a hundred bodies—impossibly old,
Extremely young—onto appalling heaps,

Democratically naked, viscous with sweat, spit and etc.,
Just so I could render the human condition
Most accurately and movingly.

ANALYZE IMAGERY

Annotate: Mark contrasting images in lines 9–10.

Interpret: What idea does this contrast help convey?

CHECK YOUR UNDERSTANDING

Answer these questions before moving on to the **Analyze the Texts** section on the following page.

1 What does the poem's use of the phrase *democratically naked* suggest?

A The speaker's motivations are political.

B Nakedness creates a natural equality among people.

C The models never feel embarrassed when they are together.

D People have voted to take off their clothes before posing.

2 Why does the speaker use such negative imagery to describe the models?

F The speaker is trying to elicit disgust in a listener or reader.

G The speaker wants to emphasize the unattractiveness of the models to a listener or reader.

H The speaker wants a listener or reader to grasp how truly ugly human beings are.

J The speaker wants a listener or reader to dwell on the flesh-and-bone reality of imperfect human bodies.

3 How would you characterize the artist's purpose in painting people?

A To see beauty in everyone

B To express anger by showing humans as ugly

C To make a statement about society's ideals

D To idealize human physical imperfections

ANALYZE THE TEXTS

Support your responses with evidence from the texts. NOTEBOOK

1. **Analyze** Which images does Browning use repeatedly in "My Last Duchess"? What does this repetition reveal about the speaker's personality?
2. **Draw Conclusions** In lines 45–46 of "My Last Duchess," the speaker says, "I gave commands; / Then all smiles stopped together." How do you interpret this statement? Why might Browning have chosen to have the duke describe his actions so ambiguously?
3. **Interpret** Browning devotes most of "My Last Duchess" to discussion of the portrait, and he ends with a description of another artwork. What theme about art and life does he develop in the poem?
4. **Analyze** What mood is created by the images of bodily imperfections and disease in "Confession"? How does this mood support the speaker's ideas about art?
5. **Draw Conclusions** Do you think the speaker of "Confession" really wants us to consider him cruel, or does he have a more idealistic reason for the way he paints? Explain your response.

RESEARCH

Feelings of jealousy have been expressed by human beings throughout the ages and across societies. How often does our entertainment industry rely on tales of jealous behavior and its consequences? Research works, such as movies, books, plays, and songs, that address the topic of jealousy. Find several examples from different time periods in a variety of media. Use the graphic organizer below to help you organize and explain your findings.

TITLE	TYPE OF MEDIA	TIME FRAME	SYNOPSIS

Extend Conduct a survey of your classmates to determine their top five favorite movies. Determine if any of the movies address the topic of jealous behavior, and discuss the themes, or messages about life or human nature, those movies express.

RESEARCH TIP

Use websites that give reviews of books, movies, and songs to discover likely titles.

Then, to gather information on years, media types, plots, and themes, search several additional websites.

CREATE AND PRESENT

Create an Oral Presentation "My Last Duchess" and "Confession" present contrasts in style, tone, and language. The speaker in "My Last Duchess" lived during the Renaissance, so he spoke very differently than the contemporary artist in "Confession." Develop an oral presentation in which you assume the persona of one of the two speakers and recite that poem as a monologue.

- ❑ Be sure you understand the emotions underlying specific words and phrases, as well as their purposes, and mark the text to indicate style of delivery.
- ❑ Plan appropriate gestures and movements along with effective intonation to guide emphasis.
- ❑ Remember to address your audience. Is the speaker talking to a listener or to himself?

Present the Monologue In a small group, present your monologue.

- ❑ Make sure your presentation helps others understand the poem.
- ❑ Be clear about the message you impart as the speaker of the poem.
- ❑ Analyze what you would do differently if you were to recite the second poem.

Go to **Giving a Presentation** in the **Speaking and Listening Studio** for more about presenting to others.

RESPOND TO THE ESSENTIAL QUESTION

What brings out cruelty in people?

Gather Information Review your annotations and notes on "My Last Duchess" and "Confession." Then, add relevant information to your Response Log. As you determine which information to include, think about:

- human nature and the human condition
- the difference between tolerance and acceptance
- ways that ego and self-obsession motivate behavior

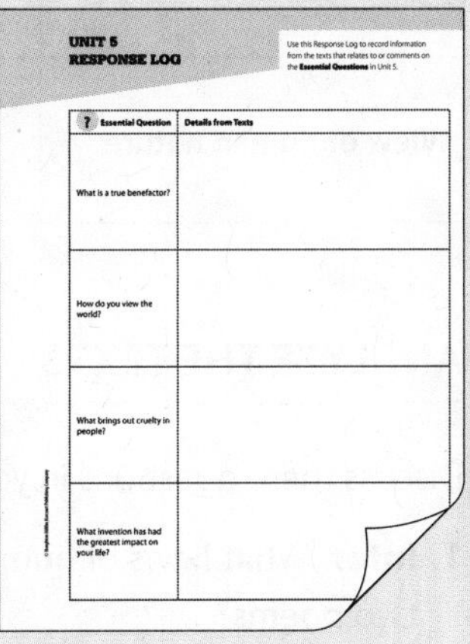

UNIT 5 RESPONSE LOG

Use this Response Log to record information from the texts that relates to or comments on the **Essential Questions** in Unit 5.

? Essential Question	Details from Texts
What is a true benefactor?	
How do you view the world?	
What brings out cruelty in people?	
What invention has had the greatest impact on your life?	

ACADEMIC VOCABULARY

As you write and discuss what you learned from the poems, be sure to use the Academic Vocabulary words. Check off each of the words that you use.

- ❑ **abandon**
- ❑ **confine**
- ❑ **confirm**
- ❑ **depress**
- ❑ **reluctance**

MY LAST DUCHESS
Poem by Robert Browning

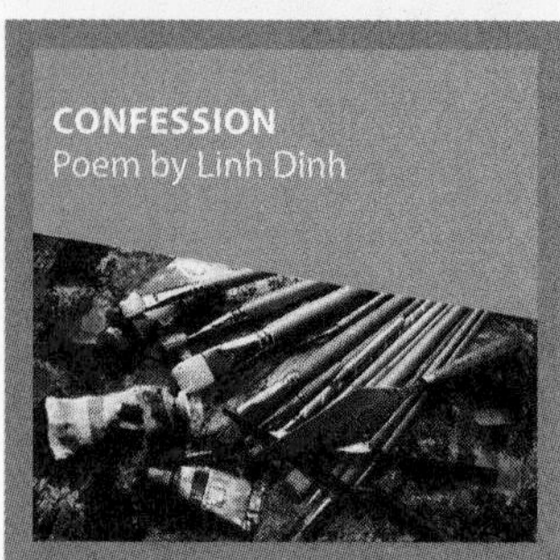

CONFESSION
Poem by Linh Dinh

Collaborate & Compare

COMPARE THEMES

"My Last Duchess" and "Confession" both focus on art, and they also address cruelty. Still, the two poems express distinct ideas about human nature.

With your group, discuss each area of focus listed in the chart below and record what you notice under the appropriate poem.

	"MY LAST DUCHESS"	"CONFESSION"
Information from the title		
Identity of the speaker		
Primary subject matter		
Use of imagery		
Implied emotions		
The role of art		
View of human nature		

ANALYZE THE TEXTS

Discuss these questions in your group.

1. **Infer** What flaws of human nature are represented by the speakers in the two poems?
2. **Interpret** How does the imagery of the two poems help reveal the identity and character of each speaker? What conclusions about the speakers can you draw based on their word choices?
3. **Compare** What similarities do Frá Pandolf and the painter in "Confession" share? What differences distinguish the two?
4. **Evaluate** How might the duke and the painter in "Confession" pose a threat to their respective societies?

COLLABORATE AND PRESENT

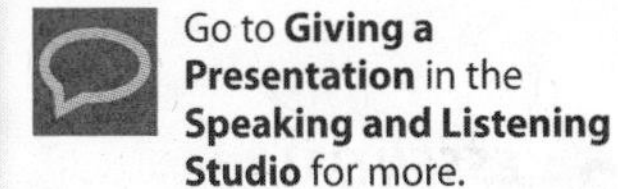

In your group, continue exploring the ideas in the poems by identifying and comparing their themes. Follow these steps:

1. **Decide on the most important details.** As a group, review the information you gathered in the previous chart. Determine which points you agree on and resolve disagreements by identifying evidence from the poems that support your ideas.
2. **Determine themes.** Write theme statements, or statements that express each poem's message about life or human nature. Use the chart below to help you track your group's ideas and identify possible themes.

	NOTES	POSSIBLE THEMES
"My Last Duchess"		
"Confession"		

3. **Compare the themes.** Work together as a group to determine similarities and differences between the themes.
4. **Develop your ideas.** Organize your ideas around your points of comparison, and provide evidence and explanations for each.
5. **Present to the class.** Determine how you will present your comparison, who will present it, and if the use of any visuals or diagrams would help clarify your points. Consider using technology as a presentation tool.

INDEPENDENT READING

? *ESSENTIAL QUESTIONS*

Review the four Essential Questions for this unit on page 587.

Reader's Choice

Setting a Purpose Select one or more of these options from your eBook to continue your exploration of the Essential Questions.

- Read the descriptions to see which text grabs your interest.
- Think about which genres you enjoy reading.

Notice & Note

In this unit, you practiced noticing and noting the signposts and asking big questions about nonfiction. As you read independently, these signposts and others will aid your understanding. Below are the anchor questions to ask when you read literature and nonfiction.

Reading Literature: Stories, Poems, and Plays	
Signpost	**Key Question**
Contrasts and Contradictions	Why did the character act that way?
Aha Moment	How might this change things?
Tough Questions	What does this make me wonder about?
Words of the Wiser	What's the lesson for the character?
Again and Again	Why might the author keep bringing this up?
Memory Moment	Why is this memory important?

Reading Nonfiction: Essays, Articles, and Arguments	
Signpost	**Key Question(s)**
Big Questions	What surprised me? What did the author think I already knew? What challenged, changed, or confirmed what I already knew?
Contrasts and Contradictions	What is the difference, and why does it matter?
Extreme or Absolute Language	Why did the author use this language?
Numbers and Stats	Why did the author use these numbers or amounts?
Quoted Words	Why was this person quoted or cited, and what did this add?
Word Gaps	Do I know this word from someplace else? Does it seem like technical talk for this topic? Do clues in the sentence help me understand the word?

INDEPENDENT READING

You can preview these texts in Unit 5 of your eBook.

Then check off the text or texts that you select to read on your own.

POEM

Sonnet 43
Elizabeth Barrett Browning

Is love an intense but simple feeling or a complex emotion with many dimensions?

POEM

Remembrance
Emily Brontë

Can love survive a loved one's death, or does it change as the survivor grows older?

ARTICLE

The Great Exhibition
Lara Kriegel

What looked like a giant greenhouse and brought visitors to London from all over the world?

SHORT STORY

Christmas Storms and Sunshine
Elizabeth Cleghorn Gaskell

Can two families divided by politics overcome their differences and discover the benefits of friendship?

ESSAY

Evidence of Progress
Thomas Babington Macaulay

During times of turmoil, how can you tell whether a nation is taking steps toward a better future?

Collaborate and Share Meet with a partner to discuss what you learned from at least one of your independent readings.

- Give a brief synopsis or summary of the text.
- Describe any signposts that you noticed in the text and explain what they revealed to you.
- Describe what you most enjoyed or found most challenging about the text. Give specific examples.
- Decide whether you would recommend the text to others. Why or why not?

Go to the **Reading Studio** for more resources on **Notice & Note.**

WRITING TASK

Write a Research Report

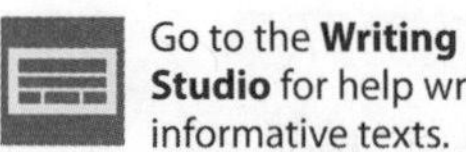

Go to the **Writing Studio** for help writing informative texts.

This unit focuses on the Victorian period, when rapid technological changes affected nearly every aspect of society, including government, transportation, communication, religious practice, and relations between classes. For this writing task, you will do some research and use outside sources to write about how technology has affected society in our own time. For an example of an essay that uses outside sources well, review the article "The Victorians Had the Same Concerns About Technology As We Do."

As you write your research report, you can use the notes from your Response Log that you filled out after reading the texts in this unit.

Writing Prompt

Read the information in the box below.

This is the topic or context for your research report.

> **Both social science research and literature often explore the effects of technological developments on our lives.**

Think carefully about the following question.

How might this Essential Question relate to your research report?

> **Which invention has had the greatest impact on your life?**

How does the research you will do relate to the topic of your report?

Write a research report about one modern invention that has changed the social order or the way people live their daily lives.

Be sure to —

Review these points as you write and again when you finish. Make any needed changes.

- ❑ develop research questions
- ❑ review many possible sources
- ❑ choose the best sources for your essay
- ❑ organize your report logically
- ❑ use evidence from your sources to support your own ideas
- ❑ cite each outside source in the text
- ❑ use quotations, paraphrasing, and summarizing; state most facts and ideas in your own words, using direct quotations when appropriate
- ❑ present a thesis statement
- ❑ include an introduction and conclusion

Plan

Once you have thought about the writing prompt, it's time to plan your research and the writing of your report. First, identify an area of focus related to the topic. It can be helpful to think about background reading you have done or personal interests that you have. As part of your planning, you must also consider your purpose and audience. Follow the steps below to get started planning your research project.

Research Report Planning Table	
Identify research questions	What are some recent inventions? How do they affect my life?
Identify ideas from background reading	
Identify personal interests related to the topic	
Focus on one question/topic	
State your purpose	
Identify your audience	

Background Reading Review the notes you have taken in your Response Log that relate to the question, "Which invention has had the greatest impact on your life?" Texts in this unit provide background reading that will help you formulate and develop the topic for your research report.

Go to **Writing Informative Texts: Developing a Topic** for help planning your research report.

Notice & Note

From Reading to Writing

As you plan your research report, apply what you've learned about signposts to your own writing. Remember that writers use common features called signposts to help convey their message to readers.

Think how you can incorporate **Quoted Words** into your report.

Go to the **Reading Studio** for more resources on **Notice & Note.**

Use the notes from your Response Log as you plan your research report.

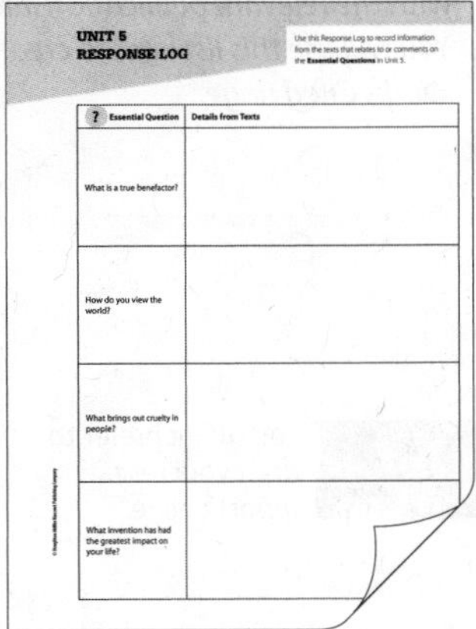

UNIT 5
RESPONSE LOG

Use this Response Log to record information from the texts that relates to or comments on the **Essential Questions** in Unit 5.

? Essential Question	Details from Texts
What is a true benefactor?	
How do you view the world?	
What brings out cruelty in people?	
What invention has had the greatest impact on your life?	

WRITING TASK

Go to **Writing Informative Texts: Organizing Ideas** for help organizing your research report.

Organize Your Ideas After you have gathered ideas in your planning table, you need to organize them in a way that will help you draft your research report. You can use the chart below to help you organize your draft before you start writing.

Organize Your Research Report	
Write a "hook." *The opening sentence of your report should grab the reader's attention.*	
Write a thesis statement. *Use your planning table to write a thesis statement for your report.*	
Outline the body of your report. *List at least three key ideas that support your thesis statement.*	
Write a conclusion. *Restate your thesis statement, and summarize your key ideas.*	
Keep a list of your sources. *List all of the sources you plan to use along with the relevant publication information. You will use this list later to create your Works Cited page.*	

2 Develop a Draft

You might prefer to draft your research report online.

Once you have completed your planning, you will be ready to begin drafting your research report. Refer to your graphic organizers as well as any notes you took as you studied the texts in this unit. This material will provide ideas for you to develop as you write. Using a word processor or online writing application makes it easier to make changes or move sentences around later when you are ready to revise your first draft.

Use the Mentor Text

Author's Craft

Your introduction should start with a "hook" to grab the reader's attention. It should also provide background on the topic. Near the end of your introduction, you should provide a thesis statement that tells the reader the main idea of your report. The thesis statement is a **claim**—something the reader might not already know or agree with. Note the introduction from "The Victorians Had the Same Concerns About Technology As We Do."

Many of us struggle with the bombardment of information we receive and experience anxiety as a result of new media. . . .

This is the background that introduces the topic.

Though the technologies may change, these fears actually have a very long history. . . . Literary, medical, and cultural responses in the Victorian age to the perceived problems of stress and overwork anticipate many of the preoccupations of our own era. . . . .

This is the thesis statement. The reader should expect the author to present evidence supporting this statement.

Apply What You've Learned Review the notes from your research and the ideas in your planning table. Then, write a statement supported by your key ideas and evidence from your research. Remember that your thesis statement should present a claim that the reader may not already know or agree with.

Genre Characteristics

When writers use evidence from their sources, they introduce the idea or fact by identifying the source. Then, they present it by paraphrasing, summarizing, or using a direct quotation. Notice how the author of the article uses signal phrases to connect her sources with the ideas the sources support.

Thomas Carlyle, for example, lamented the new lack of direct contact with society and nature. . . . Print publications were fast becoming the principal medium of public debate and influence. . . .

The author identifies the source and uses the signal phrase "for example" to show that the source supports the author's key idea.

Apply What You've Learned Introduce each source you use by giving the name of a person, organization, and/or the publication associated with the source. Use signal phrases to connect the source with the key idea it supports.

3 Revise

Go to **Writing Informative Texts: Precise Language and Vocabulary** for help revising your research report.

On Your Own Once you have written your draft, you'll want to go back and look for ways to improve your research report. As you reread and revise, think about whether you have achieved your purpose. The Revision Guide will help you focus on specific elements to make your writing stronger.

Revision Guide

Ask Yourself	Tips	Revision Techniques
1. Does the introduction engage the reader, provide background information, and clearly state the thesis?	**Circle** the engaging introduction, **underline** the background information, and **bracket** the thesis statement.	**Add** a quotation or interesting detail to hook readers. **Add** necessary background information. **Add** a thesis statement.
2. Does the body include only relevant key ideas and supporting evidence?	**Mark** the key ideas. **Number** supporting evidence for each key idea.	**Delete** irrelevant ideas and evidence. **Add** evidence to support ideas.
3. Are sources credited and citations punctuated correctly?	**Place check marks** next to material that requires citation.	**Add** parenthetical citations if necessary, and **correct** punctuation.
4. Does the conclusion restate the thesis?	**Bracket** the restatement of the thesis.	**Add** a sentence or two restating the thesis.
5. Is the Works Cited list complete and correctly formatted?	**Compare** parenthetical citations with the entries in your Works Cited list.	**Add** Works Cited entries if necessary and revise incorrectly formatted entries.

ACADEMIC VOCABULARY

As you conduct your **peer review,** be sure to use these words.

- ❑ **abandon**
- ❑ **confine**
- ❑ **conform**
- ❑ **depress**
- ❑ **reluctance**

With a Partner Once you and your partner have worked through the Revision Guide on your own, exchange research reports and evaluate each other's draft in a **peer review.** Focus on providing revision suggestions for at least three of the items mentioned in the chart. Explain why you think your partner's draft should be revised and what your specific suggestions are.

When receiving feedback from your partner, listen attentively and ask questions to make sure you fully understand the revision suggestions.

 Edit

Once you have addressed the organization, use of supporting evidence, and logical flow of ideas in your paper, you can look to improve the finer points of your draft. Edit for effective sentence structure, smooth syntax, precise word choice, and Standard English grammar and punctuation.

Language Conventions

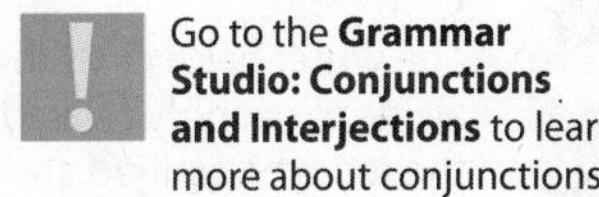

Go to the **Grammar Studio: Conjunctions and Interjections** to learn more about conjunctions.

Combining Sentences Too many short sentences can result in a stiff style that doesn't clearly show the relationship between ideas. One way that writers connect ideas is by combining sentences using coordinating and subordinating conjunctions. In the examples below, the numbers **[1]** and **[2]** show the two ideas that are combined.

Coordinating Conjunctions	Example
and, but, or, so, therefore	**[1]** Print publications were fast becoming the principal medium of public debate and influence, **[2] and** they were shaping and, in Carlyle's view, distorting human learning and communications.

Subordinating Conjunctions	Example
Time: *when, as, before, after*	**While [1]** we cannot draw too strict a line of comparison between 19th-century attitudes to such technologies as the telegraph, train, telephone, and newspaper and our own responses as a culture to the advent of the internet and the mobile phone, **[2]** there are parallels that almost argue against the Luddite position.
Contrast: *although, even though, even if, while*	
Cause/effect: *because, if, unless*	

Note that when you use a subordinating conjunction, it can come at the beginning or in the middle of the sentence.

5 Publish

Finalize your research and choose a way to share it with your audience. Consider these options:

- Share it as an article on an open web platform.
- Ask your school librarian to make your work available in the library.

WRITING TASK

Use the scoring guide to evaluate your essay.

Writing Task Scoring Guide: Research Report			
	Organization/Progression	**Development of Ideas**	**Use of Language and Conventions**
4	• The organization of the report is clear and appropriate to the purpose. • The writer has a clear thesis with all ideas strongly related to it, and the report is unified and coherent. • The writer's progression of ideas is logical, with meaningful transitions and sentence connections.	• Ideas are effectively developed; examples from outside sources are specific and well chosen. • The report is thoughtful and engaging. The writer uses material from outside sources to support personal thoughts and ideas. • The writer demonstrates a thorough understanding of research and writing.	• Word choice is purposeful and precise, maintains an appropriate tone, and contributes to the quality of the report. • The writer demonstrates a consistent command of spelling, capitalization, punctuation, grammar, and usage. • All sources cited are in correct format.
3	• The organization of the report is generally clear and appropriate to the purpose. • The writer has a clear thesis with most ideas related to it. • The paper is coherent, though it may lack unity in some places. • The writer's progression of ideas is generally logical and controlled, with smooth transitions and sentence connections.	• The development of ideas is sufficient; details and examples from outside sources are generally specific and appropriate. • The report reflects thoughtfulness. The writing is original rather than formulaic; evidence presented supports the writer's ideas. • The writer demonstrates a good understanding of research and writing.	• Word choice is mostly clear and specific, reflecting an awareness of purpose and tone, and contributing to the quality and clarity of the report. • The writer demonstrates adequate command of sentence boundaries, spelling, capitalization, punctuation, grammar, and usage. • Most sources cited are in correct format.
2	• The organizing structure of the report is evident but not always appropriate. • The report lacks clarity because the writer uses unsuitable organizational strategies. • Most ideas are related to the specified topic, but the writer's thesis is weak or unclear. • Transitions and sentence connections do not contribute to the progression of ideas.	• Ideas are only minimally developed. Examples are inappropriate or poorly presented. • The report reflects little thoughtfulness; it presents evidence from outside sources but not personal thoughts and ideas. • The writer demonstrates only a limited understanding of the task. • The writer's progression of ideas is not always logical and controlled.	• Word choice reflects only a basic awareness of the purpose of informative writing. It weakens the quality and clarity of the report. • The writer demonstrates only partial command of sentence boundaries, spelling, capitalization, punctuation, grammar, and usage. • Few sources cited are correctly formatted.
1	• The organizing structure of the report is inappropriate, and its weakness leads to a lack of clarity and direction in the report. • Most ideas are related to the specified topic, but the thesis lacks details or is unclear or illogical. • The writer fails to focus on the topic, includes extraneous information, or shifts abruptly from idea to idea.	• Ideas are poorly developed; the details and examples used are inappropriate, vague, or insufficient. • The writer's response to the prompt is vague or confused. • The report may be only weakly linked to the prompt, or developed in a manner that demonstrates a lack of understanding of the task. • The progression of ideas is weak.	• Word choice is vague or limited, reflecting little or no awareness of the purpose. It fails to establish an appropriate tone and detracts from the quality of the report. • The writer has little or no command of sentence boundaries, spelling, capitalization, punctuation, grammar, and usage. • Sources are not cited.

Give a Multimodal Presentation

You will now adapt your research report for a multimodal presentation to your classmates. You will also listen to their presentations, ask questions to better understand their ideas, and help them improve their work.

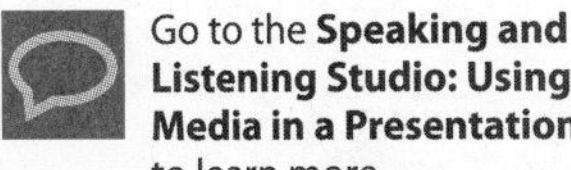

Go to the **Speaking and Listening Studio: Using Media in a Presentation** to learn more.

1 Adapt Your Report for a Multimodal Presentation

Review your research report. Use the chart below to guide you as you adapt your report to create slides and other presentation materials to convey your thesis, and present your key ideas in a clear and engaging way.

Presentation Planning Chart	
Plan Your Slides How will you present your introduction, thesis statement, key ideas and supporting evidence, and conclusion? What is the best way to convey this information on each slide?	
Use Graphics, Images, and a Consistent Design What design elements will make your slides visually appealing? How will these elements relate to the content of your report?	
Consider Adding Music, Animation, or Sound Effects Would including music, audio clips, or sound effects enhance the content of your presentation?	
Use Verbal Techniques Which sections of your report should be presented slowly? Which sections need emphasis?	
Use Nonverbal Techniques Which slides stand on their own and could be presented with little or no narration?	

2 Practice with a Partner or Group

Once you've completed your draft, practice with a partner or group to improve both your presentation and your delivery.

As you work to improve your presentations, be sure to follow discussion rules:

- ❑ **listen closely to each other**
- ❑ **don't interrupt**
- ❑ **stay on topic**
- ❑ **ask only helpful, relevant questions**
- ❑ **provide only clear, thoughtful, and direct answers**

Practice Effective Verbal Techniques

- ❑ **Enunciation** Replace words that you stumble over, and rearrange sentences so that your delivery is smooth.
- ❑ **Voice Modulation and Pitch** Use your voice to display enthusiasm and emphasis.
- ❑ **Speaking Rate** Speak slowly enough that listeners understand you. Pause now and then to let them consider important points.
- ❑ **Volume** Remember that listeners at the back of the room must be able to hear you.

Practice Effective Nonverbal Techniques

- ❑ **Eye Contact** Try to let your eyes rest on each member of the audience at least once.
- ❑ **Facial Expression** Smile, frown, or raise an eyebrow to show your feelings or to emphasize points.
- ❑ **Gestures** Stand tall and relaxed, and use natural gestures—shrugs, nods, or shakes of your head—to add meaning and interest to your presentation.

Provide and Consider Advice for Improvement

As a listener, pay close attention. Take notes about ways that presenters can improve their presentations and use verbal and nonverbal techniques more effectively. Paraphrase and summarize each presenter's thesis and key ideas to confirm your understanding, and ask questions to clarify any confusing expressions or ideas.

As a presenter, listen closely to questions and consider ways to revise your presentation to make sure your key ideas are clear and logically sequenced. Remember to ask for suggestions about how you might change onscreen text or images to make your presentation clearer and more interesting.

3 Deliver Your Presentation

Use the advice you received during practice to make final changes to your presentation. Then, using effective verbal and nonverbal techniques, present it to your classmates.

Reflect on the Unit

By completing your research report, you have created a writing product that pulls together and expresses your thoughts about the reading you have done in this unit. Now is a good time to reflect on what you have learned.

Reflect on the Essential Questions

- Review the four Essential Questions on page 587. How have your answers to these questions changed in response to the texts you've read in this unit?
- What are some examples from the texts you've read that show how technology has altered the social order and the ways in which people live their daily lives?

Reflect on Your Reading

- Which selections were the most interesting or surprising to you?
- From which selection did you learn the most about how technology affects people's lives?

Reflect on the Writing Task

- What difficulties did you encounter while working on your research report? How might you avoid them next time?
- Which parts of the research report were the easiest to write? The hardest to write? Why?
- What improvements did you make to your research report as you were revising?

UNIT 5 SELECTIONS

- **from *Jane Eyre***
- **"Factory Reform"**
- **"The Lady of Shalott"**
- **from *Great Expectations***
- **"The Victorians Had the Same Concerns About Technology As We Do"**
- **"Dover Beach"**
- **"The Darkling Thrush"**
- **"My Last Duchess"**
- **"Confession"**

UNIT 6

NEW IDEAS, NEW VOICES

MODERN AND CONTEMPORARY LITERATURE

"The English language is nobody's special property. It is the property of the imagination; it is the property of the language itself."

—Derek Walcott

Discuss the Essential Questions with your whole class or in small groups. As you read New Ideas, New Voices, consider how the selections explore these questions.

? *ESSENTIAL QUESTION:*

What makes people feel insecure?

In the modern world, safety and security seem to be emphasized more than ever before in history. Yet people continue to experience insecurity in their daily lives, their relationships, and even their sense of self. How can insecurity affect a person from within? What types of insecurity come from the world around us? How much control do we have over the sources of insecurity in our lives?

? *ESSENTIAL QUESTION:*

Why is it hard to resist social pressure?

You have probably heard many times that the company you keep can influence your thoughts and actions for good or for bad. Peer pressure is certainly a powerful force, whether it is working on individuals or groups. Why do we feel the need to go along with the crowd? What are the benefits and the dangers of conforming to society's expectations? What happens when social pressure gets out of control?

? *ESSENTIAL QUESTION:*

What is the power of symbols?

At the most basic level, a symbol is anything that represents or stands for something else. We are surrounded by symbols every day. Written symbols appear on road signs and electronic devices. Symbols for individuals and concepts appear in books, music, movies, and TV shows. Why do we use symbols? Are symbols usually more or less effective than literal representations? How do differences in interpretation affect the power of symbols?

? *ESSENTIAL QUESTION:*

When should the government interfere in our decisions?

The question of how much influence a government should have over the lives of its citizens is an old one. Over the centuries, it has sparked debates, influenced the development of political parties, and even contributed to wars. Many people agree that some governmental authority is necessary to keep peace and order, but how much interference is too much? Conversely, when does it become necessary for individual rights to yield to government authority?

MODERN AND CONTEMPORARY LITERATURE

At the turn of the 20th century, Great Britain was a nation at its peak. Under the reign of Victoria's successor, Edward VII, England was a land of prosperity, stability, and world dominance. However, vast changes were on the horizon. Over the course of the next hundred years, Britain would become embroiled in wars, experience economic depression, and face the end of its once-massive empire.

World Wars In 1914 a Serbian nationalist assassinated Archduke Franz Ferdinand, heir to the throne of Austria-Hungary. Austria declared war on Serbia, and like a line of dominoes, alliances fell into place: Austria and Germany on one side; Russia, France, and Britain on the other. Both sides became locked in bloody trench warfare. The Great War, as the conflict was then known, dragged on, devastating Europe, killing or wounding virtually an entire generation of young men, and bringing a profound sense of disillusionment to the people. In 1917 the United States entered the war, leading to Germany's capitulation the following year and an uneasy peace.

Britain had lost 750,000 men, and those who returned from World War I alive came home to unemployment and economic depression. France and Germany were hit even harder, while Russia was plunged into revolution and civil war. War-torn European nations turned to the United States for loans, but in 1929 the United States stock market crashed, causing a worldwide depression. In the economic and political chaos of the 1920s and early 1930s, dictators seized power in Italy, Russia, and Germany. In 1939 German dictator Adolf Hitler made the decision to invade Poland, prompting Britain and France to declare war on Germany. Italy and Japan allied themselves with Germany, and World War II began.

Terrible as the Great War had been, for most British citizens it was a distant tragedy on foreign battlefields. World War II was different. After the fall of France in 1940, German planes began to attack Britain. Bombs rained down on London, and the entire population mobilized to defend the home front. Britain held out against Germany until the United States entered the war in 1941, and Hitler was finally defeated in 1945.

COLLABORATIVE DISCUSSION
In a small group, review the timeline and discuss how outside events influenced British politics and literature.

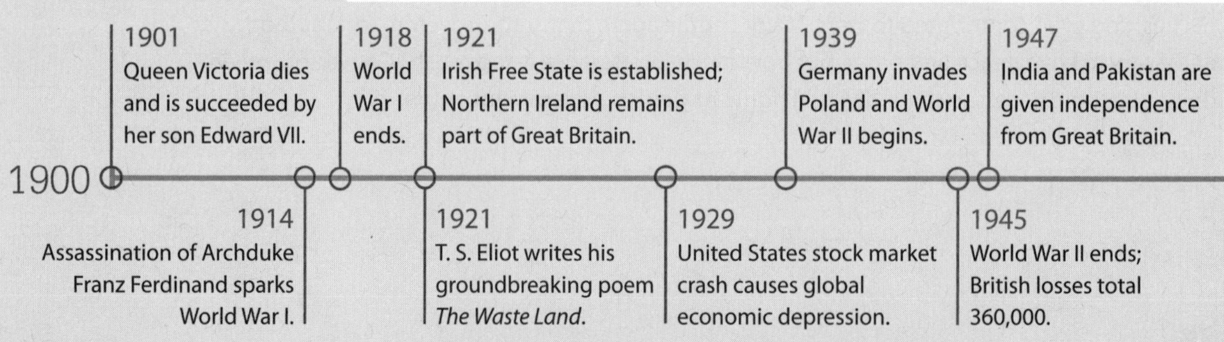

The End of Empire After World War II, Britain was financially drained, burdened by debt and the need to rebuild its cities. Everything was rationed. Determined to provide at least the basic necessities, the government transformed Britain with a new national health care system and public education. Concerned with domestic issues, leaders had little desire to cling to colonies that were all too eager for self-rule. After World War I, Britain's grasp on its empire had already begun to loosen as the spirit of nationalism swept Europe and the colonial empires. Britain granted ever-greater degrees of self-determination to its colonies, eventually making some of these lands partners in the British Commonwealth of Nations rather than continuing to treat them as possessions. Soon after World War II, Britain gave India its independence. In the decades that followed, Britain yielded to nationalistic and economic pressures and relinquished control of most of its remaining colonies.

Literature in the 20th Century and Beyond After World War I, Europe was a place of uncertainty and upheaval. In England, the previously stable social order based on community and class distinctions was giving way to the anonymity of urban life. In the arts, modernism was a way of trying to make sense of this new, fragmented world. Visual artists, composers, and writers rejected traditional forms and experimented with new styles that better reflected the realities and values of modern life.

RESEARCH
What about this historical period interests you? Choose a topic, event, or person to learn more about. Then, add your own entry to the timeline.

1949
George Orwell publishes *1984*, a nightmarish vision of a totalitarian England.

1952
Elizabeth II ascends the throne.

1979
Margaret Thatcher becomes the first female prime minister.

1997
Great Britain returns Hong Kong to China after 155 years of colonial rule.

2005
Bombs explode on the London Underground and a bus, killing 56.

2007
British Indian author Salman Rushdie is awarded a knighthood from Queen Elizabeth II.

Present

New narrative styles rejected traditional linear plot and character development, and instead placed the reader inside the character's mind. Many writers felt a sense of alienation from their own society after witnessing the horrors of war, and as a result explored themes of isolation, human relationships and vulnerabilities, and disillusionment.

The end of the British Empire also shaped and continues to shape literature. Writers from former colonies explore issues related to their countries' colonial past, while writers who have immigrated to England often address cultural tensions in their works. The multicultural perspective these writers bring has broadened the horizons of contemporary British literature.

CHECK YOUR UNDERSTANDING

Choose the best answer to each question.

1 Which most directly caused the outbreak of World War II?

A Italy's and Japan's alliance with Germany

B The crash of the United States stock market

C Hitler's seizure of power in Germany

D The invasion of Poland by Germany

2 British politicians after World War II —

F wanted to hold the British Empire together as long as possible

G believed that strengthening the colonies would help Britain recover from the war

H placed less emphasis on empire and focused more on domestic issues

J immediately granted independence to all former British colonies

3 Which was a primary aspect of modernism?

A Focus on nationalistic perspectives in the arts and literature

B Rejection of traditional forms in the arts and literature

C Focus on war recovery and domestic affairs in politics

D Rejection of colonialism and empire building in politics

ACADEMIC VOCABULARY

Academic Vocabulary words are words you use when you discuss and write about texts. In this unit, you will learn the following five words:

- [x] **arbitrary**
- [ ] **controversy**
- [ ] **convince**
- [ ] **denote**
- [ ] **undergo**

Study the Word Network to learn more about the word **arbitrary.**

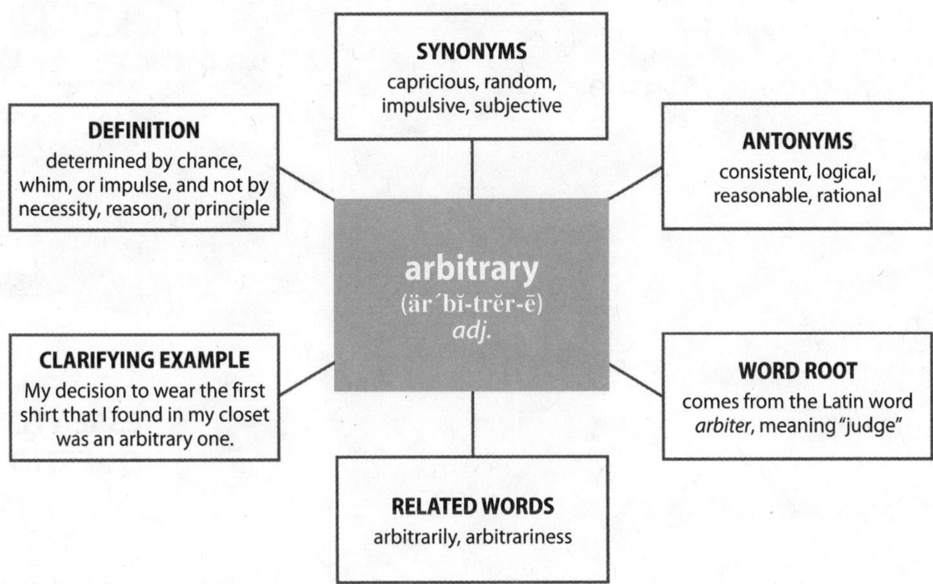

Write and Discuss Discuss your completed Word Network with a partner, making sure to talk through all of the boxes until you both understand the word, its synonyms, antonyms, and related forms. Then, fill out a Word Network for the remaining four words. Use a dictionary or online resource to help you complete the activity.

Go online to access the Word Networks.

RESPOND TO THE ESSENTIAL QUESTIONS

In this unit, you will explore four different **Essential Questions** about New Ideas, New Voices. As you read each selection, you will gather your ideas about one of these questions and write about it in the **Response Log** that appears on page R6. At the end of the unit, you will have the opportunity to write an **argument** related to one of the Essential Questions. Filling out the Response Log after you read each text will help you prepare for this writing task.

You can also go online to access the Response Log.

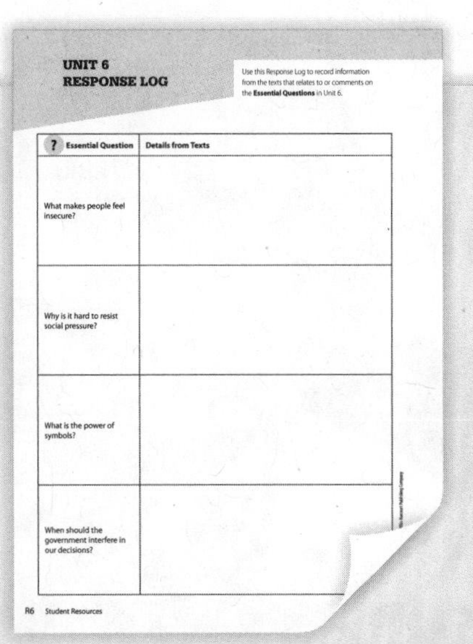

UNIT 6 RESPONSE LOG

Use this Response Log to record information from the texts that relates to or comments on the **Essential Questions** in Unit 6.

? Essential Question	Details from Texts
What makes people feel insecure?	
Why is it hard to resist social pressure?	
What is the power of symbols?	
When should the government interfere in our decisions?	

R6 Student Resources

ANALYZE & APPLY

A CUP OF TEA

Short Story by **Katherine Mansfield**

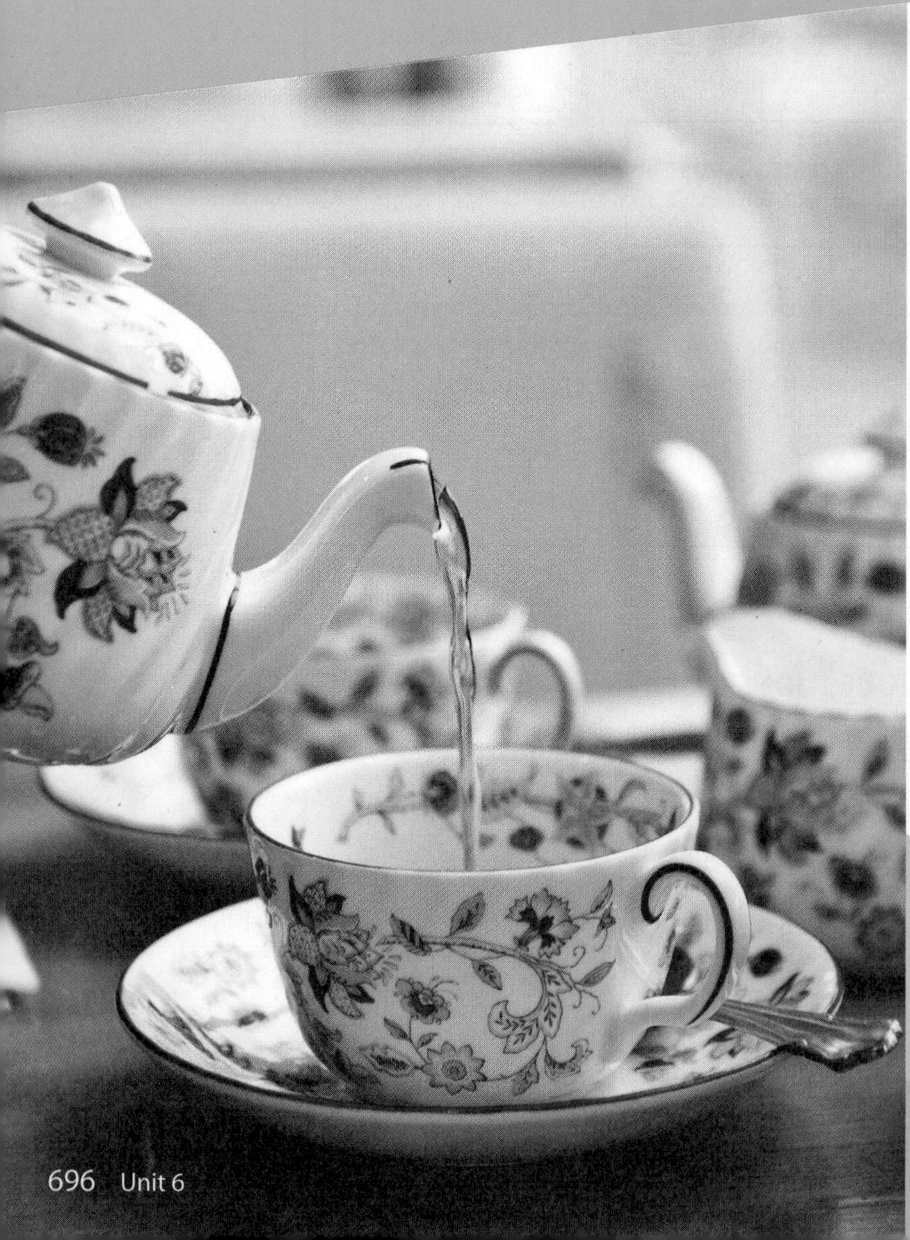

What makes people feel insecure?

QUICK START

How can social status affect a person's self-image? Discuss this question with a small group of students.

ANALYZE THIRD-PERSON POINT OF VIEW

When a writer uses the **third-person point of view,** the narrator is not a character in the story but an outside observer. Sometimes a third-person narrator is **omniscient** and can describe what all the characters are thinking and feeling. In modern fiction, authors more commonly use a **limited** third-person narrator, describing the thoughts, feelings, and observations of only one character. Readers may feel like they are looking over the shoulder of that character as the story's action unfolds. This technique often helps readers become more emotionally involved with the chosen character, but it can also lead to surprises because the narration is limited by the character's awareness and understanding of events.

In "A Cup of Tea," Katherine Mansfield's use of the third-person limited point of view influences the development of the characters. The narrator starts off describing the protagonist, Rosemary Fell, from a distance, as if discussing her with a friend. But soon the narrator focuses in on Rosemary, using slang and exaggeration to mimic Rosemary's speech and suggest how she perceives the world around her. As you read the story, notice how the narrator's conversational tone subtly reveals Rosemary's inner life.

GENRE ELEMENTS: SHORT STORY

- includes the basic elements of fiction—setting, characters, plot, conflict, and theme
- centers on a particular moment or event or follows the life of one character
- can be read in one sitting
- may be told by a first-person narrator who is a character in the story or a third-person narrator outside the story

EVALUATE A CHARACTER

Most complex characters are not entirely good or bad, and readers need to take various factors into account when evaluating them. A character's motivation may influence how you view his or her behavior; for example, a charitable donation may be motivated by compassion, vanity, or a combination of both. When evaluating a character, you should also consider the story's historical, social, and economic context. "A Cup of Tea" is set in London in the early 1900s, a time when rigid class distinctions would have made it seem improper for a wealthy woman to socialize with an impoverished one. This context influences the story's plot and theme, as well as Mansfield's characterization of the protagonist, Rosemary.

As you read "A Cup of Tea," use a chart like this one to help you evaluate Rosemary.

ACTION	MOTIVATION	OUTCOME

GET READY

CRITICAL VOCABULARY

presentable **tactfully** **listless** **vile** **engagement**

To check your familiarity with the Critical Vocabulary words, answer the following questions.

1. What word would you use to describe something you strongly dislike?
2. Which word might describe someone who has fallen ill?
3. Which word describes how you try to look to meet someone's parents?
4. What's a word for when you have social plans?
5. Which word describes how you should handle a delicate situation?

LANGUAGE CONVENTIONS

Precise Details In both fiction and nonfiction, authors use precise details to shape and inform the perception of readers. Readers evaluate an author's use of details to analyze key ideas.

> **For he took a pencil, leaned over the counter, and his pale bloodless fingers crept timidly towards those rosy, flashing ones, as he murmured gently: "If I may venture to point out to madam, the flowers on the little lady's bodice."**

In this sentence, the detail of how Rosemary perceives her own fingers in comparison to the shopkeeper's gives us an insight into her character and her habit of comparing herself favorably to others. This is a key idea in the development of the story's theme.

ANNOTATION MODEL

NOTICE & NOTE 

As you read, notice how the third-person limited point of view shapes your impression of Rosemary. Pay attention to details and word choices that provide hints about Rosemary's character and motivation. In the model you can see one student's notes about the narrator's description of Rosemary in the opening paragraph.

Rosemary Fell was not exactly beautiful. No, you couldn't have called her beautiful. Pretty? Well, if you took her to pieces . . . But why be so cruel as to take anyone to pieces? She was young, brilliant, extremely modern, exquisitely well dressed, amazingly well read in the newest of the new books, and her parties were the most delicious mixture of the really important people and . . . artists—quaint creatures, discoveries of hers, some of them too terrifying for words, but others quite presentable and amusing.

The narrator describes the protagonist as if she is talking about a friend. The tone is conversational and intimate.

The narrator is sympathetic towards Rosemary but also seems to mock her a little bit.

NOTICE & NOTE

BACKGROUND

Katherine Mansfield *(1888–1923) was born in New Zealand. She disliked her native country and was eager to leave home at 19 to settle in London, where she had attended school several years earlier. Mansfield struggled to earn a living in England and fell into some troubled romantic relationships. When she was 29 she contracted tuberculosis. In the last year of her life, Mansfield wrote some of her finest stories. By the end of her brief career, she gained recognition as a master of the modern short story, emphasizing psychological realism over dramatic action.*

A CUP OF TEA

Short Story by Katherine Mansfield

SETTING A PURPOSE

As you read, pay attention to the author's use of third-person limited point of view and think about how the story might be different if it were told in omniscient point of view.

1 Rosemary Fell was not exactly beautiful. No, you couldn't have called her beautiful. Pretty? Well, if you took her to pieces . . . But why be so cruel as to take anyone to pieces? She was young, brilliant, extremely modern, exquisitely well dressed, amazingly well read in the newest of the new books, and her parties were the most delicious mixture of the really important people and . . . artists—quaint creatures, discoveries of hers, some of them too terrifying for words, but others quite **presentable** and amusing.

2 Rosemary had been married two years. She had a duck[1] of a boy. No, not Peter—Michael. And her husband absolutely adored her. They were rich, really rich, not just comfortably well off, which is odious and stuffy and sounds like one's grandparents. But if Rosemary wanted to shop she would go to Paris as you and I would go to Bond Street.[2] If she wanted to buy flowers, the car

Notice & Note

Use the side margins to notice and note signposts in the text.

LANGUAGE CONVENTIONS

Annotate: Mark words and phrases used to describe Rosemary in paragraph 1.

Draw Conclusions: What do these details suggest about how society views her?

presentable
(prĭ-zĕn´tə-bəl) *adj.* fit for introduction to others.

---

[1] **duck:** a British expression for a darling person or thing.

[2] **Bond Street:** a London street famous for its fashionable shops.

NOTICE & NOTE

pulled up at that perfect shop in Regent Street, and Rosemary inside the shop just gazed in her dazzled, rather exotic way, and said: "I want those and those and those. Give me four bunches of those. And that jar of roses. Yes, I'll have all the roses in the jar. No, no lilac. I hate lilac. It's got no shape." The attendant bowed and put the lilac out of sight, as though this was only too true; lilac was dreadfully shapeless. "Give me those stumpy little tulips. Those red and white ones." And she was followed to the car by a thin shopgirl staggering under an immense white paper armful that looked like a baby in long clothes. . . .

3 One winter afternoon she had been buying something in a little antique shop in Curzon Street. It was a shop she liked. For one thing, one usually had it to oneself. And then the man who kept it was ridiculously fond of serving her. He beamed whenever she came in. He clasped his hands; he was so gratified he could scarcely speak. Flattery, of course. All the same, there was something . . .

4 "You see, madam," he would explain in his low respectful tones, "I love my things. I would rather not part with them than sell them to someone who does not appreciate them, who has not that fine feeling which is so rare. . . ." And, breathing deeply, he unrolled a tiny square of blue velvet and pressed it on the glass counter with his pale fingertips.

ANALYZE THIRD-PERSON POINT OF VIEW

Annotate: Mark the sentence in paragraph 5 that suggests what the shopkeeper may be thinking about Rosemary's hands.

Evaluate: Does this suggestion reflect his thoughts or Rosemary's? Explain.

5 Today it was a little box. He had been keeping it for her. He had shown it to nobody as yet. An exquisite little enamel box with a glaze so fine it looked as though it had been baked in cream. On the lid a minute creature stood under a flowery tree, and a more minute creature still had her arms around his neck. Her hat, really no bigger than a geranium petal, hung from a branch; it had green ribbons. And there was a pink cloud like a watchful cherub[3] floating above their heads. Rosemary took her hands out of her long gloves. She always took off her gloves to examine such things. Yes, she liked it very much. She loved it; it was a great duck. She must have it. And, turning the creamy box, opening and shutting it, she couldn't help noticing how charming her hands were against the blue velvet. The shopman, in some dim cavern of his mind, may have dared to think so too. For he took a pencil, leaned over the counter, and his pale bloodless fingers crept timidly towards those rosy, flashing ones, as he murmured gently: "If I may venture to point out to madam, the flowers on the little lady's bodice."[4]

6 "Charming!" Rosemary admired the flowers. But what was the price? For a moment the shopman did not seem to hear. Then a murmur reached her. "Twenty-eight guineas,[5] madam."

---

[3] **cherub** (chĕr´əb): an angel depicted as a chubby child with wings.
[4] **bodice** (bŏd´ĭs): the part of a dress above the waist.
[5] **guineas** (gĭn´ēz): units of British money equal to one pound and one shilling, used mainly for pricing luxury items.

7 "Twenty-eight guineas." Rosemary gave no sign. She laid the little box down; she buttoned her gloves again. Twenty-eight guineas. Even if one is rich . . . She looked vague. She stared at a plump teakettle like a plump hen above the shopman's head, and her voice was dreamy as she answered: "Well, keep it for me—will you? I'll . . ."

8 But the shopman had already bowed as though keeping it for her was all any human being could ask. He would be willing, of course, to keep it for her forever.

9 The discreet door shut with a click. She was outside on the step, gazing at the winter afternoon. Rain was falling, and with the rain it seemed the dark came too, spinning down like ashes. There was a cold bitter taste in the air, and the new-lighted lamps looked sad. Sad were the lights in the houses opposite. Dimly they burned as if regretting something. And people hurried by, hidden under their hateful umbrellas. Rosemary felt a strange pang.[6] She pressed her muff to her breast; she wished she had the little box, too, to cling to. Of course, the car was there. She'd only to cross the pavement. But still she waited. There are moments, horrible moments in life, when one emerges from shelter and looks out, and it's awful. One oughtn't to give way to them. One ought to go home and have an extra-special tea. But at the very instant of thinking that, a young girl, thin, dark, shadowy—where had she come from?—was standing at Rosemary's elbow and a voice like a sigh, almost like a sob, breathed: "Madam, may I speak to you a moment?"

10 "Speak to me?" Rosemary turned. She saw a little battered creature with enormous eyes, someone quite young, no older than herself, who clutched at her coat-collar with reddened hands, and shivered as though she had just come out of the water.

11 "M-madam," stammered the voice. "Would you let me have the price of a cup of tea?"

12 "A cup of tea?" There was something simple, sincere in that voice; it wasn't in the least the voice of a beggar. "Then have you no money at all?" asked Rosemary.

13 "None, madam," came the answer.

14 "How extraordinary!" Rosemary peered through the dusk, and the girl gazed back at her. How more than extraordinary! And suddenly it seemed to Rosemary such an adventure. It was like something out of a novel by Dostoyevsky,[7] this meeting in the dusk. Supposing she took the girl home? Supposing she did do one of those things she was always reading about or seeing on the stage, what would happen? It would be thrilling. And she heard herself saying afterwards to the amazement of her friends: "I simply took her home

EVALUATE A CHARACTER

Annotate: Mark words and phrases in paragraph 14 that reveal Rosemary's thoughts about this encounter.

Evaluate: What is Rosemary's motivation for inviting the girl to her home?

---

[6] **pang** (păng): a sudden sharp pain or feeling.

[7] **Dostoyevsky** (dŏs-tə-yĕf´skē): Feodor Dostoyevsky, a 19th-century Russian author who wrote a number of novels and stories dealing with the lives of the poor.

with me," as she stepped forward and said to that dim person beside her: "Come home to tea with me."

15 The girl drew back startled. She even stopped shivering for a moment. Rosemary put out a hand and touched her arm. "I mean it," she said, smiling. And she felt how simple and kind her smile was. "Why won't you? Do. Come home with me now in my car and have tea."

16 "You—you don't mean it, madam," said the girl, and there was pain in her voice.

17 "But I do," cried Rosemary. "I want you to. To please me. Come along."

18 The girl put her fingers to her lips and her eyes devoured Rosemary. "You're—you're not taking me to the police station?" she stammered.

19 "The police station!" Rosemary laughed out. "Why should I be so cruel? No, I only want to make you warm and to hear—anything you care to tell me."

20 Hungry people are easily led. The footman[8] held the door of the car open, and a moment later they were skimming through the dusk.

EVALUATE A CHARACTER
Annotate: Mark words and phrases in paragraphs 21–22 that describe how Rosemary views her treatment of the girl.
Evaluate: What do these thoughts suggest about her character?

21 "There!" said Rosemary. She had a feeling of triumph as she slipped her hand through the velvet strap. She could have said, "Now I've got you," as she gazed at the little captive she had netted. But of course she meant it kindly. Oh, more than kindly. She was going to prove to this girl that—wonderful things did happen in life, that—fairy godmothers were real, that—rich people had hearts, and that women *were* sisters. She turned impulsively, saying: "Don't be frightened. After all, why shouldn't you come back with me? We're both women. If I'm the more fortunate, you ought to expect . . ."

22 But happily at that moment, for she didn't know how the sentence was going to end, the car stopped. The bell was rung, the door opened, and with a charming, protecting, almost embracing movement, Rosemary drew the other into the hall. Warmth, softness, light, a sweet scent, all those things so familiar to her she never even thought about them, she watched that other receive. It was fascinating. She was like the little rich girl in her nursery with all the cupboards to open, all the boxes to unpack.

23 "Come, come upstairs," said Rosemary, longing to begin to be generous. "Come up to my room." And, besides, she wanted to spare this poor little thing from being stared at by the servants; she decided as they mounted the stairs she would not even ring for Jeanne, but take off her things by herself. The great thing was to be natural!

24 And "There!" cried Rosemary again, as they reached her beautiful big bedroom with the curtains drawn, the fire leaping on

[8] **footman:** a household servant, here functioning as Rosemary's chauffeur.

her wonderful lacquer furniture, her gold cushions and the primrose and blue rugs.

25 The girl stood just inside the door; she seemed dazed. But Rosemary didn't mind that.

26 "Come and sit down," she cried, dragging her big chair up to the fire, "in this comfy chair. Come and get warm. You look so dreadfully cold."

27 "I daren't, madam," said the girl, and she edged backwards.

28 "Oh, please,"—Rosemary ran forward—"you mustn't be frightened, you mustn't, really. Sit down, and when I've taken off my things we shall go into the next room and have tea and be cozy. Why are you afraid?" And gently she half pushed the thin figure into its deep cradle.

29 But there was no answer. The girl stayed just as she had been put, with her hands by her sides and her mouth slightly open. To be quite sincere, she looked rather stupid. But Rosemary wouldn't acknowledge it. She leaned over her, saying: "Won't you take off your hat? Your pretty hair is all wet. And one is so much more comfortable without a hat, isn't one?"

30 There was a whisper that sounded like "Very good, madam," and the crushed hat was taken off.

31 "Let me help you off with your coat, too," said Rosemary.

32 The girl stood up. But she held on to the chair with one hand and let Rosemary pull. It was quite an effort. The other scarcely helped her at all. She seemed to stagger like a child, and the thought came and went through Rosemary's mind, that if people wanted helping they must respond a little, just a little, otherwise it became very difficult indeed. And what was she to do with the coat now? She left it on the floor, and the hat too. She was just going to take a cigarette off the mantelpiece when the girl said quickly, but so lightly and strangely: "I'm very sorry, madam, but I'm going to faint. I shall go off, madam, if I don't have something."

33 "Good heavens, how thoughtless I am!" Rosemary rushed to the bell.

34 "Tea! Tea at once! And some brandy immediately!"

35 The maid was gone again, but the girl almost cried out. "No, I don't want no brandy. I never drink brandy. It's a cup of tea I want, madam." And she burst into tears.

36 It was a terrible and fascinating moment. Rosemary knelt beside her chair.

37 "Don't cry, poor little thing," she said. "Don't cry." And she gave the other her lace handkerchief. She really was touched beyond words. She put her arm round those thin, birdlike shoulders.

38 Now at last the other forgot to be shy, forgot everything except that they were both women, and gasped out: "I can't go on no longer

ANALYZE THIRD-PERSON POINT OF VIEW

Annotate: In paragraph 32, underline Rosemary's thoughts about the girl's behavior and circle the girl's dialogue.

Analyze: How does the use of third-person limited point of view create irony here?

NOTICE & NOTE

like this. I can't bear it. I shall *do* away with myself. I can't bear no more."

39 "You shan't have to. I'll look after you. Don't cry anymore. Don't you see what a good thing it was that you met me? We'll have tea and you'll tell me everything. And I shall arrange something. I promise. *Do* stop crying. It's so exhausting. Please!"

40 The other did stop just in time for Rosemary to get up before the tea came. She had the table placed between them. She plied the poor little creature with everything, all the sandwiches, all the bread and butter, and every time her cup was empty she filled it with tea, cream and sugar. People always said sugar was so nourishing. As for herself she didn't eat; she smoked and looked away **tactfully** so that the other should not be shy.

tactfully
(tăkt′fəl-lē) *adv.* considerately and discreetly.

41 And really the effect of that slight meal was marvelous. When the tea table was carried away a new being, a light, frail creature with tangled hair, dark lips, deep, lighted eyes, lay back in the big chair in a kind of sweet languor,[9] looking at the blaze. Rosemary lit a fresh cigarette; it was time to begin.

42 "And when did you have your last meal?" she asked softly.

43 But at that moment the door-handle turned.

44 "Rosemary, may I come in?" It was Philip.

45 "Of course."

46 He came in. "Oh, I'm so sorry," he said, and stopped and stared.

47 "It's quite all right," said Rosemary smiling. "This is my friend, Miss—"

48 "Smith, madam," said the languid figure, who was strangely still and unafraid.

49 "Smith," said Rosemary. "We are going to have a little talk."

EVALUATE A CHARACTER

Annotate: Mark references to the girl's name in paragraphs 47–49.

Evaluate: What does it suggest about Rosemary that she hasn't asked for her name until now?

50 "Oh, yes," said Philip. "Quite," and his eye caught sight of the coat and hat on the floor. He came over to the fire and turned his back to it. "It's a beastly[10] afternoon," he said curiously, still looking at that **listless** figure, looking at its hands and boots, and then at Rosemary again.

51 "Yes, isn't it?" said Rosemary enthusiastically. "**Vile**."

listless
(lĭst′lĭs) *adj.* lacking energy or disinclined to exert effort; lethargic.

vile
(vīl) *adj.* unpleasant or objectionable.

52 Philip smiled his charming smile. "As a matter of fact," said he, "I wanted you to come into the library for a moment. Would you? Will Miss Smith excuse us?"

53 The big eyes were raised to him, but Rosemary answered for her. "Of course she will." And they went out of the room together.

54 "I say," said Philip, when they were alone. "Explain. Who is she? What does it all mean?"

[9] **languor** (lăng′gər): a dreamy, lazy state.
[10] **beastly:** awful; unpleasant.

55 Rosemary, laughing, leaned against the door and said: "I picked her up in Curzon Street. Really. She's a real pick-up. She asked me for the price of a cup of tea, and I brought her home with me."

56 "But what on earth are you going to do with her?" cried Philip.

57 "Be nice to her," said Rosemary quickly. "Be frightfully nice to her. Look after her. I don't know how. We haven't talked yet. But show her—treat her—make her feel—"

58 "My darling girl," said Philip, "you're quite mad, you know. It simply can't be done."

59 "I knew you'd say that," retorted Rosemary. "Why not? I want to. Isn't that a reason? And besides, one's always reading about these things. I decided—"

60 "But," said Philip slowly, and he cut the end of a cigar, "she's so astonishingly pretty."

61 "Pretty?" Rosemary was so surprised that she blushed. "Do you think so? I—I hadn't thought about it."

62 "Good Lord!" Philip struck a match. "She's absolutely lovely. Look again, my child. I was bowled over when I came into your room just now. However . . . I think you're making a ghastly mistake. Sorry, darling, if I'm crude and all that. But let me know if Miss Smith is going to dine with us in time for me to look up *The Milliner's Gazette*."[11]

AHA MOMENT

Notice & Note: Mark the sentence in paragraph 63 that describes how Philip's comments have affected Rosemary.

Infer: Why is Rosemary rushing to give money to Miss Smith?

63 "You absurd creature!" said Rosemary, and she went out of the library, but not back to her bedroom. She went to her writing-room and sat down at her desk. Pretty! Absolutely lovely! Bowled over! Her heart beat like a heavy bell. Pretty! Lovely! She drew her checkbook towards her. But no, checks would be no use, of course. She opened a drawer and took out five pound notes, looked at them, put two back, and holding the three squeezed in her hand, she went back to her bedroom.

64 Half an hour later Philip was still in the library, when Rosemary
65 came in. "I only wanted to tell you," said she, and she leaned against the door again and looked at him with her dazzled exotic gaze, "Miss Smith won't dine with us tonight."

66 Philip put down the paper. "Oh, what's happened? Previous **engagement**?"

engagement
(ĕn-gāj´mənt) *n.* a promise or agreement to be at a particular place at a particular time.

67 Rosemary came over and sat down on his knee. "She insisted on going," said she, "so I gave the poor little thing a present of money. I couldn't keep her against her will, could I?" she added softly.

68 Rosemary had just done her hair, darkened her eyes a little, and put on her pearls. She put up her hands and touched Philip's cheeks.

[11] ***The Milliner's Gazette***: an imaginary newsletter for working-class women. A milliner is a maker of women's hats.

69 "Do you like me?" said she, and her tone, sweet, husky, troubled him.

70 "I like you awfully," he said, and he held her tighter. "Kiss me."

71 There was a pause.

72 Then Rosemary said dreamily, "I saw a fascinating little box today. It cost twenty-eight guineas. May I have it?"

73 Philip jumped her on his knee. "You may, little wasteful one," said he.

74 But that was not really what Rosemary wanted to say.

75 "Philip," she whispered, and she pressed his head against her bosom, "am I *pretty?*"

CHECK YOUR UNDERSTANDING

Answer these questions before moving on to the **Analyze the Text** section on the following page.

1 In paragraphs 3–5 what can you infer about the shopkeeper?

A He has a secret crush on Rosemary.

B He uses flattery to sell expensive things to rich people.

C He isn't very interested in money.

D He wishes he didn't have to sell his things.

2 In paragraphs 10–14, which sentence suggests Rosemary's motivation for taking Miss Smith home with her?

F *"M-madam," stammered the voice. "Would you let me have the price of a cup of tea?"*

G *There was something simple, sincere in that voice; it wasn't in the least the voice of a beggar.*

H *It was like something out of a novel by Dostoyevsky, this meeting in the dusk.*

J *And she heard herself saying afterwards to the amazement of her friends: "I simply took her home with me. . . ."*

3 How does Rosemary's husband convince her to send the girl away?

A He plays on her insecurity about her looks.

B He embarrasses her for not reading the paper.

C He scolds her about money.

D He flatters her need to feel superior.

RESPOND

RESEARCH TIP

When researching many aspects of a broad subject, look for websites run by organizations dedicated to that subject, and look through the website's menu for a "Resources" page. This is a good way to find helpful and credible sources.

ANALYZE THE TEXT

Support your responses with evidence from the text. NOTEBOOK

1. **Analyze** How does the third-person limited point of view affect your reaction to Rosemary and her plan to help Miss Smith? How might the story have been different if told by an omniscient narrator?
2. **Draw Conclusions** Reread paragraphs 60–62. Why does Philip speak so enthusiastically to his wife about Miss Smith's attractiveness? Explain.
3. **Analyze** What theme about wealthy people does Mansfield convey in "A Cup of Tea"? How do Rosemary's actions and motivation in trying to help Miss Smith relate to this theme?
4. **Connect** "A Cup of Tea" is set in a time when wealthy women did not have professions and were expected to appear fashionable. How does this context influence your evaluation of Rosemary's character?
5. **Notice & Note** Rosemary abandons her plan after Philip makes her aware of Miss Smith's beauty. Has this realization changed Rosemary? Why or why not?

RESEARCH

"A Cup of Tea" was written in 1922, at a time when British and American women's lives were undergoing radical change. Do some research to find out about some of the social changes of the 1920s, and complete the graphic organizer.

SOCIAL CHANGES FOR WOMEN IN THE 1920s	
Education	
Political Power	
Labor and Employment	
Fashion	

Extend How did these changes affect women's relationships with men on an individual and societal level?

CREATE AND DEBATE

Write a Missing Scene from Another Point of View We know that Rosemary goes back to her bedroom and gives Miss Smith some money before asking her to leave, but the scene is not in the story. Write this scene from Miss Smith's perspective using the third-person limited point of view.

- ❑ Remember that the third-person narrator is a voice outside of the story.
- ❑ The narrator should relate only Miss Smith's thoughts and feelings.

Present a Scene Read your scene to the group. Remember your presentational techniques as you convey your meaning.

- ❑ Practice reading your scene aloud.
- ❑ Determine the speed at which you will read, including where you will pause for effect.
- ❑ Select words and phrases you will emphasize.
- ❑ Determine where you might raise and lower your voice and when you will make eye contact with your audience.
- ❑ After your presentation, let the group comment or ask questions.

Go to **Writing Narratives** in the **Writing Studio** to find out more about writing fiction.

Go to **Giving a Presentation** in the **Speaking and Listening Studio** to find out more.

RESPOND TO THE ESSENTIAL QUESTION

What makes people feel insecure?

UNIT 6
RESPONSE LOG

Use this Response Log to record information from the texts that relates to or comments on the Essential Questions in Unit 6.

? Essential Question	Details from Texts
What makes people feel insecure?	
Why is it hard to resist social pressure?	
What is the power of symbols?	
When should the government interfere in our decisions?	

R6 Student Resources

Gather Information Review your annotations and notes on "A Cup of Tea." Then, add relevant information to your Response Log. As you determine which information to include, think about:

- what we base our opinions of ourselves on
- how people can use our insecurities to manipulate us
- how comparing ourselves to others can affect our self-esteem

ACADEMIC VOCABULARY

As you write and discuss what you learned from the story, be sure to use the Academic Vocabulary words. Check off each of the words that you use.

- ❑ **arbitrary**
- ❑ **controversy**
- ❑ **convince**
- ❑ **denote**
- ❑ **undergo**

CRITICAL VOCABULARY

WORD BANK
presentable
tactfully
listless
vile
engagement

Practice and Apply Complete the sentences with Critical Vocabulary words.

1. The baby is so pale and __________. She must be sick!
2. I'm sorry to cancel our plans, but I have another __________.
3. If I'd known I was having visitors I'd have tried to look __________ instead of wearing sweatpants.
4. I need to __________ remind her that she owes me money.
5. I won't tolerate such __________ language just because you are angry with me.

VOCABULARY STRATEGY: Denotation and Connotation

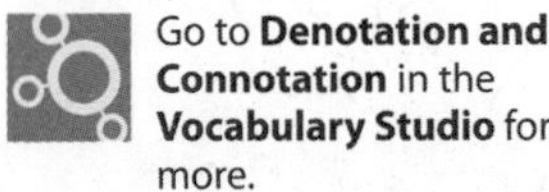

Connotation and denotation are ways of describing the meaning of words. **Denotation** is the literal definition of a word found in the dictionary. **Connotation** refers to the emotional associations of a word, which may be positive or negative. The way a word is used may influence its connotation.

> **. . . her parties were the most delicious mixture of the really important people and . . . artists—quaint creatures, discoveries of hers, some of them too terrifying for words, but others quite presentable and amusing.**

Here, the word *presentable* has a connotation of snobbery and privilege.

Practice and Apply In the sentences below from "A Cup of Tea," look up the underlined word in a dictionary and write its denotation. Then, make some notes about its connotation.

1. Her parties were the most delicious mixture of . . . people.

   Denotation:

   Connotation:

2. She saw a little battered creature with enormous eyes . . . who clutched at her coat-collar with reddened hands.

   Denotation:

   Connotation:

3. The girl stayed just as she had been put, with her hands by her sides and her mouth slightly open. To be quite sincere, she looked rather stupid.

   Denotation:

   Connotation:

LANGUAGE CONVENTIONS: Precise Details

In order to engage the reader, authors use precise details to illustrate or suggest key ideas. A good writer does not provide details arbitrarily, but rather makes very deliberate choices in using details to develop characters and themes.

> **She had a feeling of triumph as she slipped her hand through the velvet strap.**

In this sentence, the velvet strap reminds the reader that Rosemary lives a life of luxury and comfort.

> **There was a whisper that sounded like "Very good, madam," and the crushed hat was taken off.**

In this sentence, the "crushed hat" gives the reader a sense of the girl's poverty and misfortune.

Practice and Apply In the passages below from "A Cup of Tea," mark the precise details the author uses to develop the characters and theme.

> **"Don't cry, poor little thing," she said. "Don't cry." And she gave the other her lace handkerchief. She really was touched beyond words. She put her arm round those thin, birdlike shoulders.**

> **When the tea table was carried away a new being, a light, frail creature with tangled hair, dark lips, deep, lighted eyes, lay back in the big chair in a kind of sweet languor, looking at the blaze.**

How do these details contribute to the reader's understanding of the characters and the theme of the story?

THE LOVE SONG OF J. ALFRED PRUFROCK

Poem by **T. S. Eliot**

? ***ESSENTIAL QUESTION:***

What makes people feel insecure?

QUICK START

Some people appear confident in any situation, while others are filled with doubts about themselves. What circumstances can diminish a person's confidence? Write a paragraph in response to this question. Then, discuss your ideas with a partner.

UNDERSTAND MODERNIST POETRY

Modernist poets such as T. S. Eliot abandoned traditional verse forms and experimented with literary techniques to better reflect the social and technological changes of their times. Eliot's poetry can be difficult to understand because he presents a patchwork of images, symbols, and allusions that readers must connect for themselves. Consider using the following strategies to help you interpret "The Love Song of J. Alfred Prufrock":

- Read the poem aloud, pausing between sections and lingering over striking images.
- Reread the poem more than once.
- Annotate the text by marking difficult lines and passages and paraphrasing or summarizing them.
- Consult the side notes for explanations of literary allusions.

GENRE ELEMENTS: LYRIC POETRY

- expresses strong feelings or thoughts
- has a musical quality
- often deals with intense emotions surrounding events like death, love, or loss
- includes forms such as ode, elegy, and sonnet

MAKE INFERENCES

In his poetry, Eliot rarely expresses ideas in a straightforward manner. To understand and appreciate these poems, readers must make **inferences,** logical guesses based on clues found in the text. Making inferences is sometimes called "reading between the lines" because you come to an understanding of something that the author has not explicitly stated. For example, we can infer from the following lines that the speaker is going to a social gathering where he thinks he must hide his true personality or feelings from the other guests:

There will be time, there will be time
To prepare a face to meet the faces that you meet;

As you read "The Love Song of J. Alfred Prufrock," look for images that suggest thoughts and feelings. Use a chart like this one to record your inferences.

DETAILS FROM THE TEXT	MY INFERENCES

GET READY

ANALYZE STREAM OF CONSCIOUSNESS

One of the most radical breaks from convention in modernist literature was the development of **stream of consciousness.** This writing technique, used by both poets and fiction writers, presents the random flow of thoughts, emotions, memories, and associations running through the mind of a character or speaker. The goal is to re-create states of mind instead of describing them.

"The Love Song of J. Alfred Prufrock" is a dramatic monologue in which Prufrock addresses a silent listener with a tumble of thoughts, allusions, and figurative language, as in the following stanza:

> **Shall I part my hair behind? Do I dare to eat a peach?**
> **I shall wear white flannel trousers, and walk upon the beach.**
> **I have heard the mermaids singing, each to each.**

As you read the poem, try not to be put off by the seemingly nonsensical nature of the stream-of-consciousness verse, but be alert to any feelings or ideas that the images seem to suggest.

ANNOTATION MODEL

NOTICE & NOTE 

As you read, note down associations you can make between thoughts, images, and other elements in the poem. In the model, you can see one reader's notes about the opening lines of "The Love Song of J. Alfred Prufrock."

Let us go then, you and I,
When the evening is spread out against the sky
Like a patient etherised upon a table;
Let us go, through certain half-deserted streets,
The muttering retreats
Of restless nights in one-night cheap hotels
And sawdust restaurants with oyster-shells:

Prufrock addresses the listener—is that us?—with an invitation to walk with him through the city. What a strange simile he uses to describe the night sky!

He seems to be thinking about a tawdry side of town.

BACKGROUND

T. S. Eliot *(1888–1965) was one of the most influential poets and literary critics of the 20th century. He grew up in a cultured household in St. Louis, Missouri. While pursuing his graduate studies, he became involved with a circle of avant-garde writers and settled down in London. He published his first collection of poems,* Prufrock and Other Observations, *in 1917. The book baffled some reviewers but was hailed by modernists. Eliot followed it up in 1922 with* The Waste Land, *which made him internationally famous. The poem expresses the sense of alienation and spiritual loss felt by many in his generation.*

THE LOVE SONG OF J. ALFRED PRUFROCK

Poem by T. S. Eliot

SETTING A PURPOSE

As you read, consider why the speaker asks so many questions and whether or not those questions get answered.

S'io credessi che mia risposta fosse
a persona che mai tornasse al mondo,
questa fiamma staria senza più scosse.
Ma per ciò che giammai di questo fondo
non tornò vivo alcun, s'i'odo il vero,
senza tema d'infamia ti rispondo.

Let us go then, you and I,
When the evening is spread out against the sky
Like a patient etherised upon a table;
Let us go, through certain half-deserted streets,
The muttering retreats
Of restless nights in one-night cheap hotels
And sawdust restaurants with oyster-shells:
Streets that follow like a tedious argument
Of insidious intent
To lead you to an overwhelming question . . .

Notice & Note

Use the side margins to notice and note signposts in the text.

***S'io credessi . . . ti rispondo*:** These lines are from the *Inferno,* written in the early 14th century by Italian poet Dante Alighieri. As Dante visits hell, one of the damned agrees to speak of his torment only because he believes that Dante cannot return to the living world to repeat the tale.

3 etherised: given ether, a liquid used as an anesthetic.

9 insidious (ĭn-sĭd´ē-əs): more dangerous than it seems.

NOTICE & NOTE

Oh, do not ask, "What is it?"
Let us go and make our visit.

In the room the women come and go
Talking of Michelangelo.

The yellow fog that rubs its back upon the window-panes,
The yellow smoke that rubs its muzzle on the window-panes,
Licked its tongue into the corners of the evening,
Lingered upon the pools that stand in drains,
Let fall upon its back the soot that falls from chimneys,
Slipped by the terrace, made a sudden leap,
And seeing that it was a soft October night,
Curled once about the house, and fell asleep.

And indeed there will be time
For the yellow smoke that slides along the street
Rubbing its back upon the window-panes;
There will be time, there will be time
To prepare a face to meet the faces that you meet;
There will be time to murder and create,
And time for all the works and days of hands
That lift and drop a question on your plate;
Time for you and time for me,
And time yet for a hundred indecisions,
And for a hundred visions and revisions,
Before the taking of a toast and tea.

In the room the women come and go
Talking of Michelangelo.

ANALYZE STREAM OF CONSCIOUSNESS

Annotate: Mark interruptions in Prufrock's train of thought in lines 37–46.

Analyze: What connection can you make between Prufrock's thoughts about his appearance and the question he repeatedly asks in this passage?

And indeed there will be time
To wonder, "Do I dare?" and, "Do I dare?"
Time to turn back and descend the stair,
With a bald spot in the middle of my hair—
(They will say: "How his hair is growing thin!")
My morning coat, my collar mounting firmly to the chin,
My necktie rich and modest, but asserted by a simple pin—
(They will say: "But how his arms and legs are thin!")
Do I dare
Disturb the universe?
In a minute there is time
For decisions and revisions which a minute will reverse.

For I have known them all already, known them all—
Have known the evenings, mornings, afternoons,
I have measured out my life with coffee spoons;
I know the voices dying with a dying fall
Beneath the music from a farther room.
    So how should I presume?

And I have known the eyes already, known them all—
The eyes that fix you in a formulated phrase,
And when I am formulated, sprawling on a pin,
When I am pinned and wriggling on the wall,
Then how should I begin
To spit out all the butt-ends of my days and ways?
    And how should I presume?

And I have known the arms already, known them all—
Arms that are braceleted and white and bare
(But in the lamplight, downed with light brown hair!)
Is it perfume from a dress
That makes me so digress?
Arms that lie along a table, or wrap about a shawl.
    And should I then presume?
    And how should I begin?

• • • • •

Shall I say, I have gone at dusk through narrow streets
And watched the smoke that rises from the pipes
Of lonely men in shirt-sleeves, leaning out of windows? . . .

I should have been a pair of ragged claws
Scuttling across the floors of silent seas.

• • • • •

And the afternoon, the evening, sleeps so peacefully!
Smoothed by long fingers,
Asleep . . . tired . . . or it malingers,
Stretched on the floor, here beside you and me.
Should I, after tea and cakes and ices,
Have the strength to force the moment to its crisis?
But though I have wept and fasted, wept and prayed,
Though I have seen my head (grown slightly bald) brought in
    upon a platter,
I am no prophet—and here's no great matter;
I have seen the moment of my greatness flicker,
And I have seen the eternal Footman hold my coat, and snicker,
And in short, I was afraid.

54 presume: act overconfidently; dare.

55–58 And I have . . . on the wall: Prufrock recalls being scrutinized by women at other parties. He portrays himself as a live insect that has been classified, labeled, and mounted for display.

56 formulated: reduced to a formula.

MAKE INFERENCES

Annotate: Mark the metaphors in lines 55–61.

Infer: What do these metaphors suggest about how Prufrock feels among women at parties?

73–74 I should . . . silent seas: Here Prufrock presents an image of himself as a crayfish.

77 malingers (mə-lĭng′gərz): pretends illness in order to avoid duty or work.

81–83 But though . . . prophet: an allusion to the biblical story of John the Baptist, who is imprisoned by King Herod (Matthew 14; Mark 6). At the request of his wife, Herod had the Baptist's head cut off and brought to him on a platter.

NOTICE & NOTE

94 Lazarus: In the biblical story (John 11:17–44), Lazarus lay dead in his tomb for four days before Jesus brought him back to life.

105 magic lantern: a forerunner of the slide projector.

UNDERSTAND MODERNIST POETRY

Annotate: Mark the literary allusion in lines 111–119.

Summarize: Write a summary of this stanza.

115 deferential: yielding to someone else's opinion.

116 meticulous: extremely careful and precise about details.

117 obtuse: slow to understand; dull.

124–125 mermaids . . . to me: In mythology, mermaids attract mortal men by their beauty and their singing, sometimes allowing men to live with them in the sea.

And would it have been worth it, after all,
After the cups, the marmalade, the tea,
Among the porcelain, among some talk of you and me,
Would it have been worth while,
To have bitten off the matter with a smile,
To have squeezed the universe into a ball
To roll it towards some overwhelming question,
To say: "I am Lazarus, come from the dead,
Come back to tell you all, I shall tell you all"—
If one, settling a pillow by her head,
    Should say: "That is not what I meant at all.
    That is not it, at all."

And would it have been worth it, after all,
Would it have been worth while,
After the sunsets and the dooryards and the sprinkled streets,
After the novels, after the teacups, after the skirts that trail along the floor—
And this, and so much more?—
It is impossible to say just what I mean!
But as if a magic lantern threw the nerves in patterns on a screen:
Would it have been worth while
If one, settling a pillow or throwing off a shawl,
And turning toward the window, should say:
    "That is not it at all,
    That is not what I meant, at all."

• • • • •

No! I am not Prince Hamlet, nor was meant to be;
Am an attendant lord, one that will do
To swell a progress, start a scene or two,
Advise the prince; no doubt, an easy tool,
Deferential, glad to be of use,
Politic, cautious, and meticulous;
Full of high sentence, but a bit obtuse;
At times, indeed, almost ridiculous—
Almost, at times, the Fool.

I grow old . . . I grow old . . .
I shall wear the bottoms of my trousers rolled.

Shall I part my hair behind? Do I dare to eat a peach?
I shall wear white flannel trousers, and walk upon the beach.
I have heard the mermaids singing, each to each.

I do not think that they will sing to me.

I have seen them riding seaward on the waves
Combing the white hair of the waves blown back
When the wind blows the water white and black.

We have lingered in the chambers of the sea
By sea-girls wreathed with seaweed red and brown
Till human voices wake us, and we drown.

CHECK YOUR UNDERSTANDING

Answer these questions before moving on to the **Analyze the Text** section on the following page.

1 Which aspect of Prufrock's life is reflected in the simile comparing the evening to *a patient etherised upon a table*?

A His fear of the evening

B An illness he is recovering from

C His profession as a doctor

D His sense of paralysis

2 How does Prufrock feel about the guests at the party he is going to?

F He feels alienated from them.

G He feels hatred toward them.

H He feels kindness from them.

J He feels generosity toward them.

3 Lines 87–98 indicate that the woman Prufrock wants to talk to —

A feels nervous in his presence

B worries that he has gone insane

C isn't interested in what he has to say

D is trying to avoid him

RESPOND

ANALYZE THE TEXT

Support your responses with evidence from the text. NOTEBOOK

1. **Analyze** What does Prufrock compare the fog to in lines 15–22? How does this extended metaphor relate to his situation in the poem?
2. **Infer** What thought does Prufrock express in line 51 when he says, "I have measured out my life with coffee spoons"?
3. **Analyze** Read the side margin notes about the quotation from Dante's *Inferno* at the beginning of the poem and the allusion to Lazarus in line 94. What do the quotation and the allusion have in common? How are they connected to Prufrock's experience?
4. **Draw Conclusions** Why might Eliot have chosen not to clarify the nature of Prufrock's "overwhelming question" or what he wants to say to the woman at the party?
5. **Connect** Eliot wrote "The Love Song of J. Alfred Prufrock" at a time when new technology and media were rapidly changing society. How might Eliot's use of stream of consciousness reflect such changes?

RESEARCH

With a partner, find a work by each author listed in the chart that includes stream-of-consciousness writing. Choose a passage from each work and compare it to Eliot's use of this technique.

RESEARCH TIP

When researching writers from a specific era or who wrote in a specific style, focus your search on the "top" lists. Use search strings like "top modernist poets" or "best examples of stream-of-consciousness writing."

WRITER	NOTES ON STREAM OF CONSCIOUSNESS
James Joyce	
Virginia Woolf	
William Faulkner	

Extend For two minutes, write down every thought that goes through your mind. Do not worry about whether your writing is logical or coherent. Once you've finished, review your stream-of-consciousness writing and identify how your thoughts relate to one another.

CREATE AND PRESENT

Write a Poem Modernist poetry often features confusing contradictions or contrasting imagery. Using this style as your base, write a poem that includes seemingly confusing contradictions or contrasting images. Reread examples from Eliot's poem to get ideas. Review your analysis and interpretation of Eliot's creative use of metaphors and analogies to gain a better understanding of how to do this.

- ❑ Study the examples in Eliot's poem.
- ❑ Brainstorm contradictions or incongruous images.
- ❑ Write a poem that includes these contradictions.
- ❑ Use a free-verse structure, and think about where you will break lines and why.

Present a Poem Now share your poem with the class. When you and your classmates read your poems aloud, provide thoughtful feedback to each other. Discuss your interpretations of the contradictory ideas or images in your poems.

- ❑ Practice reading your poem. Experiment with stressing different syllables to bring out the musical quality in the text.
- ❑ Practice making eye contact with your audience, and use facial expressions and natural gestures to convey the meaning of the poem.
- ❑ Finally, read your poem aloud to the class.

Go to **Giving a Presentation** in the **Speaking and Listening Studio** for more on presenting.

RESPOND TO THE ESSENTIAL QUESTION

What makes people feel insecure?

Gather Information Review your annotations and notes on "The Love Song of J. Alfred Prufrock." Then, add relevant information to your Response Log. As you determine which information to include, think about:

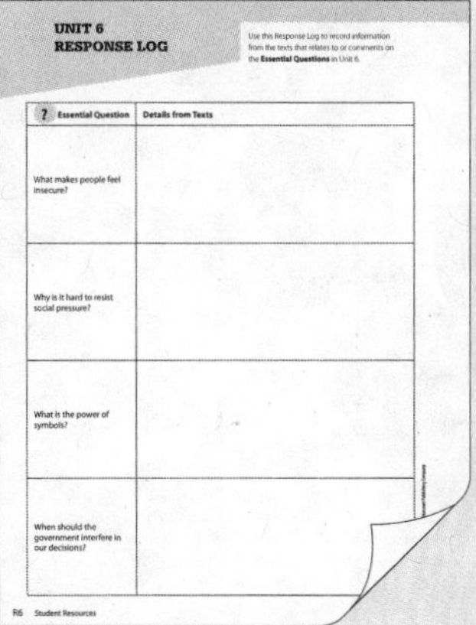

UNIT 6 RESPONSE LOG

Use this Response Log to record information from the texts that relates to or comments on the **Essential Questions** in Unit 6.

? Essential Question	Details from Texts
What makes people feel insecure?	
Why is it hard to resist social pressure?	
What is the power of symbols?	
When should the government interfere in our decisions?	

R6 Student Resources

- how you can feel insecure internally, but look confident externally
- what things might make you feel uncertain about yourself
- how important your self-talk is to how you feel about yourself

ACADEMIC VOCABULARY

As you write and discuss what you learned from the poem, be sure to use the Academic Vocabulary words. Check off each of the words that you use.

- ❑ **arbitrary**
- ❑ **controversy**
- ❑ **convince**
- ❑ **denote**
- ❑ **undergo**

SHOOTING AN ELEPHANT

Essay by **George Orwell**

ESSENTIAL QUESTION:

Why is it hard to resist social pressure?

QUICK START

Think about how you behave with your peers. Then, think about how you behave in the presence of parents or other older adults. Compare and contrast your actions, then discuss with a partner why you may behave differently in these situations.

BEHAVIOR WITH PEERS	BEHAVIOR WITH PARENTS OR ADULTS

ANALYZE REFLECTIVE ESSAY

In a **reflective essay,** the author examines a personal experience and reveals what he or she learned from it. A good reflective essay offers insight into the author's personal growth and also connects a specific observation to some larger idea about life or society. For example, in "Shooting an Elephant," Orwell reflects on an incident he experienced as a young police officer in British-ruled Burma in the 1920s. By exploring this experience, Orwell allows readers to understand what he learned about the true nature of colonialism. As you read, pay attention to the thoughts and feelings that Orwell expresses as he describes the incident.

GENRE ELEMENTS: ESSAY

- a short piece of nonfiction
- offers an opinion on a subject
- formal essays have a serious and impersonal tone
- informal essays are loosely structured and have a conversational tone
- a reflective essay examines an experience in the author's life

ANALYZE IRONY

Irony is a contrast between expectation and reality. This contrast often has the effect of surprising the reader or viewer. Irony may be subtle and easily overlooked or misunderstood. There are three main types of irony:

- **Situational irony** occurs when a character or the reader expects one thing to happen but something else actually happens.
- **Verbal irony** occurs when a character or the writer says one thing but means something quite different—often the opposite of what he or she has said.
- **Dramatic irony** occurs when the reader or viewer knows something that a character does not know.

In "Shooting an Elephant," Orwell relies on situational irony to drive home his insight about colonialism. As you read, notice how the young Orwell's expectations are overturned as he tries to carry out his responsibilities. Also pay attention to your own expectations about how he will behave in this situation.

GET READY

CRITICAL VOCABULARY

imperialism	**supplant**	**despotic**	**garish**
cowed	**prostrate**	**labyrinth**	**senility**

To see how many Critical Vocabulary words you already know, use them to complete the sentences.

1. __________ in the United States led the president to __________ the rightful queen and annex Hawaii.
2. His words were muffled as he lay __________ on the rug before the __________ ruler.
3. His __________ sometimes made his speech a tangled __________ of half-expressed thoughts.
4. She was __________ by the bright lights and loud sounds of the ________ city.

LANGUAGE CONVENTIONS

In his essay, George Orwell uses **prepositional phrases** to add clarity to his descriptions of the village, the people, and the elephant. Prepositional phrases consist of a preposition, its object, and modifiers of the object.

Common prepositions include *above, at, before, below, by, down, for, from, in, into, near, of, on, out, over, through, to, up, with,* and *without.*

ANNOTATION MODEL

NOTICE & NOTE 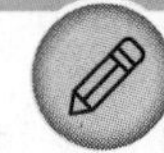

As you read the essay "Shooting an Elephant," practice taking notes, marking up the text and asking questions, to monitor your comprehension.

In Moulmein, in Lower Burma, I was hated by large numbers of people—the only time in my life that I have been important enough for this to happen to me. I was subdivisional police officer of the town, and in an aimless, petty kind of way anti-European feeling was very bitter. No one had the guts to raise a riot, but if a European woman went through the bazaars alone somebody would probably spit betel juice over her dress. As a police officer I was an obvious target and was baited whenever it seemed safe to do so.

This statement seems ironic—I expect "important" people to be respected or admired.

Orwell's attitude toward the Burmese people must have been affected by this experience of being targeted.

BACKGROUND

George Orwell *(1903–1950) was born in India. When he was 19, he joined the Indian Imperial police and left to serve in Burma, which at the time was ruled by Britain. Disillusioned with imperialism, he resigned in 1928 and decided to become a writer. In 1936 Orwell went to Spain to fight with antifascist forces in the Spanish Civil War, an experience that greatly influenced his political views. Throughout his life, Orwell spoke out against injustice. His most famous novels,* Animal Farm *and* 1984, *reflect his dedication to political freedom.*

SHOOTING AN ELEPHANT

Essay by George Orwell

SETTING A PURPOSE

Read George Orwell's essay to discover his ideas about imperialism and his role as an officer. How can you connect his turmoil with that of 21st-century officers?

1 In Moulmein, in Lower Burma,[1] I was hated by large numbers of people—the only time in my life that I have been important enough for this to happen to me. I was subdivisional police officer of the town, and in an aimless, petty kind of way anti-European feeling was very bitter. No one had the guts to raise a riot, but if a European woman went through the bazaars alone somebody would probably spit betel juice[2] over her dress. As a police officer I was an obvious target and was baited whenever it seemed safe to do so. When a nimble Burman tripped me up on the football[3] field and the referee (another Burman) looked the

[1] **Moulmein** (mo͞ol-mān´), **in Lower Burma:** the main city of British-controlled Burma, now the independent Asian nation of Myanmar. Moulmein is now usually called Mawlamyine.

[2] **betel** (bĕt´l) **juice:** the saliva created when chewing a mixture of betel palm nuts, betel palm leaves, and lime.

[3] **football:** soccer.

Notice & Note

Use the side margins to notice and note signposts in the text.

LANGUAGE CONVENTIONS

Annotate: Mark the prepositional phrases in the first sentence of paragraph 1.

Evaluate: What do these prepositional phrases suggest about the importance of the experience Orwell is about to describe?

other way, the crowd yelled with hideous laughter. This happened more than once. In the end the sneering yellow faces of young men that met me everywhere, the insults hooted after me when I was at a safe distance, got badly on my nerves. The young Buddhist priests were the worst of all. There were several thousands of them in the town and none of them seemed to have anything to do except stand on street corners and jeer at Europeans.

imperialism
(ĭm-pîr´ē-ə-lĭz əm): *n.* the extension of a nation's authority by territorial acquisition or by the establishment of economic and political dominance over other nations.

cowed
(koud): *adj.* frightened or subdued with threats or a show of force. **cow** *v.*

ANALYZE IRONY

Annotate: Mark evidence of situational irony in paragraph 2.

Analyze: Explain the situational irony in Orwell's feelings about British colonialism and about the Burmese people.

supplant
(sə-plănt´): *tr.v.* to take the place of or substitute for (another).

prostrate
(prŏs´trāt): *adj.* lying face down, as in submission or adoration.

despotic
(dĭ-spŏt´ĭk): *adj.* of or relating to a person who wields power oppressively, or a tyrant.

2 All this was perplexing and upsetting. For at that time I had already made up my mind that **imperialism** was an evil thing and the sooner I chucked up[4] my job and got out of it the better. Theoretically—and secretly, of course—I was all for the Burmese and all against their oppressors, the British. As for the job I was doing, I hated it more bitterly than I can perhaps make clear. In a job like that you see the dirty work of Empire at close quarters. The wretched prisoners huddling in the stinking cages of the lock-ups, the gray, **cowed** faces of the long-term convicts, the scarred buttocks of the men who had been flogged with bamboos—all these oppressed me with an intolerable sense of guilt. But I could get nothing into perspective. I was young and ill-educated and I had had to think out my problems in the utter silence that is imposed on every Englishman in the East. I did not even know that the British Empire is dying, still less did I know that it is a great deal better than the younger empires that are going to **supplant** it. All I knew was that I was stuck between my hatred of the empire I served and my rage against the evil-spirited little beasts who tried to make my job impossible. With one part of my mind I thought of the British Raj[5] as an unbreakable tyranny, as something clamped down, *in saecula saeculorum*,[6] upon the will of **prostrate** peoples; with another part I thought that the greatest joy in the world would be to drive a bayonet into a Buddhist priest's guts. Feelings like these are the normal by-products of imperialism; ask any Anglo-Indian official, if you can catch him off duty.

3 One day something happened which in a roundabout way was enlightening. It was a tiny incident in itself, but it gave me a better glimpse than I had had before of the real nature of imperialism—the real motives for which **despotic** governments act. Early one morning the subinspector at a police station the other end of the town rang me up on the phone and said that an elephant was ravaging the bazaar. Would I please come and do something about it? I did not know what I could do, but I wanted to see what was happening and I got on to a pony and started out. I took my rifle, an old 44 Winchester and much too small to kill an elephant, but I thought the noise might be useful

[4] **chucked up:** threw off; gave up.

[5] **British Raj:** India and adjoining areas (such as Burma) controlled by Britain in the 19th and early 20th centuries. *Raj* is the word for "kingdom" or "rule" in Hindi, a chief language of India.

[6] ***in saecula saeculorum*** (ĭn sĕk´yə-lə sĕk-yə-lôr´əm) *Latin*: forever and ever.

in terrorem.[7] Various Burmans stopped me on the way and told me about the elephant's doings. It was not, of course, a wild elephant, but a tame one which had gone "must."[8] It had been chained up as tame elephants always are when their attack of "must" is due, but on the previous night it had broken its chain and escaped. Its mahout,[9] the only person who could manage it when it was in that state, had set out in pursuit, but had taken the wrong direction and was now twelve hours' journey away, and in the morning the elephant had suddenly reappeared in the town. The Burmese population had no weapons and were quite helpless against it. It had already destroyed somebody's bamboo hut, killed a cow and raided some fruit-stalls and devoured the stock; also it had met the municipal rubbish van, and, when the driver jumped out and took to his heels, had turned the van over and inflicted violences upon it.

4 The Burmese subinspector and some Indian constables[10] were waiting for me in the quarter where the elephant had been seen. It was a very poor quarter, a **labyrinth** of squalid bamboo huts, thatched with palm-leaf, winding all over a steep hillside. I remember that it was a cloudy stuffy morning at the beginning of the rains. We began questioning the people as to where the elephant had gone, and, as usual, failed to get any definite information. That is invariably the case in the East; a story always sounds clear enough at a distance, but the nearer you get to the scene of events the vaguer it becomes. Some of the people said that the elephant had gone in one direction, some said that he had gone in another, some professed not even to have heard of any elephant. I had almost made up my mind that the whole story was a pack of lies, when we heard yells a little distance away. There was a loud, scandalized cry of "Go away, child! Go away this instant!" and an old woman with a switch in her hand came round the corner of a hut, violently shooing away a crowd of naked children. Some more women followed, clicking their tongues and exclaiming; evidently there was something there that the children ought not to have seen. I rounded the hut and saw a man's dead body sprawling in the mud. He was an Indian, a black Dravidian coolie,[11] almost naked, and he could not have been dead many minutes. The people said that the elephant had come suddenly upon him round the corner of the hut, caught him with its trunk, put its foot on his back and ground him into the earth. This was the rainy season and the ground was soft, and his face had scored a trench a foot deep and

labyrinth
(lăb´ə-rĭnth): *n.* an intricate structure of interconnecting passages through which it is difficult to find one's way; a maze.

---

[7] ***in terrorem*** (ĭn tĕ-rôr´əm) *Latin*: for terror.
[8] **gone "must":** had an attack of must, a dangerous frenzy that periodically seizes male elephants.
[9] **mahout** (mə-hout´): an elephant keeper.
[10] **constables:** police officers.
[11] **Dravidian** (drə-vĭd´ē-ən) **coolie:** a dark-skinned menial laborer from the south of India.

British troops patrolling a city in Burma

ANALYZE REFLECTIVE ESSAY

Annotate: Mark details Orwell uses to describe the corpse in paragraph 4.

Analyze: What do these details suggest about how this sight affected him?

a couple of yards long. He was lying on his belly with arms crucified and head sharply twisted to one side. His face was coated with mud, the eyes wide open, the teeth bared and grinning with an expression of unendurable agony. (Never tell me, by the way, that the dead look peaceful. Most of the corpses I have seen looked devilish.) The friction of the great beast's foot had stripped the skin from his back as neatly as one skins a rabbit. As soon as I saw the dead man I sent an orderly[12] to a friend's house nearby to borrow an elephant rifle. I had already sent back the pony, not wanting it to go mad with fright and throw me if it smelled the elephant.

5 The orderly came back in a few minutes with a rifle and five cartridges, and meanwhile some Burmans had arrived and told us that the elephant was in the paddy fields[13] below, only a few hundred yards away. As I started forward practically the whole population of

[12] **orderly:** a military aide.
[13] **paddy fields:** rice fields.

the quarter flocked out of the houses and followed me. They had seen the rifle and were all shouting excitedly that I was going to shoot the elephant. They had not shown much interest in the elephant when he was merely ravaging their homes, but it was different now that he was going to be shot. It was a bit of fun to them, as it would be to an English crowd; besides, they wanted the meat. It made me vaguely uneasy. I had no intention of shooting the elephant—I had merely sent for the rifle to defend myself if necessary—and it is always unnerving to have a crowd following you. I marched down the hill, looking and feeling a fool, with the rifle over my shoulder and an ever-growing army of people jostling at my heels. At the bottom, when you got away from the huts, there was a metalled road and beyond that a miry waste of paddy fields a thousand yards across, not yet ploughed but soggy from the first rains and dotted with coarse grass. The elephant was standing eighty yards from the road, his left side towards us. He took not the slightest notice of the crowd's approach. He was tearing up bunches of grass, beating them against his knees to clean them and stuffing them into his mouth.

6 I had halted on the road. As soon as I saw the elephant I knew with perfect certainty that I ought not to shoot him. It is a serious matter to shoot a working elephant—it is comparable to destroying a huge and costly piece of machinery—and obviously one ought not to do it if it can possibly be avoided. And at that distance, peacefully eating, the elephant looked no more dangerous than a cow. I thought then and I think now that his attack of "must" was already passing off; in which case he would merely wander harmlessly about until the mahout came back and caught him. Moreover, I did not in the least want to shoot him. I decided that I would watch him for a little while to make sure that he did not turn savage again, and then go home.

7 But at that moment I glanced round at the crowd that had followed me. It was an immense crowd, two thousand at the least and growing every minute. It blocked the road for a long distance on either side. I looked at the sea of yellow faces above the **garish** clothes—faces all happy and excited over this bit of fun, all certain that the elephant was going to be shot. They were watching me as they would watch a conjurer[14] about to perform a trick. They did not like me, but with the magical rifle in my hands I was momentarily worth watching. And suddenly I realized that I should have to shoot the elephant after all. The people expected it of me and I had got to do it; I could feel their two thousand wills pressing me forward, irresistibly. And it was at this moment, as I stood there with the rifle in my hands, that I first grasped the hollowness, the futility of the white man's dominion in the East. Here was I, the white man with his gun, standing in front of the unarmed native crowd—seemingly the leading actor of the piece; but in reality I was only an absurd puppet pushed to and fro by the will of those yellow faces behind. I perceived in this moment that when the white man turns tyrant it is his own freedom that he destroys. He becomes a sort of hollow, posing dummy, the conventionalized figure of a sahib.[15] For it is the condition of his rule that he shall spend his life in trying to impress the "natives," and so in every crisis he has got to do what the "natives" expect of him. He wears a mask, and his face grows to fit it. I had got to shoot the elephant. I had committed myself to doing it when I sent for the rifle. A sahib has got to act like a sahib; he has got to appear resolute, to know his own mind and do definite things. To come all that way, rifle in hand, with two thousand people marching at my heels, and then to trail feebly away, having done nothing—no, that was impossible. The crowd would laugh at me. And my whole

garish
(gâr´ĭsh, găr´): *adj.* overly bright or ornamented, especially in a vulgar or tasteless way; gaudy.

AHA MOMENT

Notice & Note: In paragraph 7, mark statements expressing Orwell's realization about his role as a colonial officer.

Analyze: How are these statements ironic?

[14] **conjurer** (kŏn´jər-ər): magician.

[15] **sahib** (sä´hĭb): a title of respect formerly used by native Indians to address a European gentleman.

life, every white man's life in the East, was one long struggle not to be laughed at.

8 But I did not want to shoot the elephant. I watched him beating his bunch of grass against his knees, with that preoccupied grandmotherly air that elephants have. It seemed to me that it would be murder to shoot him. At that age I was not squeamish about killing animals, but I had never shot an elephant and never wanted to. (Somehow it always seems worse to kill a *large* animal.) Besides, there was the beast's owner to be considered. Alive, the elephant was worth at least a hundred pounds; dead, he would only be worth the value of his tusks—five pounds, possibly. But I had got to act quickly. I turned to some experienced-looking Burmans who had been there when we arrived, and asked them how the elephant had been behaving. They all said the same thing: he took no notice of you if you left him alone, but he might charge if you went too close to him.

9 It was perfectly clear to me what I ought to do. I ought to walk up to within, say, twenty-five yards of the elephant and test his behavior. If he charged I could shoot, if he took no notice of me it would be safe to leave him until the mahout came back. But also I knew that I was going to do no such thing. I was a poor shot with a rifle and the ground was soft mud into which one would sink at every step. If the elephant charged and I missed him, I should have about as much chance as a toad under a steam-roller. But even then I was not thinking particularly of my own skin, only of the watchful yellow faces behind. For at that moment, with the crowd watching me, I was not afraid in the ordinary sense, as I would have been if I had been alone. A white man mustn't be frightened in front of "natives"; and so, in general, he isn't frightened. The sole thought in my mind was that if anything went wrong those two thousand Burmans would see me pursued, caught, trampled on and reduced to a grinning corpse like that Indian up the hill. And if that happened it was quite probable that some of them would laugh. That would never do. There was only one alternative. I shoved the cartridges into the magazine[16] and lay down on the road to get a better aim.

10 The crowd grew very still, and a deep, low, happy sigh, as of people who see the theater curtain go up at last, breathed from innumerable throats. They were going to have their bit of fun after all. The rifle was a beautiful German thing with cross-hair sights. I did not then know that in shooting an elephant one should shoot to cut an imaginary bar running from ear-hole to ear-hole. I ought, therefore, as the elephant was sideways on, to have aimed straight at his ear-hole; actually I aimed several inches in front of this, thinking the brain would be further forward.

ANALYZE REFLECTIVE ESSAY

Annotate: In paragraph 9, mark Orwell's explanation of what he ought to have done in this situation.

Draw Conclusions: What idea does this paragraph convey about how imperialism affects the individuals who serve it?

[16] **magazine:** the compartment from which cartridges are fed into the rifle's firing chamber.

senility
(sĭ-nĭl´ĭ-tē): *n.* relating to or having diminished cognitive function, as when memory is impaired, because of old age.

11 When I pulled the trigger I did not hear the bang or feel the kick—one never does when a shot goes home—but I heard the devilish roar of glee that went up from the crowd. In that instant, in too short a time, one would have thought, even for the bullet to get there, a mysterious, terrible change had come over the elephant. He neither stirred nor fell, but every line of his body had altered. He looked suddenly stricken, shrunken, immensely old, as though the frightful impact of the bullet had paralyzed him without knocking him down. At last, after what seemed a long time—it might have been five seconds, I dare say—he sagged flabbily to his knees. His mouth slobbered. An enormous **senility** seemed to have settled upon him. One could have imagined him thousands of years old. I fired again into the same spot. At the second shot he did not collapse but climbed with desperate slowness to his feet and stood weakly upright, with legs sagging and head drooping. I fired a third time. That was the shot that did for him. You could see the agony of it jolt his whole body and knock the last remnant of strength from his legs. But in falling he seemed for a moment to rise, for as his hind legs collapsed beneath him he seemed to tower upwards like a huge rock toppling, his trunk reaching skyward like a tree. He trumpeted, for the first and only time. And then down he came, his belly towards me, with a crash that seemed to shake the ground even where I lay.

12 I got up. The Burmans were already racing past me across the mud. It was obvious that the elephant would never rise again, but he was not dead. He was breathing very rhythmically with long rattling gasps, his great mound of a side painfully rising and falling. His mouth was wide open—I could see far down into caverns of pale pink throat. I waited a long time for him to die, but his breathing did not weaken. Finally I fired my two remaining shots into the spot where I thought his heart must be. The thick blood welled out of him like red velvet, but still he did not die. His body did not even jerk when the shots hit him, the tortured breathing continued without a pause. He was dying, very slowly and in great agony, but in some world remote from me where not even a bullet could damage him further. I felt that I had got to put an end to that dreadful noise. It seemed dreadful to see the great beast lying there, powerless to move and yet powerless to die, and not even to be able to finish him. I sent back for my small rifle and poured shot after shot into his heart and down his throat. They seemed to make no impression. The tortured gasps continued as steadily as the ticking of a clock.

13 In the end I could not stand it any longer and went away. I heard later that it took him half an hour to die. Burmans were arriving with dahs[17] and baskets even before I left, and I was told they had stripped his body almost to the bones by the afternoon.

[17] **dahs:** large knives.

14 Afterwards, of course, there were endless discussions about the shooting of the elephant. The owner was furious, but he was only an Indian and could do nothing. Besides, legally I had done the right thing, for a mad elephant has to be killed, like a mad dog, if its owner fails to control it. Among the Europeans opinion was divided. The older men said I was right, the younger men said it was a damn shame to shoot an elephant for killing a coolie, because an elephant was worth more than any damn Coringhee[18] coolie. And afterwards I was very glad that the coolie had been killed; it put me legally in the right and it gave me a sufficient pretext for shooting the elephant. I often wondered whether any of the others grasped that I had done it solely to avoid looking a fool.

ANALYZE IRONY

Annotate: Mark the opinions of the Europeans in paragraph 14.

Analyze: What is ironic about Orwell's feeling glad that the coolie had been killed?

[18] **Coringhee:** coming from a port in southeastern India.

CHECK YOUR UNDERSTANDING

Answer these questions before moving on to the **Analyze the Text** section on the following page.

1 What annoyed the narrator?

A The elephant's destruction of trees

B How the Burmans mocked soldiers

C The weather in Asia

D His small gun

2 When Orwell finally sees the elephant, it is —

F wild

G ravenous

H tame

J gentle

3 The narrator had to shoot the elephant because —

A so many people were watching

B the elephant was charging toward him

C his job was to protect the village people

D the elephant was already injured

RESPOND

ANALYZE THE TEXT

Support your responses with evidence from the text. NOTEBOOK

1. **Analyze** Reread paragraphs 5 and 6. What is ironic about Orwell's first sighting of the elephant?
2. **Evaluate** Orwell describes the shooting and slow death of the elephant in excruciating detail. How does this description support his reflections in the essay?
3. **Draw Conclusions** At the end of the essay, Orwell wonders whether other Europeans realized that he shot the elephant "solely to avoid looking a fool." Why was it so important for him to keep up appearances before the Burmans?
4. **Critique** Do you think Orwell provides a reliable account of how the Burmans viewed him? Explain why or why not.
5. **Notice & Note** Orwell says that this experience taught him that "when the white man turns tyrant it is his own freedom that he destroys." In what ways did his role as a colonial policeman end his freedom?

RESEARCH

RESEARCH TIP
Place quotation marks around your search terms to get results that include the exact wording.

Burma (now called Myanmar) was one of many colonies that Britain ruled in the early 20th century. With a partner, research the history of British colonization of Burma. Use what you learn to answer the questions:

QUESTION	ANSWER
How did Britain gain control of Burma?	
What issues fueled Burmese resentment of British rule?	
What role did Buddhist monks play in opposition to colonialism?	
How did Burma gain independence?	

Extend Conduct further research to learn about Burma's history following independence. Did Burmans enjoy greater freedom after the British left? What is life like in Myanmar today?

CREATE AND DISCUSS

Write an Informational Essay Write about a social injustice occurring today. Describe the toll that this injustice takes on individuals. Use evidence from research or what you may have witnessed.

- ❑ Begin your essay with a hook—a stirring incident or anecdote.
- ❑ Create an effective transitional sentence to blend the hook with your informational writing.
- ❑ If you're truly concerned about an injustice, write about that. If a specific social or political wrong moves you, it will come through in the essay.
- ❑ Tease out any ironies you identify in the situation to help provoke deeper thought about the issue.
- ❑ Create a memorable theme or message to share an insight.

Go to **Writing Informative Texts** in the **Writing Studio** to develop your essay.

Discuss Your Essay Use your essay to generate discussion with your peers. Allow each participant time to share an experience as well as its possible outcomes.

- ❑ Read your essay to the members of your group.
- ❑ Ask each member of the group to give you brief feedback about your essay.
- ❑ Encourage the group to discuss ideas and questions raised in your essay.
- ❑ Listen and respond as other group members read their essays.

Go to **Participating in Collaborative Discussions** in the **Speaking and Listening Studio** for more help.

RESPOND TO THE ESSENTIAL QUESTION

Why is it hard to resist social pressure?

Gather Information Review your annotations and notes on "Shooting an Elephant." Then, add relevant information to your Response Log. As you determine which information to include, think about:

- the strict roles assigned to men, women, and teens
- the consequences of being different
- social roles and responsibilities

ACADEMIC VOCABULARY

As you write and discuss what you learned from the essay, be sure to use the Academic Vocabulary words. Check off each of the words that you use.

- ❑ **arbitrary**
- ❑ **controversy**
- ❑ **convince**
- ❑ **denote**
- ❑ **undergo**

RESPOND

CRITICAL VOCABULARY

WORD BANK

imperialism	**despotic**
cowed	**labyrinth**
supplant	**garish**
prostrate	**senility**

Practice and Apply Choose the word that best completes the sentence.

1. The economic interests of __________ led the British to seize control of local governments and __________ local officials.
2. As the elephant wove through the ____________ of the village, the ____________ residents sent word to the police of the event.
3. In his __________, he would dress in ____________ costumes and relive the scene for any who would stop and listen.
4. As he gazed at the __________ form of the dead man, he felt the __________ expectation of the crowd pushing him toward an action he did not want to take.

VOCABULARY STRATEGY: Etymology

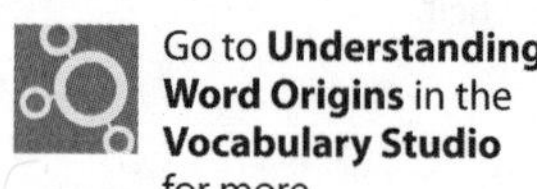

Go to **Understanding Word Origins** in the **Vocabulary Studio** for more.

Etymology is the history of a word. Most dictionary entries include etymologies that identify which language the word came from and what the original word meant. The etymology also traces the route by which a word passed into the English language.

The entry below gives the history of the Critical Vocabulary word *labyrinth*. It shows that *labyrinth* comes from the ancient Greek *laburinthos,* which refers to the Minotaur's maze in the Greek myth of Jason and the Argonauts.

> **lab·y·rinth** (lăb′ə-rĭnth): *n.* an intricate structure of interconnecting passages through which it is difficult to find one's way; a maze. [Middle English *laberinthe,* from Latin *labyrinthus,* from Greek *laburinthos;* possibly akin to *labrus,* double-headed axe used as a ritual weapon and a sign of authority in Minoan civilization, so that Greek *laburinthos* may originally have designated a Minoan palace as "the house of the double-headed axe"]

Practice and Apply Look up the remaining Critical Vocabulary words in a college-level dictionary and trace their etymology. Discuss with a partner how closely the original meaning resembles the usage of the word today.

LANGUAGE CONVENTIONS: Prepositional Phrases

A **prepositional phrase** begins with the preposition (such as *among* or *with*) and ends with its object. Prepositional phrases tell *where, when, how, what kind,* and other information that makes descriptions clearer and more vivid. Here is an example from the essay, "Shooting an Elephant."

> **The orderly came back in a few minutes with a rifle and five cartridges, and meanwhile some Burmans had arrived and told us that the elephant was in the paddy fields below, only a few hundred yards away. As I started forward practically the whole population of the quarter flocked out of the houses and followed me.**

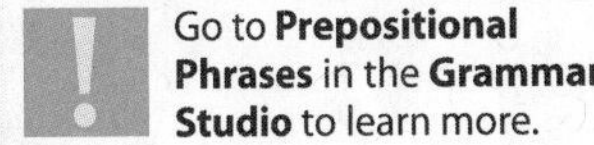

Go to **Prepositional Phrases** in the **Grammar Studio** to learn more.

Practice and Apply Identify the prepositional phrases in each sentence from "Shooting an Elephant." Then, write your own sentences, using prepositional phrases.

> **Finally, I fired my two remaining shots into the spot where I thought his heart must be.**

> **Burmans were arriving with dahs and baskets even before I left, and I was told they had stripped his body almost to the bones by the afternoon.**

> **Among the Europeans opinion was divided.**

MY DAUGHTER THE RACIST

Short Story by **Helen Oyeyemi**

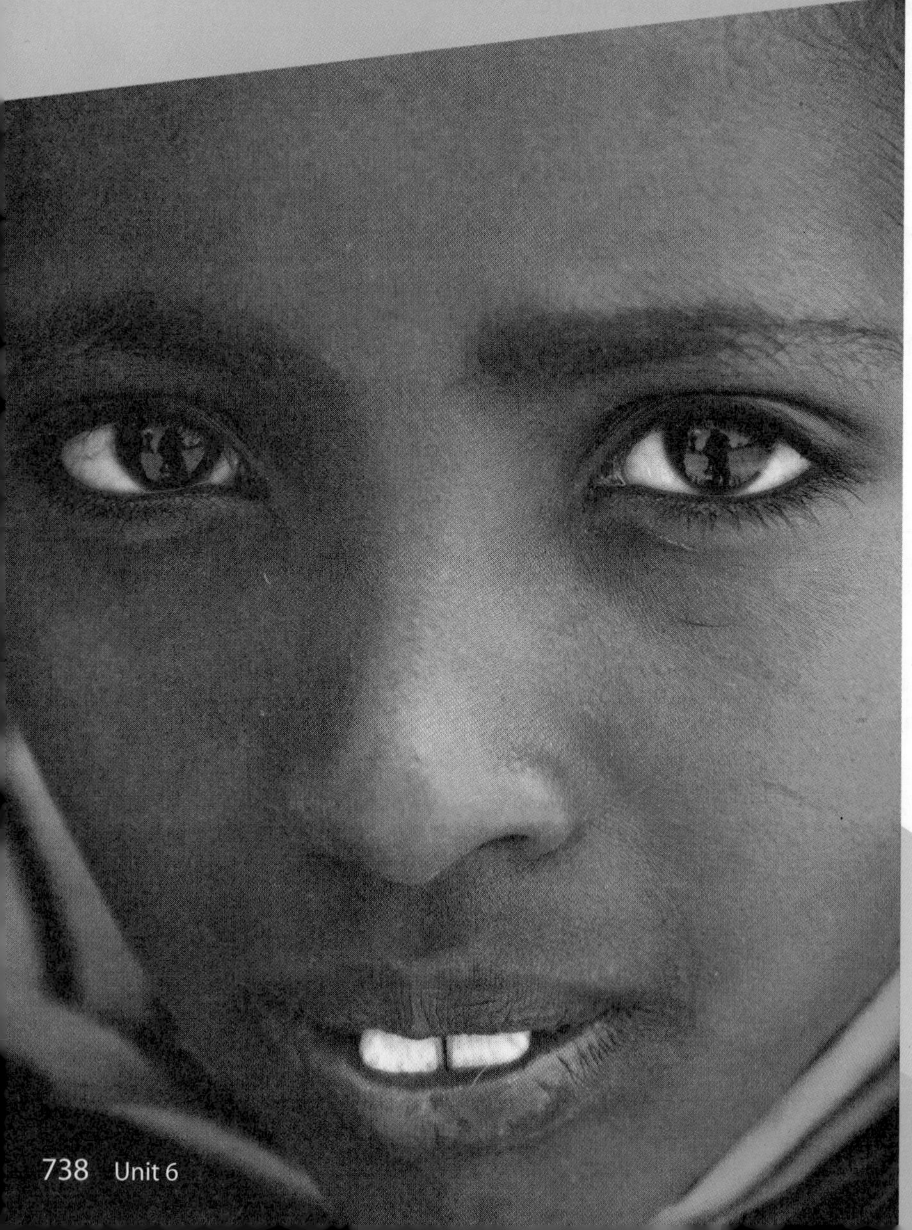

? ***ESSENTIAL QUESTION:***

Why is it hard to resist social pressure?

QUICK START

Think of a time when you stood up for something in which you believed. Freewrite about this event, making sure to explain any consequences or outcomes. Share your writing with a partner.

ANALYZE SETTING

Setting is the time and place of the action in a story. Setting also encompasses the culture and customs of the time and place. Religion, historical events, economic conditions, popular beliefs, and political climate are all part of a story's setting. "My Daughter the Racist" takes place in an unnamed country near a desert occupied by foreign troops.

As you read the story, notice how the historical and social context influence the characterization, plot, and theme of the story.

MAKE PREDICTIONS

You can use text clues to make **predictions** about what will happen next in a story. For example, near the beginning of "My Daughter the Racist," the narrator makes the following comment when discussing the tension between people in her village and foreign soldiers:

> **And that girl of mine has really begun to stare at the soldiers, too, . . .**

This remark hints that her daughter will somehow become involved in the tension between villagers and soldiers. As you read this story, try to anticipate what changes will occur in the lives of the main characters. Pay careful attention to the main characters' beliefs about themselves and their way of life, and consider how the events in the story might call these beliefs into question. Use a chart like this one to record your predictions.

GENRE ELEMENTS: SHORT STORY

- focuses on one incident and has a single plot and setting
- introduces a limited number of characters and covers a short period of time
- told from a first- or third-person point of view
- has one main conflict that the characters must resolve
- includes a theme, or message, about human nature or society

CLUE FROM TEXT	MY PREDICTION	WHAT HAPPENED

GET READY

CRITICAL VOCABULARY

balmy **loftily** **brazen** **impeccably**

To see how many Critical Vocabulary words you already know, use them to complete the sentences.

1. Loy's __________ disregard of the rules landed him in the principal's office.
2. Cree wished she could trade in this snowy day for a sunny, __________ one.
3. Kaila __________ refused to play with the young boys, claiming she was so much older and more mature.
4. Because Eliot spoke French __________, the locals could not tell he was a foreigner.

LANGUAGE CONVENTIONS

Syntax refers to the way in which words are arranged in a sentence. To keep readers interested and to draw attention to particular ideas, writers vary their syntax. For example, they might use inverted word order, alternate long sentences with short ones, or even include sentence fragments. This selection uses a mixture of short and long sentences, as well as some fragments. As you read, notice how the syntax contributes to the overall mood and tone.

ANNOTATION MODEL

NOTICE & NOTE

As you read, notice details about the setting. Underline language that helps you predict what will happen next. In the model, you can see one reader's notes about the setting.

They fight us and they try to tell us, in our own language, that they're freeing us. Maybe, maybe not. I look through the dusty window (I can never get it clean, the desert is our neighbor) and I see soldiers every day.

These details hint that the story takes place in a setting that is hot, near a desert. There is fighting taking place.

BACKGROUND

Helen Oyeyemi *(b. 1984) was born in Nigeria and raised in London. She has published novels, plays, and a collection of short stories. Oyeyemi wrote her first novel while still attending secondary school. Her story "My Daughter the Racist," which is set in an unnamed Middle Eastern or African country, was a finalist for the 2010 BBC National Short Story Award.*

MY DAUGHTER THE RACIST

Short Story by Helen Oyeyemi

SETTING A PURPOSE

As you read, notice how the narrator's wish to support her daughter's independent spirit comes into conflict with the need to protect her.

1 One morning my daughter woke up and said all in a rush: "Mother, I swear before you and God that from today onwards I am racist." She's eight years old. She chopped all her hair off two months ago because she wanted to go around with the local boys and they wouldn't have her with her long hair. Now she looks like one of them; eyes dazed from looking directly at the sun, teeth shining white in her sunburnt face. She laughs a lot. She plays. "Look at her playing," my mother says. "Playing in the rubble of what used to be our great country." My mother exaggerates as often as she can. I'm sure she would like nothing more than to be part of a Greek tragedy. She wouldn't even want a large part, she'd be perfectly content with a chorus role, warning that fate is coming to make havoc of all things. My mother is a fine woman, all over wrinkles and she always has a clean handkerchief somewhere about her person, but I don't know what she's talking about with her rubble this, rubble that—we live in a village, and it's not bad here. Not peaceful, but not bad. In

Notice & Note

Use the side margins to notice and note signposts in the text.

MAKE PREDICTIONS

Annotate: Mark details about the narrator's daughter in paragraph 1.

Predict: What expectations do you have about her personality based on these clues?

NOTICE & NOTE

ANALYZE SETTING

Annotate: Mark words and phrases in paragraph 2 that signal the social context. Mark the phrases in paragraph 3 that signal the historical context.

Infer: What do these details help you understand about the characters and plot?

cities it's worse. In the city center, where we used to live, a bomb took my husband and turned his face to blood. I was lucky, another widow told me, that there was something left so that I could know of his passing. But I was ungrateful. I spat at that widow. I spat at her in her sorrow. That's sin. I know that's sin. But half my life was gone, and it wasn't easy to look at what was left.

2 Anyway, the village. I live with my husband's mother, whom I now call my mother, because I can't return to the one who gave birth to me. It isn't done. I belong with my husband's mother until someone else claims me. And that will never happen, because I don't wish it.

3 The village is hushed. People observe the phases of the moon. In the city I felt the moon but hardly ever remembered to look for it. The only thing that disturbs us here in the village is the foreign soldiers. Soldiers, soldiers, soldiers, patrolling. They fight us and they try to tell us, in our own language, that they're freeing us. Maybe, maybe not. I look through the dusty window (I can never get it clean, the desert is our neighbor) and I see soldiers every day. They think someone dangerous is running secret messages through here; that's what I've heard. What worries me more is the young people of the village. They stand and watch the soldiers. And the soldiers don't like it, and the soldiers point their guns, especially at the young men. They won't bother with the women and girls, unless the woman or the girl has an especially wild look in her eyes. I think there are two reasons the soldiers don't like the young men watching them. The first reason is that the soldiers know they are ugly in their boots and fatigues, they are perfectly aware that their presence spoils everything around them. The second reason is the nature of the watching—the boys and the men around here watch with a very great hatred, so great that it feels as if action must follow. I feel that sometimes, just walking past them—when I block their view of the soldiers these boys quiver with impatience.

4 And that girl of mine has really begun to stare at the soldiers, too, even though I slap her hard when I catch her doing that. Who knows what's going to happen? These soldiers are scared. They might shoot someone. Noura next door says: "If they could be so evil as to shoot children then it's in God's hands. Anyway I don't believe that they could do it."

5 But I know that such things can be. My husband was a university professor. He spoke several languages, and he gave me books to read, and he read news from other countries and told me what's possible. He should've been afraid of the world, should've stayed inside with the doors locked and the blinds drawn, but he didn't do that, he went out. Our daughter is just like him. She is part of his immortality. I told him, when I was still carrying her, that that's what I want, that that's how I love him. I had always dreaded and feared pregnancy, for all the usual reasons that girls who daydream more than they live fear

pregnancy. My body, with its pain and mess and hunger—if I could have bribed it to go away, I would have. Then I married my man, and I held fast to him. And my brain, the brain that had told me I would never bear a child for any man, no matter how nice he was, that brain began to tell me something else. Provided the world continues to exist, provided conditions remain favorable, or at least tolerable, our child will have a child and that child will have a child and so on, and with all those children of children come the inevitability that glimpses of my husband will resurface, in their features, in the way they use their bodies, a fearless swinging of the arms as they walk. Centuries from now some quality of a man's gaze, smile, voice, way of standing or sitting will please someone else in a way that they aren't completely aware of, will be loved very hard for just a moment, without inquiry into where it came from. I ignore the women who say that my daughter does things that a girl shouldn't do, and when I want to keep her near me, I let her go. But not too far, I don't let her go too far from me.

6 The soldiers remind me of boys from here sometimes. The way our boys used to be. Especially when you catch them with their helmets off, three or four of them sitting on a wall at lunchtime, trying to enjoy their sandwiches and the sun, but really too restless for both. Then you see the rifles beside their lunchboxes and you remember that they aren't our boys.

7 "Mother… did you hear me? I said that I am now a racist."

8 I was getting my daughter ready for school. She can't tie knots but she loves her shoelaces to make extravagant bows.

9 "Racist against whom, my daughter?"

10 "Racist against soldiers."

11 "Soldiers aren't a race."

12 "Soldiers aren't a race," she mimicked. "Soldiers aren't a race."

13 "What do you want me to say?"

14 She didn't have an answer, so she just went off in a big gang with her schoolfriends. And I worried, because my daughter has always seen soldiers—in her lifetime she hasn't known a time or place when the cedars stood against the blue sky without khaki canvas or crackling radio signals in the way.

15 An hour or so later Bilal came to visit. A great honor, I'm sure, a visit from that troublesome Bilal who had done nothing but pester me since the day I came to this village. He sat down with us and mother served him tea.

16 "Three times I have asked this daughter of yours to be my wife," Bilal said to my mother. He shook a finger at her. As for me, it was as if I wasn't there. "First wife," he continued. "Not even second or third—first wife."

MAKE PREDICTIONS

Annotate: Mark details in paragraphs 15–23 that describe Bilal's personality.

Predict: At this point in the story, what can you predict about Bilal's involvement in the story?

17 "Don't be angry, son," my mother murmured. "She's not ready. Only a shameless woman could be ready so soon after what happened."

18 "True, true," Bilal agreed. A fly landed just above my top lip and I let it walk.

19 "Rather than ask a fourth time I will kidnap her…"

20 "Ah, don't do that, son. Don't take the light of an old woman's eyes," my mother murmured, and she fed him honey cake. Bilal laughed from his belly, and the fly fled. "I was only joking."

21 The third time Bilal asked my mother for my hand in marriage I thought I was going to have to do it after all. But my daughter said I wasn't allowed. I asked her why. Because his face is fat and his eyes are tiny? Because he chews with his mouth open?

22 "He has a tyrannical mustache," my daughter said. "It would be impossible to live with." I'm proud of her vocabulary. But it's starting to look as if I think I'm too good for Bilal, who owns more cattle than any other man for miles around and could give my mother, daughter and I everything we might reasonably expect from this life.

23 Please, God. You know I don't seek worldly things. If you want me to marry again, so be it. But please—not Bilal. After the love that I have had…you don't believe me, but I would shatter.

LANGUAGE CONVENTIONS

Annotate: Parallel structure is the repetition of a grammatical form within a sentence. Mark an example of parallel structure in paragraph 24.

Analyze: What idea does this use of parallel structure emphasize?

24 My daughter came home for her lunch. After prayers we shared some cold karkedeh,[1] two straws in a drinking glass, and she told me what she was learning, which wasn't much. My mother was there, too, rattling her prayer beads and listening indulgently. She made faces when she thought my daughter talked too much. Then we heard the soldiers coming past as usual, and we went and looked at them through the window. I thought we'd make fun of them a bit, as usual. But my daughter ran out of the front door and into the path of the army truck, yelling: "You! You bloody soldiers!" Luckily the truck's wheels crawled along the road, and the body of the truck itself was slumped on one side, resigned to a myriad of pot holes. Still, it was a very big truck, and my daughter is a very small girl.

25 I was out after her before I knew what I was doing, shouting her name. It's a good name—we chose a name that would grow with her, but she seemed determined not to make it to adulthood. I tried to trip her up, but she was too nimble for me. Everyone around was looking on from windows and the open gates of courtyards. The truck rolled to a stop. Someone inside it yelled: "Move, kid. We've got stuff to do."

26 I tried to pull my daughter out of the way, but she wasn't having any of it. My hands being empty, I wrung them. My daughter began to pelt the soldier's vehicle with stones from her pockets. Her pockets were very deep that afternoon, her arms lashed the air like whips.

[1] **karkedeh:** Egyptian drink made from dried hibiscus.

Stone after stone bounced off metal and rattled glass, and I grabbed at her and she screamed: “This is my country! Get out of here!”

27 The people of the village began to applaud her. “Yes,” they cried out, from their seats in the audience, and they clapped. I tried again to seize her arm and failed again. The truck’s engine revved up and I opened my arms as wide as they would go, inviting everyone to witness. Now I was screaming too: “So you dare? You really dare?”

28 And there we were, mother and daughter, causing problems for the soldiers together.

29 Finally a scrawny soldier came out of the vehicle without his gun. He was the scrawniest fighting man I’ve ever seen—he was barely there, just a piece of wire, really. He walked towards my daughter, who had run out of stones. He stretched out a long arm, offering her chewing gum, and she swore at him, and I swore at her for swearing. He stopped about thirty centimeters away from us and said to my daughter: “You’re brave.”

30 My daughter put her hands on her hips and glared up at him.

31 “We’re leaving tomorrow,” the scrawny soldier told her.

32 Whispers and shouts: *the soldiers are leaving tomorrow!*

33 A soldier inside the truck yelled out: “Yeah, but more are coming to take our place,” and everyone piped low. My daughter reached for a stone that hadn’t fallen far. Who is this girl? Four feet tall and fighting something she knows nothing about. Even if I explained it to her she wouldn’t get it. I don’t get it myself.

34 “Can I shake your hand?” the scrawny soldier asked her, before her hand met the stone. I thought my girl would refuse, but she said yes. “You’re okay,” she told him. “You came out to face me.”

35 “Her English is good,” the coward from within the truck remarked.

36 “I speak to her in English every day,” I called out. “So she can tell people like you what she thinks.”

37 We stepped aside then, my daughter and I, and let them continue their patrol.

38 My mother didn’t like what had happened. But didn’t you see everyone clapping for us, my daughter asked. So what, my mother said. People clap at anything. Some people even clap when they’re on an airplane and it lands. That was something my husband had told us from his travels—I hadn’t thought she’d remember.

39 My daughter became a celebrity amongst the children, and from what I saw, she used it for good, bringing the shunned ones into the inner circle and laughing at all their jokes.

MAKE PREDICTIONS

Annotate: Mark details in paragraphs 33–37 that describe the girl’s interaction with the soldier.

Predict: What do you think might happen if they meet again?

NOTICE & NOTE

40 The following week a foreigner dressed like one of our men knocked at my mother's door. It was late afternoon, turning to dusk. People sat looking out onto the street, talking about everything as they took their tea. Our people really know how to discuss a matter from head to toe; it is our gift, and such conversation on a **balmy** evening can be sweeter than sugar. Now they were talking about the foreigner who was at our door. I answered it myself. My daughter was at my side and we recognized the man at once; it was the scrawny soldier. He looked itchy and uncomfortable in his djellaba,[2] and he wasn't wearing his keffiyeh[3] at all correctly—his hair was showing.

balmy
(bä´mē) *adj.* mild and pleasant.

ANALYZE SETTING
Annotate: Mark details in paragraphs 40–51 that reveal more about the social context.
Analyze: How does the setting contribute to the plot at this point in the story?

41 "What a clown," my daughter said, and from her seat on the cushioned floor my mother vowed that clown, or no clown, he couldn't enter her house.

42 "Welcome," I said to him. It was all I could think of to say. See a guest, bid him welcome. It's who we are. Or maybe it's just who I am.

43 "I'm not here to cause trouble," the scrawny soldier said. He was looking to the north, south, east, and west so quickly and repeatedly that for some seconds his head was just a blur. "I'm completely off duty. In fact, I've been on leave since last week. I'm just—I just thought I'd stick around for a little while. I thought I might have met a worthy adversary—this young lady here, I mean." He indicated my

[2] **djellaba** (jə-lä´bə): a long, loose, hooded garment with full sleeves, worn especially in Muslim countries.
[3] **keffiyeh** (kə-fē´ə): a square of cloth, often embroidered, traditionally worn as a headdress by Arab men, either by winding it around the head or by folding it into a triangle, draping it over the head, and securing it with an agal.

daughter, who chewed her lip and couldn't stop herself from looking pleased.

44 "What is he saying?" my mother demanded.

45 "I'll just—go away, then," the soldier said. He seemed to be dying several thousand deaths at once.

46 "He'd like some tea..." my daughter told my mother. "We'll just have a quick cup or two," I added, and we took the tea out onto the verandah, and drank it under the eyes of God and the entire neighborhood. The neighborhood was annoyed. Very annoyed, and it listened closely to everything that was said. The soldier didn't seem to notice. He and my daughter were getting along famously. I didn't catch what exactly they were talking about, I just poured the tea and made sure my hand was steady. *I'm not doing anything wrong*, I told myself. *I'm not doing anything wrong*.

47 The scrawny soldier asked if I would tell him my name. "No," I said. "You have no right to use it." He told me his name, but I pretended he hadn't spoken. To cheer him up, my daughter told him her name, and he said: "That's great. A really, really good name. I might use it myself one day."

48 "You can't—it's a girl's name," my daughter replied, her nostrils flared with scorn.

49 "Ugh," said the soldier. "I meant for my daughter..."

50 He shouldn't have spoken about his unborn daughter out there in front of everyone, with his eyes and his voice full of hope and laughter. I can guarantee that some woman in the shadows was cursing the daughter he wanted to have. Even as he spoke someone was saying, May that girl be born withered for the grief people like you have caused us.

51 "Ugh," said my daughter. "I like that sound. Ugh, ugh, ugh."

52 I began to follow the conversation better. The scrawny soldier told my daughter that he understood why the boys lined the roads with anger. "Inside my head I call them the children of Hamelin."[4]

53 "The what?" my daughter asked.

54 "The who?" I asked.

55 "I guess all I mean is that they're paying the price for something they didn't do."

56 And then he told us the story of the Pied Piper of Hamelin[5] because we hadn't heard it before. We had nightmares that night, all three of us—my mother, my daughter and I. My mother hadn't even heard the story, so I don't know why she joined in. But somehow it was nice that she did.

---

[4] **Hamelin** (hăm´ə-lĭn): a city of northern Germany on the Weser River southwest of Hanover.

[5] **Pied Piper of Hamelin:** a tale of a piper who led children away from their homes using his music.

NOTICE & NOTE

57 On his second visit the scrawny soldier began to tell my daughter that there were foreign soldiers in his country, too, but that they were much more difficult to spot because they didn't wear uniforms and some of them didn't even seem foreign. They seemed like ordinary citizens, the sons and daughters of shopkeepers and dentists and restaurant owners and big businessmen. "That's the most dangerous kind of soldier. The longer those ones live amongst us, the more they hate us, and everything we do disgusts them…these are people we go to school with, ride the subway with—we watch the same movies and play the same video games. They'll never be with us, though. We've been judged, and they'll always be against us. Always."

58 He'd wasted his breath, because almost as soon as he began with all that I put my hands over my daughter's ears. She protested loudly, but I kept them there. "What you're talking about is a different matter," I said. "It doesn't explain or excuse your being here. Not to this child. And don't say 'always' to her. You have to think harder or just leave it alone and say sorry."

59 He didn't argue, but he didn't apologize. He felt he'd spoken the truth, so he didn't need to argue or apologize.

60 Later in the evening I asked my daughter if she was still racist against soldiers and she said **loftily**: "I'm afraid I don't know what you're referring to." When she's a bit older I'm going to ask her about that little outburst, what made her come out with such words in the first place. And I'm sure she'll make up something that makes her sound cleverer and more sensitive than she really was.

loftily
(lôf′tə-lē) *adv.* arrogantly; haughtily.

MAKE PREDICTIONS
Annotate: Mark details in paragraph 61 that tell how the villagers treated the narrator and her daughter.

Predict: Story plots are driven by conflict. Based on these details about conflict with their neighbors, what might happen to the narrator and her daughter as a result of their friendship with the soldier?

61 We were expecting our scrawny soldier again the following afternoon, my daughter and I. My daughter's friends had dropped her. Even the ones she had helped find favor with the other children forgot that their new position was due to her and urged the others to leave her out of everything. The women I knew snubbed me at market, but I didn't need them. My daughter and I told each other that everyone would come round once they understood that what we were doing was innocent. In fact we were confident that we could convince our soldier of his wrongdoing and send him back to his country to begin life anew as an architect. He'd confessed a love of our minarets.[5] He could take the image of our village home with him and make marvels of it.

[5] **minaret** (mĭn′ə-rĕt′): a tall slender tower attached to a mosque, having one or more projecting balconies from which a muezzin or a recording of a muezzin summons the people to prayer.

62 Noura waited until our mothers, mine and hers, were busy gossiping at her house, then she came to tell me that the men were discussing how best to deal with me. I was washing clothes in the bathtub and I almost fell in.

63 My crime was that I had insulted Bilal with my **brazen** pursuit of this soldier…

64 "Noura! This soldier—he's just a boy! He can hardly coax his beard to grow. How could you believe—"

65 "I'm not saying I believe it. I'm just saying you must stop this kind of socializing. And behave **impeccably** from now on. I mean—angelically."

66 Three months before I had come to the village, Noura told me, there had been a young widow who talked back all the time and looked haughtily at the men. A few of them got fed up, and they took her out to the desert and beat her severely. She survived, but once they'd finished with her she couldn't see out of her own eyes or talk out of her own lips. The women didn't like to mention such a matter, but Noura was mentioning it now, because she wanted me to be careful.

67 "I see," I said. "You're saying they can do this to me?"

68 "Don't smile; they can do it. You know they can do it! You know that with those soldiers here our men are twice as fiery. Six or seven of them will even gather to kick a stray dog for stealing food…"

69 "Yes, I saw that yesterday. Fiery, you call it. Did they bring this woman out of her home at night or in the morning, Noura? Did they drag her by her hair?"

70 Noura averted her eyes because I was asking her why she had let it happen and she didn't want to answer.

71 "You're not thinking clearly. Not only can they do this to you but they can take your daughter from you first, and put her somewhere she would never again see the light of day. Better that than have her grow up like her mother. Can't you see that that's how it would go? I'm telling you this as a friend, a true friend…my husband doesn't want me to talk to you anymore. He says your ideas are wicked and bizarre."

72 I didn't ask Noura what her husband could possibly know about my ideas. Instead I said: "You know me a little. Do you find my ideas wicked and bizarre?"

73 Noura hurried to the door. "Yes. I do. I think your husband spoilt you. He gave you illusions…you feel too free. We are not free."

74 I drew my nails down my palm, down then back up the other way, deep and hard. I thought about what Noura had told me. I didn't think for very long. I had no choice—I couldn't afford another visit

brazen
(brā´zən) *adj.* unrestrained by a sense of shame; rudely bold.

impeccably
(ĭm·pĕk´kə·blē) *adv.* in accordance with having no flaws; perfectly.

WORDS OF THE WISER

Notice & Note: Reread paragraphs 62–71. Mark the advice Noura gives to the narrator.

Draw Conclusions: Based on the information she tells the narrator, do you agree with Noura's advice? Explain why or why not.

NOTICE & NOTE

MAKE PREDICTIONS

Annotate: Mark the sentences in paragraph 74 that explain how the narrator made sure the villagers no longer believed that she was friendly with the soldier.

Draw Conclusions: Were you expecting this outcome or did her actions surprise you? Explain.

from him. I wrote him a letter. I wonder if I'll ever get a chance to take back all that I wrote in that letter; it was hideous from beginning to end. Human beings shouldn't say such things to each other. I put the letter into an unsealed envelope and found a local boy who knew where the scrawny soldier lived. Doubtless Bilal read the letter before the soldier did, because by evening everyone but my daughter knew what I had done. My daughter waited for the soldier until it was fully dark, and I waited with her, pretending that I was still expecting our friend. There was a song she wanted to sing to him. I asked her to sing it to me instead, but she said I wouldn't appreciate it. When we went inside at last, my daughter asked me if the soldier could have gone home without telling us. He probably hated goodbyes.

75 "He said he would come…I hope he's alright…" my daughter fretted.

76 "He's gone home to build minarets."

77 "With matchsticks, probably."

78 And we were both very sad.

79 My daughter didn't smile for six days. On the seventh she said she couldn't go to school.

80 "You have to go to school," I told her. "How else will you get your friends back again?"

81 "What if I can't," she wailed. "What if I can't get them back again?"

82 "Do you really think you won't get them back again?"

83 "Oh, you don't even care that our friend is gone. Mothers have no feelings and are enemies of progress."

84 (I really wonder who my daughter has been talking to lately. Someone with a sense of humor very like her father's...)

85 I tickled the sole of her foot until she shouted.

86 "Let this enemy of progress tell you something," I said. "I'm never sad when a friend goes far away, because whichever city or country that friend goes to, they turn the place friendly. They turn a suspicious-looking name on the map into a place where a welcome can be found. Maybe the friend will talk about you sometimes, to other friends that live around him, and then that's almost as good as being there yourself. You're in several places at once! In fact, my daughter, I would even go so far as to say that the further away your friends are, and the more spread out they are, the better your chances of going safely through the world…"

87 "Ugh," my daughter said.

CHECK YOUR UNDERSTANDING

Answer these questions before moving on to the **Analyze the Text** section on the following page.

1 Why does the narrator's daughter cut her hair?

A She wants to look pretty.

B She wants the boys to notice her.

C She wants to be able to play with the boys.

D She wants to blend in with the soldiers.

2 Why is the narrator currently unmarried?

F She is a widow.

G She hasn't found a suitor.

H She has to take care of her mother.

J She isn't allowed to marry.

3 What can be inferred about the role of women in the society in which the story is set?

A Women only work in the home.

B Women are leaders in the community.

C Women have a limited role in society.

D Women are not allowed in public spaces.

RESPOND

ANALYZE THE TEXT

Support your responses with evidence from the text. NOTEBOOK

1. **Infer** Why does the soldier come to visit the narrator and her daughter? Consider:
   - his initial encounter with the daughter
   - what he says about his home country
2. **Compare** In what ways is the narrator different from Noura? What do they have in common?
3. **Analyze** What is the theme of the story? How does this theme relate to the cultural and historical setting?
4. **Predict** How might relations between the villagers and the narrator change after the conclusion of the story? Explain the reasons for your prediction.
5. **Notice & Note** At the end of the story, the narrator tries to console her daughter with wise words about how absent friends enrich our lives, which the daughter undercuts with the comical exclamation "ugh." How has the daughter's life been enriched by her brief friendship with the foreign soldier?

RESEARCH TIP

When researching historical information, make sure you access credible and reliable primary and secondary sources that provide relevant, accurate details and accounts. Avoid blogs or other personalized sites. Instead, consult major newspapers or sites that have *.edu* or *.gov* in their URL. These sites typically belong to the government or to educational institutions and therefore are more likely to have correct information.

RESEARCH

Although Helen Oyeyemi chose not to name a specific country as the setting for her story, "My Daughter the Racist" seems to have been inspired by Western military operations in countries in the Middle East and Africa. Leaders of those operations say they want to help the people of those countries. However, the narrator reflects a common response to these claims when she says, "They fight us and they try to tell us, in our own language, that they're freeing us. Maybe, maybe not." With a partner, research involvement by Western nations in other countries and answer the following questions.

QUESTION	ANSWER
What set off the conflict?	
Why were Western troops sent to the country?	
How were ordinary citizens of the country affected by the fighting?	

Connect Think about how you would feel living in a country that has been occupied by foreign troops. How would you react? What would you do from day to day? Briefly describe what you think your experience would be like, and share your writing with a partner.

CREATE AND DISCUSS

Write a Fictional Scene In their last scene together, Noura and the narrator exchange harsh words after Noura warns the narrator to cut ties with the soldier. Write a new scene in which the two women get together after the narrator has followed Noura's advice. Will the women resume their former friendship, or does the conflict between them linger?

- ❑ Reread the scene between the narrator and Noura to refresh your memory of the disagreement between them.
- ❑ Freewrite some new dialogue between the women.
- ❑ Use the dialogue as the basis for your scene. Before you begin to write, decide whether you will stick with Oyeyemi's first-person narrator, write the scene with Noura as the narrator, or use a third-person narrator.

Go to **Writing Narratives** in the **Writing Studio** to learn more.

Critique and Discuss In a small group, share your impressions of "My Daughter the Racist," informally critiquing the short story.

- ❑ Focus on the literary devices of setting and first-person point of view. Consider what the narrator relates about the political and social context, and how the setting drives the plot and affects characters.
- ❑ Evaluate the story in terms of originality. For example, why do you think writer Helen Oyeyemi never clearly identifies the setting? What aspects of the story seem provocative or thought provoking? How are genders represented? What might the writer be expressing through these representations?
- ❑ Find evidence to support your views.

Go to **Participating in Collaborative Discussions** in the **Speaking and Listening Studio** to learn more.

RESPOND TO THE ESSENTIAL QUESTION

Why is it hard to resist social pressure?

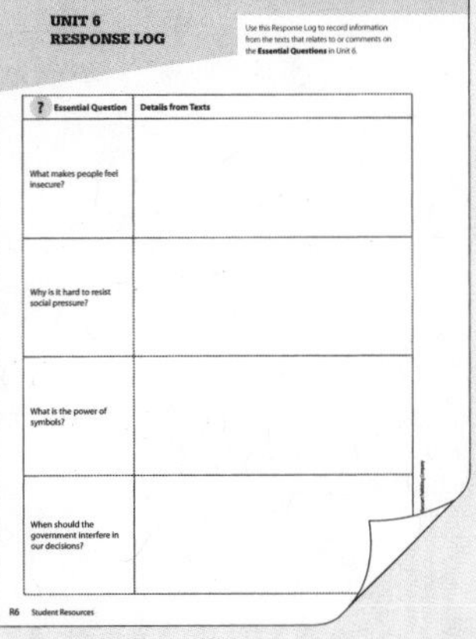

UNIT 6 RESPONSE LOG

Use this Response Log to record information from the texts that relates to or comments on the **Essential Questions** in Unit 6.

? Essential Question	Details from Texts
What makes people feel insecure?	
Why is it hard to resist social pressure?	
What is the power of symbols?	
When should the government interfere in our decisions?	

R6 Student Resources

Gather Information Review your annotations and notes on "My Daughter the Racist." Then, add relevant information to your Response Log. As you determine which information to include, think about:

- the ways in which society impacts your own views and behavior
- a time you had to resist the influence of others
- the repercussions for standing up for what you believe in

ACADEMIC VOCABULARY

As you write and discuss what you learned from the short story, be sure to use the Academic Vocabulary words. Check off each of the words that you use.

- ❑ **arbitrary**
- ❑ **controversy**
- ❑ **convince**
- ❑ **denote**
- ❑ **undergo**

CRITICAL VOCABULARY

WORD BANK
balmy
loftily
brazen
impeccably

Practice and Apply Explain whether or not the Critical Vocabulary words are used correctly in the following sentences.

1. When the weather turned **balmy,** Hillary began to shiver on the park bench.
2. Darryl spoke passionately and **loftily** when he told us about his time volunteering at the animal shelter.
3. Alice's **brazen** speech earned praise from teachers.
4. Whenever Sid's parents walk into a room, he behaves **impeccably** so he can get a reward.

VOCABULARY STRATEGY: Idioms

Go to the **Vocabulary Studio: Using Context Clues** for more on idioms.

An **idiom** is a common figure of speech whose meaning is different from the literal meaning of its words. Idioms are used in everyday speech and are often specific to a dialect. An example of an idiom in "My Daughter the Racist" appears in paragraph 24: "She made faces when she thought my daughter talked too much." *Made faces* does not mean she literally drew or crafted a face. This idiom means she tried to communicate with her granddaughter through facial expressions to prevent her from talking.

Practice and Apply Review the short story once again, this time identifying at least one additional idiom. Jot down each idiom you find and its possible meaning. Then, write a few idioms you know or use. Share your findings with a partner.

LANGUAGE CONVENTIONS: Syntax

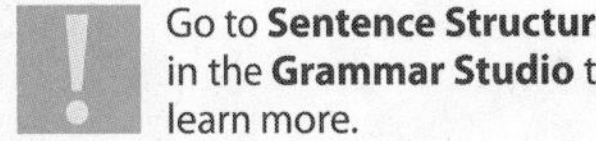
Go to **Sentence Structure** in the **Grammar Studio** to learn more.

Syntax refers to the order of words or phrases in a sentence. The author of "My Daughter the Racist" varies the syntax throughout the story to create variety, to add emphasis, and to establish a conversational tone.

For example, in paragraph 4, the narrator uses a combination of short and long sentences to call attention to the soldiers:

> **And that girl of mine has really begun to stare at the soldiers, too, even though I slap her hard when I catch her doing that. Who knows what's going to happen? These soldiers are scared. They might shoot someone. Noura next door says: "If they could be so evil as to shoot children then it's in God's hands. Anyway I don't believe that they could do it."**

The varied structure of the sentences places emphasis on the girl's boldness and suggests that something could happen between the daughter and the soldiers. By posing the question, "Who knows what's going to happen?" readers are drawn in and begin to anticipate how the plot will unfold.

In paragraph 58, the narrator uses a sentence fragment in saying:

> **"It doesn't explain or excuse your being here. Not to this child. And don't say 'always' to her. . . ."**

The sentence fragment—following a longer, complete sentence—emphasizes the narrator's protectiveness toward her child and stresses how she wants the soldier to behave. The fragment in this dialogue also mirrors the way people naturally speak. The effect is realistic-sounding dialogue.

Practice and Apply Write a brief paragraph in which you react to the plot in "My Daughter the Racist." Be sure to vary the syntax of your sentences to keep readers engaged and to emphasize certain ideas.

POEM

THE SECOND COMING

by **William Butler Yeats**

pages 759–760

COMPARE THEME

The poems you are about to read make use of symbols—a type of figurative language. As you read, look for people, places, or objects that seem likely to have a symbolic meaning, and consider how these might be related to the themes of the poems. Also make note of the similarities and differences between the two poems. After reading, you will collaborate with a small group on a final project.

? *ESSENTIAL QUESTION:*

What is the power of symbols?

POEM

SYMBOLS? I'M SICK OF SYMBOLS

by **Fernando Pessoa**

pages 762–763

QUICK START

Think about the last time you were expecting something big to happen—something you might be dreading or something you were looking forward to. What was it like to wait, anticipating a big change? How did you feel? Discuss with a partner or a small group.

UNDERSTAND SYMBOLISM

A **symbol** is a person, place, or object that has a concrete meaning in itself and also represents something beyond itself, such as an idea or feeling. This chart provides some examples of common symbols.

SYMBOL	WHAT IT REPRESENTS
dove	peace
fox	cleverness
rose	romantic love
water	purification or cleansing
winter	death

Symbolism is the practice of using symbols, and it is also the name of a literary movement that began in France in the late 19th century. The Symbolists emphasized the use of symbols to suggest states of mind and ideas that cannot be expressed directly. Like many modernist writers, Yeats was strongly influenced by this literary movement. His poems often feature complex symbols drawn from a wide variety of sources, including the Bible, Irish folklore, and occult practices.

Fernando Pessoa was also influenced by symbolism, but nothing about this Portuguese poet's work is easy to pin down. Pessoa wrote his poems through multiple personas, which he called "heteronyms." Each heteronym is a well-defined character who has his own approach to the art of poetry. The poem "Symbols? I'm Sick of Symbols" was written under the heteronym Álvaro de Campos, a naval engineer who lives in London. While some of Pessoa's heteronyms fully embrace symbolism, in this poem Campos playfully criticizes the movement.

As you read, consider which people, places, and objects could be symbolic of ideas or feelings. Also, think about how the poets develop the moods and themes of their poems through the use of symbols.

GENRE ELEMENTS: LYRIC POETRY

- expresses the thoughts and feelings of the speaker
- uses sound devices such as rhyme and rhythm to create a musical quality
- often deals with intense emotions surrounding events such as love, death, or loss

GET READY

ANALYZE RHYTHMIC PATTERNS

In poetry, **meter** is a pattern of stressed and unstressed syllables. Each unit of meter, known as a **foot,** consists of a combination of stressed and unstressed syllables. These patterns create rhythm, which brings out the musical quality of language and often serves to unify a work of literature.

An **iamb** is a foot that contains one unstressed syllable (˘) followed by one stressed syllable (´). For example, the word *apart* is an iamb. A **trochee** is a foot that contains one stressed syllable followed by one unstressed syllable, as in the word *falcon*. The chart shows the most common types of feet. It also shows terms that describe the number of feet in a line.

RHYTHMIC PATTERNS	
TYPE OF FOOT	iamb (˘ ´) trochee (´ ˘) anapest (˘ ˘ ´) dactyl (´ ˘ ˘)
NUMBER OF FEET	monometer—one dimeter—two trimeter—three tetrameter—four pentameter—five hexameter—six

Many forms of poetry are written in **iambic pentameter,** with five iambic feet in each line. In "The Second Coming," Yeats primarily uses irregular rhythms, but several of the lines are written in perfect iambic pentameter. When he uses regular metrical lines among lines with irregular meter, he creates a dramatic rhythm that helps support his theme.

Pessoa's poem, on the other hand, is written in **free verse,** which is poetry that does not follow any regular patterns of rhyme or meter. Pessoa creates a unique, irregular rhythm by using conversational language and alternating between long and short lines.

ANNOTATION MODEL

NOTICE & NOTE

As you read, mark any people, places, or objects that could be symbolic and make note of what you think they could symbolize. In the model, you can see one reader's notes about "The Second Coming."

Turning and turning in the widening gyre
The falcon cannot hear the falconer;
Things fall apart; the center cannot hold;

The poem starts off dramatically with two dactyl feet. The falcon that cannot hear the falconer may symbolize loss of control.

NOTICE & NOTE

BACKGROUND

William Butler Yeats *(1865–1939) is widely considered the finest English language poet of the 20th century. He was born in a suburb of Dublin, Ireland, but he spent much of his childhood with his grandparents in the countryside, where he learned about Irish history and mythology—subjects that would heavily influence his writing. In addition to his poetry, Yeats was a dramatist who helped found Dublin's prestigious Abbey Theatre. In 1923 he was awarded the Nobel Prize for Literature. Yeats wrote "The Second Coming" in 1919, shortly after the Russian Revolution and the end of World War I—events that traumatized Europe.*

THE SECOND COMING

Poem by William Butler Yeats

PREPARE TO COMPARE

As you read, look for places and objects in the poem that could be symbols and consider what they might represent.

Turning and turning in the widening gyre
The falcon cannot hear the falconer;
Things fall apart; the center cannot hold;
Mere anarchy is loosed upon the world,
The blood-dimmed tide is loosed, and everywhere
The ceremony of innocence is drowned;
The best lack all conviction, while the worst
Are full of passionate intensity.

Surely some revelation is at hand;
Surely the Second Coming is at hand.
The Second Coming! Hardly are those words out

Notice & Note

Use the side margins to notice and note signposts in the text.

1 gyre (jīr): spiral.

6 ceremony of innocence: the rituals (such as the rites of baptism and marriage) that give order to life.

10 Second Coming: Christ's return to Earth predicted in the New Testament to be an event preceded by a time of terror and chaos.

ANALYZE RHYTHMIC PATTERNS

Annotate: Mark the meter in lines 7–10.

Analyze: Where does Yeats vary the rhythm from iambic pentameter? What effect does this have?

NOTICE & NOTE

12 ***Spiritus Mundi*** (spîr´ĭ-to͝os mo͝on´dē) *Latin*: Spirit of the World. Yeats used this term to refer to the collective unconscious, a supposed source of images and memories that all human beings share.

14 This image suggests the Great Sphinx in Egypt, built more than 40 centuries ago.

UNDERSTAND SYMBOLISM

Annotate: Mark the symbol in line 20.

Analyze: What might this object symbolize?

When a vast image out of *Spiritus Mundi*
Troubles my sight: somewhere in sands of the desert
A shape with lion body and the head of a man,
A gaze blank and pitiless as the sun,
Is moving its slow thighs, while all about it
Reel shadows of the indignant desert birds.
The darkness drops again; but now I know
That twenty centuries of stony sleep
Were vexed to nightmare by a rocking cradle,
And what rough beast, its hour come round at last,
Slouches towards Bethlehem to be born?

CREATE AND PRESENT

Write a Response to Literature How do the poems connect to your own experiences and thoughts about symbolism? Capture your thoughts and feelings by freewriting about the use of symbols in poems. Then, use ideas from your writing to decide what feelings and emotions you want to convey in a dramatic reading of one of the poems.

- ❑ Set a time limit of 10–15 minutes for your writing.
- ❑ Write without stopping to check spelling or grammar.
- ❑ At the end of your time limit, read what you wrote and underline all the ideas you would like to convey in a dramatic poetry reading.
- ❑ If your freewriting doesn't yield any useful ideas, try another session.

Go to the **Writing Studio: Writing as a Process** for help.

Give a Dramatic Reading Work with a partner to create a dramatic reading of one of the poems.

- ❑ Begin by discussing the impact of the poet's word choices.
- ❑ Practice reading each line of your chosen poem in a way that conveys your personal connection to the poem's meaning.
- ❑ Consider how you will accompany the words with movements or gestures.
- ❑ Take turns rehearsing with a partner, giving and receiving feedback.
- ❑ Present your dramatic reading to the class, using appropriate volume, phrasing, and expression.

Go to **Giving a Presentation: Delivering Your Presentation** in the **Speaking and Listening Studio** for help.

RESPOND TO THE ESSENTIAL QUESTION

What is the power of symbols?

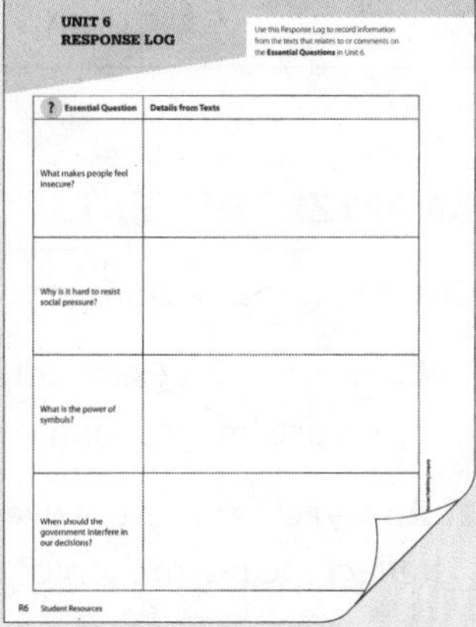

UNIT 6 RESPONSE LOG

Use this Response Log to record information from the texts that relates to or comments on the **Essential Questions** in Unit 6.

? Essential Question	Details from Texts
What makes people feel insecure?	
Why is it hard to resist social pressure?	
What is the power of symbols?	
When should the government interfere in our decisions?	

R6 Student Resources

Gather Information Review your annotations and notes on "The Second Coming" and "Symbols? I'm Sick of Symbols." Then, add relevant details to your Response Log. As you determine which information to include, think about:

- how you've used symbols to express yourself
- how symbols help you understand difficult concepts
- how symbols can express double meanings

ACADEMIC VOCABULARY

As you write and discuss what you learned from the poems, be sure to use the Academic Vocabulary words. Check off each of the words that you use.

- ❑ **arbitrary**
- ❑ **controversy**
- ❑ **convince**
- ❑ **denote**
- ❑ **undergo**

RESPOND

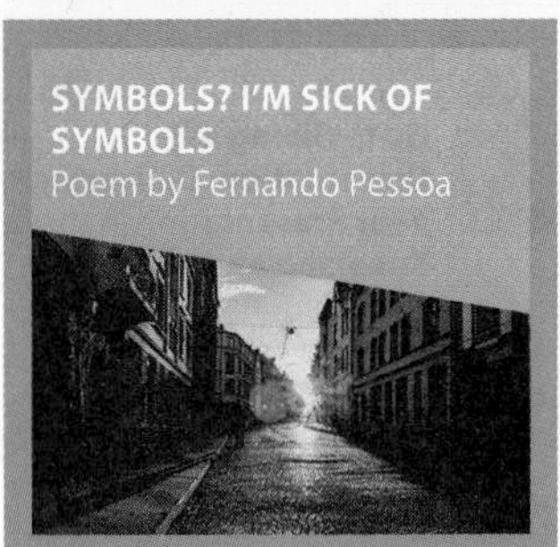

THE SECOND COMING
Poem by William Butler Yeats

SYMBOLS? I'M SICK OF SYMBOLS
Poem by Fernando Pessoa

Collaborate & Compare

COMPARE THEMES

Symbols play an important role in both "The Second Coming" and "Symbols? I'm Sick of Symbols." However, the poems are quite different from each other. Yeats uses symbols to express a grand vision, while Pessoa works on a much more modest scale to make a point about symbolism. Compare how the two authors develop their themes. As you consider the themes of the poems, think about:

- key statements made by the speaker or any characters in the poem
- central images that play important symbolic roles or evoke the theme
- tone, or the overall mood or feeling of the poem

In a small group, identify similarities and differences between the two poems. Record your thoughts in the chart.

	"THE SECOND COMING"	"SYMBOLS? I'M SICK OF SYMBOLS"
Key Statements		
Central Images, Symbols		
Tone		

ANALYZE THE TEXTS

Discuss these questions in your group.

1. **Compare** What similarities and differences do you see in how the two poets use imagery and symbols?
2. **Analyze** What is the overall tone of each poem? How does the tone reflect the poem's topic?
3. **Evaluate** Which poet expresses ideas more clearly? How might this relate to their different approaches to symbolism?
4. **Critique** Yeats's speaker expresses a prophetic view of history, while Pessoa's speaker gets emotional about something he observes on a street corner. Which poem is more likely to appeal to readers today? Explain.

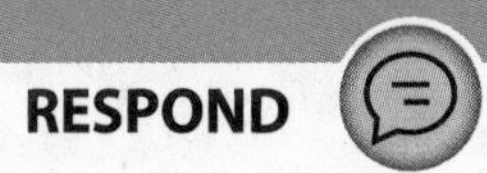

COLLABORATE AND PRESENT

Go to **Giving a Presentation** in the **Speaking and Listening Studio** for more help.

Now your group can continue exploring the ideas in these texts by identifying and comparing their themes. Follow these steps:

1. **Decide on the most important details.** With your group, review the chart you created to identify the most important details, including symbols, from each poem. Identify points you agree on, and resolve disagreements through discussion, basing your decisions on evidence from the texts.

2. **Create theme statements.** State a theme for each poem, using complete sentences. Remember, it is up to you and your group to infer the themes based on details. You can use a chart like the one shown here to determine the theme of each poem.

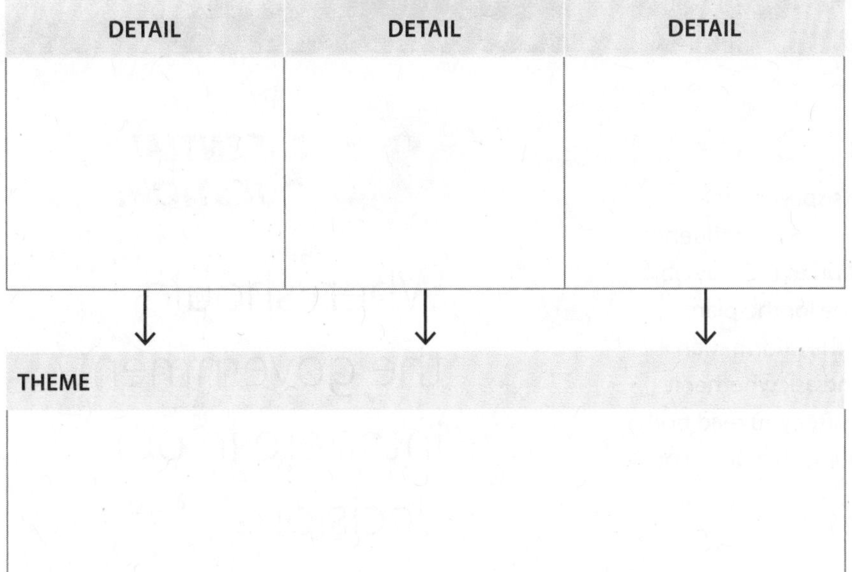

3. **Compare and contrast themes.** With your group, discuss similarities and differences in the themes of the poems. Listen actively to the members of your group, take notes, and ask the group to clarify any points you do not understand. Identify points of agreement or disagreement before you present your ideas.

4. **Present your ideas to the class.** Now it is time to present your ideas. State your conclusions about the themes of the poems. Cite text evidence from the poems to support your ideas. Discuss points of similarity and difference in the themes. You may adapt the charts you created or use other visuals to help convey your ideas to the class.

COLLABORATE & COMPARE

SPEECH

BUDGET 2016: GEORGE OSBORNE'S SPEECH

by **George Osborne**

pages 771–772

COMPARE ARGUMENTS

As you read George Osborne's speech, pay attention to the techniques he uses to influence his audience. Also pay attention to the way he uses evidence to build the case for the plan he puts forward. Notice how the information in the speech is presented, and ask whether it appeals to logic or emotion. After you read both selections, you will collaborate with a group on a final project.

ESSENTIAL QUESTION:

When should the government interfere in our decisions?

EDITORIAL

WILL THE SUGAR TAX STOP CHILDHOOD OBESITY?

by **Chris Hall**

pages 781–783

Budget 2016: George Osborne's Speech

QUICK START

Think about a time when you had to convince someone to give you permission to do or buy something. Jot down techniques you used to get what you wanted. Share with a classmate how successful you were.

EVALUATE PERSUASIVE TECHNIQUES

George Osborne delivered the speech you are about to read to members of Britain's Parliament, but it was also broadcast on television to all British citizens. His goal was to persuade both of these audiences about the merits of his government's taxing and spending policies, including a tax on sugar. **Persuasive techniques** are the methods used to influence others. Writers use these techniques to enhance their arguments and communicate more effectively with an **audience,** or the specific people to whom an argument is addressed. As you read, evaluate how well Osborne uses the following kinds of appeals:

- **Logical appeals** are arguments that use facts and evidence to support a position, appealing to an audience's reasoning or intellect.
- **Ethical appeals** invoke shared values and principles. They call upon the audience's sense of right and wrong.
- **Emotional appeals** are intended to arouse strong feelings in an audience, such as pity or fear.

GENRE ELEMENTS: SPEECH

- is a talk or public address presented to an audience
- may have one or more purposes, such as to entertain, to explain, or to persuade
- may conclude with a call to action
- may be recorded or transcribed for later reading and analysis

ANALYZE INDUCTIVE REASONING

Inductive reasoning is a method of argument in which a writer presents evidence about an issue or problem and then draws a conclusion from the evidence. This conclusion presents the writer's belief about how to resolve the issue or problem. When you analyze an inductive argument, it is important to think critically because writers sometimes introduce **logical fallacies,** or errors in logic or reasoning.

As you read and analyze the argument put forth in Osborne's speech, focus on answering these questions:

Is the evidence provided thorough?	Determine whether Osborne has provided sufficient evidence to support his conclusion.
Is the evidence valid and relevant?	Determine whether Osborne presents facts that can be verified with reputable sources.
Does the conclusion follow logically from the evidence?	Determine whether the facts and evidence provided by Osborne lead logically to the conclusion he has presented.

GET READY

CRITICAL VOCABULARY

incentive **levy** **implementation** **compulsory**

To see how many Critical Vocabulary words you already know, use them to complete the sentences.

1. It is a requirement that you attend school until a certain age. This is called __________ education.

2. The government can increase its revenue with a new __________ on services that are not currently being taxed.

3. Many times the government will provide a(n) __________, such as a tax rebate, so companies will invest in the production of energy-saving products.

4. New laws voted on by the Congress may take several years for the __________ to be fully realized.

LANGUAGE CONVENTIONS

Relative Pronouns and Relative Clauses Relative pronouns connect relative, or adjective, clauses to the words they modify in a sentence. Relative pronouns include *that, which, who, whom*, and *whose*. The noun or pronoun that a relative clause modifies is the antecedent of the relative pronoun.

> **George Osborne, who served as Chancellor of Exchequer, delivered a speech about a new tax on sugary drinks.**

In this sentence, *who* is the relative pronoun and *who served as Chancellor of Exchequer* is the relative clause. *George Osborne* is the antecedent of the relative pronoun.

ANNOTATION MODEL

NOTICE & NOTE 

As you read, make note of how the author uses facts, statistics, and other kinds of evidence to support his argument. The model shows how one reader annotated the beginning of the speech.

> Mr. Deputy Speaker, you cannot have a long-term plan for the country unless you have a long-term plan for our children's health care. Here are the facts we know.
>
> - Five-year-old children are consuming their body weight in sugar every year.
> - Experts predict that within a generation, over half of all boys and 70% of girls could be overweight or obese.

This is a logical appeal: children's health issues affect the nation's future.

These surprising facts all relate to children's health.

NOTICE & NOTE

BACKGROUND

George Osborne *(b. 1971) served as chief financial minister of the United Kingdom as Chancellor of Exchequer from 2010 to 2016. His responsibilities included controlling public spending and raising money through taxation or borrowing. He delivered a speech about the government's budget plan to the House of Commons on March 1, 2016. In this speech, he announced that a new tax on sugar in soft drinks would take effect in 2018.*

BUDGET 2016: GEORGE OSBORNE'S SPEECH

Speech by George Osborne

PREPARE TO COMPARE

As you read Osborne's speech, think about the methods he uses to persuade his audience. Paying attention to how Osborne presents his message will allow you to compare his argument to that of Chris Hall, the author of the next selection.

1 Mr. Deputy Speaker, you cannot have a long term plan for the country unless you have a long term plan for our children's health care. Here are the facts we know.

- Five-year-old children are consuming their body weight in sugar every year.
- Experts predict that within a generation, over half of all boys and 70% of girls could be overweight or obese.

2 Here's another fact that we all know. Obesity drives disease. It increases the risk of cancer, diabetes and heart disease—and it costs our economy £27 billion a year; that's more than half the entire NHS[1] paybill.

3 And here's another truth we all know. One of the biggest contributors to childhood obesity is sugary drinks. A can of cola typically has nine teaspoons of sugar in it. Some popular

Notice & Note

Use the side margins to notice and note signposts in the text.

NUMBERS AND STATS

Notice & Note: Mark the statistics Osborne includes in paragraph 1.

Evaluate: How effective are these statistics as a way to introduce the topic?

[1] **NHS:** National Health Service (United Kingdom).

NOTICE & NOTE

EVALUATE PERSUASIVE TECHNIQUES

Annotate: Mark phrases in paragraph 4 that suggest Osborne is making an ethical appeal.

Analyze: How does mentioning the steps the soft drink industry is taking strengthen Osborne's argument?

incentive
(ĭn-sĕn´tĭv) *n.* something, such as the fear of punishment or the expectation of reward, that induces action or motivates effort.

levy
(lĕv´ē) *n.* a tax or fine imposed on a person or business.

implementation
(ĭm-plə-mən-tā´shən) *n.* the process of putting into practical effect; carry out.

LANGUAGE CONVENTIONS

Annotate: Mark the relative clause in paragraph 7.

Analyze: What is the antecedent of the relative clause?

ANALYZE INDUCTIVE REASONING

Annotate: Mark sentences in paragraphs 8 and 9 that summarize the actions that Parliament wants to take to make children healthier and the results they expect to see.

Analyze: Can you find any logical fallacies in Osborne's argument for his plan to fight childhood obesity?

compulsory
(kəm-pŭl´sə-rē) *adj.* obligatory; required.

drinks have as many as 13. That can be more than double a child's recommended added sugar intake.

4 Let me give credit where credit is due. Many in the soft drinks industry recognize there's a problem and have started to reformulate their products. . . . So industry can act, and with the right **incentives** I'm sure it will.

5 Mr Deputy Speaker, I am not prepared to look back at my time here in this Parliament, doing this job and say to my children's generation: I'm sorry. We knew there was a problem with sugary drinks. We knew it caused disease. But we ducked the difficult decisions and we did nothing.

6 So today I can announce that we will introduce a new sugar **levy** on the soft drinks industry. Let me explain how it will work. It will be levied on the companies. It will be introduced in two years' time to give companies plenty of space to change their product mix. It will be assessed on the volume of the sugar-sweetened drinks they produce or import. There will be two bands—one for total sugar content above 5 grams per 100 millilitres; a second, higher band for the most sugary drinks with more than 8 grams per 100 millilitres. Pure fruit juices and milk-based drinks will be excluded, and we'll ensure the smallest producers are kept out of scope. We will of course consult with Parliament on **implementation**.

7 We're introducing the levy on the industry which means they can reduce the sugar content of their products—as many already do. It means they can promote low-sugar or no sugar brands—as many already are. They can take these perfectly reasonable steps to help with children's health. Of course, some may choose to pass the price onto consumers and that will be their decision, and this would have an impact on consumption too. We understand that tax affects behavior. So let's tax the things we want to reduce, not the things we want to encourage.

8 The OBR[2] estimate that this levy will raise £520 million. And this is tied directly to the second thing we're going to do today to help children's health and wellbeing. We're going to use the money from this new levy to double the amount of funding we dedicate to sport in every primary school. And for secondary schools we're going to fund longer school days for those that want to offer their pupils a wider range of activities, including extra sport. It will be voluntary for schools. **Compulsory** for the pupils. There will be enough resources for a quarter of secondary schools to take part—but that's just a start. . . .

9 A determination to improve the health of our children. A new levy on excessive sugar in soft drinks. The money used to double sport in our schools. A Britain fit for the future. We're not afraid to put the next generation first.

[2] **OBR:** Office for Budget Responsibility (United Kingdom).

CHECK YOUR UNDERSTANDING

Answer these questions before moving on to the **Analyze the Text** section on the following page.

1 Read this sentence from the speech.

We're going to use the money from this new levy to double the amount of funding we dedicate to sport in every primary school.

Which persuasive technique is used in the sentence?

A A logical appeal

B A legislative appeal

C An ethical appeal

D An emotional appeal

2 At the beginning of paragraphs 1, 2, and 3, the author most likely repeats the phrases facts we know and truth we know in order to make —

F himself appear trustworthy to the audience

G logical connections between the evidence he presents

H an emotional appeal

J a bandwagon appeal

3 Which one of the questions below should be asked *first* to effectively analyze Osborne's reasoning that a tax on sugary drinks will make children healthier?

A How true are the three facts that he states are already known?

B How many schools want to implement programs that promote sports?

C What are the other causes of childhood obesity?

D How much will people pay for sugary drinks?

ANALYZE THE TEXT

Support your responses with evidence from the text. NOTEBOOK

1. **Analyze** In what ways does Osborne effectively use persuasive techniques?
2. **Identify** What conclusion does Osborne draw based on the evidence he presents?
3. **Critique** Does Osborne provide adequate support for his argument?
4. **Evaluate** Osborne's speech has two audiences—the Parliament and the British people. How successful is he in addressing both of them?
5. **Notice & Note** In paragraph 6, what is the effect of providing the numbers to explain the two bands of sugar content in sweetened drinks?

RESEARCH

The national government, states, and counties levy taxes on goods and services to generate money. Research to discover the purpose of the following taxes and at which level of government they are collected. Use the empty rows in the chart to add additional taxes that you might find in your research.

TAX	PURPOSE	LEVEL (NATION/STATE/ COUNTY)
Income Tax		
State Tax		
Property Tax		
Gasoline Tax		
Capital Gains Tax		
Inheritance Tax		
Sales Tax		
Business Profit Tax		

RESEARCH TIP

Start your research by accessing your state government's website. Then, expand your search by going to your county website. Sites that end in *.gov* are websites that are managed by a government agency. However, *.com* websites may also be helpful.

Extend Many people believe they are taxed too much. Others think we need more taxes so the government can fund more programs to help keep people safe and healthy. Consider the taxes above and what you learned from your research to determine which taxes you think are the most important and which ones are the least important.

CREATE AND DEBATE

Develop a Persuasive Argument With a small group, decide on a tax you want to support or eliminate. Divide the group into two teams, each taking a *For* or *Against* stance. Both sides should take the following steps:

- ❑ Determine the facts that can be used to support your stance. This will be the basis for your logical appeal.
- ❑ Determine how the tax benefits the community or has had negative consequences. Choose words that elicit strong emotions to develop your emotional appeal.
- ❑ Develop your ethical appeal by explaining how the tax is the "right thing to do" or how the tax is "unfair and imbalanced."
- ❑ Write down your argument statements that you will use to persuade others to agree with your argument. Organize them in order so you can present a cohesive presentation.
- ❑ Be sure to anticipate the other side's argument so you can make counterarguments.

Debate Set up a time to meet in front of the class to hold a debate. Each person on the team should take part in presenting a statement using at least one kind of persuasive technique.

- ❑ Set up debate rules to define how both sides will present their arguments.
- ❑ Both sides should have the opportunity to make counterarguments.

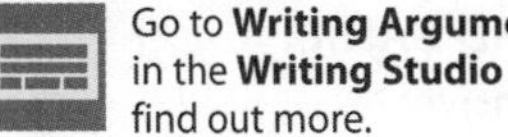

Go to **Writing Arguments** in the **Writing Studio** to find out more.

Go to **Analyzing and Evaluating Presentations** in the **Speaking and Listening Studio** to learn more.

RESPOND TO THE ESSENTIAL QUESTION

? When should the government interfere with our decisions?

Gather Information Review your annotations and notes on "Budget 2016: George Osborne's Speech." Then, add relevant details to your Response Log. As you determine which information to include, think about:

- the types of persuasive techniques that the author uses
- whether his reasoning is valid, logical, and stands on a firm premise
- what you have learned from your research and discussions

ACADEMIC VOCABULARY

As you write and discuss what you learned from the speech, be sure to use the Academic Vocabulary words. Check off each of the words that you use.

- ❑ **arbitrary**
- ❑ **controversy**
- ❑ **convince**
- ❑ **denote**
- ❑ **undergo**

RESPOND

CRITICAL VOCABULARY

WORD BANK
incentive
levy
implementation
compulsory

Practice and Apply Write the Critical Vocabulary word that has the same or similar meaning as the given word.

1. reward
2. mandatory
3. tax
4. enactment

VOCABULARY STRATEGY: Related Words

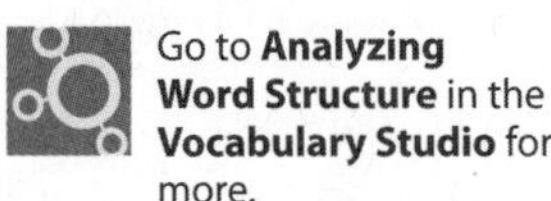

Go to **Analyzing Word Structure** in the **Vocabulary Studio** for more.

Often you can use related words to figure out the meaning of an unfamiliar word. For example, you might not know the meaning of *compulsory*. However, if you are familiar with the related word *compel,* which means "to force or require," you could guess that *compulsory* describes something that is required.

Practice and Apply Use the related word in parentheses to help you determine the meaning of each boldfaced word. Check your work by consulting a dictionary.

1. (discreet) Some people may consider calling children overweight to be an **indiscretion.**
2. (impede) Members of Parliament who disagree with Osborne might be an **impediment** to passing a sugar tax.
3. (consume) Obesity in children has been blamed on **consumption** of sugary drinks.
4. (suppose) Osborne's **presupposition** for his proposal is that sugary drinks are the main cause of childhood obesity.
5. (exclude) Osborne's proposal has **exclusionary** measures for milk and fruit juices.

LANGUAGE CONVENTIONS:
Relative Pronouns and Relative Clauses

Good writers look for opportunities to combine short, choppy sentences into longer ones. This helps to connect ideas and vary sentence structure. One way to combine sentences is to use relative pronouns and relative clauses. **Relative pronouns** are used to help identify or provide more information about the person or thing that is being discussed. The noun or pronoun that a relative clause modifies is the **antecedent** of the relative pronoun. The chart shows the relative pronouns and explains how to use them.

Go to **The Adjective Clause** in the **Grammar Studio** for more on relative pronouns and clauses.

RELATIVE PRONOUN(S)	USED TO MODIFY
who, whom	people
which	things
that, whose	people or things

Read these sentences:

The tax is intended to help reduce the amount of sugar in popular drinks.

The tax will be implemented two years from now.

Now read the sentence below, which combines the first two sentences into one by using a relative pronoun.

The tax, which will be implemented two years from now, is intended to help reduce the amount of sugar in popular drinks.

In the sentence above, *which* is used because the antecedent of the relative pronoun is a thing. The relative pronoun *which* begins a **relative clause** that describes the tax. This clause can also be called an adjective clause.

Practice and Apply Complete the table below. First, identify the antecedent. Then, use a relative clause to combine each pair of sentences. Circle the relative pronoun and underline the relative clause in your combined sentence.

SENTENCES	COMBINED SENTENCE
1. The speaker gave a speech about sugar tax. 2. The speaker answered questions that followed.	
1. The soft drink companies were aware of the problem. 2. The soft drink companies began to reduce the amount of sugar in their products.	
1. The schools sought extra funding from the government. 2. The schools agreed to lengthen school days.	

COLLABORATE & COMPARE

EDITORIAL

WILL THE SUGAR TAX STOP CHILDHOOD OBESITY?

by **Chris Hall**

pages 781–783

COMPARE ARGUMENTS

Now that you've read "Budget 2016: George Osborne's Speech," read an argument that takes a position opposing the one set forth in the speech. As you read, note the primary argument made by the writer and how he develops his argument with evidence and reasoning. Also notice whether the evidence ever causes you to question your own opinion on this matter. After you read both selections, you will collaborate with a small group on a final project.

ESSENTIAL QUESTION:

When should the government interfere in our decisions?

SPEECH

BUDGET 2016: GEORGE OSBORNE'S SPEECH

by **George Osborne**

pages 771–772

Will the Sugar Tax Stop Childhood Obesity?

QUICK START

Think about a problem or issue in your school or community. What was one proposed solution? Did the solution effectively solve the problem or issue? What solution would you have proposed? Discuss your ideas with a partner.

EVALUATE ARGUMENTS

A strong argument clearly states a **claim,** or position on an issue, and has key ideas to back up that claim. It also provides sufficient evidence to support the claim and key ideas. **Evidence** may include facts, examples, statistics, and expert opinions.

In his editorial, Chris Hall makes an argument about the effectiveness of using a sugar tax on certain beverages to combat childhood obesity. As you read, use the questions below to help you evaluate the strength of his argument.

- **Claim:** Is Hall's claim about sugary drinks and the effectiveness of taxation credible and supported by sound reasons and evidence?
- **Reasoning:** Is Hall's argument based on logic? Does he introduce any logical fallacies or errors in presenting his conclusions? For example, does he make any generalizations that are too broad?
- **Evidence:** Are the facts, examples, and other details included in the editorial valid, authoritative, relevant, and sufficient?

EVALUATE COUNTERARGUMENTS

An effective argument anticipates opposing viewpoints and provides counterarguments to challenge or disprove them. A **counterargument** is an argument made to oppose another argument. In structuring a counterargument, a writer often acknowledges an opposing viewpoint or claim and then states or implies the counterargument which refutes that viewpoint, supporting it with facts and evidence.

OPPOSING VIEW	HALL'S COUNTERARGUMENT	HALL'S FACTS AND EVIDENCE
Increased consumption of sugar-sweetened beverages is impacting rising rates of obesity and type 2 diabetes.	Sugar-sweetened beverage consumption is rising, but it is not the root of the obesity and type 2 diabetes problem.	Less than 2% of weight gain is caused by sugary drinks.

As you read the editorial, note the counterarguments Hall presents, paying attention to the quality of the facts and evidence that support them.

GENRE ELEMENTS: EDITORIAL

- states an opinion rather than being objective
- appears in a dedicated editorial/opinion section of a newspaper or broadcast
- presents the ideas of the news staff or is submitted by an independent writer
- may note opposing viewpoints and provide counterarguments to disprove them

GET READY

CRITICAL VOCABULARY

theorize **attribute** **demonize** **consumption**

To preview the Critical Vocabulary words, use context clues and your knowledge of word roots and suffixes to fill in the correct word for each sentence.

1. I know you do not agree with them, but there is no need to __________ them at every opportunity.
2. My __________ of fresh fruit increases in the summer when my favorite kinds of fruit are in season.
3. I __________ my success in school to my good teachers and study habits.
4. Historians can __________, but nobody knows for sure what Shakespeare was doing during his "lost years."

LANGUAGE CONVENTIONS

Rhetorical Questions In this lesson, you will learn how writers use **rhetorical questions** to enhance arguments and effectively convey ideas. As you read "Will the Sugar Tax Stop Childhood Obesity?" watch for questions that the author uses to get the reader to think critically about and get emotionally involved in the topic of discussion.

ANNOTATION MODEL

NOTICE & NOTE 

As you read, note how the author develops his argument. In the model, you can see one reader's notes about how the author introduces his argument.

With the release of the United Kingdom's 2016 budget, it seems everyone is talking about the sugar tax. Over the last few days I've read several opinions on whether this is a good idea and ultimately, whether it will help to halt the obesity crisis—the million dollar question!

The writer sets himself up as an authority on the topic, but he has gotten his knowledge from reading opinions. Is his argument based on solid facts, or on the opinions of others?

The writer prepares the reader for an argument against the sugar tax by questioning whether it is a "good idea" and pointing out the high stakes involved: public health and large amounts of money.

BACKGROUND

Chris Hall *is a personal trainer based in Oxford, England. As part of his stated mission, Hall feels compelled to keep up to date with the latest research on health, nutrition, and exercise. He writes articles about health-related issues for a fitness blog and for major news websites.*

WILL THE SUGAR TAX STOP CHILDHOOD OBESITY?

Editorial by Chris Hall

PREPARE TO COMPARE

As you read, pay attention to the argument that the author is making. Note any details that support his argument or errors in logic that undermine his argument. Paying attention to how he presents his message and employs reasoning will allow you to compare his argument to that of George Osborne, the author of the first selection.

Notice & Note

Use the side margins to notice and note signposts in the text.

1 With the release of the United Kingdom's 2016 budget, it seems everyone is talking about the sugar tax. Over the last few days I've read several opinions on whether this is a good idea and ultimately, whether it will help to halt the obesity crisis—the million dollar question!

2 The Government's new tax on sugary drinks will be split into two bands: the first for total sugar above 5g per 100ml, and the second for when total sugar exceeds 8g per 100ml. To give you some context, a typical cola contains 10.6g of sugar per 100ml, while typical orange juice has 8g.

3 The tax won't be placed on pure fruit juices or milk based drinks. But in an effort to drive down childhood obesity, is this the right approach?

LANGUAGE CONVENTIONS

Annotate: Mark the rhetorical question in paragraph 3.

Analyze: How does the author use this rhetorical question to develop his argument?

4 There's no denying it: our consumption of sugar-sweetened beverages (SSBs) has risen in recent decades, and there is

NOTICE & NOTE

theorize
(thē´ə-rīz, thîr´īz) *v.* to formulate theories or a theory; speculate.

attribute
(ə-trĭb´yo͞ot) *v.* to regard as arising from a particular cause or source; ascribe.

demonize
(dē´mə-nīz) *v.* to represent as evil or diabolic.

consumption
(kən-sŭmp´shən) *n.* an amount consumed.

evidence to suggest that this increase is having an impact on obesity and the rising number of cases of type 2 diabetes. But sugary drinks alone are not the root of the problem.

5 The number of articles, statements and scientific studies linking sugary drinks to weight gain makes it easy to point the finger, and come to the conclusion that sugary drinks should be eliminated. In theory, this makes a lot of sense, but when you compare the theoretical data with the observed data, you can see that the actual weight gain associated with sugary drinks is in fact ten times less than was originally **theorized,** and actually, less than 2% of weight gain can be **attributed** to drinking sugary drinks!

6 It's only in the last ten years or so that sugar has been **demonized** for our increasing waistlines. Interestingly, our total **consumption** of sugar in the UK has actually fallen by 20 per cent in the last 30 years! In fact, it is our eating patterns as a whole that are to blame. If you look at the most recent data on calorie consumption, we are both eating more (approximately 445 calories more) but also moving less than we were 40 years ago.

7 Interestingly out of the 445 extra calories we're now consuming, less than 10 percent are from sweeteners/sugar; that's only 45 calories! The remaining calories can be blamed on our increased consumption of refined grains such as french fries, potatoes, crisps[1] and baked goods, along with fats and oils.

EVALUATE COUNTERARGUMENTS
Annotate: Mark evidence in paragraphs 8–9 that contradicts the opposing view that increased prices will force people to drink healthier beverages.

Analyze: What counterargument does Hall make to refute the government's view?

8 Now, placing a tax on sugary drinks does indicate that the Government is realizing the extent of the obesity crisis and starting to do something about it. But let's be honest, the price isn't going to increase so dramatically that it will force those who buy them to find a healthier alternative. In fact, a lot of the 'healthier' alternatives are probably going to have just the same impact (if not worse!) than if you were to choose a sugary drink.

9 Milkshakes, flavored waters and off-the-shelf cold coffees can contain nearly as much sugar, if not more, than your average can of soda and they tend to be higher in calories! In fact, if you compare a standard 471ml bottle of chocolate milkshake to a can of cola you'll find the milkshake has an extra 203 calories. Yet these drinks are exempt from the tax!

EVALUATE ARGUMENTS
Annotate: In paragraphs 10–11, mark the author's recommendations for combating the obesity crisis.

Evaluate: Which claim or recommendation is best supported by the evidence the author presents? Cite examples from the article to support your answer.

10 If we are serious about tackling childhood obesity, then we must not be naive enough as to think that pushing up the cost of fizzy drinks is going to have a noticeable impact. It is more important to focus on the issue of over-eating in general, and reducing our consumption of delicious but unhealthy foods such as refined grains and fatty foods.

11 It's also crucially important that we remain active and encourage our children to put the digital tablet down, get up off the sofa and out into the fresh air. Only then do I believe we'll stand a fighting chance of tackling the obesity crisis. . . .

[1] **crisps:** a British term for potato chips.

NOTICE & NOTE

12 Any move to tackle the obesity crisis must be praised, but the issue is much more deeply rooted in our lifestyles than what we drink. Any serious attempt to tackle the crisis must face up to this fact, and make real efforts to encourage change.

CHECK YOUR UNDERSTANDING

Answer these questions before moving on to the **Analyze the Text** section on the following page.

1 Which sentence best describes the author's opinion of the sugar tax?

A The sugar tax is not a useful response to the obesity crisis.

B The sugar tax will cause a substantial decrease in purchases of sugar-sweetened beverages.

C The sugar tax will motivate British people to be more active.

D The sugar tax does not address the main causes of increased obesity rates in Britain.

2 Which of the following would the author of the editorial most likely support?

F A sugar tax that is higher than the one proposed

G A public health campaign to educate citizens on nutritious food choices

H A tax on all beverages with sugar, including milkshakes and fruit juice

J A public health campaign to educate citizens on how sugar consumption causes weight gain

3 Read this sentence from the editorial.

It's only in the last ten years or so that sugar has been demonized for our increasing waistlines.

This sentence shows that the author believes —

A the size of the average person's waistline has increased during the past ten years because of sugar consumption

B overconsumption of sugar for the past ten years is primarily responsible for the country's current obesity crisis

C scientists have found solid evidence linking obesity to sugar consumption during the past ten years

D people have put too much emphasis on the role of sugar in the obesity crisis during the past ten years

RESPOND

ANALYZE THE TEXT

Support your responses with evidence from the text. NOTEBOOK

1. **Summarize** In your own words, describe the argument the author makes about the sugar tax. Explain why he feels the tax will or will not be effective.
2. **Analyze** Consider the most likely source of the opposing viewpoints that the author addresses with his counterarguments—George Osborne's speech. Why does the author most likely choose to structure parts of his editorial using counterarguments?
3. **Infer** How does the author of the editorial view sugar-sweetened beverages?
4. **Evaluate** How well does the author develop his argument? Does it contain any errors in logic that undermine the argument?
5. **Critique** Identify an aspect of the author's argument that is weak or lacks support. How could the author strengthen that part of the argument?

RESEARCH

When Hall wrote the editorial "Will the Sugar Tax Stop Childhood Obesity?" the tax had not yet been implemented. Conduct research to locate the most recent information about how the tax works and what effects it may have had in the United Kingdom. Use the chart to record the results of your research.

IMPLEMENTATION DATE	
AMOUNT OF THE TAX	
HEALTH EFFECTS OF THE TAX	
TOTAL EARNINGS FROM THE TAX	

RESEARCH TIP

When you are looking for credible and up-to-date information on a recent or developing news story, be sure to evaluate the type of sources you find. Although opinion pieces, editorials, and blog posts can contain valuable information and give the reader insight into multiple sides of a topic, they may not always cite the most accurate or up-to-date information, and may only present information that supports the author's point of view or argument.

CREATE AND DISCUSS

Evaluate an Argument Write a three-paragraph opinion essay in which you evaluate the author's argument and use of counterarguments in "Will the Sugar Tax Stop Childhood Obesity?" Consider reviewing your notes and annotations in the text before you begin.

- ❑ Introduce your essay by identifying the author's primary argument and indicating your evaluation of the argument.
- ❑ Then, explain your evaluation of the author's argument. Include details about how the author develops specific lines of reasoning and counterarguments.
- ❑ In your final paragraph, sum up your evaluation of the author's argument and offer praise or constructive criticism as necessary.

Go to **Writing Arguments: Persuasive Techniques** in the **Writing Studio** to find out more.

Discuss In a small group, discuss your opinions about the author's arguments in "Will the Sugar Tax Stop Childhood Obesity?" Are they logical, convincing, and well supported, or illogical, unconvincing, and poorly supported? Are all parts of the argument developed equally?

- ❑ Review the editorial with your group to identify the main arguments and counterarguments the author uses.
- ❑ Then, discuss your individual evaluations of those arguments and counterarguments. As you discuss, listen closely and ask each other questions to help clarify when ideas are unclear.
- ❑ Finally, end the discussion by identifying similarities, differences, and/or common themes in the evaluations of each member of your group.

Go to **Participating in Collaborative Discussions** in the **Speaking and Listening Studio** for more.

RESPOND TO THE ESSENTIAL QUESTION

When should the government interfere in our decisions?

Gather Information Review your annotations and notes on "Will the Sugar Tax Stop Childhood Obesity?" Then, add relevant details to your Response Log. As you determine which information to include, think about:

- the role government influence plays in everyday life
- what kinds of decisions should always be left in the hands of individuals
- who gets to determine what is the "common good"

ACADEMIC VOCABULARY

As you write and discuss what you learned from the editorial, be sure to use the Academic Vocabulary words. Check off each of the words that you use.

- ❑ **arbitrary**
- ❑ **controversy**
- ❑ **convince**
- ❑ **denote**
- ❑ **undergo**

RESPOND

WORD BANK
theorize
attribute
demonize
consumption

CRITICAL VOCABULARY

Practice and Apply With a partner, discuss and then write down an answer to each of the following questions. Then, work together to write a sentence for each vocabulary word.

1. Which vocabulary word goes with *blame* and *credit*? Why?
2. Which vocabulary word goes with *hypothesis*? Why?
3. Which vocabulary word goes with *use*? Why?
4. Which vocabulary word goes with *negative*? Why?

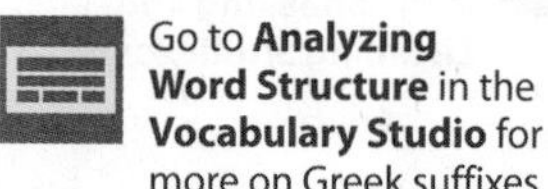

Go to **Analyzing Word Structure** in the **Vocabulary Studio** for more on Greek suffixes.

VOCABULARY STRATEGY: The Greek Suffix *-ize*

The Greek suffix *-ize* has several related meanings. A few of its meanings are listed below:

- to cause to be or become
- to cause to conform to or resemble
- to treat as
- to perform, engage in, or produce

Understanding the different meanings of the suffix *-ize* can help you determine the meaning of a word when you encounter it. Take a look at an example from "Will the Sugar Tax Stop Childhood Obesity?" below.

> **It's only in the last ten years or so that sugar has been <u>demonized</u> for our increasing waistlines.**

In the word *demonize*, the suffix *-ize* means "to treat as." Hall suggests that opponents of sugar are representing it as something evil or diabolic.

Practice and Apply Determine which meaning of the Greek suffix *-ize* helps you best understand the meaning of these words. Write your own definition of the word, incorporating the meaning of the Greek suffix.

1. agonize
2. colonize
3. familiarize
4. satirize
5. standardize

LANGUAGE CONVENTIONS: Rhetorical Questions

A **rhetorical question** is a question to which no answer is expected. Rhetorical questions are often used to emphasize meaning and evoke an emotional or thoughtful response in the reader. Writers and speakers also use them to suggest that their claims are so obvious everyone should agree with them. Employed appropriately, rhetorical questions can enhance an argument.

In "Will the Sugar Tax Stop Childhood Obesity?" Hall uses a rhetorical question in the third paragraph:

> **The tax won't be placed on pure fruit juices or milk based drinks. But in an effort to drive down childhood obesity, is this the right approach?**

Hall does not expect his readers to have a ready answer for the question. Rather, he uses the question to make readers think critically about both the claim of those who promote the sugar tax and about his own claim that the tax will not have the desired effect.

By starting the question with the word *but*, he first signals to the reader he is going to introduce a new idea that is at odds with what he just described. Then, he uses the strong phrase *drive down* to emphasize the idea that firm action and struggle will be necessary to combat childhood obesity. Finally, he uses the emotionally charged word *right*, which encourages the reader to consider the question in ethical terms of right and wrong.

Practice and Apply Reread your evaluation of Hall's argument, looking for places where you could use rhetorical questions to strengthen your position. Rewrite one of your paragraphs so it includes a rhetorical question.

BUDGET 2016: GEORGE OSBORNE'S SPEECH
Speech by George Osborne

WILL THE SUGAR TAX STOP CHILDHOOD OBESITY?
Editorial by Chris Hall

Collaborate & Compare

COMPARE ARGUMENTS

When you read just one argument, you primarily learn about only one point of view on a topic, even though the opposing point of view is usually acknowledged. Reading at least two arguments provides a more well-rounded and thorough understanding of the topic. When you compare two opposing arguments on the same topic, you can synthesize the information, taking into account all of the evidence provided by both arguments, as you evaluate each author's claim and determine your own opinion.

In a small group, complete the graphic organizer. Use the information you gather to decide whether you believe that a sugar tax will help reduce obesity in children.

OSBORNE'S CONCLUSION	HALL'S CONCLUSION
MY CONCLUSION	

ANALYZE THE TEXTS

Discuss these questions in your group.

1. **Analyze** Which elements of the arguments offered by each author are most in conflict? How might the conflict affect readers?
2. **Compare** Both authors believe that people's behaviors need to change. How do their views on the best way to change behavior differ?
3. **Synthesize** Which part of Osborne's plan would Hall be most likely to support?
4. **Evaluate** Which author's argument do you find more effective and why?

RESEARCH AND SHARE

Now your group can continue exploring the ideas in these texts by collaborating on research to present a public policy proposal for reducing obesity. Follow these steps:

1. **Develop Questions** In your group, brainstorm questions that you will need to research answers for in order to create your public policy proposal. Determine the most important questions and reach agreement on which group member will research each question. If you have more questions than group members, combine related questions before making research assignments.

2. **Gather Information** As you begin to research your question(s), make sure that the sources you consult are relevant, reliable, and credible. Although some overlap may be unavoidable, try to research only your own question(s) and not those of other group members so that each person has a meaningful share in the research process.

3. **Share Research** Once each group member has completed his or her research, discuss your findings as a group and take notes about the answer to each research question. You can use a table like the one below to track your group's research.

RESEARCH QUESTION	ANSWER

4. **Collaborate and Create** Now that your group has researched questions related to reducing obesity, it is time to develop your public policy. Discuss the findings as a group, and try to reach an agreement on a public policy addressing obesity that is supported by facts and evidence from your research. Working together and using your notes, draft a paragraph that details your public policy proposal. Be sure to explain your reasoning and back up your ideas with evidence.

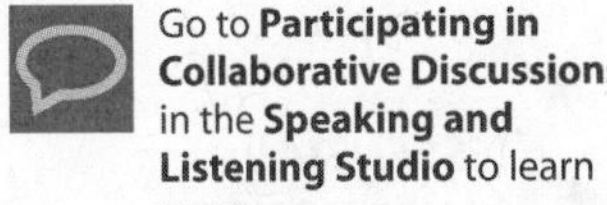
Go to **Participating in Collaborative Discussions** in the **Speaking and Listening Studio** to learn more.

INDEPENDENT READING

Reader's Choice

ESSENTIAL QUESTIONS

Review the four Essential Questions for this unit on page 691.

Setting a Purpose Select one or more of these options from your eBook to continue your exploration of the Essential Questions.

- Read the descriptions to see which text grabs your interest.
- Think about which genres you enjoy reading.

Notice & Note

In this unit, you practiced noticing and noting the signposts and asking big questions about nonfiction. As you read independently, these signposts and others will aid your understanding. Below are the anchor questions to ask when you read literature and nonfiction.

Reading Literature: Stories, Poems, and Plays	
Signpost	**Key Question**
Contrasts and Contradictions	Why did the character act that way?
Aha Moment	How might this change things?
Tough Questions	What does this make me wonder about?
Words of the Wiser	What's the lesson for the character?
Again and Again	Why might the author keep bringing this up?
Memory Moment	Why is this memory important?

Reading Nonfiction: Essays, Articles, and Arguments	
Signpost	**Key Question(s)**
Big Questions	What surprised me? What did the author think I already knew? What challenged, changed, or confirmed what I already knew?
Contrasts and Contradictions	What is the difference, and why does it matter?
Extreme or Absolute Language	Why did the author use this language?
Numbers and Stats	Why did the author use these numbers or amounts?
Quoted Words	Why was this person quoted or cited, and what did this add?
Word Gaps	Do I know this word from someplace else? Does it seem like technical talk for this topic? Do clues in the sentence help me understand the word?

INDEPENDENT READING

You can preview these texts in Unit 6 of your eBook.

Then, check off the text or texts that you select to read on your own.

☐ SHORT STORY

Araby
James Joyce

Can a poor schoolboy hope to impress a girl with a small gift?

☐ SPEECH

Professions for Women
Virginia Woolf

Woolf relates two strategies she has used to confront obstacles which all women face.

☐ POEM

Do Not Go Gentle into That Good Night
Dylan Thomas

A son pleads with his dying father to resist death and hold on to life for as long as possible.

☐ POEM

Digging
Seamus Heaney

Can a son fulfill his own life's purpose while taking a completely different path from his father?

☐ SHORT STORY

Marriage Is a Private Affair
Chinua Achebe

Nnaemeka married for love, offending his father. Can he bridge the rift he created by choosing his own path?

Collaborate and Share With a partner, discuss what you learned from at least one of your independent readings.

- Give a brief synopsis or summary of the text.
- Describe any signposts that you noticed in the text and explain what they revealed to you.
- Describe what you most enjoyed or found most challenging about the text. Give specific examples.
- Decide if you would recommend the text to others. Why or why not?

Go to the **Reading Studio** for more resources on **Notice & Note.**

Write an Argument

Go to the **Writing Studio** for help writing arguments.

This unit focuses on modern and contemporary literature. Responding to the devastation of two world wars and the loss of the once-powerful British Empire, British writers struggled to carve out a role for themselves in their new and different world. For this writing task, you will write an argument about a social or political issue in your community, such as school choice or homelessness. You can use both George Osborne's speech given to the House of Commons and Chris Hall's editorial as mentor texts to write your own argument.

As you write your argument, you can use the notes from your Response Log, which you filled out after reading the texts in this unit.

Writing Prompt

Read the information in the box below.

This is the topic or context for your argument. →

> **Think about various issues facing your own community—such as conservation efforts, homelessness, taxes, or unemployment. Consider the role of the government and what responsibilities they have to individuals and communities.**

Think carefully about the following Essential Question.

How might this Essential Question relate to your argument? →

> **When should the government interfere in our decisions?**

Choose an issue that you care about or that means something to you. →

Write an argument about a social or political issue facing your community and the government's role in helping to solve this issue.

Be sure to—

Review these points as you write and again when you finish. Make any needed changes.

- ❑ clearly state a claim, or thesis statement, about the issue you chose
- ❑ develop your argument with key ideas, supported by relevant evidence
- ❑ address opposing claims with legitimate counterarguments
- ❑ establish logical relationships between all of the elements of your argument
- ❑ use specific rhetorical devices to support your claim and counterarguments
- ❑ write a conclusion that summarizes your argument
- ❑ maintain a formal tone through the use of Standard English

1 Plan

Before you begin to write, plan your argument using the chart below. Think of two or three political or social issues that interest you—homelessness, school choice, conservation—then, choose one about which you will make a claim. Think about the government's role, as opposed to the responsibility of individual citizens on this issue. Make a list of key questions about your topic to help focus your research. Then, gather facts and evidence from reliable sources online, and talk to informed members of your community. Consider both sides of the argument carefully and use any background reading or class discussions to generate key ideas to help develop your claim, or thesis statement.

Argument Planning Chart	
Topic	
Questions to consider	
Ideas from background reading	
Ideas from class discussions	
Claim	

Background Reading Review the notes you have taken in your Response Log that relate to the question, "When should the government interfere in our decisions?" Texts in this unit provide background reading that will help you formulate your argument.

Go to **Writing Arguments: What is a Claim?** for help planning your argument.

Notice & Note

From Reading to Writing

As you plan your argument, apply what you've learned about signposts to your own writing. Remember that writers use common features, called signposts, to help convey their message to readers.

Think how you can incorporate **Numbers and Stats** into your argument.

Go to the **Reading Studio** for more resources on **Notice & Note.**

Use the notes from your Response Log as you plan your argument.

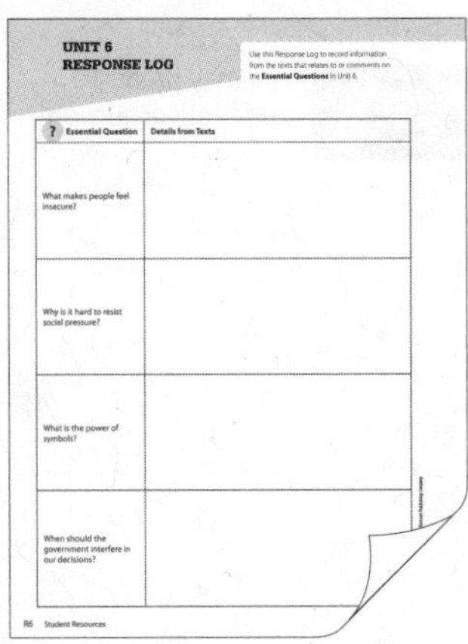

UNIT 6
RESPONSE LOG

Use this Response Log to record information from the texts that relates to or comments on the **Essential Questions** in Unit 6.

? Essential Question	Details from Texts
What makes people feel insecure?	
Why is it hard to resist social pressure?	
What is the power of symbols?	
When should the government interfere in our decisions?	

R6 Student Resources

WRITING TASK

Go to **Writing Arguments: Building Effective Support** for help organizing your ideas.

Organize Your Ideas After completing the planning chart, you should have a claim on which to base your argument. Use this chart to organize key ideas in support of your claim. Anticipate any opposing arguments and develop counterarguments. Think about how you might use rhetorical devices in supporting your claim and developing counterarguments.

Claim:		
Key ideas	**Opposing arguments**	**Counterarguments**

2 Develop a Draft

You may prefer to draft your argument online.

Once you have completed your planning activities, you will be ready to begin drafting your argument. Refer to your planning and organizational charts, as well as any notes you took as you studied the texts in this unit. These will provide a plan for you to follow as you write. Using a laptop or computer makes it easier to make changes or move sentences around later when you are ready to revise your first draft.

Use the Mentor Texts

Author's Craft

In supporting your claim, it's important to use strong, reliable, and relevant evidence. Specific details such as facts, examples, statistics, and quotations from experts contribute to a logical and effective argument. Note how George Osborne uses clear, reliable facts and statistics that are directly related to his claim and that will likely catch his listeners' attention.

Children are consuming their body weight in sugar every year.

Experts predict that within a generation over half of all boys, and 70% of girls could be overweight or obese.

. . . Obesity drives disease. . . . cancer, diabetes and heart disease . . . One of the biggest contributors to childhood obesity is sugary drinks.

A can of cola typically has nine teaspoons of sugar in it.

Osborne's serious and surprising details draw his listeners in and help them to understand his point of view. His use of statistics helps give weight to his argument that excessive sugar is harmful to children's health.

Apply What You've Learned As you search for evidence to support your claim, look for interesting facts, statistics, and examples that might surprise your reader. Be sure to use enough detail to make a convincing argument.

Genre Characteristics

An effective counterargument acknowledges the opposition with a respectful tone. In his editorial, Chris Hall recognizes the validity of the opposing view before presenting specific evidence to refute the claim about the advantage of taxing sugary drinks.

There's no denying it: our consumption of sugar sweetened beverages (SSBs) has risen in recent decades, and there is evidence to suggest that this increase is having an impact on obesity and the rising number of cases of type 2 diabetes. But sugary drinks alone are not the root of the problem.

Hall agrees that there is a problem with sugar consumption and then acknowledges the valid evidence offered by the opposing view. Note the transition sentence at the end of the paragraph. This shows he will present a counterclaim.

Apply What You've Learned Maintain a formal tone when you are making a counterargument. Begin by respectfully presenting the opposition view of a particular point. Then, transition smoothly into your counterargument.

WRITING TASK

3 Revise

Go to **Writing Arguments: Formal Style** for help revising your argument.

On Your Own Once you have written your draft, you'll want to go back and look for ways to improve your argument. As you reread and revise, think about whether you have achieved your purpose. The Revision Chart will help you focus on specific elements to make your writing stronger.

Revision Guide

Ask Yourself	Tips	Revision Techniques
1. Did I make a claim that states my position clearly?	**Highlight** your thesis statement.	If necessary, **add** a sentence or two to clarify your claim. **Add** an interesting example or related quotation to hook your reader.
2. Did I back up my claim with key ideas, supported by facts and evidence?	**Highlight** your key ideas and **underline** supporting facts and evidence.	**Read** your thesis statement aloud, followed by your key ideas. Does your argument make sense so far? **Add** more support if you can.
3. Are opposing claims addressed with well-supported counterarguments?	**Ask** a classmate to challenge your claim.	**Elaborate** by adding opposing claims and counterarguments to refute them, as needed.
4. Did I transition smoothly between ideas, paragraphs, and sentences?	**Underline** transitional words and phrases.	**Clarify** the relationship between the claim and key ideas and evidence by adding transitions.
5. Did I use rhetorical devices effectively?	**Highlight** any rhetorical devices.	**Add** appropriate rhetorical devices, such as repetition or rhetorical questions, to support and emphasize your claim and counterarguments.
6. Does my conclusion effectively restate my claim?	**Underline** your conclusion.	**Add** a statement that summarizes your claim.

ACADEMIC VOCABULARY

As you conduct your **peer review,** be sure to use these words.

- ❑ **arbitrary**
- ❑ **controversy**
- ❑ **convince**
- ❑ **denote**
- ❑ **undergo**

With a Partner Once you and your partner have worked through the Revision Guide on your own, exchange arguments and evaluate each other's draft in a **peer review.** Focus on providing revision suggestions for at least three of the items mentioned in the chart. Explain why you think your partner's draft should be revised and what your specific suggestions are. When receiving feedback from your partner, listen attentively and ask questions to make sure you fully understand the revision suggestions.

4 Edit

Now that you've revised the content of your argument, it's time to improve the finer points of your draft. Edit for the proper use of Standard English conventions and make sure to correct any misspellings or grammatical errors.

Go to **Sentence Structure** in the **Grammar Studio** to learn more.

Language Conventions

Vary Syntax for Effect Vary the **syntax,** or word order, of your sentences for more effective writing. When you use the same sentence patterns repeatedly, your writing becomes boring and your readers tend to lose interest. As you edit your argument, try the following strategies:

- To create a smooth flow, **vary sentence structure** by combining shorter sentences into compound or complex sentences.
- **Vary sentence lengths** within paragraphs to emphasize certain ideas.

The chart includes specific examples of the authors' uses of both strategies.

Strategy	Osborne	Hall
Vary sentence structure by combining shorter sentences into compound or complex sentences.	Pure fruit juices and milk-based drinks will be excluded, and we'll ensure the smallest producers are kept out of scope.	In theory, this makes a lot of sense, but when you compare the theoretical data with the observed data, you can see that the actual weight gain associated with sugary drinks is in fact ten times less than was originally theorized . . .
Vary sentence lengths within paragraphs. **(Osborne: short—long)** **(Hall: long—short)**	Obesity drives disease. It increases the risk of cancer, diabetes and heart disease—and it costs our economy £27 billion a year; that's more than half the entire NHS paybill.	Milkshakes, flavored waters and off-the-shelf cold coffees can contain nearly as much sugar as, if not more than, your average can of soda, and they tend to be higher in calories! . . . Yet these drinks are exempt from the tax!

5 Publish

Finalize your argument and choose a way to share it with your audience. Consider these options:

- Submit your argument as a letter to the editor of your local newspaper.
- Post your argument on an online news forum.

WRITING TASK

Use the scoring guide to evaluate your argument.

Writing Task Scoring Guide: Argument

	Organization/Progression	Development of Ideas and Evidence	Use of Language and Conventions
4	• Organization is appropriate to the purpose. • Claim is stated clearly, with all ideas strongly related to the claim. • Key ideas and evidence are organized consistently and logically with meaningful transitions.	• Introduction is memorable and persuasive; the claim states a position on a substantive topic. • Key ideas support the claim. • Opposing views are anticipated and addressed effectively. • Argument is supported by a variety of rhetorical devices. • Conclusion summarizes the claim.	• Writing reflects purposeful, precise word choice and maintains formal, respectful tone. • Sentences are varied. • Writing shows a consistent command of spelling, capitalization, punctuation, grammar, and usage conventions.
3	• For the most part, structure is appropriate and effective. • Claim is stated clearly, with most ideas related to the claim. Minor lapses in focus. • Organization of key ideas and evidence is confusing in a few places, and a few more transitions are needed.	• Introduction needs more to hook the reader; the claim states a position on an issue. • Key ideas support the claim but could be more convincing. • Counterarguments need further development. • Rhetorical devices do not directly support the argument. • Conclusion restates the claim.	• For the most part, writing reflects specific word choice. Style is informal in a few places and the tone defensive at times. • Sentences are reasonably varied. • Writing shows adequate command of spelling, capitalization, punctuation, grammar, and usage conventions, with few errors.
2	• Organization is evident but not always appropriate. • Irrelevant information is included or many ideas are not strongly connected to the claim. • Progression is not always logical; weak transitions, wordiness, or repetition affect the flow.	• The introduction is ordinary; the claim lacks clarity. • Key ideas are not always relevant. • Opposing views are anticipated but not addressed logically. • No clear relationship between rhetorical devices and argument. • The conclusion includes an incomplete summary of claim.	• Writing uses general or imprecise word choice, with little awareness of appropriate tone. • Sentences are often awkward, with little variation. • Writing shows only a partial command of spelling, capitalization, punctuation, grammar, and usage conventions, with some distracting errors.
1	• Organization is inappropriate to the purpose or no pattern is followed. • Claim is missing, unclear, or illogical; writing may include extraneous information or abrupt shifts between ideas. • Progression is weak; repetition, wordiness, and lack of transitions result in random or illogical presentation.	• The introduction is missing. • Significant support and evidence are missing. • Counterclaims are neither anticipated nor addressed. • Rhetorical devices are not included. • The conclusion is missing.	• Writing is vague, with limited word choice and a disrespectful tone. • Awkward sentences, fragments, and run-on sentences make the writing hard to follow. • Writing shows little or no command of spelling, capitalization, punctuation, grammar, and usage, with serious and persistent errors.

Debate an Issue

You will now adapt your argument for a debate with your classmates. You also will listen to other debate teams and prepare to critique their presentations.

Go to the **Speaking and Listening Studio: Analyzing and Evaluating a Presentation** to learn more.

1 Adapt Your Argument for a Debate

Review your written argument, and use the chart below to guide you as you adapt it and plan for a debate. Note that one team will argue for your claim, and the other will argue against it.

Plan the Debate		
Identify two debate teams with two or three members each. Team 1: ____________ ____________ Team 2: ____________ ____________	Appoint a moderator to introduce the debate and the speakers and to keep everyone on task. Moderator: ____________	Assign debate roles to each member: 1. Introduce team's argument: ____________ 2. Refute opposing team: ____________ 3. Present summary and closing statement: ____________

Prepare Briefs	Prepare Rebuttals
Identify your claim:	Identify the opposing claim:
List key ideas and evidence that support your claim:	Identify weaknesses in the opposing claim and possible counterarguments:
Summarize your argument in a closing statement:	

SPEAKING AND LISTENING TASK

As you work to improve your presentations, be sure to follow discussion rules:

- ❑ listen closely to each other
- ❑ don't interrupt
- ❑ stay on topic
- ❑ ask helpful, relevant questions
- ❑ provide clear, thoughtful, and direct answers

2 Practice with Your Team

Once you've prepared your materials, work with your team to improve the presentation of your claim, key ideas, and evidence. Also practice rebuttals. Practice listening and responding respectfully.

Practice Effective Verbal and Nonverbal Techniques

- ❑ **Voice** Enunciate your words clearly and speak slowly and loudly enough so that everyone can hear you. Use your voice to show enthusiasm and emphasis.
- ❑ **Eye Contact** Try to let your eyes rest on each member of the audience at least once.
- ❑ **Facial Expression** Smile, frown, or raise an eyebrow to show your feelings or to emphasize points.
- ❑ **Gestures** Use natural gestures to add meaning and interest to your presentation.

Provide and Consider Advice for Improvement

As you and your team practice, take notes and provide helpful advice to each other. Consider ways to revise your presentation to make sure your points are clear and logically sequenced.

3 Hold the Debate

Set up the classroom for a formal debate, with the team members facing the audience. Follow the format below:

- ❑ **Pro Speaker 1:** Present claim and supporting evidence for the "pro," or supportive, side of the argument. —5 minutes
- ❑ **Con Speaker 2:** Ask probing questions that will prompt the other team to address flaws in the argument. —3 minutes
- ❑ **Pro Speaker 2:** Respond to the questions posed by the opposing team and provide counterarguments. —3 minutes
- ❑ **Con Speaker 1:** Present the claim and supporting evidence for the "con," or opposed, side of the argument. —5 minutes
- ❑ **Pro Speaker 2:** Ask probing questions that will prompt the other team to address flaws in the argument. —3 minutes
- ❑ **Con Speaker 2:** Respond to the questions posed by the opposing team and provide counterarguments. —3 minutes
- ❑ **Pro Speaker 3:** Summarize the claim and evidence for the "pro" side and explain why your claim is more valid. —3 minutes
- ❑ **Con Speaker 3:** Summarize the claim and evidence for the "con" side and explain why your claim is more valid. —3 minutes

Reflect on the Unit

By completing your argument, you have created a writing product that pulls together and expresses your thoughts about the reading you have done in this unit. Now is a good time to reflect on what you have learned.

Reflect on the Essential Questions

- Review the four Essential Questions on page 691. How have your answers to these questions changed in response to the texts you've read in this unit?
- What are some examples from the texts you've read that show how people relate to society?

Reflect on Your Reading

- Which selections were the most interesting or surprising to you?
- From which selection did you learn the most about how people relate to society?

Reflect on the Writing Task

- What difficulties did you encounter while working on your argument? How might you avoid them next time?
- What part of the argument was the easiest to write? The hardest to write? Why?
- What improvements did you make to your argument as you were revising?

UNIT 6 SELECTIONS

- **"A Cup of Tea"**
- **"The Love Song of J. Alfred Prufrock"**
- **"Shooting an Elephant"**
- **"My Daughter the Racist"**
- **"The Second Coming"**
- **"Symbols? I'm Sick of Symbols"**
- **"Budget 2016: George Osborne's Speech"**
- **"Will the Sugar Tax Stop Childhood Obesity?"**

RESOURCES

HMH *INTO LITERATURE* STUDIOS

For more instruction and practice, visit the HMH *Into Literature* Studios.

Reading Studio

Writing Studio

Speaking & Listening Studio

Grammar Studio

Vocabulary Studio

UNIT 1 RESPONSE LOG

Use this Response Log to record information from the texts that relates to or comments on the **Essential Questions** in Unit 1.

? Essential Question	Details from Texts
What makes someone a hero?	
What is true chivalry?	
Can we control our fate?	
What happens when a society unravels?	

UNIT 2 RESPONSE LOG

Use this Response Log to record information from the texts that relates to or comments on the **Essential Questions** in Unit 2.

? Essential Question	Details from Texts
What can drive someone to seek revenge?	
How does time affect our feelings?	
What's the difference between love and passion?	
How do you defy expectations?	

UNIT 3 RESPONSE LOG

Use this Response Log to record information from the texts that relates to or comments on the **Essential Questions** in Unit 3.

? Essential Question	Details from Texts
How can satire change people's behavior?	
What is your most memorable experience?	
What keeps women from achieving equality with men?	
Why are plagues so horrifying?	

UNIT 4 RESPONSE LOG

Use this Response Log to record information from the texts that relates to or comments on the **Essential Questions** in Unit 4.

? Essential Question	Details from Texts
What can nature offer us?	
How do you define beauty?	
How can science go wrong?	
What shapes your outlook on life?	

UNIT 5 RESPONSE LOG

Use this Response Log to record information from the texts that relates to or comments on the **Essential Questions** in Unit 5.

? Essential Question	Details from Texts
What is a true benefactor?	
How do you view the world?	
What brings out cruelty in people?	
What invention has had the greatest impact on your life?	

UNIT 6
RESPONSE LOG

Use this Response Log to record information from the texts that relates to or comments on the **Essential Questions** in Unit 6.

? Essential Question	Details from Texts
What makes people feel insecure?	
Why is it hard to resist social pressure?	
What is the power of symbols?	
When should the government interfere in our decisions?	

Using a Glossary

A glossary is an alphabetical list of vocabulary words. Use a glossary just as you would a dictionary—to determine the meanings, parts of speech, pronunciation, and syllabification of words. (Some technical, foreign, and more obscure words in this book are defined for you in the footnotes that accompany many of the selections.)

Many words in the English language have more than one meaning. This glossary gives the meanings that apply to the words as they are used in the selections in this book.

The following abbreviations are used to identify parts of speech of words:

adj. adjective   *adv.* adverb   *n.* noun   *v.* verb

Each word's pronunciation is given in parentheses. A guide to the pronunciation symbols appears in the Pronunciation Key below. The stress marks in the Pronunciation Key are used to indicate the force given to each syllable in a word. They can also help you determine where words are divided into syllables.

For more information about the words in this glossary or for information about words not listed here, consult a dictionary.

Pronunciation Key

Symbol	Examples	Symbol	Examples	Symbol	Examples
ă	**pat**	m	**mum**	ûr	**urge, term, firm, word, heard**
ā	**pay**	n	**no, sudden*** (sud´n)	v	**valve**
ä	**father**	ng	**thing**	w	**with**
âr	**care**	ŏ	**pot**	y	**yes**
b	**bib**	ō	**toe**	z	**zebra, xylem**
ch	**church**	ô	**caught, paw**	zh	**vision, pleasure, garage**
d	**deed, milled**	oi	**noise**	ə	**about, item, edible, gallop, circus**
ĕ	**pet**	ŏŏ	**took**	ər	**butter**
ē	**bee**	ōō	**boot**		
f	**fife, phase, rough**	ŏŏr	**lure**		
g	**gag**	ôr	**core**		
h	**hat**	ou	**out**	**Sounds in Foreign Words**	
hw	**which**	p	**pop**	KH	*German* **ich, ach;** *Scottish* **loch**
ĭ	**pit**	r	**roar**	N	*French*, **bon** (bôN)
ī	**pie, by**	s	**sauce**	œ	*French* **feu, œuf;** *German* **schön**
îr	**pier**	sh	**ship, dish**	ü	*French* **tu;** *German* **über**
j	**judge**	t	**tight, stopped**		
k	**kick, cat, pique**	th	**thin**		
l	**lid, needle*** (nēd´l)	*th*	**this**		
		ŭ	**cut**		

***In English the consonants *l* and *n* often constitute complete syllables by themselves.**

Stress Marks

The relative emphasis with which the syllables of a word or phrase are spoken, called stress, is indicated in three different ways. The strongest, or primary, stress is marked with a bold mark (**´**). An intermediate, or secondary, level of stress is marked with a similar but lighter mark (´). The weakest stress is unmarked. Words of one syllable show no stress mark.

GLOSSARY OF ACADEMIC VOCABULARY

abandon (ə-băn′dən) *v.* to withdraw one's support or help, especially in spite of duty, allegiance, or responsibility.

ambiguous (ăm-bĭg′yo͞o-əs) *adj.* open to more than one interpretation.

anticipate (ăn-tĭs′ə-pāt) *v.* to see as a probable occurrence; expect.

appreciate (ə-prē′shē-āt) *v. tr.* to recognize the quality, significance, or magnitude of.

arbitrary (är′bĭ-trĕr-ē) *adj.* determined by chance, whim, or impulse, and not by necessity, reason, or principle.

collapse (kə-lăps′) *v.* to break down or fall apart suddenly and cease to function.

conceive (kən-sēv′) *v.* to understand or form in the mind; to devise.

confine (kən-fīn′) *v.* to keep within bounds; restrict.

conform (kən-fôrm′) *v.* to be similar to or match something or someone; to act or be in accord or agreement.

controversy (kŏn′trə-vûr-sē) *n.* public disagreement, argument.

convince (kən-vĭns′) *v.* persuade or lead to agreement by means of argument.

denote (dĭ-nōt′) *v.* to serve as a symbol for the meaning of; signify.

depress (dĭ-prĕs′) *v.* to cause to be sad or dejected.

displace (dĭs-plās′) *v.* to move, shift, or force from the usual place or position.

drama (drä′mə) *n.* a prose or verse composition intended to be acted out.

encounter (ĕn-koun′tər) *n.* to confront in battle or competition.

exploit (ĭk-sploit′) *v.* to take advantage of; to use for selfish or unethical purposes.

insight (ĭn′sīt) *n.* the ability to discern the true nature of a situation.

integrity (ĭn-tĕg′rĭ-tē) *n.* the quality of being ethically or morally upright.

intensity (ĭn-tĕn′sĭ-tē) *n.* a high degree of concentration, power, or force.

invoke (ĭn-vōk′) *v.* to call on for assistance, support, or inspiration.

military (mĭl′ĭ-tĕr-ē) *n.* the armed forces of a nation considered collectively; *adj.* of, related to, or characteristic of members of the armed forces.

persist (pər-sĭst′) *v.* to hold firmly to a purpose or task in spite of obstacles.

radical (răd′ĭ-kəl) *adj.* departing markedly from the usual or customary; extreme or drastic.

reluctance (rĭ-lŭk′təns) *n.* the state of being reluctant; unwillingness.

subordinate (sə-bôr′dn-ĭt) *adj.* subject to the authority or control of another.

undergo (ŭn-dər-gō′) *v.* to experience or be subjected to.

violate (vī′ə-lāt) *tr. v.* to disregard or act in a manner that does not conform to (a law or promise, for example).

visual (vĭzh′o͞o-əl) *adj.* seen or able to be seen by the eye; visible.

widespread (wīd′sprĕd′) *adj.* occurring or accepted widely.

GLOSSARY OF CRITICAL VOCABULARY

abate (ə-bāt´) *v.* to reduce in amount, degree, or intensity; lessen.

abrogate (ăb´rə-gāt) *v.* to revoke or nullify.

abyss (ə-bĭs´) *n.* an immeasurably deep chasm, depth, or void.

accolade (ăk´ə-lād, -läd) *n.* a special acknowledgement; an award.

affairs (ə-fârz´) *n.* personal business.

affliction (ə-flĭk´shən) *n.* something that causes suffering or pain.

aghast (ə-găst´) *adj.* struck by shock, terror, or amazement.

algorithm (ăl´gə-rĭ*th*-əm) *n.* a finite set of unambiguous instructions that, given some set of initial conditions, can be performed in a prescribed sequence to achieve a certain goal and that has a recognizable set of end conditions.

anecdote (ăn´ĭk-dōt) *n.* a short account of an interesting or humorous incident.

appraise (ə-prāz´) *tr. v.* 1. to estimate the price or value of: appraise a diamond; appraise real estate. 2. to make a considered judgment about.

ardor (är´dər) *n.* intensity of emotion, especially strong desire, enthusiasm, or devotion.

artifice (är´tə-fĭs) *n.* cleverness or ingenuity in making or doing something.

attribute (ə-trĭb´yo͞ot) *v.* to regard as arising from a particular cause or source; ascribe.

aversion (ə-vûr´zhən) *n.* a fixed, intense dislike; repugnance.

autonomy (ô-tŏn´ə-mē) *n.* the condition or quality of being autonomous; independence.

bailiff (bā´lĭf) *n.* an overseer of an estate; a steward.

baleful (bāl´fəl) *adj.* harmful or malignant in intent or effect.

balmy (bä´mē) *adj.* mild and pleasant.

bequeath (bĭ-kwē*th*´, -kwēth´) *tr. v.* to pass (something) on to another; hand down.

bereft (bĭ-rĕft´) *adj.* 1. deprived of something. 2. lacking something needed or expected.

brazen (brā´zən) *adj.* unrestrained by a sense of shame; rudely bold.

brooding (bro͞o´dĭng) *adj.* thinking about something moodily.

cacophony (kə-kŏf´ə-nē) *n.* jarring, discordant sound; dissonance.

calamity (kə-lăm´ĭ-tē) *n.* an event that brings terrible loss, lasting distress, or severe affliction; a disaster.

chafe (chāf) *v. intr.* to cause irritation by rubbing or friction: The high collar chafed against my neck.

chow (chou) *n.* food; victuals.

collateral (kə-lăt´ər-əl) *adj.* concomitant or accompanying.

commence (kə-mĕns´) *v.* to begin or start.

commend (kə-mĕnd´) *tr. v.* to commit to the care of another; entrust.

compulsory (kəm-pŭl´sə-rē) *adj.* obligatory; required.

condone (kən-dōn´) *v.* to overlook, forgive, or disregard (an offense) without protest or censure.

congenial (kən-jēn´yəl) *adj.* agreeable, sympathetic.

consumption (kən-sŭmp´shən) *n.* an amount consumed.

cowed (koud) *tr. v.* to frighten or subdue with threats or a show of force.

GLOSSARY OF CRITICAL VOCABULARY

curate (kyŏŏr´āt) *tr. v.* to gather and present to the public.

demonize (dē´mə-nīz) *v.* to represent as evil or diabolic.

deprivation (dĕp-rə-vā´shən) *n.* the condition of being deprived; lacking the basic necessities or comforts of life.

despotic (dĭ-spŏt´ĭk) *adj.* of or relating to a person who wields power oppressively, or a tyrant.

discourse (dĭs´kôrs) *n.* verbal exchange or conversation.

dismay (dĭs-mā´) *v.* to upset or distress.

dissimulation (dĭ-sĭm´yə-lā-shən) *n.* deceit or pretense.

dogged (dô´gĭd, dŏg´ĭd) *adj.* stubbornly persevering; tenacious.

domain (dō-mān´) *n.* a sphere of activity, influence, or knowledge.

dominion (də-mĭn´yən) *n.* rule or power to rule; mastery.

double entendre (dûb´əl än-tän´drə) *n.* an expression having a double meaning.

emulation (ĕm´yə-lā-shən) *n.* competitive imitation.

encumbrance (ĕn-kŭm´brəns) *n.* a burden or impediment.

engagement (ĕn-gāj´mənt) *n.* a promise or agreement to be at a particular place at a particular time.

entail (ĕn-tāl´) *v.* involve as a consequence.

ersatz (ĕr´zäts, ĕr-zäts´) *adj.* being a usually inferior imitation or substitute; artificial.

eschew (ĕ-shŏŏ´, ĕs-chŏŏ´) *tr. v.* to avoid using, accepting, participating in, or partaking of.

esprit de corps (ĕ-sprē´ də kôr´) *n.* a spirit of devotion and loyalty among group members.

evanescent (ĕv-ə-nĕs´ənt) *adj.* vanishing or likely to vanish like vapor.

exorbitant (ĭg-zôr´bĭ-tənt) *adj.* beyond what is reasonable or customary, especially in cost or price.

expound (ĭk-spound´) *v.* to explain in detail; elucidate.

extract (ĭk-străkt´) *v.* to draw or pull out, often with great force or effort.

extremist (ĭk-strē´mĭst) *adj.* advocating or resorting to measures beyond the norm, especially in politics.

feeble (fē-bəl) *adj.* lacking strength.

finite (fī´nīt) *adj.* having bounds; limited.

flotsam (flŏt´səm) *n.* discarded or unimportant things.

forebear (fôr´bâr) *n.* a person from whom one is descended; an ancestor.

forge (fôrj) *v.* to form (metal, for example) by heating in a forge and beating or hammering into shape.

garish (gâr´ĭsh, găr´-) *adj.* overly bright or ornamented, especially in a vulgar or tasteless way; gaudy.

genre (zhän´rə) *n.* a category within an art form, based on style or subject.

gilded (gĭl´dĭd) *adj.* covered with or having the appearance of being covered with a thin layer of gold.

guile (gīl) *n.* clever trickery; deceit.

hierarchy (hī´ə-rär-kē) *n.* a ranking of status within a group.

huddle (hŭd´l) *v.* to crowd together, as from cold or fear.

ignoble (ĭg-nō´bəl) *adj.* not noble in quality, character, or purpose; base or dishonorable.

immersion (ĭ-mûr´zhən, -shən) *n.* the act or instance of engaging in something wholly or deeply.

impeccably (ĭm-pĕk´ə-blē) *adv.* in accordance with having no flaws; perfectly.

imperialism (ĭm-pîr´ē-ə-lĭz-əm) *n.* the extension of a nation's authority by territorial acquisition or by the establishment of economic and political dominance over other nations.

implementation (ĭm-plə-mən-tā´shən) *n.* the process of putting into practical effect; carry out.

inanimate (ĭn-ăn´ə-mĭt) *adj.* not having the qualities associated with active, living organisms.

inarticulate (ĭn-är-tĭk´yə-lĭt) *adj.* uttered without the use of normal words or syllables; incomprehensible as speech or language.

incentive (ĭn-sĕn´tĭv) *n.* something, such as the fear of punishment or the expectation of reward, that induces action or motivates effort.

inculcate (ĭn-kŭl´kāt, ĭn´kŭl-) *v.* to impress (something) upon the mind of another by frequent instruction or repetition; instill.

incumbent (ĭn-kŭm´bənt) *adj.* required as a duty or an obligation.

inducement (ĭn-dōōs´mənt, -dyōōs´-) *n.* an incentive.

infantry (ĭn´fən-trē) *n.* the branch of an army made up of units trained to fight on foot.

infuse (ĭn-fyōōz´) *v.* to fill or cause to be filled with something.

inoculate (ĭ-nŏk´yə-lāt) *v.* to safeguard as if by inoculation; to protect.

labyrinth (lăb´ə-rĭnth) *n.* an intricate structure of interconnecting passages through which it is difficult to find one's way; a maze.

levy (lĕv´ē) *v.* to impose (a tax or fine, for example) on someone.

listless (lĭst´lĭs) *adj.* lacking energy or disinclined to exert effort; lethargic: felt tired and listless.

loathsome (lōth´səm) *adj.* causing loathing; abhorrent.

loftily (loft´ĭ-ly) *adv.* arrogantly; haughtily.

luddite (lŭd´īt) *n.* one who opposes technical or technological change.

malady (măl´ə-dē) *n.* a disease, disorder, or ailment.

manacle (măn´ə-kəl) *v.* to restrain the action or progress of something or someone.

mandatory (măn´də-tôr-ē) *adj.* required or commanded by authority; obligatory.

meme (mēm) *n.* a unit of cultural information, such as a cultural practice or idea, that is transmitted verbally or by repeated action from one mind to another.

mire (mīr) *v.* to hinder, entrap, or entangle.

misdeed (mĭs-dēd´) *n.* a wrong or illegal deed; a wrongdoing.

misogyny (mĭ-sŏj´ə-nē) *n.* hatred or mistrust of women.

monetize (mŏn´ĭ-tīz, mŭn´-) *tr. v.* to convert into a source of income.

morose (mə-rōs´, mô-) *adj.* sullen or gloomy.

odious (ō´dē-əs) *adj.* extremely unpleasant; repulsive.

ominous (ŏm´ə-nəs) *adj.* menacing; threatening.

pension (pĕn´shən) *n.* a sum of money paid regularly as a retirement benefit.

pervasive (pər-vā´sĭv,-zĭv) *adj.* having the quality or tendency to pervade or permeate.

plateau (plă-tō´) *intr. v.* to reach a stable level; level off.

plight (plīt) *n.* a situation, especially a bad or unfortunate one.

posit (pŏz´ĭt) *tr. v.* to assume or put forward, as for consideration or the basis of argument.

preamble (prē´ăm-bəl, prē-ăm´-) *n.* a preliminary statement.

precipice (prĕs´ə-pĭs) *n.* an overhanging or extremely steep mass of rock; the brink of a dangerous or disastrous situation.

prerogative (prĭ-rŏg´ə-tĭv) *n.* an exclusive right or privilege held by a person or group, especially a hereditary or official right.

prescient (prĕsh´ənt) *adj.* of or relating to prescience—which means knowledge of actions or events before they occur.

presentable (prĭ-zĕn´tə-bəl) *adj.* fit for introduction to others.

prodigious (prə-dĭj´əs) *adj.* enormous.

prognosis (prŏg-nō´sĭs) *n.* a prediction of the probable course and outcome of a disease.

promiscuously (prə-mĭs´kyōō-əs-lə) *adv.* lacking standards of selection; acting without careful judgment; indiscriminate.

GLOSSARY OF CRITICAL VOCABULARY

prostrate (pros´trāt) *adj.* lying face down, as in submission or adoration.

pyrrhic victory (pĭr´ĭk vĭk´tə-rē) *n.* a victory that is offset by staggering losses.

quell (kwĕl) *tr. v.* to pacify; quiet.

ransack (răn´săk) *tr. v.* to go through (a place) stealing valuables and causing disarray.

realm (rĕlm) *n.* kingdom.

rebuke (rĭ-byo͞ok´) *tr. v.* to criticize (someone) sharply; reprimand.

recoil (rĭ-koil´) *v.* to shrink back, as in fear or repugnance.

redress (rĭ-drĕs´) *n.* repayment for a wrong or an injury.

repine (rĭ-pīn´) *v.* to be discontented; complain or fret.

rotation (rō-tā´shən) *n.* regular and uniform variation in a sequence or series.

ruddy (rŭd´ē) *adj.* having a healthy reddish glow.

rudiment (ro͞o´də-mənt) *n.* fundamental element, principle, or skill.

salutation (săl-yə-tā´shən) *n.* a polite expression of greeting or goodwill.

satire (săt´īr) *n.* a literary work in which human foolishness or vice is attacked through irony, derision, or wit.

scorn (skôrn) *n.* contempt or disdain.

scrounge (skrounj) *v. intr.* to obtain by salvaging or foraging; round up.

scrupulous (skro͞o´pyə-ləs) *adj.* conscientious and exact; having scruples.

sea change (sē chānj) *n.* a marked transformation.

self-possessed (sĕlf-pə-zĕst´) *adj.* having calm and self-assured command of one's faculties, feelings, and behavior.

senility (sĭ´nĭl-ĭ-tē) *n.* relating to or having diminished cognitive function, as when memory is impaired, because of old age.

sentient (sĕn´shənt) *adj.* having sense perception; conscious.

smart (smärt) *v.* to suffer acutely, as from mental distress, wounded feelings, or remorse.

sovereignty (sŏv´ər-ĭn-tē, sŏv´rĭn-) *n.* complete independence and self-government.

spoof (spo͞of) *n.* a satirical imitation; a parody or send-up.

succinct (sək-sĭngkt´) *adj.* characterized by clear, precise expression in few words; concise and terse.

summon (sŭm´ən) *v.* to bring into existence or readiness.

superficial (so͞o-pər-fĭsh´əl) *adj.* apparent rather than actual or substantial; shallow.

supplant (sə-plănt´) *tr. v.* to take the place of or substitute for (another).

sustenance (sŭs´tə-nəns) *n.* something, especially food, that sustains life or health.

tactfully (tăkt´fəl-lə) *adv.* considerately and discreetly.

theorize (thē´ə-rīz, thîr´īz) *v.* to formulate theories or a theory; speculate.

treachery (trĕch´ə-rē) *n.* an act of betrayal.

trinket (trĭng´kĭt) *n.* a small ornament, such as a piece of jewelry.

tumult (to͞o´mŭlt) *n.* a state of agitation of the mind or emotions.

undaunted (ŭn-dôn´tĭd, -dän´-) *adj.* not discouraged or disheartened; resolutely courageous.

underpin (ŭn-dər-pĭn´) *tr.* v. to give support or substance to.

usurp (yo͞o-sûrp´) *v.* to seize unlawfully by force.

Utopian (yo͞o-tō´pē-ən) *adj.* excellent or ideal but impracticable; visionary.

valor (văl´ər) *n.* courage, bravery.

veracity (və-răs´ĭ-tē) *n.* conformity to fact or truth; accuracy.

verandah (və-răn´də) *n.* a porch or balcony.

vexation (vĕk-sā´shən) *n.* a source of irritation or annoyance.

vigilance (vĭj´ə-ləns) *n.* alert watchfulness.

vile (vīl) *adj.* unpleasant or objectionable.

vindication (vĭn-dĭ-kā´shən) *n.* justification.

virtue (vûr´cho͞o) *n.* *Archaic* chastity, especially in a woman.

visitation (vĭz-ĭ-tā´shən) *n.* a gathering of people in remembrance of a deceased person.

vogue (vōg) *adj.* the prevailing fashion, practice, or style.

wail (wāl) *v.* to make a long, loud, high-pitched cry, as in grief, sorrow, or fear.

writ (rĭt) *n.* a written order issued by a court, commanding the party to whom it is addressed to perform or cease performing a specified act.

INDEX OF SKILLS

INDEX OF TITLES AND AUTHORS

ACKNOWLEDGMENTS

Excerpts from *Beowulf* translated by Seamus Heaney. Translation copyright © 2000 by Seamus Heaney. Reprinted by permission of W. W. Norton & Company, Inc., and Faber & Faber Ltd.

Excerpt from "Budget 2016: George Osborne's Speech" by George Osborne from www.gov.uk. Contains Parliamentary information licensed under the Open Parliament License v3.0.

"Chivalry" from *Smoke and Mirrors* by Neil Gaiman. Text copyright © 1998 by Neil Gaiman. Reprinted by permission of Writers House, LLC.

"Confession" from *Borderless Bodies* by Linh Dinh. Text copyright © 2005 by Linh Dinh. Reprinted by permission of Linh Dinh.

"A Cup of Tea" from *The Short Stories of Katherine Mansfield* by Katherine Mansfield. Text copyright © 1923 by Penguin Random House LLC, renewed by J. Middleton Murry. Reprinted by permission of Alfred A. Knopf, an imprint of the Knopf Doubleday Publishing Group, a division of Penguin Random House LLC. All rights reserved. Any third-party use of this material, outside of this publication, is prohibited. Interested parties must apply directly to Penguin Random House LLC for permission.

"Education Protects Women from Abuse" by Olga Khazan as first published in *The Atlantic Magazine*, May 14, 2014. Text copyright © 2014 by The Atlantic Media Co. Reprinted by permission of Tribune Content Agency, LLC. All rights reserved. Distributed by Tribune Content Agency, LLC.

"For Army Infantry's 1st Women, Heavy Packs and the Weight of History" by Dave Phillips from *The New York Times*, May 27, 2017. Text copyright © 2017 by *The New York Times*. Reprinted by permission of PARS International Corps on behalf of *The New York Times*. All rights reserved. Protected by the Copyright Laws of the United States. Any printing, copying, redistribution, or retransmission of this content without express written permission is prohibited. www.nytimes.com

Excerpt from "Frankenstein: Giving Voice to the Monster" by Langdon Winner from www.langdonwinner.com, July 7, 2017. Text copyright © 2017 by Langdon Winner. Reprinted by permission of Langdon Winner.

Excerpt from "Hamlet's Dull Revenge" by René Girard from *Stanford Literature Review 1*, Fall 1984. Text copyright © 1984 by René Girard. Reprinted by permission of Martha Girard.

Excerpt from *Inferno: A Doctor's Ebola Story* by Steven Hatch. Text copyright © 2017 by Steven Hatch. Reprinted by permission of St. Martin's Press and Blackstone Publishing.

Excerpt from *Le Morte D'Arthur: King Arthur and the Legends of the Round Table* by Sir Thomas Malory, a new rendition by Keith Baines. Text copyright © 1962 by Keith Baines. Text copyright renewed © 1990 by Francesca Evans. Any third-party use of this material, outside of this publication, is prohibited. Interested parties must apply directly to Penguin Random House LLC for permission. Reprinted by permission of New American Library, an imprint of Penguin Publishing Group, a division of Penguin Random House LLC. All rights reserved.

"Loneliness" from *Second Childhood* by Fanny Howe. Text copyright © 2014 by Fanny Howe. Reprinted by permission of The Permissions Company, Inc., on behalf of Graywolf Press. www.graywolfpress.org

"The Love Song of J. Alfred Prufrock" from *Collected Poems 1909–1962* by T.S. Eliot. Text copyright © 1930, 1940, 1941, 1942, 1943, 1958, 1962, 1963 by T.S. Eliot, renewed 1970 by Esme Valerie Eliot. Reprinted by permission of Faber and Faber Ltd.

"My Daughter the Racist" from *Mr. Fox* by Helen Oyeyemi. Text copyright © 2011 by Helen Oyeyemi. Any third-party use of this material, outside of this publication, is prohibited. Interested parties must apply directly to Penguin Random House LLC for permission. Reprinted by permission of Riverhead, an imprint of Penguin Publishing Group, a division of Penguin Random House LLC, Penguin Canada, a division of Penguin Random House Canada Limited, and Wylie Agency LLC. All rights reserved.

"My Syrian Diary: Parts 1–3" by Marah from www.NewsDeeply.com. Text copyright © 2014 by Syria Deeply. Reprinted by permission of News Deeply, Inc.

Excerpt from *The Pastons: A Family in the War of the Roses* edited by Richard Barber. Text copyright © 1981 by Richard Barber. Reprinted by permission of Boydell & Brewer Ltd.

Quote from *A Dance with Dragons: A Song of Ice and Fire: Book Five* by George R. R. Martin. Text copyright © 2011 by George R. R. Martin. Any third-party use of this material, outside this publication, is prohibited. Interested parties must apply directly to Penguin Random House LLC for permission. Reprinted by permission of Bantam Books, an imprint of Random House, a division of Penguin Random House LLC and HarperCollins Publishers Ltd. All rights reserved.

From "Derek Walcott, the Art of Poetry No. 37," an interview by Edward Hirsch, originally published in *The Paris Review*, Issue 101, Winter 1986. Text copyright © The Paris Review, Inc. Reprinted by permission of Wylie Agency LLC.

"Satire is dying - the internet is killing it" by Arwa Mahdawi from www.theguardian.com, August 19, 2014. Text copyright © 2014 by The Guardian News & Media Ltd. Reprinted by permission of The Guardian News & Media Ltd.

"The Second Coming" from *The Collected Works of W. B. Yeats, Volume I: The Poems, Revised* by W. B. Yeats, edited by Richard J. Finneran. Text copyright 1924 by The Macmillan Company, renewed 1952 by Bertha Georgie Yeats. Reprinted by permission of Scribner, a division of Simon & Schuster, Inc. All rights reserved.

"Shooting an Elephant" from *Shooting an Elephant and Other Essays* by George Orwell. Text copyright © 1950 by Sonig Brownell, renewed © 1978 by Sonig, Pitt-Rivers. Reprinted by permission of Houghton Mifflin Harcourt Publishing Company, Penguin Books Ltd., and Bill Hamilton as the Literary Executor of the Estate of the Late Sonia Brownell Orwell. All rights reserved.

"Song of a Thatched Hut Damaged in Autumn Wind" by Du Fu, translated by Tony Barnstone and Chou Ping from *The Anchor Book of Chinese Poetry: From Ancient to Contemporary, the Full 3000-Year Tradition* edited by Tony Barnstone and Chou Ping. Text copyright © 2005 by Tony Barnstone and Chou Ping. Reprinted by permission of Penguin Random House LLC. All rights reserved. Any third-party use of this material, outside of this publication, is prohibited. Interested parties must apply directly to Penguin Random House LLC for permission.

"Symbols? I'm Sick of Symbols" by Fernando Pessoa from *Fernando Pessoa & Co.: Selected Poems*, edited and translated by Richard Zenith. Translation copyright © 1998 by Richard Zenith. Reprinted by permission of Grove Atlantic, Inc.

"Poem III" from *Twenty-One Love Poems* (retitled from "Part III") from *Collected Poems: 1950-2012* by Adrienne Rich. Text copyright © 1978 by Adrienne Rich, renewed © 2016 by the Adrienne Rich Literary Trust. Reprinted by permission of W. W. Norton & Company and The Frances Goldin Literary Agency.

"The Victorians Had the Same Concerns About Technology as We Do" by Melissa Dickson from www.theconversation.com, June 21, 2016. Text copyright © 2016 by Melissa Dickson. Reprinted by permission of Melissa Dickson.

"The Wanderer" from *Poems and Prose from the Old English* translated by Burton Raffel. Text copyright © 1997 by Yale University Press. Reprinted by permission of Yale University Press.

Excerpt from "The Wife of Bath's Tale" from *The Canterbury Tales* by Geoffrey Chaucer, translated by Nevill Coghill. Translation copyright © 1951 by Nevill Coghill, renewed 1958, 1960, 1975, 1977 by Nevill Coghill. Reprinted by permission of Penguin Books Ltd. and Curtis Brown Group Ltd, London on behalf of the Estate of Nevill Coghill. All rights reserved.

Excerpt from "Will the Sugar Tax Stop Childhood Obesity?" by Chris Hall from the HuffPost blog, March 22, 2016. Text copyright © 2016 by Chris Hall. Reprinted by permission of Chris Hall.